The Found

Sheffield Hallam University
Learning and IT Services
Collegiate Learning Centre
Collegiate Crescent Campus
Sheffield   S10 2BP

D0494231

101 973 825 8

From Stock

The Foundations of Public Law

Principles and Problems of Power in the British Constitution

Keith Syrell

Reader in Law, School of Law, University of Bristol

palgrave
macmillan

© Keith Syrett 2011

All rights reserved. No reproduction, copy or transmission of this publication may be made without written permission.

No portion of this publication may be reproduced, copied or transmitted save with written permission or in accordance with the provisions of the Copyright, Designs and Patents Act 1988, or under the terms of any licence permitting limited copying issued by the Copyright Licensing Agency, Saffron House, 6–10 Kirby Street, London EC1N 8TS.

Any person who does any unauthorized act in relation to this publication may be liable to criminal prosecution and civil claims for damages.

The author has asserted his right to be identified as the author of this work in accordance with the Copyright, Designs and Patents Act 1988.

First published 2011 by
PALGRAVE MACMILLAN

Palgrave Macmillan in the UK is an imprint of Macmillan Publishers Limited, registered in England, company number 785998, of Houndmills, Basingstoke, Hampshire RG21 6XS.

Palgrave Macmillan in the US is a division of St Martin's Press LLC, 175 Fifth Avenue, New York, NY 10010.

Palgrave Macmillan is the global academic imprint of the above companies and has companies and representatives throughout the world.

Palgrave® and Macmillan® are registered trademarks in the United States, the United Kingdom, Europe and other countries

ISBN 978–0–230–23643–1

This book is printed on paper suitable for recycling and made from fully managed and sustained forest sources. Logging, pulping and manufacturing processes are expected to conform to the environmental regulations of the country of origin.

A catalogue record for this book is available from the British Library.

10   9   8   7   6   5   4   3   2   1
19 18 17 16 15 14 13 12 11 10

Printed and bound in Great Britain by
Thomson Litho, East Kilbride

SHEFFIELD HALLAM UNIVERSITY
wl
342
Sy
COLLEGIATE LEARNING CENTRE

For Paula

Acknowledgements

This book is the product of nearly two decades of reading, researching and teaching public law and British politics. Fading memory and limited space preclude me from thanking all of those whose writings, words of personal encouragement or sheer enthusiasm for the subject matter may have influenced me during that period, but I should particularly like to acknowledge Rodney Barker, Danny Nicol, Tony Prosser, Mike Radford and Andy Thomas for the inspiration which they have offered at various times. Special thanks are also due to Paula Giliker, Phil Syrpis, and three anonymous reviewers for their comments on sections of this book and to Rob Gibson at Palgrave Macmillan for his invaluable assistance and patience. Finally, I owe an enormous debt of gratitude to my family for the support and love without which this project would never have come to fruition.

I intend to provide brief updates on constitutional developments on an annual basis, in or around September each year. These updates will be available on the book's companion website at **www.palgrave.com/law/ syrett**.

The law is stated as at 1 January 2011.

Contents

Table of Cases

Table of Legislation

UK legislation

Legislation from other jurisdictions, treaties and international conventions

Canada

European Convention for the Protection of Human Rights and Fundamental Freedoms 1950

European Union

Chapter 1

An introduction to the study of public law

What is public law?[1]

Public law (sometimes called constitutional and administrative law) is one of the foundational subjects of study in all legal systems. Indeed, without a functioning system of public law, there would be no other forms of law within a state, since it is by means of the network of principles and rules which make up public law that authority is conferred upon institutions such as Parliament and the courts to make law within that state. However, it is a subject whose meaning and functions are sometimes unclear. This is especially the case in the United Kingdom (UK), where, as discussed below, the usual starting point for study of the subject is notably absent and, relatedly, a powerful academic tradition has tended to reject the idea that this should constitute a distinctive field of law at all.[2] This chapter therefore seeks to provide a brief introduction to the nature of the subject matter and to offer some words of advice on how to approach it successfully.

Public law is concerned with three matters which are fundamental to the operation of any modern state. First, it entails study of the institutional structure of government and of the rules which underpin this structure.[3] Second, and relatedly, it sets out the relationships which the various institutions of government have with each other and the limits beyond which they cannot go. Third, it is concerned with the relationship between the individual and the state. This aspect of public law has become of particular significance in Britain in recent years. Although individual freedoms

---

[1] For a fuller and more theoretically developed engagement with this question, see M. Loughlin, *The Idea of Public Law* (Oxford: OUP, 2003).

[2] *ibid*, 4. For further discussion, see M. Loughlin, *Public Law and Political Theory* (Oxford: Clarendon Press, 1992), especially Chapter 7; J. Mitchell, 'The causes and effects of the absence of a system of public law in the United Kingdom' [1965] *Public Law* 95.

[3] Some of the important 'rules' which apply in the case of the United Kingdom are not legally enforceable, but are nonetheless regarded as binding by those to whom they apply. For discussion of such 'constitutional conventions', see further chapter 4.

have always received some protection in the law, the Human Rights Act 1998 has provided a clearer, more positive statement of the rights which individuals possess against the state in this country, and such issues have accordingly moved to the forefront of the political, media and judicial agenda. We shall need to pay careful attention to the implications of this important (and controversial) piece of legislation as we move through the pages of this book.

There are, of course, other subjects of legal study in which the relationship between the individual and the state is of central significance. Perhaps the most obvious of these is criminal law, in which Parliament prohibits certain conduct which is considered to represent a threat to the safety and welfare of the public. The centrality of the state is signified here by the fact that prosecutions for infringement of criminal laws are carried out in its name (although in the United Kingdom, the term used in this context is 'the Crown'). However, although criminal law can be regarded as a particular species of public law for this reason, the relevant framework of legal rules is so complex and extensive that the subject is always studied in its own right. The same might be said of other areas in which, to a greater or lesser extent, the state and the individual may come into conflict, such as family law, environmental law, housing law, the law of taxation and others.

There is another group of subjects, the study of which will normally occupy the bulk of a student's time on an undergraduate law degree, which may be labelled 'private law': this group includes subjects such as contract, tort, property law and trusts. On the face of it, this category is easily distinguishable from public law, in that the focus here is upon the legal relationship between private citizens, or between corporate bodies, or between private citizens and corporate bodies. The state plays no *direct* role, although (as noted in the first paragraph of this chapter) state organs such as Parliament and the courts are largely responsible for establishing the legal framework through which these relationships are regulated, in the form of legislation – such as the Law of Property Act 1925 – and/or judicial decisions which establish guiding legal principles within which those relationships operate – such as the famous decision of the House of Lords in *Donoghue v Stevenson*.[4]

However, the distinction is not as clear-cut as may appear at first sight. Just as a private citizen or corporate body may enter into contracts, own property or engage in activity which constitutes a tort, so may the government do so. In some countries, such as France, special legal regimes apply to the state's exercise of private law powers. In broad terms, this is not the

---

4   [1932] AC 562.

case in the UK: the common law principles of contract, tort *etc* apply to the state, albeit with certain increasingly important modifications. For this reason, public lawyers tend not to dwell at length upon this type of legal relationship, at least outside of more advanced courses in the subject. Nonetheless, it is important to understand that government may also often act through the medium of private law. This is especially necessary because there has been a significant trend over the past thirty years for activities which were formerly performed by the state (such as refuse collection services provided on behalf of local government, or the provision of long-term care facilities for the elderly) to be handed over to the private sector, in an attempt to ensure efficiency and value for money in the delivery of public services. In this sense, the boundary between 'public' and 'private' has become increasingly blurred and, as will be noted in chapter 5, this has at times caused classification difficulties for judges who have had to decide upon the correct legal procedure applicable in cases brought before them.

Earlier it was noted that 'public law' is sometimes studied under the heading of 'constitutional and administrative law'. It is not especially important which title is used: classification tends to be a matter of academic preference rather than a reflection of any real distinction of substance in the subject matter. Nevertheless, it is perhaps useful to explain the meaning of the latter phrase briefly at this point. *Constitutional law* refers to that body of laws which defines the institutions of government, which determines their functions and which regulates their relationship with each other and with individual citizens. *Administrative law* relates to the duties and powers of administrative agencies: that is, those bodies which are charged with putting the law into effect within society. The dividing line between these two areas is not always readily apparent, especially since (as will shortly be seen) the United Kingdom lacks a single document which might be classified as 'a constitution', which would give a clearer indication as to which laws were to be regarded as constitutional and which were not. For this reason, this book uses the broader phrase 'public law' to describe its subject matter. However, examples may clarify matters here. The question of whether a government minister has an obligation to resign when s/he has misled Parliament (and, if so, whether this applies only when the minister has 'knowingly' done so),[5] is constitutional in nature: it speaks to the relationship between two institutions of government – the legislature (Parliament) and the executive (the minister). By contrast, the legality of a local council's decision to prohibit the hunting of deer on land which it manages is a question of administrative law. If this

---

[5] Such questions were at issue in the Scott Inquiry on the export of arms to Iraq, below p.31 (n.37).

were to be challenged, a court might be asked to decide (using the process of judicial review which is discussed in chapter 5) whether a decision which was premised on the moral beliefs of the councillors had taken the administrative agency (in this instance, the local council) outside of the scope of its legal powers to manage land for specific statutory purposes.[6]

What is public law for?

At first sight, this might seem a peculiar question to be posing, particularly to those who are new to the study of law. It might be thought that the primary job of a lawyer is to become acquainted with the (very large body of) legal rules which exist in any given legal system and to understand how they work, applying them as necessary to the facts of the case before them. We might call this the *expository* approach to the study of law, and it necessitates that the student of law should develop particular skills, especially the capacity to comprehend and memorise legislation, cases, legal principles *etc* and then to reproduce these when called upon to do so by a tutor (and later, by a client).

It is true that this forms part of the task of the lawyer and law student and that this book will engage in exposition in various places: indeed, one of the fundamental objectives of this text is to map the sources of power in the British constitution. But there is a further approach to legal study in general, and to that of public law in particular. This might be labelled the *functional* approach: it focuses upon the *job which law actually performs within society*. From this perspective, we are not only interested in what legal rules say, but in what they do and how well they do it. Importantly, it makes two demands of the student. First, it requires development of an awareness of the *context in which law operates* so that we can understand the societal role which the law should perform. In the case of public law, as discussed further below, this will mean some degree of familiarity with the political environment. Secondly, it obliges the student to take a *critical approach to the law*: that is, to evaluate its success or otherwise in achieving its societal objectives and, if possible, to propose alternative frameworks, institutions or principles which might do the job better.

Successful study of public law will almost certainly depend upon your capacity to understand and apply the second approach to the subject matter, while of course not neglecting the task of explaining what the law is where it is necessary to do so. This is an aspect of the subject which some will find challenging. It is important to grasp that, while the views of those teaching you, or those whose work you read, can provide some guidance

---

[6] See *R v Somerset County Council, ex parte Fewings* [1995] 1 All ER 513 (QBD).

in this regard, it is crucial that you formulate your own opinions as to the appropriate role which law should be playing in a particular context and whether it is discharging that role in a satisfactory manner.

This having been said, it may be useful at this point to flag up two possible answers to the question 'what is public law for?' which have been influential in the academic literature in this field, and elements of which may be discerned both within the case law and within the institutional framework of public law. You might wish to begin considering which of these accords most closely with your own perspective and, as you proceed through the pages of this book, to ask yourself how far the institutions and principles which are being analysed fit within either of these models (while noting that, in most instances, this is unlikely to be clear-cut).

The first approach, which has traditionally tended to dominate thinking in this field and which especially continues to underpin most external perceptions of public law (such as those which are expressed within the media), is that the law functions as a *control mechanism*. That is, it sets parameters for the actions and/or decisions which governmental institutions can take, restricting their sphere of activity. We might conceive of this approach as negative in the sense that it focuses upon unlawfulness and seeks to provide a retrospective form of redress for those who are harmed by actions or decisions which exceed the legal authority which a particular governmental institution has been allocated. It is negative, also, in respect of the view which is taken of state (that is, governmental) activity: the assumption is that the state must be kept within appropriate bounds and prevented from undue interference with the freedom which individuals possess to plan and live their lives as they choose. For these reasons, it may be helpful to conceive of this model of public law's function through the use of the 'traffic light' metaphor developed by Harlow and Rawlings: this may be seen as the 'red light' theory of public law.[7]

A significant, albeit still minority, body of opinion rejects this view of the function of public law, adopting instead a 'green light' view.[8] As the metaphor implies, governmental activity is regarded in a more positive light within this model and the function of the law is not therefore to set limits to such activity; but rather to provide a framework which will *facilitate the achievement of objectives by governmental institutions*. Law will act to structure, channel and guide public decision-making, and will seek to ensure that those decisions are, prospectively, as good as they can be (that is, that they are in the interests of society as a whole) before they are given effect. Subscribers to this model do not necessarily reject the notion of

---

[7] C. Harlow and R. Rawlings, *Law and Administration* (Cambridge: CUP, 3rd ed., 2009), Chapter 1.

[8] *ibid*, Chapter 3.

individual freedom and autonomy which is at the heart of the 'red light' approach, but they also place value upon liberties which may best be realised in a collective manner and view intervention by the state as being the best means of securing these. The 'green light' position has been lucidly summarised by Adam Tomkins:

'the goal of the state might be to house the homeless, to feed the hungry, to care for the sick, to educate the young, and so on, and the role of ... law is to help the state perform these tasks well, to distinguish between good and bad administrative practices, and to encourage and facilitate the former as well as to minimise the latter.'[9]

What can readily be deduced from these brief summaries is that the view which one takes of the function of public law will hinge largely upon a perception of the appropriate role for government within society. This is, of course, fully consonant with a functional approach to the subject matter: the role of law can only be understood in the context of the environment in which it operates – here, the governing political principles of a society – and our evaluation of the success of law in achieving its objectives is not primarily a matter for empirical observation, but rather depends upon our personal perspective or opinion. To put the matter another way, and to express it more broadly: public law is not a subject where we can say, without fear of contradiction, that a particular legal principle, decided case, process or institutional framework is 'good' or 'bad', 'right' or 'wrong'. It is a subject where differing conclusions on such matters are wholly acceptable, provided always that they are backed by sufficient evidence and are cogently argued.

Public law and power

In the preceding discussion, public law was viewed as a mechanism either for controlling and constraining, or for structuring, channelling and guiding *decisions and actions taken by governmental institutions*. A different way of putting this would be to say that public law is centrally concerned with the *exercise of power* by such institutions.

This is, in fact, not an especially surprising observation. Elements of law in various of its forms connect to the concept of power, whether that power is physical (criminal law, tort law), economic (contract law, competition law, property law), military (international law), industrial (labour law) or familial (family law): moreover, law itself may be seen as a particular type

---

[9] A. Tomkins, 'In Defence of the Political Constitution' (1992) 22 *Oxford Journal of Legal Studies* 157, 159.

of power structure. It would be beyond the scope of an introductory text such as this fully to explore the meaning of 'power', especially as this is a matter for considerable debate.[10] However, as a shorthand definition for the purposes of our study,[11] we might note Loughlin's explanation that political power – which is the type of power with which public law is concerned – refers to 'the ability [that is, of governmental institutions] to produce intended effects. We experience power in this sense by observing the behaviour of actors as decisions are made, action is taken and consequences follow'.[12]

Public law has much to say about power in this sense. In its expository dimension, it provides us with a map of where (political) power resides within a particular state. That is, it explores the questions of where power comes from, by whom it is exercised and in what ways, and seeks to identify where the limits to that power lie. As the next section will outline, there are greater difficulties in locating such a 'power map' in the British case than there are in other states: but such an exercise can nonetheless be undertaken.

From a functional perspective, taking first the 'red light' approach, public law is concerned with the questions of: (a) whether a governmental institution actually possesses the power which it is purporting to exercise: that is, whether it is acting within or in excess of its allotted power; and (b) whether power which the institution *does* have authority to exercise has nonetheless been abused in some manner. In both instances, the law seeks to prevent government from misusing its power, so that the autonomy of individuals may be safeguarded. Alternatively, on the 'green light' approach, public law provides a 'toolkit' of principles and values of 'good decision-making' which can facilitate the exercise of power by government, so that it can act in a manner which is beneficial to society as a whole.

It will be noted that the approach to power adopted here places emphasis upon the *making of decisions* by governmental actors.[13] It is important to unpack this notion a little further. In some instances, such actors will be obliged to adopt a particular course of action: in such cases, we may say that they are acting under a *duty*. A failure to fulfil such a duty may give rise to challenge through mechanisms of public law (particularly when the duty is a relatively specific one) or through political channels (these may be more appropriate where the duty is general in nature, or ethical – as distinct from legal – in character). However, as generally understood, the

---

10 See S. Lukes, *Power: a Radical View* (Basingstoke: Macmillan, 1974), 9.
11 With which Lukes, for one, would take issue: *ibid*, Chapter 7.
12 M. Loughlin, *Sword and Scales* (Oxford: Hart, 2000), 12–13.
13 See Lukes, n.10, 15.

essence of decision-making resides in the ability to make a *choice* between different courses of action. In public law, the capacity to exercise such a choice is captured by the concept of *discretionary power*. It is fundamental to an understanding of the role of public law – especially in its 'red light' incarnation – to grasp the fact that law may set limits to the exercise of such choices, even in situations where the decision-maker would seem to have complete free rein to act as it wishes. The rationale for legal intervention into decision-making of this type will be explored in greater depth in chapter 2 of this book.

A further concept which is of immense significance to the study of public law in the UK is that of *sovereignty*. Further space will be devoted to this idea in chapter 3, but it is useful here to briefly outline its relationship with power. The term was defined by the sixteenth-century legal theorist Jean Bodin as 'supreme power over citizens and subjects, unrestrained by the laws',[14] which, as Loughlin notes, simply equates it with (political) power understood in the manner described above, that is as the capacity to bring about intended effects and consequences.[15] However, during the nineteenth century, this idea of *political* sovereignty became detached from that of *legal* sovereignty, particularly in the work of the great Victorian constitutional theorist, Professor Albert Venn Dicey, about whom this book will have considerably more to say in due course. Political sovereignty connoted the ultimate source of political power within a state, while legal sovereignty spoke to the question of which institution possessed *ultimate authority within a legal system*, enabling us to identify the types of rules which are superior to others. Understood in this way, it is perfectly possible for sovereignty to reside in different places: for example, political sovereignty might rest with the electorate, while legal sovereignty might be located in Parliament.

Where can the rules of public law be found?

Those undertaking courses in public law elsewhere in the world have considerably more obvious starting points for their studies than those in the UK. In many countries, the rules of public law (in some cases, both constitutional law and administrative law, in others, just the former) are *codified*, meaning that they are collected together and incorporated in a legally-binding statement or code. The most important aspect of this is the existence of a written constitutional document setting out the rules which establish and regulate the institutions of government within that state. It should be noted, however, that even in such countries, such a document

---

[14] See W. Dunning, 'Jean Bodin on Sovereignty' (1896) 11 *Political Science Quarterly* 82, 92.
[15] Loughlin, n.12, 125.

will not contain *all* of the rules which are of importance in this regard, and the student of public law will need also to consider the political practices which have grown up around the formal, legal constitutional rules in order to develop a full picture of the manner in which the institutions of government operate and the ways in which they are constrained.

The UK is virtually unique in not having a codified constitution of this type (though it is less unusual in not possessing a code of administrative law),[16] a fact which is normally explained by the absence of a historical break such as civil war or independence.[17] It would be wrong, however, to claim that the British constitution (and, of course, there is a British constitution in the sense that there exist legal and non-legal rules pertaining to the institutional structure of government and its relationship with the individual)[18] is unwritten. More accurately, it can be described as a constitution of multiple sources. The student of public law must, therefore, search widely to discover the rules of public law, considering primary and secondary legislation,[19] judicial decisions, laws and customs of Parliament and 'constitutional conventions'.[20]

However, the absence of a codified constitution carries implications beyond those entailed in locating the sources of law. A constitution serves not only to define the institutions of government and to distribute power between them – to act as a 'power map'[21] – but also acts as a mechanism for the *limitation* of governmental power. This might be thought necessary for a number of reasons: to identify and protect the relative powers of central (national) governmental institutions and those functioning at a regional or local level, especially in a federal state such as the United States (US), Canada or Australia; to express a commitment to the protection of the rights and liberties of individual citizens *vis-a-vis* the state (which will normally take the form of a 'bill of rights', either contained within the original constitutional document as in South Africa or as amendments to it, as in the US); or, more broadly, because political power may be easily and dangerously abused. As Ridley comments, 'whatever the reasons, the purpose of constitutions generally is to restrict the powers government

---

[16] New Zealand and Israel are also commonly regarded as having unwritten constitutions.

[17] Readers with knowledge of British history will be aware that a civil war did take place in the 1640s; and, in fact, the subsequent republican government of Oliver Cromwell operated under two successive documents which may be described as constitutions, the Instrument of Government and the Humble Petition and Advice. These did not survive the restoration of the monarchy in 1660.

[18] However, for a critique of this view, see F. Ridley, 'There is no British Constitution: a Dangerous Case of the Emperor's Clothes' (1988) 41 *Parliamentary Affairs* 340.

[19] The distinction between these two types of legislation will be explored in chapter 3.

[20] The latter are examined further in chapter 4.

[21] See I. Duchacek, *Power Maps: Comparative Politics of Constitutions* (Santa Barbara: Clio Press, 1973).

may take'.[22] This is captured in the notion of 'constitutionalism', which might briefly be defined as 'the concept of limited government under a higher law'.[23]

When viewed as a means of controlling political power – as demanded by the 'red light' approach – the absence of a codified constitution in the UK would seem to be very troubling. A constitution functions as a type of 'higher law' against which actions and decisions of government may be evaluated, with some mechanism (such as a constitutional court) being empowered to invalidate those measures which exceed the limits imposed by the constitution. This form of control is seemingly absent in the UK. Indeed, the problem appears to be even greater than we might appreciate at first sight. The doctrine of parliamentary sovereignty, which will be explored at length in chapter 3, appears to confer unfettered power upon Parliament to change the shape of the British constitution at will, even if the measures thus adopted might publicly be viewed as abuses of power in that they trample on individual rights or disturb existing and long-standing relationships between institutions of government for short-term political gains. Without a codified constitution, what is to prevent such action from occurring?

Leaving aside the fact that proponents of a 'green light' approach would caution against taking such a negative view of the exercise of governmental power in any event, those concerned at this prospect may take comfort from three related observations, upon which subsequent discussion will expand further. First, control mechanisms *do* exist within Britain's constitutional arrangements: it is simply that, at least until recently, they have primarily taken a political, rather than legal character. Secondly, and following from the first point, recent constitutional developments and changing judicial approaches have combined to strengthen legal forms of control of political power to the degree that it has been claimed that 'the courts of the United Kingdom, though acknowledging the sovereignty of Parliament, apply principles of constitutionality little different from those which exist in countries where the power of the legislature is expressly limited by a constitutional document'.[24] Thirdly, as this statement implies, the lack of a codified constitution does not mean that 'higher order' constitutional principles are absent from the arena of public law: indeed, we shall examine certain of these principles in chapters 2 and 3 of this book. It is true that the content of these principles may be more difficult to determine and delineate than is the case where a written constitution exists, and there is consequently considerable

---

22 Ridley, n.18, 351.

23 D. Fellman, 'Constitutionalism', in P. Wiener (ed.), *Dictionary of the History of Ideas: Studies of Selected Pivotal Ideas* (New York: Scribner, 1973), vol.1, 492.

24 *R v Secretary of State for the Home Department, ex parte Simms* [2000] 2 AC 115, 131 (Lord Hoffmann).

debate among scholars as to their meaning and extent. For example, as will be explored in the next chapter, some hold that such principles relate only to 'formal' questions relating to the procedures by which laws are passed and the 'surface' characteristics of such laws (such as clarity), while others argue that they give effect to certain democratic values upon which society is founded.[25] Nonetheless, the developing consensus among judges and academic analysts is that limited government under the law, not majority rule through the exercise of political power, characterises the modern British constitutional order.[26] In that sense the absence of a codified constitutional document functioning as a form of 'higher law' to limit the abuse of power by governmental institutions may be of decreasing practical significance, albeit that it remains a peculiarity which is undoubtedly worthy of comment.

Shifting power: from the 'political constitution' to the 'legal constitution'

The preceding discussion should alert readers to the fact that, as a map of power, a constitution is not set in stone: the distribution of power within a political society may change and constitutional arrangements correspondingly evolve to reflect this. In fact, such change may be more difficult to bring about in states with codified constitutions than is the case in the UK. Since it acts both as a form of 'higher law' and also establishes the foundations of a political system and a legal order, a constitution ought not to be easily altered at the whim of a transient political majority. It will therefore ordinarily be subject to a greater or lesser degree of *entrenchment*: that is, protection against repeal or amendment by way of special procedures for change (such as a two-thirds majority in the legislature or approval of the electorate by means of a referendum). In principle, the doctrine of parliamentary sovereignty precludes such entrenchment in the UK, since Parliament can make or unmake any law whatsoever, including those which alter constitutional arrangements.[27] This, it is said, makes the British constitution flexible, although it should be noted that the flexibility of constitutional arrangements is not merely a matter of legal form but also of political context. A commitment to historical continuity (the value

---

[25] For examples of each approach, see H. Wade, *Constitutional Fundamentals* (London: Stevens, 1980); T. Allan, *Constitutional Justice: a Liberal Theory of the Rule of Law* (Oxford: OUP, 2001).

[26] See *eg* J. Jowell, 'Beyond the rule of law: towards constitutional judicial review' [2000] *Public Law* 671, especially 671, 682; *Jackson v Attorney-General* [2005] UKHL 56, [102] (Lord Steyn), [107] (Lord Hope).

[27] But see *Jackson, ibid*, especially [102] (Lord Steyn), [159] (Baroness Hale); and further, *Thoburn v Sunderland City Council* [2002] EWHC 195. These cases are discussed further in chapters 2 and 3.

of tradition) has often rendered extensive constitutional change problematic in the UK, albeit that the reforms introduced since 1997, which will be discussed in the pages of this book, have been described as amounting to a 'constitutional revolution'.[28]

Just as the distribution of power may change, so may the means which exist for the control of such power. In this regard, it is important to develop the first two observations made at the end of the preceding section of this chapter. The traditional mode of subjecting exercises of governmental power in the UK to scrutiny and constraint has been through *political* mechanisms. On a day-to-day basis, the most important of these is the convention of ministerial responsibility to Parliament and the associated processes for enforcement of this, which will be examined in detail in chapters 3 and 4. More sporadically – but potentially more tellingly – the electorate is provided with the opportunity to call government to account *via* the ballot box at election time.[29] By contrast, legal institutions played a limited role. In particular, at least until the mid-1960s, the process of judicial review, by which courts subjected the lawfulness of governmental decisions and actions to scrutiny and review (which had been in existence since the early modern period) had become relatively dormant.[30]

The most powerful case in favour of the predominance of political forms of control was made in 1979 in a celebrated journal article by Professor J.A.G. Griffith, entitled 'The Political Constitution'. He argued that:

'law is not and cannot be a substitute for politics. This is a hard truth, perhaps an unpleasant truth. For centuries political philosophers have sought that society in which government is by laws and not by men. It is an unattainable ideal. Written constitutions do not achieve it. Nor do Bills of Rights or any other devices. They merely pass political decisions out of the hands of politicians and into the hands of judges or other persons. To require a supreme court to make certain kinds of political decisions does not make those decisions any less political. I believe

[28] See A. Gamble, 'The Constitutional Revolution in the United Kingdom' (2006) 36 *Publius* 19.

[29] Note also the role of the print and broadcast media as a means of scrutiny of government activity, albeit one that is heavily influenced both by commercial considerations and (in the case of the press) by the political preferences of newspaper proprietors. For discussion, see *eg* M. Saward, 'The News Media and the Public Relations State' in P. Dunleavy, R. Heffernan, P. Cowley and C. Hay (eds.), *Developments in British Politics 8* (Basingstoke: Palgrave Macmillan, 2006).

[30] See S. Sedley, 'The Sound of Silence: constitutional law without a constitution' (1994) 110 *Law Quarterly Review* 270, 277, referring to 'the long sleep of judicial review'. The 'reawakening' of the courts is normally traced to the decision of the House of Lords in *Ridge v Baldwin* [1964] AC 40.

firmly that political decisions should be taken by politicians. In a society like ours this means by people who are removable. It is an obvious corollary of this that the responsibility and accountability of our rulers should be real and not fictitious. And of course our existing institutions, especially the House of Commons, need strengthening. And we need to force governments out of secrecy and into the open. So also the freedom of the Press should be enlarged by the amendment of laws which restrict discussion. Governments are too easily able to act in an authoritarian manner. But the remedies are political. It is not by attempting to restrict the legal powers of government that we shall defeat authoritarianism. It is by insisting on open government.'[31]

Not everyone shared this preference for political remedies. At the time of writing, Griffith sought to contrast his vision of the constitution with that expressed by judges whom he considered to have largely conservative views. Notable amongst these was the former Lord Chancellor, Lord Hailsham, who had famously spoken out against the 'elective dictatorship' of the executive branch of government and had called for the establishment of a number of legal safeguards against this phenomenon, including a Bill of Rights, legal limitation on the unlimited capacity of Parliament to legislate, and devolved power to the countries of the UK.[32] During the following two decades, such demands – particularly that for a legally enforceable statement of individual rights – were increasingly taken up by judges of a more liberal persuasion, in part as a response to perceived encroachments upon individual liberties by the Conservative governments of 1979–1997.[33] Concurrently, as will be noted in chapter 5, the simplification of the process by which an application for judicial review could be made resulted in a significant increase in the number of cases, offering the judiciary ample opportunity to develop the grounds for, and scope of, this jurisdiction as a means of scrutiny of governmental activity. Underlying this evolution was a judicial perception that the political forms of control were increasingly inadequate and that legal controls were necessary to 'mitigate the democratic deficit'.[34] This view was, perhaps, most cogently expressed by Lord Mustill in 1995 in the following terms:

---

[31] (1979) 42 *Modern Law Review* 1, 16.

[32] See Lord Hailsham, *The Dilemma of Democracy: Diagnosis and Prescription* (London: Collins, 1978).

[33] See *eg* Lord Woolf, '*Droit public* – English style' [1995] *Public Law* 57, 70.

[34] The phrase derives from Lord Irvine, 'Judges and Decision-Makers: the Theory and Practice of *Wednesbury* review' [1996] *Public Law* 59.

'Parliament has its own special means of ensuring that the executive, in the exercise of its delegated functions, performs in a way which Parliament finds appropriate. Ideally, it is these latter methods which should be used to check executive errors and excesses; for it is the task of Parliament and the executive in tandem, not of the courts, to govern the country. In recent years, however, the employment in practice of these specifically Parliamentary remedies has on occasion been perceived as falling short, and sometimes well short, of what was needed to bring the performance of the executive into line with the law, and with the minimum standards of fairness implicit in every Parliamentary delegation of a decision-making function. To avoid a vacuum in which the citizen would be left without protection against a misuse of executive powers, the courts have had no option but to occupy the dead ground in a manner, and in areas of public life, which could not have been foreseen thirty years ago.'[35]

Judicial activity has, however, not been the only factor which has served to enhance the potency of legal forms of control of governmental power. Since 1972, a number of pieces of legislation have brought about significant changes in British constitutional arrangements. These will be examined in more detail later in this book, but a brief roster would include the European Communities Act 1972, the Human Rights Act 1998, the statutes which devolve varying degrees of power to new political institutions in Wales, Scotland and Northern Ireland,[36] the Freedom of Information Act 2000 and the Constitutional Reform Act 2005. These developments are important in two regards. First, they provide a *written foundation for existing, modified or new constitutional arrangements, principles and rights* such as the rule of law, the appointment of the judiciary, the relationship between central and regional governmental institutions, civil and political rights, and access to information held by governmental bodies. In this sense, the gap between the British constitution and written, legally enforceable constitutions elsewhere in the world can be said to have narrowed, although a single code of constitutional rules still appears to be some distance away.[37] Secondly, the potential for the courts to act as mechanisms for scrutiny and control of other branches of government has been significantly enhanced. For example, notwithstanding the doctrine of parliamentary sovereignty, courts may now strike down legislation on the

---

[35] *R v Secretary of State for the Home Department, ex parte Fire Brigades Union* [1995] 2 AC 513, 567. For further discussion of this case, see pp.27–28.

[36] Respectively, the Government of Wales Acts 1998 and 2006, the Scotland Act 1998 and the Northern Ireland Act 1998.

[37] See 'Written Constitution is a long way off, says Straw', *The Guardian*, 13 February 2008.

basis that it conflicts with European Union law, while both governmental actions and decisions, and legislation are subject to review for compatibility with the rights protected by the European Convention on Human Rights. When performing these functions, the courts are operating in a manner which is broadly comparable to constitutional courts in other jurisdictions, albeit that their powers of review – especially of primary legislation – are more limited than those of, for example, the US Supreme Court.[38]

Increasingly, then, the arena in which attempts are made to control governmental power is the courtroom, not Parliament. Although rightly described as 'one of the most fundamental realignments of the constitutional order since the end of the seventeenth century',[39] this change in the constitution is perhaps less startling when set in a comparative social and political context. It has been contended that, generally, 'in the post-war period, European democracies have experienced a profound, multifaceted judicialisation of politics' impacting both upon high-level constitutional matters and more prosaic day-to-day administrative disputes,[40] and that, more broadly, this may be illustrative of the spread of an American-style 'litigation culture'.[41] Nonetheless, the implications of this development are potentially profound. In particular, it appears to place non-elected judges centre-stage, in consequence raising questions as to their mode of appointment, representativeness and relationship with other branches of government; and, more fundamentally, as to the democratic character of the modern British constitutional order.

Public law and politics

It should be apparent from the discussion so far that, even if one does not subscribe to Griffith's view that 'laws are merely statements of a power relationship and nothing more',[42] there is a profound and intimate connection between public law and politics. On the one hand, public law may be seen as a means of achieving political ends, as the 'outcome of an institutionalised political process, thus presenting law as an instrument of

---

[38] See above, n.24.

[39] A. Tomkins, *Public Law* (Oxford: OUP, 2003), 23.

[40] R. Kelemen, 'The Americanisation of European law? Adversarial legalism *à la Européene'* (2008) 7 *European Political Science* 32, 32.

[41] See R. Kelemen and E. Sibbitt, 'The Globalization of American Law' (2004) 58 *International Organization* 103. There is continued debate about the existence of a 'litigation (or compensation) culture' in the United Kingdom, even within the field of tort law, where the phenomenon appears to be most applicable. For discussion, see A. Morris, 'Spiralling or Stabilising? The Compensation Culture and our Propensity to Claim Damages for Personal Injury' (2007) 70 *Modern Law Review* 349.

[42] Griffith, n.31, 19.

government'.[43] On the other, public law may be seen as establishing the foundations for political relationships within the state and setting parameters for political activity and decision-making, 'forming the cordon within which politics is allowed to take place'.[44] It is true that, in principle, the notion of public law as a means of constraint and limitation of governmental action implies an elevation of neutral, rational legal principle above the often self-interested struggles of politics. Something of this distinction between the two spheres is captured in the idea of the rule of law, which will be examined in depth in the next chapter. However, as Nicol notes, the developments outlined in the preceding section – and particularly the Human Rights Act 1998, which (as will be seen) demands that judges should formulate some vision of what is 'necessary in a democratic society', understood as one which embodies the principles inherent in a modern European liberal democracy[45] – have conclusively 'propelled into the courtroom decision-making which in former days would have fallen within the domain of the politician'.[46]

This interpenetration of law and politics is a matter which often alarms students of public law, many of whom profess themselves to be uninterested in politics. There is some misunderstanding here. There is no necessity for students to possess a detailed knowledge of *party politics* in the form of speeches made by politicians, policy proposals or election manifestos except in so far as these relate to issues which form part of the subject matter of public law (such as constitutional reform). Nor is a comprehensive understanding of British political history required, although a nodding familiarity with key historical events will certainly do no harm. What is important – and, as the discussion in this chapter has sought to demonstrate, unavoidable – is an appreciation of the *nature* of politics, particularly its character as a struggle for power and as an arena for debate as to alternative conceptions of what constitutes a good society (for example, one in which protection of individual autonomy is the primary goal, or one in which the good of the collectivity necessitates some degree of state intervention). It is only against this backdrop that the role of public law can properly be understood and its success evaluated.

Structure and objectives of this book

The idea of power constitutes a central thread running through the remainder of this book. We shall be concerned to identify the *types of power*

---

43 Loughlin, n.12, 218.
44 D. Nicol, 'Law and Politics after the Human Rights Act' [2006] *Public Law* 722, 722.
45 See Jowell, n.26, 681.
46 Nicol, n.44, 732.

which exist, *which institutions exercise such power* and *how far power extends vis-a-vis* other constitutional actors. That is, to utilise the terminology adopted above, part of the task of this text is to draw up a map of power within the British constitutional order.

A starting point for such an exercise is afforded by the doctrine of the separation of powers, which seeks to identify the distinct functions performed by the several branches of government within a state, and to allocate these functions to different institutions. Chapter 2 will explain the meaning of this idea. In the following three chapters, each type of power will be examined in turn, in the context of the institutional arrangements of the British constitutional order. While, as will be seen, application of this model to the British constitution is necessarily imprecise, it nonetheless offers a useful means of classifying and understanding the various types of governmental power which exist.

However, as noted earlier in this chapter, the shape of such a map may alter over time. While such changes will be considered throughout the book, chapter 6 will focus particularly upon shifts in relations of power within the British constitutional order as a consequence of recent developments. It will consider both how such developments may have displaced power from the institutions considered in the three preceding chapters, and how the balance of power may have altered as a consequence of those developments.

While the mapping of power within the British constitutional order represents an obvious framework for the structure of the text, it is important not to lose sight of the functional dimension of public law. A further goal will therefore be to identify the doctrines and mechanisms which exist to enable the various branches of government to carry out their functions in a manner which is to the benefit of society as a whole, and those which exist to restrain any abuse or excess of power. We shall be concerned, therefore, to examine the *constitutional principles* – both facilitating and constraining – *which regulate the exercise of power*. This task is undertaken throughout the book, but chapters 2 and 3 afford a particular focus upon three key underlying principles. In addition to the separation of powers, as outlined above, we shall consider the notion of the 'rule of law', which may be said to be the guiding principle by means of which the objectives of 'constitutionalism' may be realised in the United Kingdom in the absence of a codified constitution; and the principle of the sovereignty of Parliament, which expresses the source of ultimate legal authority within the British constitutional order and which has been described as 'the dominant characteristic of our political institutions'.[47]

---

[47] A. Dicey, *Introduction to the Study of the Law of the Constitution* (London: Macmillan, 10th ed., 1959), 39.

In keeping with the need to adopt a critical approach to our subject matter, the text will also seek to identify areas in which the exercise of power gives rise to awkward constitutional problems. In undertaking this task, the key principles examined in chapters 2 and 3 will provide useful yardsticks. For example, we may say that certain institutional arrangements amount to a violation of the separation of powers, and that they should therefore be reformed. However, we shall also have occasion to consider the compatibility of exercises of power with certain other fundamental precepts of modern government, such as accountability and democracy.

You should be aware that this is not a textbook. It does not offer a fully comprehensive coverage of the entirety of the subject matter of a course in public law or constitutional and administrative law. Rather, what it seeks to do (as the title indicates) is to provide a grounding in fundamental principles, institutions, mechanisms and questions of the British constitution, which will equip you with a solid foundation for your studies. You may choose to read the book from beginning to end relatively early on, so that you develop a sound grasp of issues which you will later cover in depth. Alternatively – or additionally – you may wish to consult this book alongside the more detailed descriptions of specific topics addressed in a textbook, to provide you with an alternative reading and to assist you in building a more sophisticated understanding of them, one which is (wherever possible) rooted in recent developments and the wider political context in which public law operates. In either event, you will need to make full use of primary sources such as case law, legislation and official publications, and secondary sources such as books and journal articles relating to specific aspects of the British constitution. Particularly through the provision of footnotes, this book provides you with assistance in locating such sources.

Chapter 2

Classifying and controlling power

Before commencing the study of particular institutions of British government, it is important to gain an understanding of certain broad fundamental principles which appear to underpin the UK's constitutional order. As noted in chapter 1, the absence of a codified constitutional document makes it more difficult both to identify such principles and to determine their significance. The consequence is that (as we shall see) different 'constitutional actors' – such as academic commentators, judges and politicians – hold varying views as to the meaning of the principles or, indeed, whether it makes sense to speak of them at all in relation to the British constitution. We are also confronted with the issue of fluidity: the principles to be discussed may have waxed or waned in significance as time has passed so that we cannot say with certainty that any one of them takes priority over the others. For example, it has long been thought that the central underlying principle of the British constitution, whose meaning will be explored in full in chapter 3, is that Parliament is legislatively supreme. However, a number of recent developments have combined to put pressure upon this principle while, concurrently, the two principles to be discussed in this chapter may be said to have become more potent in recent years.

Difficulties of this nature should not, however, prompt us to abandon the task of locating and comprehending the key underlying principles of the British constitution. This is a valuable exercise for a number of reasons. First, the principles may act as *organising concepts*: that is, they can offer guidance on how we might classify and comprehend particular elements or phenomena of the constitutional order. This makes the task of understanding complex institutions, processes, events or doctrines somewhat more straightforward since, rather than analysing each of these individually and discretely, we can seek to relate them to a limited number of central ideas. There is, of course, a danger of oversimplification or reductionism if we proceed blithely down this road and you should therefore be wary of assuming too readily that everything in public law can easily be explained in terms of the underlying principles, not least because you will constantly be uncovering aspects or incidents which appear to be exceptions to them. Nonetheless, if used with appropriate care, the principles – especially the first, the separation of powers – can assist in building a *constitutional taxonomy*, a means of classifying or categorising, which can form a foundation for study of the subject and which provides the basis of the organisation of this book.

Secondly, an appreciation of the two principles described in this chapter, the separation of powers and the rule of law, together with the third – parliamentary sovereignty, which is explored in chapter 3 – is important for an understanding of the relationship between public law and power, the theme introduced in chapter 1. From this perspective, the principles might be regarded in the following manner: the separation of powers is concerned with the *distribution* of power between institutions of government, the rule of law with the *control* of power and parliamentary sovereignty with the *exercise* of power. This categorisation is not completely watertight. As will be seen, aspects of the doctrine of the separation of powers – particularly the notion of 'checks and balances' – also perform a control function (and, indeed, the separation of powers is often regarded as being a constituent part of the rule of law in this regard).[1] Nonetheless, it provides a rough rule of thumb. The significance of this for a study of British constitutional arrangements lies in the absence of a codified constitutional document. As discussed in chapter 1, we would normally look to such a document (and/or to a court's interpretation of its meaning) to define the types of power which exist, to which institutions of government such powers are allocated, what such institutions are required or permitted to do, and – most crucially of all – where the limits to their powers lie. The absence of a 'higher order law' in the form of a constitutional document means that we must look elsewhere for such matters, and it is the principles to be discussed here which provide us with a basis for answering these fundamental constitutional questions in the UK context.

Thirdly, by acquiring a knowledge of the three key principles, we may also develop an understanding of the interrelationship between public law and politics. Since the principles are fundamentally concerned with the manner in which society should be governed, there is an inherent connection to particular philosophical theories of politics. This, however, is not necessarily a straightforward matter. Commentaries on the constitution, such as Dicey's *Introduction to the Study of the Law of the Constitution*, may purport to adopt a descriptive or historical approach to the subject matter,

---

[1] See below p.39.

with the principles and doctrines which are analysed being said to represent accounts of what is, as distinct from what ought to be. However, upon closer inspection they may in fact reflect unstated conceptions of the proper role of government within society and thus constitute expressions of the ideological preferences of the author. It is important to attempt to identify these underlying predispositions if we are to take a critical approach to the study of public law. If we fail to do so, we run the risk of evaluating institutions, processes and concepts from a perspective which may not match our own, and which also may be historically outdated.

A. The separation of powers

Meaning and function of the principle

The first of the principles which might be considered to underpin British constitutional arrangements is the separation of powers. While this doctrine is of classical antiquity, its modern origins lie in the writings of the French commentator, Montesquieu, who presented what appears to be an idealised version of the English constitution as the basis for his framework.[2] Montesquieu's work offered a threefold division of the functions of government into 'that of enacting laws, that of executing the public resolutions, and of trying the causes of individuals'. In modern parlance, these are referred to as legislative, executive and judicial tasks. The legislative function entails making laws, the executive function entails putting the law into effect, and the judicial function entails the settlement of disputes arising from the application or interpretation of the laws. Furthermore, there are particular agencies or branches of government which undertake these functions: legislature, executive and judiciary.

In the following three chapters we shall have cause to identify and analyse the institutions which perform these functions in the UK. However, probably the clearest exposition of the separation of powers doctrine is to be found in the Constitution of the US. The opening three Articles of the Constitution allocate the three functions of government to particular institutions, as follows:

'All legislative Powers herein granted shall be vested in a Congress of the United States, which shall consist of a Senate and House of Representatives ...

---

[2] C. Montesquieu, *The Spirit of the Laws* (trans. A. Cohler, B. Miller and H. Stone) (Cambridge: CUP, 1989). For further discussion, see M. Vile, *Constitutionalism and the Separation of Powers* (Indianapolis: Liberty Press, 2nd ed., 1998), Chapter 4.

The executive Power shall be vested in a President of the United
States of America ...

The judicial Power of the United States shall be vested in one
supreme Court, and in such inferior Courts as the Congress may from
time to time ordain and establish ...'

Provisions such as these both classify the types of political power exercised
within a society and allocate that power to particular institutions. They are
therefore fundamental components of a constitutional 'power map'.
However, the idea of the separation of powers extends well beyond mere
descriptive categorisation of the functions of government. It is also *normative* in orientation: that is, the principle expresses a conception of how
government *ought* to be ordered. This raises the question of the purpose
served by the division of power to different institutions. Montesquieu
wrote:

'When legislative power is united with executive power in a single
person or in a single body of the magistracy, there is no liberty ... Nor
is there liberty if the power of judging is not separate from legislative
power and from executive power. If it were joined to legislative power,
the power over the life and liberty of the citizens would be arbitrary, for
the judge would be the legislator. If it were joined to executive power,
the judge could have the force of an oppressor.'[3]

Similarly, James Madison, the principal author of the US Constitution,
argued that 'the accumulation of all powers, legislative, executive, and
judiciary, in the same hands, whether of one, a few, or many, and whether
hereditary, self-appointed or elective, may justly be pronounced the very
definition of tyranny'.[4] These passages indicate that the underlying rationale for the principle is a concern that concentration of the various types of
political power in one individual or institution will create the potential for
dictatorship. In this sense, the principle connects to notions of limited
government and, in turn, to political liberalism with its focus upon the
freedom of the individual.

Such a goal can be achieved in a number of ways. The most comprehensive manner of realising the objective would be to ensure that there is
separation of both personnel and of functions. Thus, for example,
members of the judiciary (that is, judges) should not sit in the legislature
(Parliament) or hold ministerial office as part of the executive branch

---

[3] *ibid*, book XI, Chapter 6.
[4] J. Madison, *Federalist* No. 47, 'The Particular Structure of the New Government and the
Distribution of Power Among its Different Parts' (1788).

(usually referred to as 'government'). Similarly, and again by way of illustration, organs of central or local government such as the Cabinet or local councils, which fall under the executive, should not make laws (legislative function) or adjudicate upon disputes (judicial function). This relatively rigid form of separation is frequently labelled the 'pure' separation of powers.

The 'pure' version represents an idealised form of the principle. It is unlikely to be workable in practice since total isolation of the branches of government from one another might result in deadlock within the political system. This may be especially true in a situation of *divided government*, that is, where the executive branch fails to command majority support in at least one chamber of the legislature, normally because the branches are controlled by different political parties. In such a situation, the disconnection between the component parts of government which is inherent in the pure separation of powers can develop into tension and conflict, exacerbated by partisan preferences, and result in stalemate. This has sometimes been the case in the US,[5] even though the US Constitution does not, in fact, exemplify a pure version of the principle.

A more realistic approach, and that which in fact characterises most constitutions, is a partial form of separation of powers. The objective remains the same: that is, to prevent the concentration of power in any one branch of government, but it is not considered imperative to ensure that functions and personnel are entirely separately allocated to the appropriate branches. Instead, the emphasis is upon the existence of a series of checks and balances exercised by each branch of government over the others to constrain any excess of power. It is clear from the writings of Madison that this was the approach he favoured for the nascent United States of America:

> 'It is agreed on all sides, that the powers properly belonging to one of the departments, ought not to be directly and completely administered by either of the other departments. It is equally evident, that neither of them ought to possess directly or indirectly, an overruling influence over the others in the administration of their respective powers. It will not be denied, that power is of an encroaching nature, and that it ought to be effectually restrained from passing the limits assigned to it. After discriminating therefore in theory, the several classes of power, as they may in their nature be legislative, executive, or judiciary; the next and most difficult task, is to provide some practical security for each against

---

[5] For discussion, see A. Ware, 'Divided Government in the United States' in R. Elgie (ed.), *Divided Government in Comparative Perspective* (Oxford: OUP, 2001).

the invasion of the others. What this security ought to be, is the great problem to be solved.'[6]

In consequence, the US Constitution contains a number of provisions by means of which control may be exercised by one branch over another. For example, the President has power to veto legislation passed by Congress, although this veto may be overridden by a two-thirds majority in each House.[7] The President makes nominations to certain public offices, including ministers, ambassadors and justices of the Supreme Court, but these appointments are subject to the 'advice and consent' of the Senate.[8] And courts possess the power of judicial review of executive acts and legislation for compliance with the Constitution: this power was not explicitly set out in the document, but was assumed by the Supreme Court in the early case of *Marbury v Madison*.[9]

Just as there are difficulties with the 'pure' variant of the separation of powers doctrine, so the partial version is not unproblematic. One particular concern which arises, especially in the US context, is the so-called 'counter-majoritarian difficulty' of judicial review.[10] Put simply, why should unelected judges be able to nullify the actions or decisions of those elected members of the executive or legislative branches who represent the will of the majority? This raises broad questions as to the legitimacy of judicial review to which we shall return in chapter 5, although it will be noted there that the problem is not nearly as serious in the UK. However, even if we categorise this problem as one which is particularly acute in the US, other difficulties may arise in a system characterised by checks and balances. For example, approval by the legislative branch of appointments to (or, for that matter, of dismissals from) public office by the executive branch presuppose that the former is in possession of sufficient information to make a meaningful judgment upon competence to perform the task in question. In practice, it may only be the executive branch which possesses such information, with the consequence that the involvement of the legislature interferes with the efficient conduct of government for no palpable benefit.[11]

---

[6] J. Madison, *Federalist*, No. 48, 'These Departments Should Not Be So Far Separated as to Have No Constitutional Control Over Each Other' (1788).

[7] Article I, section 7.

[8] Article II, section 2.

[9] 5 U.S. (1 Cranch) 137 (1803).

[10] The phrase derives from A. Bickel, *The Least Dangerous Branch: the Supreme Court at the Bar of Politics* (New Haven: Yale University Press, 2nd ed., 1986), 16.

[11] For a discussion along these lines, see E. Barendt, 'Separation of powers and constitutional government' [1995] *Public Law* 599, 602.

Separation of powers in the British constitution: does it exist?

The US Constitution has explanatory value in affording a useful illustration of the meaning and operation of the separation of powers doctrine. However, this book is concerned with the UK. We need therefore to explore the relevance of the principle to the British constitutional order.

At the most basic level, the separation of powers is, of course, applicable to the UK. As is the case in any other state, government performs executive, legislative and judicial functions and it is possible to identify bodies which fulfil such roles. The next three chapters of this book will seek to undertake this task. Nevertheless, as will be seen, this is a far from straightforward exercise in the British context, especially in the absence of a written document delineating and allocating such powers. This raises questions as to whether the principle can be said to apply in a meaningful way.

A significant number of eminent constitutional commentators have concluded that the principle has little relevance to the UK. Prominent amongst these are Sir Ivor Jennings, who doubted that it was, in fact, possible to identify material differences between the three functions of government such that we might allocate particular functions to particular agencies,[12] and Geoffrey Marshall, who contends that the principle 'may be counted little more than a portmanteau of arguments for policies that should be supported or rejected on other grounds'.[13] This rejection of the doctrine, Munro argues, is attributable to two factors.[14] First, the modern origins of the doctrine – which, as we have seen, lie with Montesquieu and Madison in the eighteenth century – postdate the settlement of the English constitution at the end of the seventeenth century, so it would be impossible for the constitution to be *based* upon the principle, although it may have had subsequent influence upon constitutional reform. Secondly, the development of the British constitution has primarily been the product of gradual historical evolution rather than of principled argument, in stark contrast to the United States where the Constitution was the outcome of the deliberations of the delegates at the Philadelphia Convention of 1787. A third factor, identified by Barendt,[15] is that the separation of powers is not readily compatible with the doctrine of the legislative supremacy of Parliament which accords the legislature unchecked power to make laws which might violate the principle in either its pure or partial variants, for example by interfering with

---

[12] I. Jennings, *The Law and the Constitution* (London: University of London Press, 5th ed., 1959), Appendix 1.

[13] G. Marshall, *Constitutional Theory* (Oxford: Clarendon Press, 1971) at 124.

[14] C. Munro, *Studies in Constitutional Law* (London: Butterworths, 2nd ed., 1999), 302.

[15] Above n.11, 604.

the independence of the judiciary or legislating to abolish the process of judicial review.

Both Munro[16] and Barendt,[17] along with others, take a different view from those who reject the doctrine, considering both that the ideas inherent in the separation of powers doctrine have been influential in the development of the British constitution, and that such influence is to be welcomed. Perhaps the most comprehensive attempt to develop a normative case for the significance of the principle in the UK is to be found in the work of Trevor Allan. He writes that 'the principle of the separation of powers enables the law to serve as a bulwark between governors and governed, excluding the exercise of arbitrary power',[18] and views it as a fundamental component of the rule of law.

It may be pertinent that these more positive analyses of the principle are relatively recent. This may suggest that the doctrine possesses greater contemporary explanatory and/or normative validity than was previously the case. We shall explore whether there is justification for such a view later in this chapter.

If we turn now to statements of English judges concerning the separation of powers principle, we find further support for the relevance of the principle to British constitutional arrangements, but also some uncertainty as to its precise meaning. In *Duport Steels v Sirs*, Lord Diplock utilised the principle as a rationale for a restrained approach by the court to a matter of significant political controversy, in this case the legality of 'secondary' industrial action (that is, the extension of strike action to employees of companies not involved in the original dispute). His Lordship expressed the principle as follows:

'it cannot be too strongly emphasised that the British constitution, though largely unwritten, is firmly based upon the separation of powers; Parliament makes the laws, the judiciary interpret them. When Parliament legislates to remedy what the majority of its members at the time perceive to be a defect or a lacuna in the existing law (whether it be the written law enacted by existing statutes or the unwritten common law as it has been expounded by the judges in decided cases), the role of the judiciary is confined to ascertaining from the words that Parliament has approved as expressing its intention what that intention was, and to giving effect to it.'[19]

---

[16] Above n.14, 332.
[17] Above n.11, 619.
[18] Above p.11 (n.25), 3.
[19] [1980] 1 WLR 142, 157. Lord Scarman took a similar view: 169.

Similarly, in *M v Home Office*, Lord Templeman stated that 'Parliament makes the law, the executive carry the law into effect and the judiciary enforce the law'.[20]

These judicial dicta might be regarded as simple affirmations of the classificatory reading of the idea of the separation of powers or, from a normative perspective, as acknowledgments of the value of a 'pure' approach to the principle. They contain no reference to checks and balances and are fully compatible with a constitutional system in which Parliament is the legally sovereign power. We may contrast this with the approach taken by Lord Mustill in *R v Secretary of State for the Home Department, ex parte Fire Brigades Union*, who, in a dissenting judgment (part of which has already been cited in chapter 1),[21] sets out his interpretation of the principle:

'It is a feature of the peculiarly British conception of the separation of powers that Parliament, the executive and the courts have each their distinct and largely exclusive domain. Parliament has a legally unchallengeable right to make whatever laws it thinks right. The executive carries on the administration of the country in accordance with the powers conferred on it by law. The courts interpret the laws, and see that they are obeyed. This requires the courts on occasion to step into the territory which belongs to the executive, to verify not only that the powers asserted accord with the substantive law created by Parliament but also that the manner in which they are exercised conforms with the standards of fairness which Parliament must have intended. Concurrently with this judicial function Parliament has its own special means of ensuring that the executive, in the exercise of delegated functions, performs in a way which Parliament finds appropriate.'[22]

This passage repays careful study. Barendt argues that, in common with Lord Diplock's dictum in *Duport Steel v Sirs*, it may be said to support the 'pure' version of the separation of powers.[23] It is true that, in the first half of the statement, the judge appears to expound a view of the constitution in which powers are allocated to separate branches of government which are functionally separate from each other ('their distinct and ... exclusive domain'). However, this is qualified by the word 'largely', the meaning of which becomes apparent in the second part of the passage. Here, his Lordship sets out, albeit in somewhat veiled terms, the 'checks and balances' which exist in the British constitution. Courts 'step into the

---

[20] [1994] 1 AC 377, 395.
[21] Above, p.14 (n.35).
[22] *ibid*, 567
[23] Above n.11, 616.

territory which belongs to the executive' when exercising the jurisdiction of judicial review of administrative action, considered below in chapter 5. Through this mechanism, they ensure that executive bodies do not exceed the powers allocated to them by statute ('verify ... that the powers asserted accord with the substantive law created by Parliament') and that such bodies comply with common law principles of 'natural justice' ('conform ... with the standards of fairness that Parliament must have intended'). Alongside this check upon the executive runs another exercised by Parliament ('its own special means of ensuring that the executive ... performs in a way in which Parliament finds appropriate'), which takes the form of the constitutional convention of ministerial responsibility and the institutional arrangements for giving effect to this, which are explored (respectively) in chapters 4 and 3.

It is thus apparent that, notwithstanding Barendt's view, Lord Mustill adheres to the partial model of the separation of powers. That said, he is aware of the risks inherent in this model, in particular the danger of excessive judicial encroachment into the 'political' realms occupied by the executive and legislature which may be said to give rise to a variant of the counter-majoritarian difficulty: 'As the judges themselves constantly remark, it is not they who are appointed to administer the country.'[24] Thus, while he perceives the expansion of judicial review as a necessary counterweight to the relative inadequacy of the legislature's check on the executive through the mechanisms of ministerial responsibility ('For myself, I am quite satisfied that this unprecedented judicial role has been greatly to the public benefit'),[25] he goes on to caution that the checks and balances must not be abused: 'Absent a written constitution much sensitivity is required of the parliamentarian, administrator and judge if the delicate balance of the unwritten rules evolved (I believe successfully) in recent years is not to be disturbed, and all the recent advances undone.'[26]

Separation of powers and institutions of British government

It appears, therefore, that there is a difference of opinion amongst academic commentators and judges as to the relevance and meaning of the separation of powers in the British context. What light may be cast upon this seemingly contentious issue by an analysis of the institutions of government themselves, and of the relationships between them? We are, of course, somewhat hampered here by the fact that we have yet to analyse these institutions in depth, so you may wish to revisit this section once

---

[24] Above n.21, 567.
[25] *id.*
[26] *id.*

you have a more detailed knowledge of the various branches of government and their roles, as described in the next three chapters. Nonetheless, some picture of the extent to which the separation of powers is realised at an institutional level is necessary at this stage if we are to reach a meaningful conclusion on whether it may be considered to operate as an underlying principle of the constitution.

i Legislature and judiciary

Let us first consider whether there are any overlaps in personnel or functions between Parliament and the judges. Judges holding full-time appointment are disqualified from sitting in the House of Commons under section 1 of the House of Commons Disqualification Act 1975. There is no equivalent provision regarding membership of the House of Lords and, until October 2009, the highest court in the United Kingdom was a committee of the House of Lords, the Appellate Committee.[27] Its members, the Lords of Appeal in Ordinary (generally known as 'Law Lords') were life peers who were entitled to sit and vote in the chamber and, as such, sometimes played a significant role in parliamentary debate, for example on the bill which became the Human Rights Act 1998.[28] By constitutional convention, however, the Law Lords sat as 'cross-benchers' (that is, they were independent of political parties). Furthermore, in considering whether to participate in a debate or to vote, Law Lords were expected to recognise that it was 'not ... appropriate to engage in matters where there is a strong element of party political controversy' and that 'they might render themselves ineligible to sit judicially if they were to express an opinion on a matter which might later go to an appeal to the House'.[29]

This particular overlap in personnel, which was described as 'a unique arrangement among leading liberal democracies',[30] has now come to an end as a result of the changes initiated by the Constitutional Reform Act 2005, which will be described in the next section of this chapter. However, functional overlaps between the two branches of government remain. Parliament's power to enforce its own privileges, the rights and immunities possessed by members of Parliament which enable them to carry out their duties effectively, means that it exercises a judicial function in the trial and

---

[27] Except for Scottish criminal matters. It is necessary also to consider the position of the European Court of Justice, for discussion of which see chapters 3 and 6.

[28] For critical discussion of judicial involvement in such debate, see K. Ewing, 'The Human Rights Act and Parliamentary Democracy' (1999) 62 *Modern Law Review* 79, 85–86.

[29] Joint Committee on Human Rights, 'Implementation of the Human Rights Act 1998', HL 66-iii/HC 332-iii (2000–01), q.105 (Lord Bingham).

[30] A. Bradley and K. Ewing, *Constitutional and Administrative Law* (Harlow: Pearson Education, 14th ed., 2007), 393.

punishment of violations.[31] More importantly, the judges perform a law-making function both through their interpretation of the meaning of statutory provisions and the development of 'judge-made' principles of common law. Illustrations of this power in the particular context of public law will be provided in chapter 5.

How far do these two branches of government exercise checks and balances over each other? A major impediment to judicial checking of Parliamentary power is afforded by the doctrine of parliamentary sovereignty, explored at length in chapter 3. English courts have traditionally possessed no power, akin to that asserted by the US Supreme Court in *Marbury v Madison*, to declare primary legislation void. By contrast, Parliament may legislate in such a manner that the effect of a judicial decision is reversed, even on occasion doing so with retrospective effect.[32] This clearly puts Parliament in a constitutionally superior position *vis-a-vis* the judiciary, although the dynamics of this relationship are also shifting as a result of recent constitutional changes, as subsequent discussions will make apparent. Parliament also possesses the theoretical power to remove judges from office (removal takes place by way of an address presented to the Queen by both Houses of Parliament),[33] but this power has only been exercised once in three centuries and it would be virtually unthinkable for it to be used today. However, parliamentary censure of judges is restricted by rules of Parliament, including the principle that the conduct of judges or the judiciary in general should not be criticised except by way of a formal motion for debate, while the *sub judice* rule generally precludes parliamentary discussion of matters which are awaiting adjudication in a court of law.

ii Executive and judiciary

There are relatively few overlaps in practice as regards personnel in the executive and judicial branches.[34] The monarch retains a symbolic role as the figure in whose name justice is administered. Consequently, the courts are the Queen's courts, the judges are Her Majesty's judges and criminal prosecutions are carried out in the name of the Crown: however, the monarch has no personal involvement in the administration of justice. The

---

[31] For a recent situation in which parliamentary privilege was held not to apply, see *R v Chaytor and others* [2010] UKSC 52.

[32] *Eg Burmah Oil Co. Ltd v Lord Advocate* [1965] AC 75, in which the House of Lords held that destruction of property by British troops during the Second World War carried an entitlement to compensation for the company. Parliament passed the War Damage Act 1965 which exempted the Crown from liability to pay such compensation, both in respect of past and future actions.

[33] Senior Courts Act 1981, s.11(3); Constitutional Reform Act 2005, s.33.

[34] However, for discussion of the Lord Chancellor, see below, pp.36–37.

Judicial Committee of the Privy Council, established by the Judicial Committee Act 1833, is in form a component of an executive body (the Privy Council being the primary mechanism for government during the Tudor era in the sixteenth century), but in practice is an independent court which hears appeals from certain Commonwealth states and, prior to the opening of the new Supreme Court in 2009, resolved disputes as to the jurisdiction of the devolved regional legislatures (see further chapters 3 and 6). The Law Officers of the Crown, the Attorney-General and Solicitor-General, who are members of government who provide it with legal advice, perform certain quasi-judicial functions, though they are not judges. For example, the consent of the Attorney-General is required for prosecutions under the Official Secrets Act 1989 and s/he may enter an application of *nolle prosequi* which functions to stop a criminal prosecution.

There are further functional overlaps between the branches in addition to the last mentioned. One of the most notable is the appointment of judges by government to chair independent inquiries. Such inquiries are frequently established to investigate matters of acute political controversy or significant public interest, such as the Hillsborough stadium disaster,[35] the events of 'Bloody Sunday' in Northern Ireland,[36] the 'arms to Iraq' affair,[37] and the death of Dr David Kelly, the Ministry of Defence weapons expert.[38] This strategy is beneficial to a government which seeks to demonstrate that it is taking serious action in response to such incidents, since judges are seen as apolitical and authoritative. However, there is a danger that judges undertaking such work may be exposed to political criticism, that they may become drawn into the work of government with implications for impartiality in future cases which they may have to decide, and that the public perceives judges as being used for political ends, which may decrease confidence in the judiciary.[39]

Relatedly, we should also briefly consider the work of various mechanisms of 'administrative justice', which are explored at greater length in chapter 6. Tribunals, inquiries, ombudsmen and internal appeal or complaints processes all perform dispute resolution functions which might otherwise be assigned to the courts, although certain of these bodies do not operate in a manner which resembles the form of adversarial adjudication which is characteristic of the judicial model in the UK. It is difficult to

---

[35] *The Hillsborough Stadium Disaster* (the 'Taylor Report'), Cm 962 (1990).

[36] *Report of the Bloody Sunday Inquiry*, HC 29-I – HC 29-X (2010–11).

[37] *Report of the Inquiry into the Export of Defence Equipment and Dual-Use Goods to Iraq and Related Prosecutions* (the 'Scott Report'), HC 115 (1995–96).

[38] *Report of the Inquiry into the Circumstances surrounding the death of Dr David Kelly CMG* (the 'Hutton Report'), HC 247 (2003–04).

[39] See further J. Beatson, 'Should judges conduct public inquiries?' (2005) 121 *Law Quarterly Review* 221.

determine whether these institutions operate within the executive or judicial branches, or are somehow distinct from both.[40] This is in part because such bodies have tended to be created in a somewhat *ad hoc* manner, with little consideration given to systemic design, although there have been some important recent changes in this regard as will be noted below. Elsewhere, the existence of such mechanisms reflects a desire on the part of government to retain control of decision-making, for example because it is necessary to consider it as part of a wider policy context (as may be the case with certain planning inquiries) or because it is speedier, cheaper and more responsive to resolve matters internally (as is the case with many complaints about the performance of public services).

As for checks and balances, the executive has power of appointment of judges and there is no requirement for confirmation by the legislature, as there is in the US. The most senior judges are appointed by the Queen on the advice of the Prime Minister, and others by the Queen on the advice of the Lord Chancellor, with the Judicial Appointments Commission providing recommendations to the executive.[41] However, once appointed, judges have security of tenure (subject to the power of removal exercisable by Parliament which was outlined above) and their salaries are governed by statute and are not subject to parliamentary debate.[42] In principle, they should also be insulated from ministerial criticism or pressure relating to particular decisions or to the judiciary generally, although in recent years this principle has been subject to some erosion.[43]

For its part, the judiciary possesses a powerful mechanism for checking any abuse of power by the executive branch, in the form of judicial review of administrative action. This process will be discussed at much greater length in chapter 5. It will merely be noted briefly here that the judicial review jurisdiction is only exercised by the superior courts (High Court level and above) and that it extends to all bodies which perform a public function, not simply the institutions which make up the 'core executive' (such as central government departments).

iii *Legislature and executive*

While there are clearly some overlaps, both as regards personnel and functions, between the judiciary and the other two branches of government within the British constitution, there does broadly appear to be an under-

---

[40] This reflects a broader difficulty of distinguishing judicial from executive functions, which lay at the heart of Jennings' dismissal of the relevance of the doctrine. See p.25 (n.12), 303–04.

[41] See Constitutional Reform Act 2005, Part 4, Chapters 1 & 2.

[42] Judges' Remuneration Act 1965; Constitutional Reform Act 2005, s.34.

[43] For discussion see below, chapter 5.

lying commitment to the notion of judicial independence which Montesquieu had identified as a particularly important aspect of the separation of powers.[44] By contrast, the final relationship within the tripartite division which the principle establishes has been described by the Victorian constitutional commentator Walter Bagehot as 'the close union, the nearly complete fusion, of the legislative and executive powers'.[45] The key to this connection, in Bagehot's view, was the Cabinet, which he saw as 'a hyphen which joins, a buckle which fastens' the two branches of government.[46]

The close connection was, in Bagehot's view, a positive facet of the British constitution, but it is potentially problematic for two reasons. First, in studying the constitution, it is relatively easy to confuse 'government' with 'Parliament' given that key personnel from the former sit in the latter. This is one reason why developing an early understanding of the taxonomy developed by theorists such as Montesquieu and Madison is vital: armed with this knowledge, you will be better able to distinguish the two. Secondly, if the two branches are as 'fused' as Bagehot suggests, there is a clear danger that one may easily control the other and thereby secure a predominant constitutional position, restrained only by the third branch of government, the judiciary. It is precisely this type of dominance, with its attendant risk of abuse, that the principle of the separation of powers was intended to prevent. Let us now consider how far these concerns may be justified by analysing overlaps in personnel, functions and the existence of checks and balances.

Certain executive office holders are statutorily disqualified from membership of the House of Commons under section 1 of the House of Commons Disqualification Act 1975. These include civil servants, members of the armed forces, members of police forces, and office holders in a large number of other public bodies listed in Schedule 1 of the Act. Crucially, of course, this does not include holders of ministerial office and, indeed, it is a constitutional convention that ministers should be members of one of the Houses of Parliament and that the Prime Minister should be a member of the House of Commons so that the latter can hold the government accountable for its actions. However, the 1975 Act does limit the number of ministers in the House of Commons to 95.[47] If more ministers are required they must, therefore, be members of the House of Lords. Nonetheless, when combined with strong party loyalty enforced through the whip system and the significant parliamentary majorities which a governing party may

---

[44] See Vile, n.2, 96.
[45] W. Bagehot, *The English Constitution* (P. Smith (ed.), Cambridge: CUP, 2001), 9.
[46] *ibid*, 10
[47] s.2(1).

secure as a result of the UK's current absolute majority or 'first past the post' system for elections to Westminster (see further below, chapter 3), the fact that government ministers are drawn from Parliament does create the strong possibility of executive dominance over the legislature.

This is not to say that checks and balances do not exist which might enable Parliament to assert some degree of control over the executive. The conventions of collective and individual ministerial responsibility, realised through parliamentary mechanisms such as questions and select committees, fulfil the checking function and their operation and effectiveness will be analysed in depth subsequently. Furthermore, government is ultimately dependent for its existence upon the support of the House of Commons: if the government loses the vote in the House on a motion of no confidence, the Prime Minister must, by convention, seek a dissolution of Parliament, which causes a general election to be held.[48] Such was the fate of the Labour government of James Callaghan in 1979.

The most significant functional overlap between the legislative and executive branches arises through the making of secondary or delegated legislation, primarily by ministers although also by local councils (in the form of byelaws applicable to a particular locality). Parliament possesses unlimited power to delegate its law-making functions to others, and may therefore pass an 'enabling' Act which sets the framework for law in a particular field but which then delegates authority to another body, such as a minister, to complete the details required to render the law operational, generally by way of a statutory instrument. On occasion, the powers delegated may even extend to amendment of primary legislation (that is, legislation made by Parliament itself in the form of Acts): a controversial example of a provision conferring such a power (known as a 'Henry VIII clause') being section 10 of the Human Rights Act 1998.[49] Such legislation is subject to parliamentary scrutiny,[50] but the large volume of it – for example, there were 3,327 statutory instruments issued in 2008 – coupled with its often technical content is generally thought to render such scrutiny deficient as a means of control, even though it is now accepted that such legislation is inevitable given the extensive functions exercised by modern government.[51]

---

[48] But see now the Fixed-Term Parliaments Bill 2010, discussed below p.132.

[49] See below, p.223.

[50] Secondary legislation may also be reviewed by the courts to ensure that it is within the powers allocated by the enabling Act.

[51] This was not always the case. In 1929, the then Lord Chief Justice, Lord Hewart, published a scathing attack on delegated legislation under the title *The New Despotism* (London: Benn). You might reflect upon how far differing perspectives on the acceptability of extensive delegated legislative powers reflect changing ideological perspectives on the proper role of government in society (see above, pp.5–6).

Constitutional reform and the separation of powers

The preceding survey of institutional relationships affords ample explanation for the sceptical attitude towards the principle of the separation of powers which is apparent in the writings of many eminent academic commentators. Descriptively, it is abundantly clear that the UK does not adhere to a 'pure' approach to the principle, given the significant overlaps between personnel and functions within the three branches of government (although judicial independence is generally upheld). Even the more pragmatic, 'partial' approach, whereby we might regard the separation of powers as a 'network of rules and principles which ensure that power is not concentrated in the hands of one branch',[52] faces the difficulty of accounting for the close relationship between executive and legislature which seems to undercut the principle.

However, as noted previously, the separation of powers is not merely a vehicle for explaining the governmental structures within a particular system. It also has normative value: it offers a prescription for the manner in which government *should* be arranged. If we apply this reading of the principle to the British constitution, we acquire a theoretical model which enables us to critically evaluate present institutional arrangements and propose reforms thereto (assuming, of course, that we endorse the underlying objective of the principle, that is to prevent concentration of power in any particular part of government and the abuses which may result).

From this perspective, it is interesting to analyse a number of recent reforms which appear to propel the British constitution in the direction of the separation of powers. Undoubtedly the most significant of these is the Constitutional Reform Act 2005, which implemented a number of reforms to 'put the relationship between the executive, the legislature and the judiciary on a modern footing, which takes account of people's expectations about the independence and transparency of the judicial system'.[53] For the first time, this legislation imposed a statutory duty upon the Lord Chancellor, ministers and 'all with responsibility for matters relating to the judiciary or otherwise to the administration of justice' to uphold the continued independence of the judiciary,[54] and proscribed any attempt to influence particular judicial decisions through any special access to the judiciary.[55]

In addition to this somewhat intangible statutory duty, the Act made concrete changes to institutional arrangements. Prominent amongst these

---

[52] Barendt, n.11, 608–09.
[53] Department for Constitutional Affairs, *Constitutional Reform: a Supreme Court for the United Kingdom* (2003), 10.
[54] s.3(1).
[55] s.3(5).

was the creation of a Supreme Court, which began work in October 2009. Exercising the jurisdiction of the former Appellate Committee, coupled with that on devolution previously exercised by the Privy Council, the new court is separated both geographically and in respect of personnel from the House of Lords. It occupies premises on the opposite side of Parliament Square from the Houses of Parliament, and while the first Justices of the Supreme Court are the former Law Lords,[56] they no longer sit and vote as members of Parliament.[57] Lord Phillips, the first President of the court, commented upon the changes as follows:

'For the first time, we have a clear separation of powers between the legislature, the judiciary and the executive in the United Kingdom. This is important. It emphasises the independence of the judiciary, clearly separating those who make the law from those who administer it.'[58]

As well as changes to the process for judicial appointments, noted briefly above, the Act also had a significant impact upon the office of Lord Chancellor. The holder of this office, which dates back at least as far as the Norman Conquest, was formerly the head of the judiciary in England and Wales and the presiding officer of the House of Lords (the equivalent of Speaker of the House of Commons), as well as a Cabinet minister with responsibility for matters such as constitutional reform and administration of the court system. As such, the Lord Chancellor had important roles within all three branches of government, a position which may be described as 'unsustainable on the basis of the separation of powers'.[59] The Act ended the judicial role of the Lord Chancellor and precluded the holder of that office from being a judge, although the person appointed may still be a qualified lawyer or a legal academic.[60] The Lord Chief Justice became head of the judiciary in England and Wales,[61] and the Speakership of the House of Lords became a separate office, filled by internal election in the House of Lords. The office of Lord Chancellor continues to exist and its incumbent continues to serve as a Cabinet minister, with responsibility for the new Ministry of Justice established in 2007.

---

[56] Future vacancies in the Supreme Court will be filled by a process administered by an *ad hoc* Selection Commission which will report to the Lord Chancellor who then makes a recommendation to the Prime Minister. See Constitutional Reform Act 2005, ss.26–31 and Schedule 8.

[57] s.137(3). Retired Justices of the Supreme Court will be eligible to sit and vote in the House of Lords.

[58] Supreme Court Press Notice 01/09 (1 October 2009).

[59] D. Woodhouse, *The Office of Lord Chancellor* (Oxford: Hart, 2001), 20.

[60] s.2.

[61] s.7.

If we utilise the separation of powers as a normative model for the evaluation of constitutional arrangements, these reforms are clearly welcome. However, it is a more difficult task to ascertain how far commitment to the principle represented a motivating factor for the UK Government. Indeed, it has been suggested that the reforms contained within the 2005 Act were driven by a mixture of pragmatic political and personal factors as much as engagement with ideas of constitutionalism.[62]

Nonetheless, one legal impetus which is worthy of highlighting is Article 6 of the European Convention on Human Rights, which provides for the right to a fair trial by an independent and impartial tribunal.[63] In *McGonnell v United Kingdom*,[64] the European Court of Human Rights had ruled that there had been a violation of this right where the Bailiff of Guernsey, an official who performed executive, legislative and judicial functions, had presided over a case in which a landowner argued that there should be a departure from a development plan which had been approved by the legislature, over which the Bailiff had also presided. Despite the fact that the court had maintained that 'neither Article 6 nor any other provision of the Convention requires states to comply with any theoretical constitutional concepts as such' and notwithstanding that the then Lord Chancellor stated that he would never sit in a case involving legislation in the passage of which he had been involved, nor in a case where the interests of the executive were directly engaged, the case may be viewed as casting doubt (by analogy) upon the continued lawfulness of the exercise of all three types of function by the Lord Chancellor.[65] Similarly, and despite the Law Lords' self-denying ordinance on involvement in the legislative process,[66] the creation of the Supreme Court can be viewed as necessary to ensure compliance with Article 6.[67]

---

[62] See A. LeSueur, 'Judicial Power in the Changing Constitution', in J. Jowell and D. Oliver (eds.), *The Changing Constitution* (Oxford: OUP, 5th ed., 2005).

[63] For further discussion, see below p.201. It should be noted that the UK has been bound by Article 6 as a matter of international law ever since the Convention entered into force in 1953. However, the enactment of the Human Rights Act 1998, which gave domestic effect to the rights contained in the Convention, served both to render the rights more visible and to raise the prospect that UK courts might be called upon to adjudicate upon an alleged violation of Article 6 in respect of British constitutional arrangements.

[64] (2000) 30 EHRR 289. See further LeSueur, n.62, 334–36.

[65] See D. Woodhouse, 'The Constitutional Reform Act 2005 – defending judicial independence the English way' (2007) 5 *International Journal of Constitutional Law* 153, 154–55.

[66] Above, n.29.

[67] See the Department for Constitutional Affairs consultation paper, n.53, 11: 'The Human Rights Act, specifically in relation to Article 6 of the European Convention on Human Rights, now requires a stricter view to be taken not only of anything which might undermine the independence or impartiality of a judicial tribunal, but even of anything which might appear to do so. So the fact that the Law Lords are a Committee of the House of Lords can raise issues about the appearance of independence from the legislature.'

Article 6 of the European Convention also appears to have had an impact upon recent reform of the system of tribunals. These reforms will be discussed in chapter 6.

Each of the above reforms can therefore be viewed as enhancing judicial independence from the other two branches of government. In this respect, they contribute to a strengthening of the separation of powers in the British constitution in the direction of the 'pure' model: that is, they are designed to ensure a separation of personnel. However, recent constitutional reforms have also contributed to a reinforcement of the checks and balances which exist within the constitution, altering the balance between executive, legislature and judiciary. We shall consider the impact of these changes throughout the book, but especially in chapters 5 and 6.

Conclusion

The separation of powers principle is an extremely useful means of classifying governmental functions and institutions. It considerably facilitates the tasks of identification and analysis, and for this reason it will be adopted as the primary basis for the organisation of this book. Furthermore, as a normative model of liberal democracy, it has substantial value as a foundation both for the critique of current constitutional arrangements and for their reform.

In the absence of a codified constitution comparable to that of the US, the extent to which the principle is followed in the UK is difficult to measure. Certainly, significant functional and personnel overlaps between the branches – particularly the executive and legislature – are clearly at odds with a 'pure' version of the principle. However, it is submitted that the dismissive attitude to the separation of powers which is evident in the work of certain commentators is misplaced. The UK *does* possess a network of rules (whether in the form of laws or constitutional conventions), which seek to ensure that there is not excessive concentration of power in a particular branch of government, albeit that some of these mechanisms work better than others. And recent constitutional developments suggest that the principle continues to have potency, particularly in the context of the independence of the judiciary, even if commitment to it is merely one amongst several motivations for constitutional change in the UK.

B. The rule of law

We turn now to examine the second of the three principles which may be said to underpin the British constitution, the rule of law. This is a broader and somewhat more abstract principle than the separation of powers, in so far as it less overtly expresses a connection to a particular form of institutional arrangement. However, it fulfils similar objectives in that it operates to ensure that governmental power is not abused. Indeed, as noted above, the separation of powers is often (though not always) viewed as a component of the rule of law.[68] It is therefore fundamental to ideas of constitutionalism,[69] although it may be argued that this concept refers more properly to constitutional structures, institutions and arrangements while the rule of law expresses certain ideas as to the qualities which a legal system should possess.[70]

The rule of law has a lengthy history which can be traced back to classical civilisation. It commands widespread support, notably – but far from exclusively – from Western liberal democracies: indeed, it has been described as '*the* preeminent legitimating political ideal in the world today'.[71] However, it is also 'an exceedingly elusive notion'.[72] It has been observed that 'there are almost as many conceptions of the rule of law as there are people defending it'.[73]

Exploration of the multiplicity of meanings which have been attached to the principle, while fascinating, would take us too far beyond the subject matter of this book.[74] Instead, the focus here will be upon the meaning(s) attached to the concept in the context of English public law, the mechanisms through which it is given effect and the function it performs within the constitution.

The rule of law in British constitutional thought: from Bracton to Dicey

Many accounts of the meaning of the rule of law in the context of the British constitutional order commence with the work of Dicey.[75] Dicey's

---

[68] See *eg* Allan, above p.11 (n.25), 31; D. Meyerson, 'The Rule of Law and the Separation of Powers' [2004] *Macquarie Law Journal* 1; R. Bellamy (ed.), *The Rule of Law and the Separation of Powers* (Aldershot: Ashgate, 2005). By contrast, Dicey, for whom the rule of law was a fundamental tenet of the British constitution, virtually ignored the separation of powers, referring to it as 'the offspring of a double misconception': above p.17 (n.47), 338.

[69] See above p.10.

[70] See C. Ten, 'Constitutionalism and the Rule of Law' in R. Goodin, P. Pettit and T.Pogge (eds.), *A Companion to Contemporary Political Philosophy* (Malden: Blackwell, 2007), 493.

[71] B. Tamanaha, *On the Rule of Law: History, Politics, Theory* (Cambridge: CUP, 2004), 4.

[72] *ibid*, 3.

[73] O. Taiwo, 'The Rule of Law: the new Leviathan?' (1999) 12 *Canadian Journal of Law and Jurisprudence* 151, 154.

[74] Readers seeking such an analysis are directed to Tamanaha, n.71; A. Hutchinson and P. Monahan (eds.), *The Rule of Law: Ideal or Ideology?* (Toronto: Carswell, 1987); F. Neumann, *The Rule of Law: Political Theory and the Legal System in Modern Society* (Leamington Spa: Berg, 1986).

[75] See *eg* J. Jowell, 'The Rule of Law Today' in J. Jowell and D. Oliver (eds.), *The Changing Constitution* (Oxford: OUP, 6th ed., 2007); I. Loveland, *Constitutional Law, Administrative Law and Human Rights: a critical introduction* (Oxford: OUP, 2009), 53.

account of the principle has undoubtedly been of considerable influence (although, as will be seen, not necessarily of a wholly positive character), but, as Loughlin has noted,[76] it was rooted in earlier ideas. As far back as the thirteenth century, Henry de Bracton had written that 'The king must not be under man but under God and under the law, because the law makes the king'.[77] Then, in the seventeenth century, Chief Justice Coke ruled that the monarch could not determine legal disputes himself, but must act through his judges who, through 'long study and experience' had acquired the necessary knowledge and skill to adjudicate upon the basis of the 'artificial reason and judgment of law': consequently, 'the law was the golden metwand and measure to try the causes of the subjects: and which protected His Majesty in safety and peace'.[78] Coke's dicta allude to the important role played by a particular mindset on the part of the judges: a disposition, enhanced by knowledge of and training in the law, towards objectivity and fairness rather than passion and self-interest.[79] Such an attitude of mind, especially if shared by other actors within the branches of government, would serve to restrain excesses and abuses of power.[80] As we shall see, this line of thinking represented an important strand in Dicey's model of the rule of law, to which we next turn. Furthermore, it assists in resolving one of the key difficulties which arises from a reading of Dicey, that is, achieving congruence between the apparently incompatible principles of the rule of law and parliamentary sovereignty, an issue which will be analysed further in chapter 3.

Albert Venn Dicey was Vinerian Professor of English Law at Oxford University from 1882 to 1909.[81] In 1885, a collection of his lectures was published as *Introduction to the Study of the Law of the Constitution*. His intention in writing the work was to identify for students of constitutional law, 'two or three guiding principles which pervade the modern constitution of England'.[82] The work was immediately popular and sold out within months of publication, running to six further editions prior to Dicey's retirement. McEldowney explains why:

---

[76] Above p.1 (n.2), 151.

[77] H. Bracton, *On the Laws and Customs of England* (trans., S. Thorne) (Cambridge, Mass.: Harvard University Press, 1968) vol. II, 33.

[78] *Prohibitions del Roy* (1607) 12 Co Rep 63.

[79] For a somewhat different reading of Coke's judgment in this case, see Tomkins, above p.15 (n.39), 56–58.

[80] See J. Shklar, *Political Thought and Political Thinkers* (S. Hoffmann, ed.) (Chicago: University of Chicago Press, 1998), 24.

[81] For a biography, see R. Cosgrove, *The Rule of Law: Albert Venn Dicey, Victorian Jurist* (London: Macmillan, 1980).

[82] Dicey, above p.17 (n.47), v.

'The immediate attraction of a work of constitutional law as distinct from constitutional history was obvious for English lawyers who lacked a written constitution. In the absence of a written constitution lawyers had traditionally found it difficult to discover principles of constitutional law to explain the relationship between Parliament, the institutions of government and the law ... Dicey's clarity of style and economy of expression commended his writings to a wide audience both nationally and internationally. Students of constitutional law were attracted by Dicey's convenient format which encouraged certainty and precision in a subject which was vague and imprecise. British lawyers gained a legal language to discuss political institutions and issues. Although the British constitution remained unwritten, after Dicey's book it was presentable in a written form to American or European lawyers who were more familiar with written constitutions.'[83]

The authoritative standing which Dicey's work has enjoyed is not without its drawbacks. As Johnson notes:

'like most striking simplifications in any field of discourse, this one carried the risk of tempting future generations to treat its terms as holy writ. His principal conclusions came to be reiterated as clichés. All too often in later years Dicey was cited as *the* constitutional authority and it was felt that that must settle the argument.'[84]

In addition to the type of intellectual laziness to which this passage alludes – that is, resolving debates as to the British constitution by simple reference to the work of Dicey without further reflection, an uncritical acceptance of Dicey's analysis is problematic for at least two further reasons. First, it has tended to stultify the evolution of certain areas of English public law. This is especially true of administrative law, which Dicey considered not to exist at all in England. For several decades, this view was highly influential in preventing the development of a distinctive set of institutions or principles of administrative justice.[85] Secondly, although Dicey sought to apply an analytical or expository methodology to his subject matter, it would be wrong to assume that his writings were somehow 'scientifically' neutral.

---

[83] J. McEldowney, 'Dicey in Historical Perspective – a Review Essay' in P. McAuslan and J. McEldowney (eds.), *Law, Legitimacy and the Constitution* (London: Sweet & Maxwell, 1985), 40–41.

[84] N. Johnson, 'Dicey and his influence on Public Law' [1985] *Public Law* 717, 719. Emphasis in original.

[85] See *eg* W. Wade and C. Forsyth, *Administrative Law* (Oxford: OUP, 7th ed., 2000) 7, commenting that Dicey 'long threw a chilly shadow over administrative law'. W. Robson, 'The Report of the Committee on Ministers' Powers' (1932) 3 *Political Quarterly* 346, 359 wrote of the 'dead hand of Dicey'.

Rather, they reflected certain ideological preferences regarding the role of the state in society which were themselves shaped by the economic, social and political environment in which he worked. This is perhaps especially true of his account of the rule of law, which Hibbitts has argued 'is revealed not as a timeless truth but as a highly contingent historical phenomenon'.[86]

Dicey's model of the rule of law consisted of three elements, which he considered to be reflective of the state of the British constitution in his day.[87] It is worth setting these out in full before analysing the meaning of each in detail and assessing whether they can be regarded as descriptively accurate:

> 'No man is punishable or can lawfully be made to suffer in body or goods except for a distinct breach of the law established in the ordinary legal manner before the ordinary courts of the land. In this sense the rule of law is contrasted with every system of government based on the exercise of wide, arbitrary, or discretionary powers of constraint ...

> 'No man is above the law ... every man, whatever be his rank or condition, is subject to the ordinary law of the realm and amenable to the jurisdiction of the ordinary tribunals ...

> 'The general principles of the constitution ... are with us the result of judicial decisions determining the rights of private persons in particular cases brought before the courts.'[88]

The first of these principles can be divided into two components. Dicey tells us that there can be no punishment – whether in terms of deprivation of personal liberty or some form of monetary penalty – in the absence of a breach of the law. If we move somewhat beyond Dicey's formulation of this principle in the language of criminal law, we might express this as the notion that any infringement of individual autonomy by the state must be grounded in law: government must have legal authority for any action which it takes which impinges upon the individual. We might think of this as the simplest meaning of the rule of law. It essentially expresses the idea that 'powerful people and people in government, just like anybody else, should obey the law',[89] and it connects back to Bracton's statement above. A useful illustration of this aspect of the rule is afforded by the well-known

---

[86] B. Hibbitts, 'The Politics of Principle: Albert Venn Dicey and the Rule of Law' (1994) 23 *Anglo-American Law Journal* 1, 2.

[87] In fact, Dicey uses the phrase '*English* constitution' throughout his work.

[88] Dicey, above p.17 (n.47), 188–196.

[89] J. Raz, 'The Rule of Law and its Virtue' (1977) 93 *Law Quarterly Review* 195, 197.

case of *Entick v Carrington*, in which Lord Camden cj observed succinctly that 'If it is law, it will be found in our books. If it is not to be found there, it is not law'.[90] On this basis, the Court of Common Pleas ruled that entry onto premises and seizure of papers under purported power of a 'general warrant' issued by the Home Secretary, for which there was no authority either in statute or common law, was unlawful.

But Dicey goes further than this, particularly in the second sentence of the first passage quoted above, and in his subsequent summation of the three elements. Here, the rule of law is set in opposition to 'the influence of arbitrary power, and excludes the existence of arbitrariness, of prerogative, or even of wide discretionary authority on the part of government'.[91] His central concern is that governmental power should be exercised in a manner which is relatively certain, clear, open and predictable, free from the whim or personal prejudice of the decision-maker. It is readily apparent that instances of indefinite detention without trial, or laws which impose retrospective legal liability, or laws which are kept secret from citizens, would offend against this aspect of the rule of law, and most of us would be likely to agree that such laws should generally be impermissible. What is less clear – and significantly more controversial – is how far broadly formulated laws which could be used for a variety of purposes and which vest extensive discretionary power in the recipient,[92] can and should be considered not to comply with the rule of law, especially given their utility in realising the goals of modern government.

The second component of Dicey's model of the rule of law is centred upon equality before the law. He tells us that, in the British constitution, no one, regardless of their social status or position, is above the law and that the same law – the 'ordinary law of the land' administered by 'the ordinary tribunals' – is applicable to all. This seems unobjectionable: most of us would regard it as problematic if (for example) legal processes overtly favoured men over women, rich over poor, or Christians over Muslims.[93] As Jennings comments, 'among equals the law should be equal and should be equally administered, that like should be treated alike. The right to sue and be sued, to prosecute and be prosecuted, for the same kind of action should be available for all citizens of full age and understanding, and without distinction of race, religion, wealth, social status or political influence'.[94]

---

[90] (1765) 19 How. St. Tr. 1029, 1066.

[91] Dicey, above p.17 (n.47), 202.

[92] For the meaning of discretionary power, see above p.8.

[93] Of course, there is a substantial academic literature which seeks to demonstrate that, however *formally* neutral the law may appear, it does in practice favour certain interests over others.

[94] Above n.12, 50.

However, this form of equality was not Dicey's fundamental concern, and still less was he concerned that there should be *substantive* equality between citizens, for example by the redistribution of wealth from the rich to the poor. He goes on to state that 'With us every official, from the Prime Minister down to a constable or a collector of taxes, is under the same responsibility for every act done without legal justification as any other citizen'.[95] The rule of law therefore 'excludes the idea of any exemption of officials or others from the duty of obedience to the law which governs other citizens or from the jurisdiction of the ordinary tribunals'.[96] We can see here again a connection to Bracton's notion that the King should be under the law (assuming, of course, that we substitute 'government' for 'King'), but Dicey also articulates a view as to the applicable legal system for adjudication upon disputes involving 'officials'.[97] Such cases are to be dealt with in the 'ordinary courts of the land' by reference to 'ordinary law': that is, the same courts which determine disputes between private individuals, on the basis of principles of law which are equally applicable to government official and citizen alike. Dicey draws an explicit comparison with the French system of *droit administratif*, a specialised system of institutions and legal rules for cases involving state bodies, which he considered to operate unfairly to exempt officials from the ordinary law and which, for this reason, was 'utterly unknown to the law of England, and indeed is fundamentally inconsistent with our traditions and customs'.[98]

The third element of Dicey's model of the rule of law expresses a conception that individual rights were protected through the common law rather than by way of codified constitutions or bills of rights. Dicey described the 'English' constitution as 'a judge-made constitution',[99] its principles being 'inductions or generalisations based upon particular decisions pronounced by the courts as to the rights of given individuals',[100] which were articulated through *private* law rather than by way of a distinct form of constitutional adjudication. He pointed in particular to the importance which judges attached to the establishment of remedies for wrongdoing in English common law, and contrasted this with the more general (and, to his mind, less easily enforceable) guarantees of rights contained in constitutional documents elsewhere. It is clear, however, that Dicey regarded this as more than mere description of the state of constitutional arrangements: it also amounted to a normative

---

[95] Above p.17 (n.47), 193.
[96] *ibid*, 202–03.
[97] Defined by Dicey as 'all persons employed in the service of the state': *ibid*, 195.
[98] *ibid*, 203.
[99] *ibid*, 196.
[100] *ibid*, 197–98.

account of the arrangements which he considered to be preferable. This is readily apparent from the following:

> 'The matter to be noted is, that where the right to individual freedom is a result deduced from the principles of the constitution, the idea readily occurs that the right is capable of being suspended or taken away. Where, on the other hand, the right to individual freedom is part of the constitution because it is inherent in the ordinary law of the land, the right is one which can hardly be destroyed without a thorough revolution in the institutions and manners of the nation.'[101]

Let us now address the issue of the accuracy of Dicey's discussion of the meaning of the rule of law in relation to the state of the British constitution at the end of the nineteenth century, recalling that his objective in writing the text was to offer a *descriptive* account of certain general principles of constitutional law. In this task we are assisted by those, such as Sir Ivor Jennings and William Robson (writing between the World Wars), who adopt a 'functional' approach to public law,[102] which sought critically to expose the linkages between law and politics. Thus, Jennings pointed out that 'public authorities do in fact exercise wide discretionary powers'[103] – for example, the seizure of property without compensation in an emergency, or compulsory purchase of property for planning or public health purposes – and that many of these powers existed in Dicey's day.[104] Furthermore, he noted that officials were not, in practice, subject to the same laws as ordinary citizens: 'all public officials, and especially public authorities, have powers and therefore rights which are not possessed by other persons. Similarly, they must have special duties',[105] and (in common with Robson), criticised Dicey for a misunderstanding of the French system, whose purpose was 'not to exclude public officials from liability for wrongful acts, but to determine the powers and duties of public authorities and to prevent them from exceeding or abusing their powers'.[106] Finally, Jennings observed that 'the powers of administrative authorities in respect of "fundamental liberties" are mainly contained in statutes',[107] as distinct from the common law (as Dicey believed) and

---

[101] *ibid*, 201.
[102] See above, p.4.
[103] Above n.12, 55.
[104] Particularly those relating to public health. For an account of the historical development of governmental powers in this field during the Victorian era, see A. Wohl, *Endangered Lives: Public Health in Victorian Britain* (London: Dent, 1983).
[105] Above, n.12, 312.
[106] *ibid*, 313.
[107] *ibid*, 314.

pointed to the centrality of the sovereignty of Parliament, which operated as a fundamental law in the same manner as a 'higher order' constitution would do in other legal systems.

If the rule of law, as Dicey understood it, was not an accurate description of the state of the British constitution when he wrote his famous text, it is even less so today. The primary reason for this is the development of the welfare state in the UK, particularly after the Second World War. As the state took greater responsibility for provision of health care, education, social security for those who were disadvantaged, housing and certain key industries such as coal and water (among other activities), so it became necessary for legislation to vest significant discretionary powers in public bodies and individual officials. Discretionary power was necessary for at least three related reasons. First, the sheer range of functions performed by government meant that it was not feasible for Parliament to legislate in detail in respect of all of the powers which government might need, and although secondary legislation could fill certain of the details, it was nonetheless likely that officials would be left with a degree of freedom of manoeuvre in carrying out their tasks. Secondly, it was not possible to foresee every possible eventuality in respect of the use of these powers in advance. Thirdly, it would frequently be preferable to leave discretion to officials who actually administered the service in question since they would have greater knowledge than Parliament as to how those powers were used in practice. Accordingly, 'experience is clear that it is not possible to draft effective legislation in many regulatory and welfare areas without leaving leeway for the exercise of administrative judgment in rule-making and adjudication'.[108]

The other components of Dicey's model are equally questionable from a contemporary perspective. As we shall see in chapter 5, the significant growth of judicial review in recent years has effectively created a 'separate' system of administrative law, especially when viewed alongside the numerous non-judicial mechanisms of administrative justice which now exist (to be discussed in chapter 6), such as tribunals, ombudsmen, inquiries and internal review and complaints mechanisms. Although 'officials' may still be held accountable to the 'ordinary courts' through principles of tort and contract,[109] it is the supervisory jurisdiction of the Administrative Court which is of primary significance in regulating the relationship between individual and state. Dicey's third 'meaning' of the rule, meanwhile, is

---

[108] H. Jones, 'The Rule of Law and the Welfare State' (1958) 58 *Columbia Law Review* 143, 152.

[109] Although even in these areas of law, legal principles have been modified to reflect the distinction between governmental bodies and private individuals or organisations, reflecting at least a partial acceptance of the 'green light' argument that public bodies may warrant differential treatment since they perform functions which are in the interests of society in general. For discussion, see Harlow and Rawlings, above p.5 (n.7), especially Chapters 8–9, 17.

problematic from three perspectives. First, the existence of the second of Dicey's central principles of the British constitution, parliamentary sovereignty, means that liberties established by way of the common law can easily be eroded or removed by legislation. Secondly, research into the composition of the judiciary has exposed its lack of representativeness,[110] with the consequence that the present-day public is likely to be less confident than was Dicey in the capability of judges objectively to uphold individual liberties. Thirdly, following from the preceding point, there is now a widespread belief in the value of declarations of individual rights, reflected – for example – in the enactment of legislation such as that dealing with discrimination, the Human Rights Act 1998 and the Freedom of Information Act 2000.

It would be perfectly reasonable for a reader of this book to pause at this point and ponder why, if Dicey's model of the rule of law is descriptively inaccurate to the extent suggested, such time and space should be devoted to a discussion of it. Three responses to this question may be posited. First, Dicey's account is of historical value in understanding the evolution of English public law. As noted above, the powerful influence exercised by Dicey as the first author to attempt a descriptive analysis of the fundamental principles of the British constitution helps us to understand in particular why a system of administrative law was so slow to develop and why, even today, it lacks the coherence and distinctiveness of a system such as the French. Secondly, there are components of Dicey's approach to the rule of law which feature in most subsequent understandings of the principle: for example, notions of predictability, generality, absence of arbitrariness and non-retrospectivity, which may be drawn especially from the first of the Diceyan meanings, are fundamental to 'formal' approaches to the rule of law, as discussed below. Thirdly – and perhaps most significantly – a critical analysis of Dicey's model brings to light the ideological underpinnings which are inherent in conceptions of the rule of law and, by extension, serves to illustrate the interconnectedness between law and politics which was emphasised in chapter 1. Let us pursue this latter point further by attempting to identify the political preferences which underlie Dicey's version of the rule.

It is not difficult to discern a powerful current of liberal individualism underpinning Dicey's version of the rule of law. His basic political beliefs – shaped, of course, by personal and social influences – are well described by Hibbits:[111]

---

[110] Notably J. Griffith, *The Politics of the Judiciary* (London: Fontana, 5th ed., 1997). See further below, pp.178–80.

[111] Above n.86, 3, 9.

'Dicey clearly regarded the individual – not classes or groups – as the essential social unit. The individual's good was the ultimate political and legal value ... Through the realisation of individual goods the good of the social collectivity – the nation – would be achieved ... The complement of Dicey's individualism was a suspicion of, indeed an aversion to, government and legislation for any except the most limited of ends. Dicey considered these acceptable ends to be the removal of restrictions in the way of individuals pursuing their own interests and happiness, and the prevention of harm to others. Dicey, with many others of his time, appeared to consider the individual and government largely antithetical, and their respective spheres of activity mutually exclusive.'

Dicey's disquiet over arbitrary and wide discretionary powers can therefore be understood as a preference for clear, fixed rules which would leave a sphere of individual autonomy insulated from 'interference' by government. His conception of equality before the law reflected a belief that the state possessed – and that it *should* possess – capacity and powers which were no more extensive than those of private individuals or organisations; likewise, his aversion to French *droit administratif* was rooted in a (mistaken) belief that it would give preferential treatment to government at the expense of the individual. His trust in the judiciary coupled with the principles and processes of 'ordinary law' can be explained by a perception that the common law was individualist in orientation: that is, that its function was 'to define the respective spheres of government and the individual, setting limits beyond which the state on the one hand and the individual on the other could not go'.[112] Conversely, his aversion to codified constitutions and bills of rights may be seen as shaped by a fear that a sovereign Parliament could readily sweep away all the liberties which free-born Englishmen had acquired over the course of several centuries, particularly if it were infiltrated by those who favoured socialism.[113]

It follows that if, like Robson and Jennings, we do not share Dicey's liberal individualist perspective on the proper role of the state in society and the function of law in relation to this – for example, if we are (to use the terminology deployed in chapter 1) more of a 'green light' persuasion – then we would not accept his analysis of the meaning of the rule of law. To provide just one illustration of this: a believer in state intervention would be likely to regard it as necessary both that public bodies and officials should have greater powers than those exercised by private individuals and

---

[112] *ibid*, 16.
[113] On Dicey's fear of socialism, see *ibid*, 12–15.

organisations since this will facilitate actions and decision-making which are for the benefit of society as a whole; and that distinct principles and processes of law may be appropriate for such bodies and officials given the need to offer them some protection so that they can discharge their functions effectively.

We may conclude that, while Dicey purported to offer a descriptive or expository account of principles of the constitution, his work on the rule of law carried (perhaps unconsciously)[114] a normative dimension: it implicitly expressed a conception of how the constitution should be arranged in order to give best effect to his political beliefs on the proper role of government in society. It is important, therefore, that we do not simply utilise Dicey's model as a neutral measuring stick to evaluate the appropriateness or otherwise of processes, principles and institutions within public law, but are aware of the liberal individualist outlook which fundamentally informs it.

The rule of law in British constitutional thought: from Dicey to the present day

Although the work done by Robson and Jennings between the World Wars undoubtedly served to call into question the rule of law as it had been articulated by Dicey, the principle did not disappear. As noted above, it continues to have significant impact across the globe as a fundamental component of a commitment to ideals of liberal democracy, albeit that these are not always viewed in the same individualist terms with which Dicey would have been comfortable. In the context of the UK, there have been a number of more modern attempts to conceptualise the notion of the rule of law, three of which will be briefly considered here.

i Friedrich von Hayek

Hayek was an Austrian-born economist who worked at the London School of Economics. In 1944, he published *The Road to Serfdom*, which expressed his opposition to centralised state planning of economic activities and governmental intervention in society, on the basis that this would readily develop into dictatorship and the consequent diminution of individual freedoms. Hayek saw the rule of law and the existence of a welfare state as fundamentally incompatible, stating that 'any policy aiming directly at a

---

114 Jennings wrote that 'Dicey honestly tried ... to analyse, but, like most, he saw the constitution through his own spectacles, and his vision was not exact': n.12, 316.

substantive ideal of redistributive justice must necessarily lead to a destruction of the rule of law'.[115]

This conflict arose as a consequence of the definition of the rule of law which Hayek adopted: 'that government in all its actions is bound by rules fixed and announced beforehand – rules which make it possible to foresee with fair certainty how the authority will use its coercive powers in given circumstances, and to plan one's individual affairs on the basis of this knowledge'.[116] Hayek therefore shared Dicey's distaste for discretionary powers – which, as we have seen, are integral to the realisation of a welfare state – since these would lack the element of predictability which was necessary if individuals were to be free to plan and live their lives as they chose. He viewed the function of the judiciary as being the protection of the individual against the state and was opposed to any 'green light' notion of using legal processes and principles to assist government bodies and officials in the discharge of their tasks. It is readily apparent, therefore that his conception of the rule of law connected to a preference for limited governmental power, but he is much more explicit than Dicey in acknowledging this fact, observing that his approach 'implies limits to the scope of legislation' in social and economic matters.[117]

Hayek's theories were especially influential upon the governments of Margaret Thatcher from 1979–1990. His conception of the rule of law played a particular role as justification for legislative action against the trade unions,[118] which had been granted immunity from legal liability in tort for acts done 'in contemplation of furtherance of a trade dispute' by the Trade Disputes Act 1906. Hayek, following Dicey,[119] considered that such immunity rendered unions 'uniquely privileged institutions to whom the general rules of law do not apply',[120] and argued that the 'coercion' that they were thereby able to exercise prevented the market from operating freely and was the chief cause of unemployment and the decline of the British economy.[121]

---

[115] F. Hayek, *The Road to Serfdom* (London: Routledge & Kegan Paul, 1944), 59.

[116] *ibid*, 54.

[117] *ibid*, 61–62.

[118] Especially Employment Act 1982, s.15 which removed union immunity.

[119] Dicey had argued that the 1906 Act made 'a trade union a privileged body exempted from the ordinary law of the land. No such privileged body has ever before been deliberately created by an English Parliament': A. Dicey, *Lectures on the relation between law and public opinion in England during the nineteenth century* (London: Macmillan, 2nd ed., 1914), xlvi. For discussion of the necessity of immunities to counteract the individualist tendencies of common law, see *eg* K. Wedderburn, *Employment Rights in Britain and Europe: Selected Papers in Labour Law* (London: Lawrence & Wishart, 1991).

[120] F. Hayek, *The Constitution of Liberty* (London: Routledge & Kegan Paul, 1960), 267.

[121] See F. Hayek, *1980s Unemployment and the Unions* (London: Institute of Economic Affairs, 2nd ed., 1984).

ii Joseph Raz

Raz is a legal philosopher working within the positivist tradition, which holds that there is no necessary connection between law and morality. In an important journal article,[122] he advances a conception of the rule of law which takes as its starting point Hayek's definition of the principle and which focuses upon the characteristics which render obedience to the law a feasible prospect: 'if the law is to be obeyed it must be capable of guiding the behaviour of its subjects. It must be such that they can find out what it is and act upon it'.[123]

Raz identifies eight such qualities of law, while admitting that his list is 'incomplete': laws should be prospective, open and clear; laws should not be changed too often; there should be open, clear, general and stable rules and procedures for making laws; there should be an independent judiciary; the principles of natural justice (such as fair hearings and an absence of bias) should be observed; the courts should have powers of review to ensure that the other components of the rule of law are upheld; courts should be easily accessible; and the police and prosecuting authorities should not be permitted to use their discretion to 'pervert the law' (*eg* decisions not to prosecute certain types of offence or classes of offenders).

In conformity with his positivist orientation, Raz does not argue that compliance with these principles means that laws, or a legal system, are necessarily 'good' in a moral sense. He draws an instructive analogy with a knife: sharpness is a virtue of knives, but a sharp knife may be put to good or bad uses.[124] Similarly, conformity of a legal system with the rule of law through realisation of the listed qualities does not necessarily mean that the laws within such a system will be directed to morally good ends, but it does ensure that law has the ability to perform its function. That function, the 'basic idea' of the doctrine, is the guidance of people's behaviour.[125] Hence, Raz concludes that:

> 'The rule of law is essentially a negative value. The law inevitably creates a great deal of arbitrary power – the rule of law is designed to minimise the danger created by the law itself. Similarly, the law may be unstable, obscure, retrospective etc., and thus infringe people's freedom and dignity. The rule of law is designed to prevent this danger as well. Thus the rule of law is a negative value in two senses: conformity to it does

---

[122] Above n.89.
[123] *ibid*, 208. Emphasis removed.
[124] *ibid*, 198.
[125] *id*.

not cause good except through avoiding evil and the evil which is avoided is evil which could only have been caused by the law itself.'[126]

iii Trevor Allan

The most comprehensive recent analysis of the meaning and value of the rule of law has been offered by Allan. Allan regards the rule as a 'necessary component' of any genuine liberal or democratic political system, defining 'liberal' as 'any modern democratic regime that protects a range of familiar civil and political liberties and in which governmental action is constrained by law, interpreted and applied by independent judges'.[127] He contends that the core of the rule of law is not, as Raz has argued, the idea that law should be capable of guiding people's behaviour, but rather the 'more fundamental principle that people are entitled to be treated with the respect that their equal dignity as citizens demands'.[128] This requires moving beyond those notions of generality, non-retrospectivity and protection from arbitrariness which are articulated in the work of Hayek and Raz, and embracing a conception of the rule of law which ensures that 'any interference with people's liberty or property is regulated by general rules, *whose purposes are the promotion of some genuine public good*',[129] the latter being publicly stated and open to public debate. This does not preclude differential treatment of certain classes of the public – thus, Allan might be supportive of measures of positive discrimination in favour of women or ethnic minorities, or redistribution to the poor[130] – but any such differential treatment must be justified in terms of its capacity to contribute to the realisation of the 'common good'.

Allan's notion of the rule of law as entailing a requirement of equal citizenship, with any departure from such equal treatment requiring justification by reference to conceptions of the common good, obliges courts to play a significant role. It is assumed that members of the legislature are elected 'in order to advance the public good, by enactment of just laws, according to their moral convictions',[131] but the legislature may sometimes permit infringement of individual rights and violations of equality by granting powers to the executive, powers which the latter will willingly

---

[126] *ibid*, 206.
[127] Above p.11 (n.25), 1.
[128] *ibid*, 38.
[129] *ibid*, 39. Emphasis added.
[130] Allan describes his model of the rule of law as one which 'embodies a conception of constitutional equality that may be compared to that embraced by Dicey and Hayek, but which does not share their hostility to administrative discretion or governmental interference in economic affairs: *ibid*, 21.
[131] *ibid*, 22.

assume in light of its tendency to 'exaggerate' what is needed in the interests of public safety and short-term political gain.[132] In this situation, the courts must carefully scrutinise any such infringements which serve only temporary political ends, seeking assurances that the legislature has genuinely given its approval, although judges must remain respectful of the legitimacy and sovereignty of Parliament. In this manner, argues Allan, 'courts and legislature can share responsibility for deciding what qualifications and limitations of existing rights are necessary and appropriate for the common good'.[133]

There is much which is controversial in Allan's account. It may be argued that it places too much faith in legislators pursuing a 'common good' when they are more inclined to seek short-term party political gains. Moreover, in the absence of a codified constitutional document, it may be difficult to identify which (if any) principles may be regarded as 'constitutionally fundamental' in the UK. In addition, the focus upon the role of the courts sets up a tension with the principle of parliamentary supremacy which might be viewed as constitutionally questionable, although Allan argues that 'there is no opposition in this scheme between Parliament and the judiciary'.[134] Nonetheless, significant components of this model do reflect recent developments in public law in England, particular as regards the judiciary's approach to interpretation of legislation to achieve conformity with individual rights. These will be examined further below.[135]

Classifying theories of the rule of law: formal and substantive variants

The range of views as to the meaning of the rule of law – and those discussed above merely represent a small number, selected for their pertinence to public law in the UK – might appear bewildering. However, one useful means of understanding them is to classify them as either *formal* or *substantive* in character.[136]

Formal conceptions of the rule of law are concerned with the manner in which the law comes into existence and the 'surface' characteristics or qualities of the law. Thus, an exponent of a formal approach would consider whether the law was created by an institution which was authorised to make laws within a particular legal system, according to the correct procedures for law-making. A formalist would also regard it as imperative that laws are

---

[132] *ibid*, 48.

[133] *ibid*, 45.

[134] T. Allan, 'Legislative Supremacy and the Rule of Law: Democracy and Constitutionalism' (1985) 44 *Cambridge Law Journal* 111, 130.

[135] See pp.58–59.

[136] See P. Craig, 'Formal and Substantive Conceptions of the Rule of Law: an Analytical Framework' [1997] *Public Law* 467.

clear, accessible, general and non-retrospective. However, such a person would not be interested in the *content* of the laws – that is, the objectives which they serve. We may recall here Raz's analogy with a knife. Sharpness of a knife is the quality that renders it fit for purpose, but a sharp knife may be used for good or bad ends, such as slicing vegetables or committing murder. Similarly, formalists are concerned with the features of the law, not with the goals which it serves. By contrast, those embracing a substantive conception of the rule of law do not reject the notion that laws should take a certain form, but seek to move beyond this. Laws are also valued for their content: generally, for their compliance with certain fundamental values such as human rights. For a person adopting a substantive approach, the use to which a knife is put, not just its sharpness, *is* an important matter.

Neither of these approaches is unproblematic. The neutrality of the formal conception as to the content of laws means that it is compatible with all manner of inequalities between citizens (such as slavery) and that oppressive, tyrannical regimes may be in compliance with it.[137] The substantive version avoids these pitfalls, but runs the risk of simply 'collapsing' into a broader vision of what constitutes a good society. That is, the notion of the rule of law carries no independent meaning in itself but just reflects the preferences that the particular theorist holds as to the appropriate goals of governmental action *eg* that this should bring about redistribution of wealth or protect certain individual rights *etc*. Raz expresses both problems powerfully in his claim (which he acknowledges will 'alarm many') that:

> 'If the rule of law is the rule of the good law then to explain its nature is to propound a complete social philosophy. But if so the term lacks any useful function. We have no need to be converted to the rule of law just in order to discover that to believe in it is to believe that good should triumph ... . It is not to be confused with democracy, justice, equality (before the law or otherwise), human rights of any kind or respect for persons or for the dignity of man. A non-democratic legal system, based on the denial of human rights, on extensive poverty, on racial segregation, sexual inequalities and religious persecution may, in principle, conform to the requirements of the rule of law better than any of the more enlightened Western democracies. This does not mean that it will be better than those Western democracies. It will be an immeasurably worse legal system, but it will excel in one respect: in its conformity to the rule of law.'[138]

---

[137] See Tamanaha, n.71, 95–96.
[138] Above n.89, 195–96.

If we apply the formal/substantive classification to the theorists discussed above, then it becomes apparent that both Hayek and Raz (notwithstanding the latter's appreciation of the risks inherent in a formal approach) are formalists, concerned with law's outward appearance. Allan, by contrast, sits within the substantive camp: he acknowledges that he seeks to articulate 'a limited conception of the good law',[139] as his references to 'the common good' and the purposes served by law indicate. Dicey is rather more problematic to classify. Craig considers him to be a formalist, arguing that he does not provide us with any criterion for establishing that the content of a law is 'bad';[140] but Allan contends that Dicey takes a substantive view, pointing to his third meaning of the rule of law, by means of which the common law gives effect to certain general principles of a substantive nature, which we might describe as civil and political rights.[141]

The difficulty, as Allan notes,[142] is that even formal conceptions of the rule of law, which are purportedly neutral as to the ends which law serves, rest upon substantive foundations. We can see this clearly if we look at the work of both Hayek and Dicey (if we share Craig's view that Dicey takes a formal approach). At base, these conceptions are rooted in notions of individual autonomy and limited government. The function of the rule of law on these accounts (and that of Raz, who is somewhat less hostile to state intervention) is to set predictable limits on the powers exercised by the state, so that individuals can reliably take account of these powers as they plan and lead their lives in the manner which they choose. As Waldron notes, this 'brings the rule of law ideal close to the nerve of liberal philosophy':[143] and this represents a substantive vision of a good society, albeit one which is widely shared, at least in the West. In consequence, while the formal/substantive divide may be superficially helpful in classifying models of the rule of law, we should remain alert to the (often implicit) political philosophies which underpin *all* such models.

The rule of law in practice

It will not have escaped the notice of readers that the discussion of the rule of law to date has been conducted almost exclusively in theoretical terms. This is demonstrative of the status of the rule primarily as a political or jurisprudential principle rather than as a definable ground of review which

---

[139] Above n.134, 114.

[140] Above n.136, 472.

[141] Above p.11 (n.25), 18–19. Dicey cites the right to personal liberty and the right of public meeting as examples of the 'general principles of the constitution' which are articulated through the common law: above p.17 (n.47), 195.

[142] Above p.11 (n.25), 23, 25.

[143] J. Waldron, 'The Rule of Law in Contemporary Liberal Theory' (1989) 2 *Ratio Juris* 79, 84.

judges may utilise to determine the outcome of a dispute between the individual and the state. In part, this is due to Dicey's failure clearly to articulate the scope and content of the rule in a form which was sufficiently clear and coherent that it might govern judicial decision, in stark contrast to the doctrine of parliamentary sovereignty. Thus, Allan has observed of the rule that 'its implications are recognised in a variety of contexts, but there has been little attempt at systematic exposition. Judicial references to the rule of law tend to be rather acknowledgments of the importance of constitutionalism, as a form of government, than conscientious attempts to articulate the specific requirements of the legal principle'.[144]

i Constitutional Reform Act 2005, s.1 and judicial review

This view, expressed in 1985, needs to be modified somewhat to take account of more recent developments within the British constitution. Most strikingly of all, the rule of law has now been given statutory recognition through section 1 of the Constitutional Reform Act 2005, which provides that the Act does not affect 'the existing constitutional principle of the rule of law', nor the Lord Chancellor's role in respect of that principle. However, neither the Act nor the explanatory notes which accompany it provide further definition of the principle, an omission which has been seen as a deliberate choice on the part of the legislative branch which may well 'have preferred to leave the task of definition to the courts if and when occasion arose',[145] although there is some debate as to how far the meaning of this open-ended provision could, in practice, be determined by a court.[146] At a minimum, however, statutory reference to the principle would seem to mean that judges will 'not [be] free to dismiss the rule of law as meaningless verbiage, the jurisprudential equivalent of motherhood and apple pie, even if they were inclined to do so'.[147]

Section 1 of the 2005 Act has been cited in argument in a very limited number of cases. In *FP (Iran) v Secretary of State for the Home Department*, the Court of Appeal held that rejection of two applications for asylum was unlawful where appeal hearings had taken place in the absence of the individuals because the individuals' lawyers had failed to notify the Asylum and Immigration Tribunal of a change of address. Sedley LJ stated that 'unless a minimum level of fairness is achieved, the principle of the rule of law will be infringed',[148] cited Dicey's second meaning of the rule and

---

[144] Above n.134, 114–15.
[145] Lord Bingham, 'The Rule of Law' (2007) 66 *Cambridge Law Journal* 67, 68. See also generally T. Bingham, *The Rule of Law* (London: Allen Lane, 2010).
[146] See Bingham, *ibid* (2007), n.11.
[147] Bingham, *ibid*, 69.
[148] [2007] EWCA Civ 13, [59].

opined that 'it must follow that a person must have an opportunity to bring before the court his claim that he is entitled to a certain right, or his claim that some obligation should not be imposed upon him. It also follows that the opportunity must be a real one'.[149] He concluded that such an opportunity had been denied in this instance: 'a situation in which a party is given a right and then it is taken away before he has a chance to exercise it is not one, in my judgment, which is fair, nor in my judgment is it one which fulfils the basic requirements of the rule of law'.[150] In *R (on the application of Corner House Research) v Director of the Serious Fraud Office*, the Administrative Court determined that the decision of the Director to cease investigations into allegations of bribery by a British aircraft company in relation to an arms deal with Saudi Arabia, on the ground that the continued investigation would harm the public interest, was unlawful. Moses LJ noted that debate continued as to the meaning of the principle, but observed that it lay 'at the heart of the obligations of the courts and of the judges',[151] which were obliged to 'patrol the boundary between the territory which they safeguard and that for which the executive is responsible'.[152] He considered that the rule of law entailed that the courts should ensure the independence of a decision-maker free from pressure, and that the action of the Director in yielding to threats made by Saudi representatives was consequently unlawful. However, this decision was overturned by the House of Lords,[153] which held that the Director had not stepped beyond the lawful bounds of his discretion in determining that the public interest in pursuing an important investigation was outweighed by the public interest in protecting the lives of British citizens.

These cases do not provide us with a great deal of assistance in defining the meaning of the rule of law as articulated in section 1 of the 2005 Act, although they do illustrate the breadth of activity to which the principle may be pertinent. It is notable that, in both cases, the courts' decisions could have rested upon other legal principles: in the first case, the right to a fair hearing and, in the second, unlawful delegation of discretionary power to another individual or body (see further, chapter 5). This suggests that the enactment of the provision contained in the 2005 Act may have made little practical difference to the courts. That is, the rule of law does not operate as a distinct and independent principle upon which judicial review of executive action may be founded, but rather functions to underpin and

---

[149] *ibid*, [60].
[150] *ibid*, [74].
[151] [2008] EWHC 714 (Admin), [62]–[63].
[152] *ibid*, [66].
[153] [2008] UKHL 60. For criticism, see Lord Steyn, 'Civil Liberties in Modern Britain' [2009] *Public Law* 228, 233–35.

legitimise review on the basis of those grounds which already exist. We might conclude from this – as do the courts – that to develop an understanding of how the rule is given practical effect in the British constitution, it is therefore crucial to analyse the manner in which 'the principles of judicial review give effect to the rule of law'.[154] We shall accordingly return to this issue in chapter 5.

ii Statutory interpretation: the 'principle of legality'

The rule of law also plays a practical role as the basis of judicial interpretation of the meaning of legislative provisions in certain situations. This function of the judiciary will, again, be considered in more detail in chapter 5, but brief mention will be made here of the 'principle of legality' which functions as a presumption of interpretation (that is, an assumption made by the court as to what Parliament must have intended). In *R v Secretary of State for the Home Department, ex parte Pierson*, the House of Lords was called upon to review the Home Secretary's decision to increase the minimum period which a prisoner had to serve before being considered for parole from that which had originally been recommended by the trial judge and Lord Chief Justice. There was no issue of the minister having followed an incorrect procedure in increasing the sentence; nonetheless, the court held that the increase was unlawful in offending the rule of law, Lord Steyn stating that 'Unless there is the clearest provision to the contrary, Parliament must be presumed not to legislate contrary to the rule of law, and the rule of law enforces minimum standards of fairness, both substantive and procedural'.[155] This approach was endorsed in the subsequent case of *R v Secretary of State for the Home Department, ex parte Simms*, which concerned the right of a prisoner to communicate with journalists with a view to challenging his conviction. Here, Lord Hoffmann stated:

'Parliamentary sovereignty means that Parliament can, if it chooses, legislate contrary to fundamental principles of human rights. The Human Rights Act 1998 will not detract from this power. The constraints upon its exercise by Parliament are ultimately political, not legal. But the principle of legality means that Parliament must squarely confront what it is doing and accept the political cost. Fundamental rights cannot be

---

[154] *R (on the application of Alconbury Developments Ltd) v Secretary of State for the Environment, Transport and the Regions* [2001] UKHL 23, [73]. This dictum was cited with approval by both the Administrative Court and the House of Lords in the *Corner House Research* case: nn.151 and 153, [62] and [41] respectively.

[155] [1998] AC 539, 591.

overridden by general or ambiguous words. This is because there is too great a risk that the full implications of their unqualified meaning may have passed unnoticed in the democratic process. In the absence of express language or necessary implication to the contrary, the courts therefore presume that even the most general words were intended to be subject to the basic rights of the individual.'[156]

We may observe in these cases that the courts have developed a notion of the rule of law which gives effect to certain fundamental rights, which then function as the basis for judicial control of executive action and – more controversially, given the potential for conflict with the principle of parliamentary sovereignty – for a particular interpretive approach to the meaning of legislation. This clearly takes us well beyond a formal model of the rule of law into a substantive reading of the concept.

iii The Human Rights Act 1998

It is noteworthy that the Human Rights Act 1998 had not come into effect at the date when these cases were decided. The enactment of that legislation has further strengthened the trend toward a substantive conception of the rule of law based around fundamental human rights and freedoms. As will be discussed in more detail in chapter 5, the executive branch of government is obliged by section 6 of the statute to act in compliance with the Convention rights and a court may declare an action or decision to be unlawful if a right has been violated. Furthermore, section 3 of the Act obliges courts to interpret legislation in a manner which is compatible with Convention rights, so far as it is possible to do so. Although cases in which these provisions are at issue are more likely to be phrased in the language of 'rights' than that of the rule of law, the close connection between the two is evident from the statement of the European Court of Human Rights that the Convention on Human Rights and Fundamental Freedoms, from which the rights contained in the Human Rights Act are drawn, 'draws its inspiration' overall from the notion of the rule of law.[157] An important recent extra-judicial analysis of the meaning of the rule by Lord Bingham has therefore included 'adequate protection of human rights' as a component.[158]

---

[156] Above p.10 (n.24), 131.

[157] *Engel v The Netherlands* (No. 1) (1976) 1 EHRR 647, [69].

[158] Above n.145 (2007), 75. However, Bingham concurs with the view expressed by Jowell, n.75, 23, that the rule of law is insufficiently elastic to accommodate the *full range* of human rights which are protected by the Human Rights Act or other statements of rights. On this basis, Jowell suggests that the courts have in fact moved 'beyond' the rule of law when upholding certain rights: see J. Jowell, 'Beyond the rule of law: towards constitutional judicial review' [2000] *Public Law* 671.

The function of the rule of law in the British constitution

The rule of law is therefore given practical effect in public law through the principles of judicial review, in the interpretation of statutes, and by way of the Human Rights Act 1998, to all of which we will return in more detail in chapter 5. But before we conclude our analysis of this elusive concept, one significant question remains, namely: what role does it play within the British constitutional order?

Let us return first to some of the theoretical discussions of the principle. As noted previously, Raz tells us that the rule of law is 'essentially a negative value', which operates to minimise the danger of arbitrary power and of infringement of individual freedom and dignity. He believes also that there is no moral virtue in compliance with the rule for its own sake, arguing that 'conformity to it does not cause good except through avoiding evil'.[159] Allan, by contrast, does regard compliance as possessing moral value, claiming that 'it rests on the truth that there are many kinds of good that cannot be attained without the law, properly and fairly administered in accordance with the rule of law'.[160] However, even for him, the rule is primarily viewed as a 'bulwark or barrier against the exercise of arbitrary state power'.[161]

It is evident from these passages that the rule of law is regarded as a central component of constitutionalism by adherents to the formal and substantive approaches alike. The principle operates as a restraining force upon government, checking and controlling power (especially, power which might be used in an arbitrary manner) and thereby demarcating a sphere of individual autonomy within which people may plan and live their lives as they choose. The difference between formalists like Raz and substantivists like Allan lies not so much in their commitment to this central objective of the rule, but rather in their approaches to the criteria of justice against which the validity of governmental power is measured. Raz would argue that the only exercises of power which should be considered unacceptable are those which violate the 'surface' characteristics of law such as clarity, non-retrospectivity, access to courts *etc.*, while Allan would also wish to discount exercises of power which offend the 'public good'.

Now, as we noted in chapter 1, in most legal systems the task of restraining governmental power is primarily performed by the provisions of a constitutional document, usually enforced by some form of constitutional

---

[159] Above, n.89, 206. Compare Jowell, *ibid*, 19, who argues that the rule also functions as a principle of 'institutional morality', providing guiding principles to the legislature and executive on the form which laws should take.

[160] Above p.11 (n.25), 58

[161] *ibid*, 61.

court. Constitutions therefore perform a 'disabling' function: they establish limitations to the exercise of (political) power. By contrast, in the UK this role is primarily performed by the unwritten principle of the rule of law, sometimes in tandem with the related idea of the separation of powers. The rule of law is therefore of profound significance to British constitutional arrangements, a fact acknowledged by Lord Hope in the highly significant case of *Jackson v Attorney-General*, when he stated that 'the rule of law enforced by the courts is the ultimate controlling factor on which our constitution is based'.[162] Furthermore, its importance has increased over time, with the Human Rights Act providing a particular stimulus to judicial activity in this regard. Indeed, a case can be made that it should now be regarded as a legal principle superior to that of parliamentary sovereignty, contrary to the view expressed by Dicey.[163] We shall return to this controversial issue in chapter 3.

A useful illustration of the disabling function performed by the rule of law and of its growing potency as a constitutional principle is afforded by cases relating to issues of national security in the UK. Courts have traditionally been reluctant to call into question the measures which the executive considers to be necessary in order to secure the safety and security of the British public in time of war or other public emergency. This is exemplified by the Second World War case of *Liversidge v Anderson*, in which – notwithstanding a powerful dissent by Lord Atkin – the House of Lords held that it would not inquire as to the reasonableness of the Home Secretary's belief that individuals were of 'hostile origin or association' and should therefore be detained under Defence Regulations authorised by the Emergency Powers (Defence) Act 1939.[164] However, in more recent times, the courts have taken a much more critical stance, grounded in the rule of law, as regards the exercise of wide powers by the executive in response to the perceived security threat to the UK following the 9/11 attacks in the United States. In *A v Secretary of State for the Home Department*, the House of Lords issued a declaration of incompatibility in respect of section 23 of the Anti-Terrorism, Crime and Security Act 2001, which provided for indefinite detention without trial of suspected international terrorists who could not be deported from the UK. Lord Nicholls stated that 'indefinite imprisonment without charge or trial is anathema in any country which observes the rule of law', while Lord Hoffmann referred more obliquely to the principle, in stating that the case called into question 'the very existence of an ancient liberty of which this country has until now been very

---

[162] Above p.11 (n.26), [107].
[163] See J. Jowell, 'Parliamentary sovereignty under the new constitutional hypothesis' [2006] *Public Law* 562.
[164] [1942] AC 206.

proud: freedom from arbitrary arrest and detention. The power which the Home Secretary seeks to uphold is a power to detain people indefinitely without charge or trial. Nothing could be more antithetical to the instincts and traditions of the people of the United Kingdom'.[165] Similarly, in *A(FC) v Secretary of State for the Home Department*, individuals who had been imprisoned under the same provision successfully argued that evidence against them which might have been obtained by way of torture inflicted by foreign nationals without the complicity of the British government was inadmissible, in part because obtaining evidence in such a manner was a violation of the rule of law. Lord Hope described torture as 'one of the most evil practices known to man' and noted that, unless restrained by the law, the executive was prone to make use of the practice:

> 'The lesson of history is that, when the law is not there to keep watch over it, the practice is always at risk of being resorted to in one form or another by the executive branch of government. The temptation to use it in times of emergency will be controlled by the law wherever the rule of law is allowed to operate. But where the rule of law is absent, or is reduced to a mere form of words to which those in authority pay no more than lip service, the temptation to use torture is unrestrained.'[166]

Even more recently, the Administrative Court has ruled that disclosure of evidence of abuse and torture of an individual alleged to be engaged in acts of terrorism did not infringe the principle of executive control over intelligence information, despite the argument that this would threaten the UK's national security and intelligence-sharing arrangements with the US. Thomas LJ stated that 'the suppression of wrongdoing by officials ... is inimical to the rule of law. Championing the rule of law, not subordinating it, is the cornerstone of democracy'.[167]

Although some commentators have argued that the courts could have gone further still in limiting the powers claimed and exercised by the executive in the name of national security,[168] these cases nonetheless demonstrate that the judges regard the principle of the rule of law as a highly valuable tool for the justification and legitimation of judicial control over executive power. We might view the rule of law as a means by which courts are able to 'democratise' their judgments and thereby respond to the

---

[165] [2004] UKHL 56, [74], [86]. For further discussion, see pp.223–24.

[166] [2005] UKHL 71, [101].

[167] *R (on the application of Mohamed) v Secretary of State for Foreign and Commonwealth Affairs* [2009] EWHC 152 (Admin), [73].

[168] See K. Ewing and J-C. Tham, 'The continuing futility of the Human Rights Act' [2008] *Public Law* 668. For criticism, see A. Kavanagh, 'Judging the judges under the Human Rights Act: deference, disillusionment and the "war on terror"' [2009] *Public Law* 287.

'counter-majoritarian' problem of judicial review. That is, through appeal to a principle which is regarded as central to liberal democratic forms of government, the courts seek to stave off criticism (whether from the executive, the public or the media) that unelected judges are limiting the capacity of elected officials to act in accordance with their judgment of what the public interest might require in situations of risk or emergency. Of course, they are not always successful in this regard.[169]

It will be noted, however, that while the rule of law is conceptualised in these cases as a form of 'shield' between the individual and excessive governmental power, its precise content and application continues to lack clarity. This is further demonstrated by the House of Lords decision in *R (on the application of Anufrijeva) v Secretary of State for the Home Department*. Here, the Home Office had refused an application for asylum and had passed this decision on to the Benefits Agency, which terminated her income support as permitted by legislation. The asylum decision was not, however, communicated to the individual and she was unable to attend subsequent meetings with an immigration officer as she could not afford the train fare. More than four months elapsed before the decision was communicated to the applicant and she argued that she should have continued to receive income support until that date. The court agreed. Lord Steyn, giving the leading judgment for the majority, stated that 'notice of a decision is required before it can have the character of a determination with legal effect because the individual concerned must be in a position to challenge the decision in the courts if he or she wishes to do so', noting that this was simply an application of the right of access to justice.[170] Lord Bingham, however, took a different view, arguing that the legislative provisions clearly expressed the intention of Parliament that the right to income support should be terminated on the date when the Home Office determined the asylum application and not when it was communicated to the individual concerned.

This case is interesting for a number of reasons. First, we might note the subject matter. While the treatment of asylum-seekers does, of course, generate significant public interest, the date from which benefit could lawfully be terminated for such individuals was rightly described by Lord Steyn as 'a rather technical issue'.[171] While we should not seek to downplay the importance to the person concerned, this was an administrative decision of the sort of which many thousands – perhaps, millions – are taken every week. Yet the House of Lords still considered that the principle

---

[169] See *eg* 'Hysterical and human rights obsessed judges are imperilling our liberty and security', *Daily Mail*, 17 October 2005. The issue is discussed further in chapter 5.

[170] [2003] UKHL 36, [26].

[171] *ibid*, [21].

of the rule of law was applicable to the case. The rule of law is not, there-fore, simply concerned with 'high level' cases of constitutional significance (such as those relating to national security), but may apply to any exercise of power by the executive branch. Secondly, the case offers another exam-ple of the employment by the courts of the 'principle of legality' as an aid to the interpretation of legislation.[172] This approach is constitutionally contentious because it is not always easy to ascertain what Parliament intended, with the consequence that judges may end up giving effect to *their* interpretations. The majority view in this case was that, since Parliament had not *explicitly* legislated contrary to fundamental constitu-tional principles (here, access to justice), the court could 'read into' the legislation an intention to comply with such principles. However, Lord Bingham considered that the words used *were* clear and, accordingly, that the court was obliged to give effect to them even if the consequences were 'distasteful'.[173] We can see here that the work of statutory interpretation, to which we shall return in chapter 5, leaves ample scope for judicial discretion and differences of opinion, a matter about which we may be concerned in light of the undemocratic nature of the judiciary. Furthermore, it raises questions as to the commitment of some judges to the principle of parliamentary sovereignty. Lord Steyn's somewhat glib statement that 'the semantic arguments of counsel for the Home Secretary cannot displace ... constitutional principles'[174] certainly suggests that there is a tension between that principle and the rule of law (as expressed through the principle of legality).

Thirdly, and perhaps most significantly, the case demonstrates the 'inherent elasticity of the rule of law'.[175] Both Lord Steyn and Lord Bingham invoke the principle in their judgments, but they have differing understandings of its meaning and reach different conclusions based upon it. For Steyn, the rule of law connotes predictability (connecting to individ-ual autonomy through the opportunity to plan one's life), absence of arbi-trary power and access to justice. He argues that the rule 'requires that a constitutional state must accord to individuals the right to know of a deci-sion before their rights can be adversely affected. The antithesis of such a state was described by Kafka: a state where the rights of individuals are over-ridden by hole in the corner decisions or knocks on doors in the early hours. That is not our system'.[176] For his part, Bingham is also concerned with predictability as an aspect of the rule of law, but rather than regarding

---

172 *ibid*, [27].
173 *ibid*, [20].
174 *ibid*, [33].
175 Jowell, n.75, 22.
176 Above n.170, [28].

this as a foundation for individual rights, as the majority appear to do, he views it in more formal terms as expressive of the clarity of laws made by the legislature: 'it is ... a cardinal principle of the rule of law ... that subject to exceptions not material in this case effect should be given to a clear and unambiguous legislative provision'.[177] There is a striking paradox here. As we have seen throughout the preceding discussion – and as the judgments in *Anufrijeva* confirm – certainty lies at the heart of most accounts of the rule of law. Yet the principle itself is uncertain in its meaning. It is impossible to predict the outcome of a case in which the principle is invoked with any degree of assurance. Indeed, it is probably misleading to refer to it as a 'rule' at all.

Conclusion

Yet it is this very uncertainty which arguably invests the principle of the rule of law with its constitutional weight. If we accept the need for the existence of some mechanism to limit the power of government – and it is arguable that such a 'disabling' tool is especially imperative in the UK in the absence of a codified constitution and in light of the strength of the executive branch which is derived, in large part, from its fusion with the legislature – then the flexibility inherent in the rule of law is a welcome quality. It means that government must be acutely cautious in its actions and decision-making in order not to conflict with the ambiguous principle.

However, this will not be regarded as a wholly satisfactory state of affairs by all. The assumption that governmental power can and should be limited by the law is likely to be questioned both by those who favour broad state intervention and by those who are concerned about the democratic legitimacy of judicial activity. We should not, therefore, unthinkingly regard the rule of law (as some commentators have) as an 'unqualified human good'.[178] Rather, we should remain critically attuned to the varying meanings which are attached to the notion and to the implications which its use carries both for the relationships between the branches of government and, more broadly, for society as a whole.

---

[177] *ibid*, [20].

[178] The phrase is, perhaps somewhat surprisingly, that of a Marxist historian: E. Thompson, *Whigs and Hunters* (London: Allen Lane, 1975), 266. For criticism of this view, see M. Horwitz, 'The Rule of Law: an unqualified human good?' (1977) 86 *Yale Law Journal* 561.

Chapter 3
The legislature

We commence our analysis of the three institutions of government which were identified in the previous chapter by considering the legislative branch.[1] Here, our focus will primarily be upon the Parliament of the United Kingdom which sits at Westminster, but it is important to recall that the fact that there is no 'pure' separation of powers within the British constitution means that other bodies may in practice undertake some of the tasks which are traditionally seen as falling within Parliament's remit, especially that of making laws. We have already noted that government ministers (who are key members of the executive branch) possess extensive power to make secondary legislation, and that local councils also possess a law-making power with respect to their localities. Law-making power may also be exercised by regional institutions, such as the Scottish Parliament sitting in Edinburgh, and by supranational bodies of which the UK is a member, such as the European Union. These will be further examined in chapter 6.

In such cases, Parliament itself has allocated the power to make laws to other institutions through the passage of a statute which has this effect. But, in order to understand Parliament's present-day role and position within the British constitutional order, it is necessary also to consider the somewhat more subtle manner in which the other branches of government may encroach upon Parliament's traditional functions, thereby altering the balance of power between the three constituent constitutional elements. For example, as we shall see in this chapter, the executive exercises significant influence over the process by which law is made by the legislature such that even though legislative authority continues to rest with Parliament as a matter of constitutional principle, the government might be said to act as the real law-maker in terms of the political reality. Furthermore (and leaving to one side the fact that judges, in developing

---

[1] It is extremely common for students of public law to confuse the word *legislature* with the word *legislative*. The former is a noun and the latter an adjective: the Westminster Parliament is the *legislature* for the United Kingdom and, in making laws, it undertakes *legislative* functions.

principles of common law in cases which they decide, effectively make law) the need for interpretation of the meaning of the wording of statutes opens up a possibility that judicial understandings of the law as passed by Parliament may not be exactly equivalent to that which was originally intended. As will be noted in more detail in chapter 5, this is especially pertinent in situations where it is alleged that a provision contained in a statute is incompatible with the rights contained in the European Convention on Human Rights, as given effect in English law by the Human Rights Act 1998. Here, judges may come very close on occasion to performing a legislative function of the type which is constitutionally allocated to Parliament, even though the Human Rights Act ostensibly places limits upon their capacity to act in such a manner.

This discussion should serve to underline an aspect of the unwritten and relatively flexible British constitution which was commented upon in chapter 1 of this book. In public law, we need to be attentive to the distinctions which may frequently exist between the power which exists as a matter of theoretical legal principle, and the power which can, in fact, be exercised in light of the realities of practical politics (including, in this context, what we might refer to as *judicial* politics). This will become especially significant in developing an understanding of the third of the underlying principles of the constitution, parliamentary sovereignty, which is discussed in the latter part of this chapter. We will see that, while Parliament formally retains the constitutional power to make or repeal laws on any subject which it chooses – albeit subject now to important restrictions arising from the UK's membership of the European Union – in practical terms there are a number of limitations to what it can do. While certain of these have arguably always existed (and were acknowledged by Dicey), others have become apparent as a consequence of more recent developments, demonstrating that the meaning of parliamentary sovereignty – as is the case with the two other principles described in chapter 2 – is not fixed but rather subject to a process of continuous evolution.

However, before analysing this fundamental principle of the British constitution, this chapter will consider Parliament from an institutional perspective, focusing in particular upon its composition (including the balance of power between the constituent elements) and its functions.[2]

---

[2] For an authoritative account, see R. Blackburn and A. Kinnon, *Griffith and Ryle on Parliament: Function, Practice and Procedures* (London: Sweet & Maxwell, 2nd ed., 2001).

A. Composition of Parliament

The bicameral legislature

The United Kingdom Parliament is made up of three constituent elements: the House of Commons, House of Lords and the Crown.[3] The involvement of the latter is essentially formal. The monarch opens each session of Parliament and sets out the legislative agenda in a speech delivered to both Houses of Parliament – however, the speech is written by the current government with the Prime Minister having the final say upon its contents. The monarch's assent is also necessary for bills which have proceeded through their parliamentary stages to pass into law but, as will be noted in the next chapter, such assent is in practice always given, although it is just possible to imagine a highly extreme set of circumstances in which it might be constitutionally appropriate for it to be refused. While the monarch's modern role in respect of Parliament is, therefore, of a largely symbolic character, her presence is a reminder of Parliament's historical origins as the body by way of whose consent the Crown secured funds to enable it to govern the realm.

Setting aside the role of the Crown, the Westminster Parliament is, as are many legislative assemblies across the globe, *bicameral*.[4] This form of institutional arrangement may be adopted for a number of reasons: for example, it may be intended to be representative of different strata of society, or to afford a guaranteed place in the legislature for particular geographical, regional or ethnic identities. Additionally, however, bicameralism functions to preserve stability and to improve the quality of legislation.[5] A second parliamentary chamber possesses the capacity to restrain legislative acts which constitute kneejerk, ill-considered responses to transient political crises, or which unacceptably infringe the interests of minorities, although its power to do so will not necessarily be unconstrained. It also offers a second opportunity to consider the content of proposed legislation, extending the range of views and contributions in a manner which should enhance the quality of the law which is ultimately passed. This might be said especially to be the case when the composition of the second chamber differs from that of the first: for example if it is elected upon a different basis or consists partly of members other than 'career' politicians who possess expertise in various fields.

---

[3] For further discussion of the meaning of this latter term, see chapter 4.

[4] For a scholarly analysis of this form of institutional legislative arrangement, see G. Tsebelis and J. Money, *Bicameralism* (Cambridge: CUP, 1997).

[5] The importance of bicameralism as a component of limited government was recognised by Madison: see J. Madison, *Federalist* No. 62, 'The Senate' (1788).

As a bicameral legislature, the Westminster Parliament consists of two legislative chambers, or 'Houses'. The lower House (a designation which does not reflect the relative importance of the chamber, but rather its origins as the assembly of the lower nobility and its status as the originator of most legislation), the House of Commons, is elected by way of universal suffrage, presently through a system of simple plurality voting (commonly known as 'first past the post': the individual obtaining the largest number of votes is declared the winner, even if s/he does not attain a majority of all votes cast) in geographical constituencies, of which there were 650 across the United Kingdom at the 2010 general election.[6] The vast majority of the Members of Parliament (MPs) who are thus elected are selected by political parties, although a handful of independent MPs have also secured election to the Commons since the rise of political parties in the nineteenth century.

By contrast, the upper House, the House of Lords, is presently unelected. Prior to 1999, the majority of its members were hereditary peers: that is, those who had acquired a title and privilege to sit in the upper chamber through inheritance. The House of Lords Act 1999 removed the automatic entitlement of hereditary peers to sit in the House, but 92 such peers remained in place pending further reform, elected by fellow hereditary peers or, in the case of 15 officers of the House, by the entire chamber. As a consequence, the Lords is now dominated by those with life peerages under the Life Peerages Act 1958. These individuals are conferred with a peerage for life (that is, the title ceases to exist upon the death of the holder) and a seat in Parliament by the monarch. Recommendations for such peerages were formerly made by the Prime Minister alone, but in 2000, a House of Lords Appointments Commission was created, which possesses power to make recommendations for appointments of non-party political life peers (popularly known as 'people's peers') and which also scrutinises the appointment of life peers nominated by the leaders of the political parties for propriety. Nonetheless, the Prime Minister continues to play a major role in appointment in so far as he determines the number of life peers who are to be appointed, the number allocated to each party and the timing of appointments.

There are two further categories of members of the House of Lords, who also hold seats for life only. First, peers appointed under the Appellate Jurisdiction Act 1876 to undertake the judicial functions of the House of Lords were formerly entitled to sit and vote in the House. In 2009, as noted

---

[6] The Coalition Government led by David Cameron will hold a referendum on reforming the electoral system and intends to reduce the number of parliamentary constituencies: see Parliamentary Voting System and Constituencies Bill 2010.

in chapter 2, the judicial work of the House of Lords was transferred to the new Supreme Court, but those peers who became the first Justices of the Supreme Court retain their membership of the House of Lords, even though they are no longer permitted to sit and vote.[7] Retired Law Lords also continue to sit in the House of Lords (and may participate in debates and vote). Secondly, 26 Archbishops and Bishops of the Church of England sit in the House: these are the Archbishops of Canterbury and York, the Bishops of London, Durham and Winchester and the next 21 most senior bishops. There is no guaranteed place for representatives of other religions, although other faiths may of course be represented among the life peers.

The issue of the composition of the House of Lords has proved to be one of the most intractable problems of the British constitution. Numerous attempts have been made to reform the House, dating back to the late nineteenth century. The central problem is easily stated. The upper House is unelected and unaccountable to the public, and – even following the removal of the majority of those peers who were present merely by accident of birth – this does not sit easily with conceptions of democracy.[8] It might therefore be thought that the solution is also straightforward: assuming that we retain a commitment to a bicameral legislature,[9] the second chamber should be elected, as is the first. This was the view expressed by the House of Commons in a vote on government proposals for reform which took place in March 2007,[10] the preference being for a fully-elected upper House rather than for various combinations of election and appointment. However, a clear demonstration of the difficulty of reforming the composition of the Lords was afforded by the vote in that House the following week, which was strongly in favour of a 100 per cent appointed House.

While election of the second chamber appears an intuitively attractive option, it may be problematic for a number of reasons. First, it would be likely to prove more costly than the current arrangement given that processes of election are expensive to administer. Secondly, it would almost certainly result in a House in which 'career' politicians dominated with the consequence that the breadth of experience and variety of backgrounds which is said to be characteristic of the current membership would be lost, and a more adversarial atmosphere would be likely to ensue. Thirdly, and perhaps most significantly, an elected upper chamber would acquire

---

[7] Constitutional Reform Act 2005, s.137(3).

[8] Canada also retains an appointed upper legislative chamber.

[9] Retention of a bicameral legislature was favoured by 416 votes to 163 in the House of Commons vote of March 2007. Not all states have bicameral legislatures: in addition to the regional assemblies in Scotland, Wales and Northern Ireland, a significant number of other countries, including New Zealand, Sweden, Israel, Greece and Portugal are unicameral.

[10] HM Government, *The House of Lords: Reform*, Cm. 7027 (2007).

greater public legitimacy, but this might alter the balance of power with the Commons which is examined below. If the upper House was elected at the same time and on the same basis as the lower, it would be likely to end up as a 'mirror-image' of the latter, with little purpose to its continued existence. On the other hand, if it was elected on a different cycle, and perhaps via a different electoral system (such as one which sought to be proportional to the number of votes cast for each party, or which was based upon regional or ethnic factors), it might acquire *greater* democratic legitimacy than the Commons with the consequence that conflicts between the two Houses would become more frequent, thereby stultifying the legislative process. It is because of concerns such as these that a combination of elected and appointed members has frequently been the favoured option for reform,[11] although (as the March 2007 votes proved), fixing upon an appropriate and acceptable proportion between elected and non-elected members is liable to be highly contentious.[12]

Relations between the two Houses: the Parliament Acts

As a matter of constitutional law, the two Houses were of equal status until the twentieth century, with the exception of financial matters upon which the Commons claimed predominance. However, at least from 1832 onwards, when the right to vote was extended beyond the landowning classes and the system of geographical representation was reformed, the House of Commons could claim to be the more legitimate of the two chambers in that it reflected the political preferences of (at least some of) the populace. Consequently, when conflict occurred between the two Houses, the Lords would tend to give way to the Commons, although it is important to stress that such a stance was reflective of political pragmatism, rather than an obligation of constitutional law:

> 'The Lords chose not to frustrate the Commons. This choice may have been influenced by the fear that the government might ask the monarch to swamp the upper chamber with new peers if the Lords rejected a Commons Bill. But there was no legal impediment to the Lords simply blocking government policy'.[13]

---

[11] See *eg ibid* [12.2]; Department for Constitutional Affairs, *The House of Lords: Completing the Reform* Cm 5291 (2001), [36].

[12] The Coalition Government has indicated that it will establish a committee to bring forward proposals for a wholly or mainly elected upper chamber on the basis of proportional representation: *HM Government: the Coalition: our programme for government* (2010) 27.

[13] Loveland, above p.39 (n.75), 162.

However, this uneasy truce comprehensively broke down in the early years of the twentieth century when the Liberal Government which took power in 1906 introduced a programme of social reform. Matters came to a head when the Lords, with an inbuilt Conservative majority as a result of its hereditary membership, rejected the 1909 Finance Bill in which the Chancellor, Lloyd George, sought to increase taxes. It was argued that the terms of the Bill had not been clearly approved by the electorate at the general election in 1906 and that therefore the Lords were justified in demanding that such popular consent should be signified, notwithstanding the Commons' pre-eminent role on matters of finance. Parliament was dissolved and the Liberals were returned to office, albeit without an overall majority. The Lords agreed to pass the Finance Bill but (unsurprisingly) rejected further proposed legislation which would have limited the constitutional powers of the second chamber. A second general election resulted in the return of the Liberal Government, underpinned by a (secret) commitment by the King to create sufficient peers to ensure passage of the legislation restricting the powers of the Lords. When the undertaking given by the monarch was disclosed by the Prime Minister, Asquith, the upper House gave way and the Parliament Act 1911 was passed.

The Act provides that the maximum period between general elections should be five years, rather than seven.[14] However, its chief importance for this discussion lies in its regulation of the relationship between the two Houses. Section 1 provides that a Bill which has been certified by the Speaker as a 'money Bill' can be given royal assent after a month notwithstanding failure to pass through the Lords,[15] while Section 2 provides that other public Bills can be granted royal assent in the absence of approval by the Lords after a delay of two years if passed by the Commons in three successive sessions of Parliament. The latter provision was later amended by the Parliament Act 1949 to provide for a maximum period of delay of one year where the Bill in question has been passed by the Commons in two successive sessions.

The Acts therefore remove the power of the Lords to veto legislation passed by the Commons, with the exception of legislation to extend the life of Parliament,[16] and substitute for that power a power to delay. They clearly signal that the lower House is the predominant partner, in legal terms just as in practical politics. This position was strengthened by the undertaking given by Lord Salisbury, leader of the Conservative (majority)

---

[14] s.7. The Fixed-Term Parliaments Bill 2010 will, if passed, fix the maximum (and usual) length of a Parliament at five years: clause 1. See further pp.132–33 below.

[15] 'Money Bills' are defined in section 1(2), while section 1(3) provides that such Bills shall be certified by the Speaker of the House of Commons.

[16] s.2(1).

peers in the House of Lords during the period of the Labour Government of Clement Attlee from 1945–51, that the upper House would not oppose policies which had been set out in a governing party's election manifesto.[17] The combination of the 'Salisbury Doctrine' and the Parliament Acts, coupled with processes of negotiation between the two Houses, means that outright conflict between the Commons and Lords tends to be rare. Prior to 1991 only the Welsh Church Act 1914, the Government of Ireland Act 1914 and the Parliament Act 1949 became law by way of the Parliament Act procedure, although initiation of the process has in certain other instances secured the agreement of the Lords,[18] while other pieces of legislation have been lost as a result of opposition from the Lords without the procedure being used. In more recent times, the Parliament Act procedure has been used with somewhat greater regularity: the War Crimes Act 1991, the European Parliamentary Elections Act 1999, the Sexual Offences (Amendment) Act 2000 and the Hunting Act 2004 were all passed in this manner. While it is important not to read too much into this latter fact given the still limited number of instances in which the Parliament Acts procedure has been used, this small recent upsurge might suggest that the relationship between the Commons and the Lords is fluid rather than fixed, with the upper House on occasion showing a willingness to be more assertive in fulfilling its constitutional tasks. Possible explanations for this will be explored below in the context of consideration of the contemporary role of the Lords.

Validity of the Parliament Act 1949

As was noted above, the Parliament Act 1949 reduced the delaying power of the Lords from two years to one. From 1949 onwards, it would therefore appear that, if the Lords refused to pass legislation which had passed through the Commons in two successive sessions, the lower House need only wait for a year before Royal Assent could be obtained and the Bill in question would pass into law.

However, the correctness of that assumption rests upon the validity of the 1949 Act itself. As we shall see later in this chapter, the doctrine of parliamentary sovereignty, as traditionally applied, means that courts cannot ordinarily question the validity of an Act of Parliament. But can we consider Acts passed under the Parliament Act procedure to be 'normal'

---

[17] G. Dymond and H. Deadman, *The Salisbury Doctrine*, House of Lords Library Note, LLN 2006/006 (2006).

[18] This was the case for the Temperance (Scotland) Act 1913, the Trade Union and Labour Relations (Amendment) Act 1976 and the Aircraft and Shipbuilding Act 1977: see R. Kelly, *The Parliament Acts*, House of Commons Library Standard Note SN/PC/675 (2007),10.

Acts? The argument advanced by some eminent constitutional commentators was that the legal effect of the 1911 Act was to *delegate* authority to the Commons and monarch as a legislative body with power to act only in specified circumstances. This body was necessarily subordinate to the tripartite Parliament of Commons, Lords and monarch.[19]

It is perfectly open to Parliament to delegate legislative power – as will be noted below, statutes frequently delegate such power to ministers, local councils and a multiplicity of other institutions. But any such body to which power is delegated cannot *expand* the scope of that power without express permission from Parliament, since to do so would be to encroach upon Parliament's position as the ultimate source of all law-making authority in the British constitution: effectively, the delegate would be awarding itself powers which Parliament had not allocated to it.[20] Consequently, laws passed by the delegate body might be invalidated if they exceed the powers allocated by Parliament. On this analysis, it could be argued that the 1949 Act – which had been passed by the 1911 Act procedure and to which a 'full' Parliament had therefore not given its consent – *did* effectively expand the power of the 'delegate body' of Commons and monarch by increasing the number of situations in which that body could pass a law, in that it reduced the power of the Lords to delay legislation from two years to one. Hence, it would be open to a court to declare the 1949 Act invalid.

These issues remained the subject of mere academic debate until 2004, when opponents of the Labour Government's ban on foxhunting sought to challenge the validity of the Hunting Act 2004, which had been passed by way of the procedure set out in the Parliament Act 1949. In *Jackson v Attorney-General*, the House of Lords rejected the argument that the 1949 Act was legally invalid (which would have had the consequence that *all* Acts subsequently made by the process set out in that Act, including the Hunting Act, would also have been invalid). Lord Bingham disagreed with the claim that the effect of the 1911 Act was to delegate legislative power to the Commons and monarch acting alone, holding that:

'The overall object of the 1911 Act was not to delegate power: it was to restrict, subject to compliance with the specified statutory conditions, the power of the Lords to defeat measures supported by a majority of the Commons, and thereby obviate the need for the monarch to create

---

[19] See especially W. Wade, 'The basis of legal sovereignty' (1955) 13 *Cambridge Law Journal* 172.

[20] In addition to the problems which arise with respect to the doctrine of parliamentary sovereignty, an expansion of powers in such a manner would give rise to concerns under both the rule of law and the separation of powers principles.

(or for any threat to be made that the monarch would create) peers to carry the government's programme in the Lords.'[21]

Accordingly, he considered that the 'Commons, when invoking the 1911 Act, cannot be regarded as in any sense a subordinate body'.[22] This being the case, the procedure set out in section 2 of the Parliament Act 1911 could be used to pass *any* statute, whether or not it served to increase the power of Commons and monarch acting alone, subject to the two exceptions of a money Bill (which is covered by the provisions of section 1 of the Act) and a Bill to extend the life of Parliament. The Parliament Act 1949 was consequently valid, with the necessary consequence being that the Hunting Act 2004 was also valid. The other judges also dismissed the challenge to the validity of the 2004 Act.

The conclusion reached by the House of Lords has the considerable merit of pragmatism. Since, as Lord Bingham observed, 'for the past half century it has been generally, even if not universally, believed that the 1949 Act had been validly enacted, as evidenced by the use made of it by governments of different political persuasions',[23] it would clearly be highly disruptive for a court sitting in 2005 to rule that the Act was invalid. It is less clear, however, that *Jackson* is satisfactory as regards key constitutional principles. In part this is because, as will be discussed later in the chapter, it appears to be based upon a misapprehension of the nature of parliamentary sovereignty as a doctrine which can be altered by law, rather than a reflection of the political facts upon which the constitution is based. But it is also problematic because, as his Lordship concedes, it implies that a House of Commons which is dominated by the executive can circumvent many of the checks and balances of the constitution through an over-zealous use of the Parliament Acts process:

'It has been a source of concern to some constitutionalists ... that the effect of the 1911, and more particularly the 1949, Act has been to erode the checks and balances inherent in the British constitution when Crown, Lords and Commons were independent and substantial bases of power, leaving the Commons, dominated by the executive, as the ultimately unconstrained power in the state. There is nothing novel in this perception. What, perhaps, is novel is the willingness of successive governments of different political colours to invoke the 1949 Act not for the major constitutional purposes for which the 1911 Act was invoked (the Government of Ireland Act 1914, the Welsh Church Act

---

[21] Above p.11 (n.27), [25].
[22] *ibid*, [36].
[23] *ibid*, [36].

1914, the 1949 Act) but to achieve objects of more minor or no constitutional import (the War Crimes Act 1991, the European Parliamentary
Elections Act 1999, the Sexual Offences (Amendment) Act 2000 and
now the 2004 Act). There are issues here which merit serious and objective thought and study.'[24]

For this reason, proponents of limitations on executive power would be
likely to favour the decision of the Court of Appeal in *Jackson* over that of
the House of Lords. That court had held that, while the Parliament Act
1949 was valid in so far as it represented only a 'relatively modest and
straightforward amendment' to the 1911 Act, 'the greater the scale of the
constitutional change proposed by any amendment, the more likely it is
that it will fall outside the powers contained in the 1911 Act' and would
hence require the assent of *all three* constituent elements of Parliament.[25]
This having been said (and as was noted in chapter 2), there are statements
in the House of Lords decision in *Jackson* which suggest that the sovereignty of Parliament has lost some force as the pre-eminent doctrine of the
British constitution, which may serve partially to mitigate concerns as to
the degree of power which accrues to the executive as a result of its dominance of a sovereign legislature. We shall return to the present status of
parliamentary sovereignty at the end of this chapter.

B. Functions of Parliament

i Making the law

Within the doctrine of the separation of powers, as articulated by theorists
such as Montesquieu,[26] or expressed in cases such as *Duport Steel v Sirs* and
M v Home Office,[27] the role of the legislative branch is seen as being to
enact or make the law. This function does indeed occupy a substantial
proportion of Parliament's time: for example, approximately 60 per cent of
the activity of the House of Lords is devoted to legislation.[28] However, the
extent of Parliament's impact upon the process of making law is contested.
While it is necessary for any bill to pass through a series of stages in both
chambers (subject, as described previously, to use of the Parliament Acts
process) in order to become law, the opportunities for MPs or peers to make

---

[24] *ibid*, [51].
[25] [2005] EWCA Civ. 126, [98], [100].
[26] See above, pp.21–22.
[27] See above, pp.26–27.
[28] See http://www.direct.gov.uk/en/Governmentcitizensandrights/UKgovernment/Parliament/
DG_073604

a practical difference to the content of legislation would seem to be limited. This has led some to view Parliament merely as a 'rubber stamp' for policy proposals which emanate primarily from the executive branch (government).[29] However, others identify a more meaningful role for the institution,[30] albeit that it may be necessary to modify the idealised view that Parliament 'makes the law' in order to account for the realities of modern-day politics.

The process through which Parliament scrutinises *primary legislation*, that is, statute law which is enacted by the Queen in Parliament (normally) following passage through both Houses and which is embodied in the form of an Act of Parliament, can usefully be divided into three broad stages: pre-legislative scrutiny, legislative scrutiny, and post-legislative scrutiny.[31] The following analysis will consider the role which Parliament plays at each of these stages. *Secondary legislation* (also known as subordinate or delegated legislation), that is law which is made by a person or body (frequently, a minister) under powers granted by primary legislation, will be considered subsequently.

Self-evidently, before the legislative process 'proper' can commence, an idea for legislation must emerge. In most instances, primary legislation is initiated by government, sometimes from policies put forward in an election manifesto, or as a response to events or issues of public concern. There may also be a decision to respond to recommendations of law reform bodies, commissions of inquiry, non-departmental public bodies or pressure groups. Additionally it may be necessary to respond to a court judgment or to pass legislation to give effect to treaty obligations, including those which the UK has assumed as a consequence of its membership of the European Union. Parliament's role in this aspect of the pre-legislative stage is minimal, although it is possible that a parliamentary debate or select committee report may prompt government to act. The only real exception to this general rule is the private members' Bill process, whereby an MP or peer with no governmental responsibility may introduce legislation. The most likely route to success for such a Bill is through a ballot held in the Commons at the beginning of each parliamentary session, from which 20 Members are given priority for passage of their Bills on Fridays.

---

[29] See *eg* P. Norton, *Does Parliament Matter?* (Hemel Hempstead: Harvester Wheatsheaf, 1993), Chapter 5.

[30] See especially A. Brazier, S. Kalitowski and G. Rosenblatt, *Law in the Making: Influence and Change in the Legislative Process* (London: Hansard Society, 2008).

[31] This is the classification adopted by the Constitution Committee, *Parliament and the Legislative Process*, HL 173 (2003–04), [9]. The Report of the Hansard Commission on the Legislative Process, *Making the Law* (London: Hansard Society, 1993), which is described by the Committee as 'seminal' (*ibid*, [2]), divides the process into six stages: initiation, preparation, drafting, parliamentary scrutiny and passage, implementation and post-legislative review: 6–9.

Even in this case, the idea for legislation may not emanate from Parliament:

> 'Over 400 Members normally enter the ballot, however, a substantial proportion have no particular subject for a bill in mind. If they are drawn high in the ballot, they will be contacted by pressure groups, other organisations and their own colleagues who will suggest subjects and offer draft bills. The government may also offer so called "handout" bills often but by no means exclusively to its own backbenchers.[32] These are usually bills for which the government has not been able to find time in its programme or, for some other reason, does not want to present itself.'[33]

Such Bills are unlikely to pass through the legislative stages without some degree of government support, particularly in the form of allocation of time. However, a number of private members' Bills do secure passage in most sessions of Parliament.[34]

Proposals for legislation are now regularly put out for consultation by government to interested parties in order to expand the range of evidence available, to identify possible problems in advance, and to secure some degree of public legitimacy for the proposed action. Ministers retain discretion not to consult upon proposals, but will frequently abide by the principles articulated in a *Code of Practice* which sets out the framework for consultation (including the principles that consultations should normally last for 12 weeks and should be accessible to and targeted at those people that the exercise is intended to reach).[35] Following the completion of any consultation process, the proposal must be adopted as part of the government's legislative programme, by way of approval by Cabinet Committee.[36] The Bill is then drafted by the Office of Parliamentary Counsel on instructions drawn up by the sponsoring government department.

At this point, some Bills move straight to the second stage of the three identified above and are presented to Parliament at First Reading. However, an increasingly common practice in recent times has been to prepare Bills

---

[32] A backbench MP is one who does not hold ministerial office or a post as a spokesperson for the Opposition party.

[33] House of Commons Information Office, *Private Members' Bills Procedure*, Factsheet L2 (London: House of Commons, 2010), 2–3.

[34] Since the beginning of the 1979–80 parliamentary session, 340 such Bills have received Royal Assent. Those which were passed in the 2009–10 session included the Sunbeds (Regulation) Act 2010, the Anti-Slavery Day Act 2010 and the Mortgage Repossessions (Protection of Tenants etc.) Act 2010.

[35] HM Government, *Code of Practice on Consultation* (2008).

[36] Cabinet Committees are discussed below, pp.152–53.

in draft form for parliamentary pre-legislative scrutiny, normally by a departmental select committee or joint committee of the Commons and Lords. This process has been welcomed as 'enhancing the capacity of Parliament to influence legislation at a formative stage'.[37] While the impact of such scrutiny may vary from case to case, there are occasions on which it can have a significant effect: the Constitution Committee cites the example of the draft Civil Contingencies Bill, the committee report on which occupied 227 pages and which contained recommendations which the government largely accepted in full or in part.[38]

Bills may be introduced into either House of Parliament, although most government Bills originate in the Commons. The primary opportunities for parliamentary input into legislation occur at Second Reading (a debate upon the general principles of the Bill), at Committee stage (at which the Bill is examined clause by clause, usually by a Public Bill Committee which can take evidence from witnesses) and at the Report stage (where the Bill will be reported back to the House as a whole and at which significant changes may be made). Once the Bill has completed its passage through one chamber, it moves to the other from where, subject to agreement on any amendments made in the latter, it is submitted for Royal Assent.

The Constitution Committee has commented that 'many regard legislative scrutiny as the most deficient part of the way in which Parliament does its job'.[39] A key problem relates to the allocation of time for adequate scrutiny of legislative proposals, particularly in the Commons. Here, a specific difficulty arises at the Report stage. This has been described as 'the only opportunity for the House as a whole to engage with proposed legislation and debate and decide its principal provisions in any detail', but only a maximum of five hours is normally available and new clauses and amendments proposed by ministers are given priority, meaning that backbench or Opposition proposals are frequently not debated at all.[40] More broadly, there is a belief that the government has too much power over the allocation of time for scrutiny and that it may use various mechanisms to curtail debate upon legislation.[41] This concern has been forcibly expressed by the House of Commons Reform Committee:

---

[37] Constitution Committee, n.31, [25].

[38] *ibid*, [23].

[39] Above n.31, [75].

[40] House of Commons Reform Committee, *Rebuilding the House*, HC 1117 (2008–09), [110]–[112].

[41] These include programme orders and guillotine motions: for discussion, see House of Commons Information Office, *Programming of Government Bills*, Factsheet P10 (London: House of Commons, 2008).

'It is wrong in principle that, in addition to controlling its own legislative timetable, the government rather than the House decides what is discussed, when, and for how long. It is entirely right that a democratically elected government should have a priority right to put its legislative and other propositions before the House at a time of its own choosing, and to be able to plan for the conclusion of that business. But it should be for the House as a whole to determine how much time to devote to such debate and scrutiny.'[42]

In an attempt to alleviate some of these problems, MPs voted in March 2010 to establish a Backbench Business Committee which would seek to improve scheduling of business to ensure more effective scrutiny of legislation, especially at Report stage and in consideration of amendments made by the Lords, while guaranteeing that government has time and first choice of dates to ensure passage of its legislation. It remains to be seen how effective these changes may prove. However, an underlying problem remains: the growing complexity of legislation. Figures provided by the Hansard Society vividly illustrate the increasing length of statute law over the past century or so. In 1901 forty public general Acts were passed, occupying 247 pages in a collected volume of statutes. In 2005, exactly the same number of Acts were passed, but these occupied 2,712 pages.[43] To some extent, this trend is inevitable both because a greater number of amendments to earlier legislation will be needed as time goes by, and because the range of activities carried out by modern government is significantly greater than was the case at the end of the Victorian era. But it does raise serious questions as to the capacity of Parliament to exercise meaningful scrutiny given both pressures on time and the relative lack of specialist legal knowledge which is likely to be needed, particularly in the Commons.

A further hindrance to Parliament's effectiveness at the stage of legislative scrutiny is partisanship. Some regard its 'essentially factional, adversarial approach to the legislative process'[44] as positive: the Constitution Committee comments that 'the clash between the parties is a basic and necessary feature of a healthy political system'.[45] Nevertheless, a considerable danger exists that, rather than engaging in a process of objective, critical analysis of proposed legislation in the public interest, parliamentarians will merely attempt to score party political points and seek to impress those who are in a position to advance their careers (primarily, party leaders). The

---

[42] Above n.40, [161]–[162].
[43] See above, n.30 and n.31, 230 and 399 respectively.
[44] Loveland, above p.39 (n.75), 141.
[45] Above n.31, [154].

problem is exacerbated by a perception, underpinned by the language used, that significant changes made to legislation in Parliament amount to 'defeats' for the government. Success in passing legislation is seen as indicative of a government's strength and considerable efforts will therefore be made to ensure that its proposals are supported. The system of party discipline is crucial in this regard. Party managers (known as 'whips') operate to put pressure upon MPs to vote in accordance with the party line, and make them aware of the significance to the party of particular items of parliamentary business (including debates on legislation) by providing a weekly circular upon which such items are underlined, with a 'three line whip' indicating that attendance and voting with the party is expected, the potential sanction being expulsion from the parliamentary party. This means that 'backbench revolts' are a relatively rare occurrence,[46] and that even if there is opposition within the party, a government – even with a relatively small majority of sitting MPs – can normally expect that its legislation will be passed by the Commons.

The situation is somewhat different in the Lords, where party political loyalties and discipline are not as strong and where there are significant numbers of crossbench peers who do not take a party whip.[47] These factors, coupled with the broader extent of expertise in the upper House, are frequently said to render it more effective than the Commons in carrying out the task of legislative scrutiny,[48] and mean that the government is less likely to dominate.[49] It must be recalled, however, that the Lords is constitutionally subordinate to the Commons and that its lack of democratic legitimacy is likely to render it an unsuitable arena for the introduction of legislation which is of great political controversy.

The third stage of legislative scrutiny occurs *after* the Bill has received Royal Assent and passed into law. The Hansard Commission identifies the issues which arise at this stage as follows: 'are the policies applied by the Bill still desired or acceptable; what problems have there been in interpreting, enforcing, administering and complying with the Act … are the orders, regulations *etc* [that is, delegated legislation] made under the Act working effectively?' In particular, it is important to establish whether the legislation is achieving its intended objectives and, if not, whether there are alternative means of doing so.

---

[46] But such revolts are far from unknown. See *eg* P. Cowley, *The Rebels: How Blair mislaid his Majority* (London: Politico's, 2005).

[47] Following the general election of May 2010, there were 186 crossbenchers out of a total of 707 peers.

[48] See *eg* Loveland, above p.39 (n.75), 180; Hansard Commission, n.31, [279]; Brazier, Kalitowski and Rosenblatt, n.30, 182–84.

[49] See M. Russell and M. Sciara, 'Why does the Government get defeated in the House of Lords? The Lords, the Party System and British Politics' (2007) 2 *British Politics* 299.

In some cases, specific arrangements may be made to review the working of legislation after it has been enacted. A notable example is afforded by recent statutes seeking to deal with the threat of terrorism.[50] Similarly, statutes may be subject to post-legislative scrutiny in instances where clear problems have emerged in their implementation. But, formerly, no framework existed through which Parliament (or any other body) could consistently scrutinise legislation once it has been passed. The Constitution Committee considered this situation to be unsatisfactory. Indeed, it argued that a lack of post-legislative scrutiny constituted the 'biggest gap' in Parliament's involvement in the legislative process.[51]

The government subsequently requested the Law Commission to undertake a study of the options for how post-legislative scrutiny could best be achieved. The Commission proposed the establishment of a dedicated parliamentary committee whose function would be to conduct post-legislative scrutiny on a regular basis.[52] However, the government considered that the function would be better performed by departmental select committees (see section iii below). These would choose whether to conduct a review following receipt of a memorandum issued by the relevant government department which would include a preliminary assessment of how the legislation had worked in practice and which would be issued between three and five years from Royal Assent.[53] This process now applies to the majority of Acts which have received Royal Assent in or after 2005. It is perhaps still too early to reach a definitive conclusion upon its effectiveness, although it will be noted that the Law Commission's proposal envisaged a more extensive role for the *legislature* in undertaking such review than the measures which were ultimately implemented.

Parliament's role in the scrutiny of *secondary* legislation is still more marginal. The importance of this form of legislation should not be understated. The volume of such legislation significantly exceeds that of primary legislation, and, as noted in chapter 2, it raises significant questions as to the separation of powers. The majority of secondary legislation is subject to the processes laid down in the Statutory Instruments Act 1946, with the choice of method being specified in the Act which delegates the powers in question. The *affirmative resolution* procedure necessitates the approval of Parliament. The majority of statutory instruments subject to this process are laid before Parliament in draft form but will not come into effect until a motion is passed approving the instrument; others come into effect

---

[50] See Terrorism Act 2000, s.126; Anti-Terrorism, Crime and Security Act 2001, s.122; Terrorism Act 2006, Part 3.

[51] Above n.31, [193].

[52] Law Commission, *Post-legislative Scrutiny*, Law Com No. 302 (2006).

[53] Office of the Leader of the House of Commons, *Post-legislative Scrutiny – the Government's Approach*, Cm 7320 (2008).

immediately but cannot remain in force unless approved by Parliament within a certain period. Statutory instruments subject to the *negative resolution* procedure become law unless Parliament objects. In such cases an instrument may either come into effect immediately, subject to annulment should Parliament pass a motion to that effect (normally within 40 days), or it may be laid before Parliament in draft form but will not come into effect if Parliament objects to it within 40 days.

This brief description should serve to demonstrate the significant limitations to Parliament's capacity for scrutiny. Only instruments subject to the affirmative resolution procedure require parliamentary approval, and these only amount to some 10 per cent of the total number.[54] Even here, debates on the floor of the House of Commons are rare, given the pressures on parliamentary time, and most consideration tends to take place in Delegated Legislation Committees. In addition, there is a Joint Committee on Statutory Instruments, which focuses upon the question of whether the statutory instrument falls within the powers granted by the primary legislation in question; and a Merits of Statutory Instruments Committee in the Lords, which examines the policy benefits of secondary legislation which is subject to parliamentary procedure.[55] Nevertheless, despite the existence of these mechanisms, there remains a powerful case for arguing that 'the scrutiny of statutory instruments in Parliament is inadequate and unsatisfactory',[56] not least because their sheer volume and technicality renders such scrutiny highly problematic.

ii Maintaining government in office

In its historical origins, Parliament provided authority and finance to enable the executive to govern, and this role – which Bagehot regarded as the primary function performed by the legislature[57] – remains central to its operation today in two senses.

First, as Munro notes, the British constitution is characterised by a 'parliamentary executive'.[58] As was observed in chapter 2, constitutional convention prescribes that all government ministers shall be members of one of the two Houses, and the Prime Minister is the person who is best able to command the confidence of the House of Commons. Relatedly, the

---

[54] House of Commons Information Office, *Statutory Instruments*, Factsheet L7 (London: House of Commons, 2008), 5.

[55] Note also the Delegated Powers and Regulatory Reform Committee, which examines primary legislation to assess whether it inappropriately delegates legislative power or subjects the exercise of legislative power to an inappropriate degree of parliamentary scrutiny.

[56] Hansard Commission on the Legislative Process, n.31, [264].

[57] Bagehot, above p.33, (n.45), 154–55.

[58] Above p.25, (n.14), 322.

government holds office by virtue of its ability to command the confidence of the Commons, and should that confidence be lost, the Prime Minister will be expected to resign or to seek a dissolution of Parliament (triggering a general election).[59] The government is therefore formed through Parliament and relies upon the support of Parliament (or, more specifically, the House of Commons) to sustain its existence.[60]

Secondly, Parliament provides the financial resources for government to carry out its work, as specified by Article 4 of the Bill of Rights 1689, which provides 'that levying money for or to the use of the Crown by pretence of prerogative, without grant of Parliament, for longer time, or in other manner than the same is or shall be granted, is illegal'. A government which fails to secure the acceptance of its financial proposals by the House of Commons will be expected to resign or to seek a dissolution of Parliament. While such a course of events is unusual,[61] the obligation to seek authorisation from Parliament for the raising of resources through taxation provides an opportunity for scrutiny of the government's financial proposals on an annual basis through debate upon the Budget, which is followed by passage of the Finance Act. Similarly, most expenditure by the government must be approved by Parliament on an annual basis, although in practice debate upon proposals for expenditure very rarely takes place and the power of the House of Commons over expenditure has been described as 'very close' to 'a constitutional myth'.[62]

iii Scrutiny of the executive

If the obligation to seek financial supply from the Commons presents the latter with a theoretical possibility to exercise a certain degree of oversight of government, there are more tangible manifestations of Parliament's role as a check and balance to executive power to be detected elsewhere. An understanding of this aspect of the legislature's work, and its effectiveness in carrying it out, is crucial to an appreciation of the dynamics of the modern British constitution, especially the perceived deficiencies of political forms of control which (at least in part) provide a rationale for the recent elevation of *legal* forms of accountability, as noted in chapter 1. We shall accordingly have cause to return to this subject both later in this chapter – when we consider how Dicey attempted to square his conception of the unlimited power of Parliament with a commitment to a balanced

---

[59] See Cabinet Office, *The Cabinet Manual – Draft* (2010), [56].

[60] See now the proposals on confidence contained in the Fixed-Term Parliaments Bill 2010, discussed below pp.132–33.

[61] The events of 1909 afforded an exception to the general rule: see the discussion above, p.72.

[62] Procedure Committee, *Resource Accounting and Budgeting*, HC 438 (1997–98), [10].

constitution[63] – but also in chapter 4, where we examine the conventional practices which regulate ministerial responsibility to Parliament. The present section may, therefore, most profitably be read in conjunction with those subsequent discussions. The focus here is upon the *procedural mechanisms and institutional structures* within Parliament which provide it with an opportunity to hold the government to account for its decisions, actions and policies.

As the executive branch in the British constitution is parliamentary in character (by contrast, for example, with the US President who sits outside Congress), various occasions exist within the legislature's schedule during which MPs are able to monitor the government's discharge of its executive functions. The most well-known of these is question time. In the Commons, a period of an hour is set aside at the commencement of parliamentary business on Mondays to Thursdays, during which departmental ministers respond to questioning on a rota system, with questions to the Prime Minister lasting for 30 minutes every Wednesday. In the Lords, question time lasts for up to 30 minutes and questions are directed at the government as a whole, rather than a particular departmental minister. Such questions may take either written or oral form, with only a small number of the latter being answered in each case (questions which do not receive an oral reply will be answered in written form). Questions are submitted in advance, providing ministers with an opportunity to formulate a response, but MPs may ask supplementary questions for which notice has not been given. Prime Minister's Question Time is a more open affair, during which MPs frequently table questions which ask the Prime Minister to list his engagements, enabling them to follow up with an unanticipated supplementary question, while the leader of the opposition is not obliged to table questions in advance at all. These exchanges attract a degree of media interest, especially since televising of Commons proceedings commenced in 1989, but it is doubtful how far they can be said to constitute an effective means of oversight of the executive branch. Although described by some as 'highly interactive, combative and spontaneous',[64] oral questions have frequently been seen as a means of scoring party political points, as Loveland claims in respect of Prime Minister's Question Time:

'For opposition MPs, the opportunity to speak is little more than a chance to attract a good deal of publicity by indulging in splenetic rhetoric designed to demonstrate their ideological purity either to their

---

[63] Below, pp.104–06.
[64] A. Kaiser, 'Parliamentary Opposition in Westminster Democracies: Britain, Canada, Australia and New Zealand' (2008) 14 *Journal of Legislative Studies* 20, 28.

party leaders or to their local constituency activists. Government backbenchers, in contrast, are likely to produce questions which enable the
Prime Minister to lavish praise on particular aspects of government
policy.'[65]

For this reason, written questions and answers may be a more fruitful
mechanism for holding government to account, in that they are apt to be
less partisan and more focused in content. They serve partially to redress
the imbalance in the availability of information which hinders
Parliament's capacity to oversee the executive,[66] providing a basis for
further investigation by the MP concerned.

Debates also provide an opportunity for both Houses to scrutinise the
activities of government. In the Commons,[67] half-hour adjournment
debates take place at the close of business, during which a backbench MP
who is selected by ballot may raise a matter with advance notice, enabling
an appropriate minister to reply.[68] Emergency debates may also be held on
issues which should receive urgent consideration, although such debates
are rare. More important are the 'Opposition Days', twenty days allocated
annually to general debates on topics chosen by opposition parties.
Opportunities also now exist for the initiation of debates by backbenchers
in Westminster Hall, as noted in section v below.

These procedures now need to be read against the previously-noted
establishment of a Backbench Business Committee,[69] which will have
control over the scheduling of parliamentary business on days, or parts of
days, which are set aside for non-ministerial business. It remains to be seen
whether the existence of this Committee significantly affects the balance
of power between backbench MPs and those with ministerial roles, or
between the executive and Parliament more broadly, but the ambitions
which have been expressed for it are far-reaching:

'Without in any way compromising Government's ability to have its
own initiatives discussed and scrutinised, this Committee will take clear
charge of part of the agenda for at least one day a week or its equivalent
for the House collectively to discuss those matters that Members feel
should be prioritised. It will create new opportunities for all Members,

---

[65] Above p.39 (n.75), 145.
[66] See further below, p.167.
[67] Adjournment debates do not take place in the Lords, but Questions for Short Debate in
that House allow for a debate of up to 90 minutes.
[68] The Speaker chooses the topic for debate on Thursdays.
[69] See *House of Commons Debates*, 15 June 2010, col. 778. The Coalition Government has
indicated that a House Business Committee, with responsibility for management of government
business, will be established by the third year of the current Parliament: see above n.12, 27.

giving them a greater sense of ownership and responsibility for what goes on in their own House. It will make debates more responsive to public concerns, as fed in to Members by their constituents.'[70]

Brief mention should also be made of Commons Early Day Motions, which are written motions tabled by individual members calling for debates on particular issues, to which other members may append their signatures. Debates rarely take place on such motions, but they serve as a means of drawing ministerial, media and public attention to campaigns or other matters of interest or concern.[71]

None of these processes appear ideally designed to perform the type of informed and sustained scrutiny of government which would seem to be necessary if Parliament is to act as a meaningful check and balance to executive power. However, the legislature has another mechanism at its disposal in the form of the system of select committees. Although dating in an identifiably modern form from the mid-nineteenth century, the present system derives from a reform in 1979 when it was recommended that committees should be established in the House of Commons to scrutinise the work of each government department, with the membership (of between 11 and 14 MPs) fixed for the lifetime of a Parliament and upon which neither ministers nor frontbench Opposition spokespersons would serve. The committees have formal power to summon witnesses and to call for papers and records (although they normally proceed by way of invitation) and may appoint specialist advisers. Each committee chooses the topics which it will investigate within a general remit to examine and comment upon the policy, expenditure and administration of the department (the latter including the department's executive agencies, non-departmental public bodies and other associated bodies),[72] and to assist the House in debate and decision.[73] Evidence, both written and oral, is taken and a report is drawn up which reflects the consensus position of the membership and which contains recommendations for action. The report is laid before Parliament and may be the subject of debate on the floor of the House or in Westminster Hall. The government must normally respond to a select committee report within two months.

There are also committees in the House of Lords, but these do not 'shadow' the work of particular government departments: they focus instead upon broad themes, including science, Europe, economics and the

---

[70] House of Commons Reform Committee, n.40, [181].

[71] For example, motions tabled on 21 June 2010 marked Vocational Qualifications Day, maintained that there should be no further weakening of trade union rights, and congratulated the Northern Irish golfer Graeme McDowell on winning the US Open, among other matters.

[72] See further below pp.157–59.

[73] Liaison Committee, *Annual Report 2004*, HC 419 (2004–05), [7].

constitution. Additionally, there are committees in both Houses which have cross-cutting responsibilities, including the Public Administration Committee (which examines the quality and standards of administration in the civil service and scrutinises the reports of the Parliamentary and Health Service Ombudsman) and the powerful Public Accounts Committee (which scrutinises government expenditure focusing upon economy, effectiveness and efficiency). Other committees, such as the previously-mentioned Backbench Business Committee, the Procedure Committees and the Liaison Committee (which co-ordinates and oversees the select committee system and before which the Prime Minister appears twice a year) deal with the business of the legislature itself.

Academic commentators offer differing perspectives on the effectiveness of the select committee system. Loveland notes that they command limited resources (especially when contrasted to the powerful Congressional committees which operate in the United States) and that they have frequently experienced difficulty in obtaining information or obliging witnesses to attend or answer questions despite the formal power to summon.[74] Furthermore, it is difficult to disentangle the impact of committee reports and recommendations upon government policy from other factors which may be of influence. On the other hand, Tomkins praises the committees for providing 'a forum in which parliamentarians feel, and are, able to co-operate across the party divide, rather than routinely and unthinkingly to divide along party lines'.[75] This comment is illustrative of the fact that, while the composition of departmental select committees reflects the overall balance of parties in the Commons, some committees are chaired by Opposition politicians and, as noted, reports seek to reflect a consensus position with the consequence that partisanship is considerably less apparent than is the case on the floor of the House. Additionally, the process of gathering evidence (both from within government and beyond) by committee members who, over the course of years, can acquire some degree of expertise on a particular topic, may be said to result in an accumulation of information on the activities of government which would be beyond the compass of Parliament as a collective entity to obtain. Such information renders the task of scrutiny of the executive – whether carried out by MPs or by extraparliamentary means, such as the media – a more feasible and meaningful task.

Once again in this context, recent developments demonstrate that Parliament's position in relation to the executive is not fixed but rather continues to evolve. In March 2010, MPs approved proposals emanating from the House of Commons Reform Committee that chairs of select

---

[74] Above p.39 (n.75),150.
[75] Above p.15 (n.39) 168.

committees should in future be elected by the whole House at the start of every Parliament and that members of the committees should be chosen by secret ballot within parties. This reform is intended to reduce the previously decisive influence which the party whips exercised over membership, the Committee contending that 'it should be for the House and not the Executive to choose which of its Members should scrutinise the Executive'.[76] The first elections took place in June 2010.

iv Redress of grievances

Historically, there was a close connection between Parliament's function as the source of authorisation of governmental revenue and the redress of grievances against the Crown. Ridley comments that 'the traditional role of Parliament, centuries older than the establishment of democracy, was as a channel for complaints against government. Before the feudal Parliament voted the King the taxes he required, it pressed for the redress of collective grievances'.[77] With the advent of representative democracy, MPs in the House of Commons acquired a role as intermediaries between government and their constituents (individuals residing in the electoral area which an MP represents), and might contact or seek an appointment with a minister or raise an issue in the House of Commons on behalf of those whom they represent. The scope for such action is wide, and is not restricted (as is judicial review of administrative action) to decisions which have already been taken or policies which have already been implemented:

'Members [of Parliament] intervene at all stages of decision-making, not just to have a decision reversed. Attempts are made to sway a matter under consideration. MPs are called on to expedite matters, to press for a decision or push a person to the head of a queue. They are sought out for information and advice or to lend weight to an application still to be made.'[78]

However, as Rawlings also notes, there is considerable variability in the manner in which different MPs approach this task,[79] which renders this a somewhat haphazard means for the citizen to obtain redress against government. Consequently, other avenues, such as judicial review or

---

[76] House of Commons Reform Committee, n.40, [72].
[77] F. Ridley, 'The Citizen against Authority: British approaches to the redress of grievances' (1984) 37 *Parliamentary Affairs* 1, 2.
[78] R. Rawlings, 'The MP's Complaints Service' (1990) 53 *Modern Law Review* 22, 22.
[79] *ibid*, 165.

ombudsmen (respectively described in chapters 5 and 6) may prove more fruitful for the individual.

Relatedly, MPs – especially those who also hold ministerial office – may struggle to meet the additional workload presented by constituency matters, especially given the deficiencies in parliamentary resources which were identified above. The Select Committee on Modernisation of the House of Commons has referred to a 'tidal wave' of constituency work, with MPs receiving an average of over 300 letters a week (by comparison with 12–15 per week in the 1950s and 1960s), a figure which does not include emails, faxes and telephone calls.[80] Thus, although it appears that 'MPs regard themselves primarily as representing their constituencies [and] ... spend more time on constituency work than any other part of their job',[81] it is far from clear that they are able to discharge this function as effectively as might be wished.

v Forum for debate and constitutional watchdog

If the grievance redress role is necessarily performed primarily by the House of Commons (since that chamber consists of representatives elected by constituents), the House of Lords is rather better placed than the lower chamber to act as a focus for discussion and deliberation upon matters of public concern and importance. The Lords is less dominated by party than the Commons (in part because the party whipping system does not operate with as much rigour as in the lower House and in part because of the significant number of crossbenchers), is free from pressure to be re-elected, and contains a breadth of expertise on a wide variety of topics. From the beginning of the parliamentary session (traditionally in November in a non-election year) until the end of June, general motions for debate have precedence over legislative and other business on Thursdays in the Lords, and the fourth of four oral questions directed at the government as a whole from Tuesday to Thursday is a 'topical question' selected by ballot.[82] The range of topics addressed in general debate is wide. For example, between March and July 2008, there were debates upon the impact of government policies upon women, voting systems, crime, encouraging high-quality architecture, the role played by post offices in local communities, interfaith dialogue, reserves in the armed forces, disability rights, data protection, Britishness, the rule of law and higher education, amongst other matters.

---

[80] Select Committee on the Modernisation of the House of Commons, *Revitalising the Chamber: the Role of the back bench Member*, HC 337 (2006–07), [15]–[16].

[81] *ibid*, Ev. 32, [8] (M. Rush and P. Giddings).

[82] Cabinet Office, *Guide to Parliamentary Work* (2010), [4.34], [4.41].

By contrast, as noted in section i above, the partisan nature of proceedings in the Commons and the relative lack of parliamentary time would seem to act as hindrance to deliberation on issues of general public interest. However, its capacity to function in this regard has been enhanced since 1999 by the use of an additional chamber for debate, a grand committee room just off Westminster Hall in the Palace of Westminster.[83] This has alleviated some of the pressure on time in the Commons, and provides an opportunity for back-bench MPs to initiate general debates, for questions on cross-cutting issues that involve the work of more than one department, and for debate on Select Committee reports. Sittings take place three times a week.

In addition to its function as a debating chamber on matters of general public concern, Parliament may have a more specific deliberative part to play. The preceding discussion of scrutiny of the executive indicates that an important dimension of the role of the legislature is to function as a check and balance with respect to other branches of government, as a 'partial' reading of the separation of powers doctrine requires. However, that function may be said to amount to rather more than the oversight of policies, decisions and actions of the executive, extending to a broader role as a guardian of fundamental constitutional principles.

Given executive dominance of the lower Chamber in modern times, this is not a task which the House of Commons can easily assume, although there will be occasions when an appeal to constitutional values is made in the course of debate upon government proposals or actions; furthermore, certain MPs have acquired a reputation for particular concern with matters of constitutional principle.[84] Additionally, the House of Commons plays a role, albeit limited, in ensuring observance of the provisions of the European Convention on Human Rights (as given effect in English law by the Human Rights Act 1998) in that section 19 of the latter Act obliges a government minister in charge of a bill to make a statement confirming its compatibility with the Convention prior to its second reading in the House.[85] More tangibly, the Commons is represented on the Joint Committee on Human Rights,[86] which examines bills for compatibility with the Convention, monitors the government's response to court judgments and considers human rights issues in general, including treaties and issues beyond the scope of the European Convention.[87]

---

[83] Select Committee on Modernisation of the House of Commons, *Sittings of the House in Westminster Hall*, HC 194 (1998–99).

[84] The most notable recent example is Tony Benn. See *eg*, T. Benn and A. Hood, *Common Sense: a new Constitution for Britain* (London: Hutchinson, 1993).

[85] This applies in whichever House the Bill is introduced.

[86] A Joint Committee is a Select Committee containing members from both Houses.

[87] See *eg* Joint Committee on Human Rights, *The UN Convention on Human Rights of Persons with Disabilities* HL 9/HC 93 (2008–09).

Once again, however, it is the less executive-dominated House of Lords which is in the best position to fulfil the function of 'constitutional watchdog', upholding fundamental constitutional values against any attempted incursion by the government. Thus, Oliver has argued that 'functions performed by supreme courts or constitutional courts or councils of state or constitutional councils in other countries are being institutionalised and internalised in the second chamber. They are intra-, not extra-parliamentary'.[88] We might attribute the increased willingness to assume such a role in recent years to three factors. First, the removal of most of the hereditary peers in 1999 (which had the consequential effect of removing an inbuilt Conservative Party majority in the House) has endowed the Lords with a greater degree of legitimacy, albeit that, in the absence of election, it cannot be described as democratic. This has apparently led it to be more assertive *vis-a-vis* the Commons: for example, in 2005 the Prevention of Terrorism Bill 'evoked a level of resistance from the second chamber unprecedented since the constitutional crisis sparked by Lloyd George's budget in 1909',[89] with the shadow Lord Chancellor, Lord Kingsland, observing in debate that 'we have our constitutional duty in this House ... It would be wholly wrong for us to shirk it'.[90] Secondly, a Select Committee on the Constitution was established in the House of Lords in 2001, which examines public bills for constitutional implications, investigates broad constitutional issues and seeks to clarify the government's position on constitutional issues by taking evidence from the Lord Chancellor. The Committee has produced reports on a number of issues of constitutional concern, including Parliament's role in respect of the prerogative war power,[91] relations between the executive, judiciary and Parliament,[92] and referendums in the United Kingdom.[93] Finally, although more speculatively, it might be supposed that an awareness of the situation to which Lord Mustill (who is himself, of course, a member of the House of Lords) drew attention in the *Fire Brigades Union* case – that is, of the inadequacies of Parliamentary means 'of ensuring that the executive, in the exercise of its delegated functions, performs in a way which Parliament finds appropriate'[94] – has permeated the House more generally and that it has consequently sought to strengthen its constitutional role.

---

[88] D. Oliver, 'The "Modernization" of the UK Parliament?' in Jowell and Oliver (eds.), above p.39 (n.75), 178.

[89] M. Russell and M. Sciara, *The House of Lords in 2005: a more representative and assertive chamber?* (London: UCL Constitution Unit, 2006), 10. The government suffered 18 defeats on provisions of the Bill in the Lords, on six such occasions being defeated by more than 100 votes.

[90] *House of Lords Debates*, 10 March 2005, col. 1003.

[91] HL 236-I (2005–06). See further below p.143 (n.68).

[92] HL 151 (2006–07).

[93] HL 99 (2009–10).

[94] Above p.14 (n.35).

Does Parliament matter?[95]

The preceding discussion of Parliament's functions within the British constitution could usefully be summarised under three broad headings. First, Parliament provides authority for the executive to govern: by providing the necessary financial resources; by ensuring the passage of the government's legislative agenda; and by delegating powers to ministers and other components of the executive. Secondly, Parliament has an impact upon the content of legislation, although it would appear to be an over-statement of its contribution to suggest that it actually *makes* the law. Thirdly, Parliament scrutinises the executive's policies, decisions and actions both on a day-to-day basis and with a view to their compatibility with long-term fundamental constitutional values.

This analysis would suggest that some modification of the theory of the separation of powers – especially the 'pure' variant – is necessary if we are to understand the position which the legislature occupies within the British constitutional order. Rather than viewing Parliament as an institution standing on an equal footing with the executive branch (as well as the judiciary), it would be more accurate to see the executive as the dominant player, with Parliament's primary role being to act as a check and balance to executive power. Such a perspective is adopted by Adam Tomkins, who suggests that 'we should abandon the notion that Parliament is a legislator, and conceive of it instead as a scrutineer'.[96] It reflects the fact that, as a matter of political reality as distinct from abstract constitutional theory, the executive dominates the House of Commons (and, by extension, Parliament as whole, in view of the fact that the House of Lords is the constitutionally subordinate partner). Senior members of government, including the Prime Minister, are present in the House and can employ the techniques of party discipline in order to ensure that the majority which they possess in the chamber, as a consequence of an electoral system which frequently produces an outright victory for a single party, translates into support for the government's position. The consequence is that the executive can normally enforce its will against Parliament, a situation that has, in essence, prevailed since the rise of political parties in the mid-nineteenth century.

---

[95] See Norton, n.29.

[96] A. Tomkins, 'What is Parliament For?' in N. Bamforth and P. Leyland (eds.) *Public Law in a Multi-Layered Constitution* (Oxford: Hart, 2003), 76. Such a view is not fully consonant with other studies, notably that of Brazier, Kalitowski and Rosenblatt, who argue that 'legislative proposals *do* change measurably as they make their way through the legislative process': n.30, 16 (emphasis in original). However, even these authors refer to 'parliamentary scrutiny' of legislation: *ibid*, 173, suggesting that any disagreement with Tomkins is a matter of degree rather than principle.

An evaluation of the acceptability or otherwise of this position will be dependent to some extent upon perceptions of the proper function of public law and of the role of the state, as discussed in chapter 1. If government intervention is seen as necessary for the pursuit of the collective good of society, then Parliament's subservience to the executive branch might seem less troubling since there is a predominant need for strong government (although it should be noted that an adherent to this view will, on occasion, have to tolerate a government exercising control over the legislature which is not to his/her ideological taste). On the other hand, if a more cautious approach to the role of the state is taken, with concern expressed as to government's capacity to infringe individual autonomy and freedoms, then Parliament's weakness relative to the executive would seem problematic, especially when read alongside the legal doctrine of parliamentary sovereignty, which is explored in the next section of this chapter. Disquiet of this type may be seen to underpin Lord Hailsham's familiar warning as to the dangers of 'elective dictatorship'.[97] If such a view is taken, then it is important either to bolster the legal checks and balances which exist within the British constitution to compensate for the legislature's inadequacies – the development which Lord Mustill notes in his dictum in the *Fire Brigades Union* case[98] – or to reinvigorate Parliament by enhancing its position *vis-a-vis* the executive: or to pursue both of these approaches. In short, some degree of 'rebalancing' of the three institutions of government is needed.

The flexible nature of the British constitution means, however, that relationships between the branches of government are fluid and dynamic. The upshot is that – to a large extent – such 'rebalancing' may occur on an ongoing, incremental basis, rather than by way of formal amendment to the constitution as is likely to be necessary in other jurisdictions. The preceding discussion offers a number of illustrations of this, including the evolution of the select committee system from 1979, enhanced processes for pre- and post-legislative scrutiny in recent years, the establishment of a supplementary debating chamber in Westminster Hall and the more assertive stance taken by the House of Lords since removal of most of the hereditary peers in 1999. Each of these developments has strengthened Parliament's position relative to the executive and each serves as a reminder of the point made in chapter 1, that power relations within the British constitutional order are constantly changing.

Furthermore, it is important to be aware not only of recent changes which may affect the balance of power between the institutions of government, but also to explore possible future trends. In this context, the recent decisions

---

[97] Above p.13 (n.32).
[98] Above p.14 (n.35).

to establish a Backbench Business Committee and to elect chairs and members of select committees from June 2010 onwards are worthy of particular note as reforms which may enhance Parliament's future standing. We should also note the proposal to introduce fixed-term Parliaments and to specify how an earlier election may be triggered, which are discussed in chapter 4, and possible changes to the voting system, as favoured by the Liberal Democrat party within the present governing coalition.[99] The latter would be likely to have a significant effect upon the balance of power given that the current 'first past the post' system has a normal tendency to produce governments with a Commons majority, frequently of a significant nature. A different system would be more likely to produce a Commons in which no single party possessed an overall majority, as has frequently been the case in the regional assemblies of Scotland and Wales since devolution in 1999.[100] This would seem, in principle, to make it more difficult for government to enforce its will upon Parliament.[101]

These emergent factors also neatly illustrate the fact that it is not always easy to predict the nature or timing of events which might lead to alterations in constitutional power relations. The proposals for a Backbench Business Committee and elections to select committees emerged as part of a package of reforms designed to reinvigorate Parliament in light of the scandal over parliamentary expenses, when a significant number of MPs and peers were found to have abused the rules as to the sums which could be claimed in support of their work.[102] Similarly, the prospect of reform to the electoral system moved significantly closer as a consequence of the

---

[99] Above n.12, 27. These proposals have been said to 'strengthen Parliament's power over the executive': *House of Commons Debates*, 5 July 2010, col. 24 (N. Clegg).

[100] The system proposed for elections to Westminster (the 'alternative vote' system) differs from that used in Scottish Parliament and Welsh Assembly elections (the 'additional member' system). Since devolution, governments in both Scotland and Wales have either been coalitions between two parties or minority governments in which a single party governs despite not having an overall majority of seats.

[101] Such an analysis supposes that it will be more difficult for a coalition government to enforce party discipline upon two parties than it would be for a single party government to enforce discipline upon one. Another possibility should, however, be considered: that a coalition government of two (or more) parties will tend to dominate Parliament to an even greater extent than is the case for a single party government because there will be fewer parties in opposition.

[102] See House of Commons Reform Committee: 'We have been set up at a time when the House of Commons is going through a crisis of confidence not experienced in our lifetimes. This is largely, but not exclusively, because of the revelations about Members' expenses, bringing with it a storm of public disapproval and contempt. Public confidence in the House and in Members as a whole has been low for some time, but not as low as now. It is not too much to say that the institution is in crisis ... Without the shock of recent events, it is unlikely that this Committee would have been established ... We have a rare window of opportunity. There is an appetite for reform inside the House and among the public at large': above n.40, [1], [4], [5].

outcome of the general election of May 2010, following which the Conservative Party (which has traditionally opposed any reform to the electoral system) entered into a coalition with the Liberal Democrats (who are in favour of change), a central condition of which was the holding of a referendum upon electoral reform. Even the most perceptive of commentators could not necessarily have foreseen the precise manner in which these events unfolded, demonstrating that medium to long-term shifts in power relations between branches of government may arise from transient (albeit highly significant) political events at least as frequently as they do from a process of dispassionate, apolitical and perhaps painstaking theorising about optimal constitutional design. To that extent, as we saw in chapter 1, public law cannot and should not be isolated from the political environment which surrounds it.

C. The sovereignty of Parliament

In chapter 1, we noted the importance of the concept of sovereignty to the study of public law and observed that a distinction may need to be drawn between *political* and *legal* sovereignty in denoting the location of ultimate decision-making authority within a constitutional order. In a democracy, political sovereignty resides with the people, while in most states the ultimate source of legal authority resides in the constitutional text. In fact, there is a danger of creating too rigid a divide here: as will be seen, parliamentary sovereignty as a legal rule within the British constitution connects, at least to some extent, to historical events and, in its modern-day form, amounts to an expression of the democratic character of the state. Nonetheless, it is with parliamentary sovereignty as a *doctrine of constitutional law* that we shall primarily be concerned in the ensuing discussion. We commence with Dicey, who has offered the most influential reading of the meaning of the principle in the context of the British constitution, but it should be noted that the doctrine predates his work in the late nineteenth century and we shall accordingly have need to reach further back into history in order better to understand its origins.[103]

---

[103] For a comprehensive and scholarly account of the history of parliamentary sovereignty, see J. Goldsworthy, *The Sovereignty of Parliament* (Oxford: OUP, 1999).

The meaning and nature of parliamentary sovereignty

Dicey's account of parliamentary sovereignty is relatively straightforward to express. It consists of two components, a positive limb and a negative limb. The positive dimension is articulated in the principle that 'Parliament ... has under the English constitution, the right to make or unmake any law whatever', while the negative aspect embodies the notion that 'no person or body is recognised by the law of England as having a right to override or set aside the legislation of Parliament'.[104] Dicey considered these propositions together to amount to 'the very keystone of the law of the constitution'.[105]

It is important to note that Dicey regarded his definition to be limited in scope. He explained that parliamentary sovereignty was the dominant characteristic of political institutions 'from a legal point of view',[106] indicating clearly that the doctrine should be seen only as a rule expressing the relationship between the legislature and the courts. He went on to express the distinction between types of sovereignty which was identified above in the following manner:

'The word "sovereignty" is sometimes employed in a political rather than in a strictly legal sense. That body is "politically" sovereign or supreme in a state the will of which is ultimately obeyed ... In this sense of the word the electors of Great Britain may be said to be ... the body in which sovereign power is vested ... But this is a political, not a legal fact ... The political sense of the word "sovereignty" is, it is true, fully as important as the legal sense or more so. But the two significations ... are essentially different.'[107]

This explanation enables us to understand that Dicey was not trying to identify (as might a political scientist) the location of the ultimate source of political power in the British state. If that had been his goal, then locating it in Parliament would clearly be mistaken from a modern perspective (given what has been said earlier in this chapter about the balance of power between legislature and executive), and would arguably have been problematic even at the time when he wrote, in light of the rise to dominance of the Cabinet and the growth of the party system. Nonetheless, as in the case of his account of the rule of law, Dicey's seemingly objective legal analysis of the fundamental principles of the British constitution concealed certain ideological political preferences on his part. As Craig

---

[104] Dicey, above p.17 (n.47), pp.39–40.
[105] *ibid*, 70.
[106] *ibid*, 39.
[107] *ibid*, 73–74.

notes, 'Dicey's theories were themselves explicitly premised upon certain assumptions concerning representative democracy, and the way in which it operated'. In particular, they reflected a commitment to a 'self-correcting majoritarian democracy'.[108] The meaning and implications of this will be explored in the next section.

Setting aside the political dimension of Dicey's theories for the time being, the doctrine of the sovereignty of Parliament might be said to provide us with a crucial component of what the legal theorist Herbert Hart has described as a 'rule of recognition'.[109] This is a rule, sitting at the apex of the hierarchy of laws within a legal system, which specifies the criteria which determine which other rules should be recognised as valid within the system. If Hart's analysis is applied in the context of the British constitution, we may say that 'whatever the Queen in Parliament enacts is law'.[110] This rule is 'entirely a matter of fact. It is whatever rule that system's most senior officials, including its judges, do in fact accept and apply in identifying valid laws of the system, irrespective of its merits from the perspective of political morality'.[111]

This approach therefore seeks to identify the rule of recognition on an empirical basis: we can establish its existence by observing behaviour, and 'its content depends upon a morally neutral description of whichever standard of official behaviour officials accept at any given point in time'.[112] On this reading, the notion that 'whatever the Queen in Parliament enacts is law' constitutes the ultimate basis of legal validity in the state rests upon an observable consensus to that effect: as Goldsworthy claims, 'the historical evidence demonstrates that for several centuries, at least, all three branches of government in Britain have accepted the doctrine that Parliament has sovereign law-making authority'.[113] This provides us with an important means of understanding the origins and character of parliamentary sovereignty as a defining characteristic of the British constitution. Although it is a legal rule in so far as it establishes the relationship between the courts and the legislature, parliamentary sovereignty cannot be *created* by judges as a principle of common law, because this would beg the question of what gave the judges the authority to make common law in the first place. But equally, parliamentary sovereignty cannot owe its origins to statute because – leaving aside the obvious point that no statute which

---

[108] P. Craig, 'Unitary, Self-Correcting Democracy and Public Law' (1990) 106 *Law Quarterly Review* 105, 105, 109.

[109] H. Hart, *The Concept of Law* (Oxford: Clarendon Press, 2nd ed., 1994), 94.

[110] *ibid*, p.148.

[111] Goldsworthy, n.103, 238.

[112] S. Lakin, 'Debunking the Idea of Parliamentary Sovereignty: the Controlling Factor of Legality in the British Constitution' (2008) 28 *Oxford Journal of Legal Studies* 709, 717.

[113] Above, n.103, 236.

confers sovereignty upon Parliament exists – Parliament cannot logically confer sovereign power upon itself since the validity of that statute would depend upon the existence of the very sovereign power which Parliament was seeking to confer. This appears to leave us with only one possibility: namely, that the source of parliamentary sovereignty resides in the 'consciousness' of judges, legislators and other key actors in the constitutional system – that is, their *acceptance* that this is the ultimate rule.

To establish the origins of that acceptance would be a lengthy historical task well beyond the scope of this text. Goldsworthy argues that it is articulated in the work of a variety of political and legal thinkers dating from the thirteenth century onward.[114] However, as a matter of political history – as distinct from political theory – the crucial event was the constitutional settlement which followed the 'Glorious Revolution' of 1688, when Parliament offered the throne to William and Mary of Orange on condition that the monarch's powers to govern through the use of prerogative powers would, in future, be significantly circumscribed.[115] The Bill of Rights 1689, which established Parliament's rights against the Crown and restricted the exercise of monarchical prerogative power, can be regarded as inherently expressing the principle of the supremacy of Parliament in the law. Accordingly, the acceptance by the branches of government of parliamentary sovereignty as a fundamental rule of legal validity can be said to be rooted in historical political reality even if it had been formulated as a theoretical construct at an earlier stage.[116]

This analysis raises some important and controversial questions. First, if the existence of the doctrine of parliamentary sovereignty is explained, at least in part, by acceptance of a political reality, what would happen if that political reality were to change? As Bradley puts it, 'if the rule of legislative sovereignty came about from a historical process, rather than as a result of a "big bang" creation of a fundamental rule, can we be certain that this area of constitutional evolution has come to a full stop?'[117] Secondly, is it in fact correct to say that acceptance of the rule that 'whatever the Queen in Parliament enacts is law' is a mere matter of fact, or can adherence to it be explained by commitment to deeper moral or political principles? If the latter is true, then the possibility exists that such principles might not always be consistent, in every situation, with Parliament's wishes. If this is so, might the courts be prepared to call into question Parliament's expression of its will through statute in order to give

---

[114] Above, n.103.

[115] For further discussion, see below, pp.135–37; also Wade, above n.19.

[116] Wade, *ibid*.

[117] A. Bradley, 'The Sovereignty of Parliament – Form or Substance?' in Jowell and Oliver (eds.), above p.39 (n.75), 30.

effect to these deeper values, notwithstanding the 'negative' limb of Dicey's definition?

These difficult issues will be explored in the subsequent discussion of the present status of parliamentary sovereignty in the British constitution. Prior to this, however, it is necessary to explore some of the ramifications of Dicey's account of parliamentary sovereignty in more depth.

Implications of the positive and negative limbs of parliamentary sovereignty

The statement that 'Parliament ... has the right to make or unmake any law whatever' defines the Westminster Parliament as legislatively omni-competent. No subject matter is, in principle, out of bounds: it can make whatever laws it wishes. One particular consequence of this is that funda-mental constitutional changes can be effected by the Westminster Parliament without the need to progress through a process of formal constitutional amendment, as is necessary in most other democratic states. Legislation which might be regarded as constitutional in content or impact may be passed by the two Houses (or, exceptionally, by the Commons alone) by simple majority in precisely the same manner as was (to cite a recent example) the Sunbeds (Regulation) Act 2010. This has been espe-cially apparent since 1997, as the Blair and Brown Governments imple-mented a significant package of constitutional change by way of legislation, including the Human Rights Act 1998, the Scotland Act 1998, the Northern Ireland Act 1998, the Government of Wales Acts 1998 and 2006, the House of Lords Act 1999, the Freedom of Information Act 2000, the Constitutional Reform Act 2005 and the Constitutional Reform and Governance Act 2010, among other measures.

This demonstrates that 'the sovereignty of Parliament provides a remarkably flexible and efficient instrument of constitutional reform'.[118] However, the simplicity of effecting constitutional reform through Parliament cuts both ways. Since Parliament can also 'unmake' any law whatever, any such measure can, in principle, also be repealed by way of simple parliamentary majority as well. Indeed, the Conservative Party manifesto for the 2010 general election promised repeal of the Human Rights Act 1998,[119] and, more broadly, the Conservative-Liberal Democrat coalition government formed subsequently to that election has indicated that it will seek passage of a 'Great Repeal Bill' which will overturn certain pieces of legislation which restrict civil liberties or

---

[118] *ibid*, 37.
[119] Conservative Party, *Invitation to Join the Government of Britain* (2010), p.79. For further discussion, see below, pp.236–37.

which impose unnecessary offences or excessive regulation upon business or civil society organisations (although there is no indication as yet that this Bill will include any measures which might be described as 'constitutional' in character).[120] In short, the existence of parliamentary sovereignty and the absence of a 'higher-order' constitutional text means that legally, no entrenchment of constitutional law is possible in the United Kingdom. But it is important here, again, to distinguish between the legal and political situations. For example, repeal of the Scotland Act 1998 could *legally* be brought about by legislation passed by the Westminster Parliament by a simple majority; but *politically* this is highly unlikely to happen, at least in present circumstances, especially given that the Scottish people indicated their support for the establishment of a Parliament at Edinburgh by a clear majority in a referendum which preceded the passage of the 1998 Act.

As this discussion indicates, the one thing which the otherwise omnicompetent Westminster Parliament cannot, in principle, do is to bind future Parliaments. A clause contained (for example) in the Human Rights Act 1998 which forbade future Parliaments from repealing the legislation would be of no legal effect (although it might possess some political and/or moral weight). For Dicey, sovereignty had a *continuing* character: each successive Parliament is equally free as each preceding Parliament to legislate exactly as it wishes. This aspect of sovereignty has, however, prompted widespread academic debate. Putting aside recent constitutional developments, which will be considered below, three questions have proved especially problematic. First, it has been argued that the Treaty of Union 1707, which united the kingdoms of England and Scotland and which was approved by Parliaments in both nations by way of legislation prior to the creation of a single Parliament for Britain, imposed certain limitations upon future Parliaments:[121] for example that the two kingdoms should 'for ever after be united into one kingdom',[122] and that alterations to 'laws which concern private right' should not be made 'except for evident utility of the subjects within Scotland'.[123] Secondly, we might question whether, if 'Parliament may surrender its sovereign power over some territory ... to another person or body ... after such a surrender, any legislation which Parliament purports to enact for that territory is not merely ineffective there but is totally void, in this country as elsewhere, since Parliament has surrendered the power to legislate'.[124] For example, does section 4 of

---

[120] HM Government, above n.12, 11.

[121] For discussion, see Munro, above p.25 (n.14), 137–142.

[122] Article I.

[123] Article XVIII.

[124] *Manuel v Attorney-General* [1983] Ch. 77, 95 (Sir Robert Megarry VC).

the Statute of Westminster 1931, which states that Acts of Parliament passed after that date shall not extend or be deemed to extend to a 'Dominion' (such as Canada, New Zealand, Australia and South Africa) without a declaration of the latter's consent, limit the legislative sovereignty of future Parliaments? And thirdly, there is debate as to whether Parliament can limit its successors by specifying that certain procedures must be followed in the passage of future legislation (the 'manner and form' argument), or by redefining its composition (for example, by specifying that future legislation on a particular subject matter cannot be passed without the support of the majority of the electorate – or a section of it – in a referendum).

Considerable academic ink has been spilled in an analysis of these scenarios, with the 'manner and form' argument attracting particular support from opponents of the orthodox Diceyan approach to parliamentary sovereignty.[125] However, if we return to the analysis offered in the previous section, the decisive question which we need to ask is: do key actors in the British constitution (especially judges, given that we are concerned with sovereignty in its *legal* sense, but also legislators and ministers) continue to accept that, in these cases, Parliament can make or unmake any law whatever?

The answer to this question would seem to be positive. Although there are *obiter dicta* in Scottish cases which raise the possibility that some provisions of the Treaty of Union may be entrenched,[126] other cases contradict this position,[127] and no English court (including the House of Lords and Supreme Court, acting as Scotland's highest civil court) has supported it. Furthermore, the Westminster Parliament has passed legislation on a number of occasions which effect alterations to the Treaty of Union, including provisions whose wording appears to render them entrenched.[128] Similarly, courts have explicitly stated that Parliament could, if it wished, pass legislation applying to former Dominions without a declaration of their consent, while observing that such legislation would be of no practical political effect.[129] Moreover, the Westminster Parliament *did* pass legislation, the Southern Rhodesia Act 1965, which reasserted its right to legislate in the wake of a unilateral declaration of independence by a colony which had enjoyed legislative autonomy and self-government for

---

[125] See *eg* Jennings, above p.25 (n.12), 151–56; R. Heuston, *Essays in Constitutional Law* (London: Stevens, 1961), Chapter 1; G. Marshall, above p.25 (n.13), Chapter 3.
[126] See *MacCormick v Lord Advocate* 1953 SC 396; *Gibson v Lord Advocate* 1975 SLT 134.
[127] *Sillars v Smith* 1982 SLT 539.
[128] *Eg* Universities (Scotland) Act 1853.
[129] *British Coal Corporation v R* [1935] AC 500.

a number of years.[130] And judicial support for the manner and form/rede-finition thesis derives from cases relating to the legislatures of New South Wales, South Africa, and Ceylon (now Sri Lanka),[131] in which legislation had been set aside by courts on the basis that it had not been passed in accordance with specified procedures. But it is not at all clear that these cases are relevant to the British constitutional context, since they concern legislatures whose powers had been conferred on them by constituent instruments: that is, a fundamental, higher order law which establishes institutions of government and confers powers upon them. There is no such instrument within the British constitutional order, and judicial authority tends to suggest that Parliament cannot bind its successors in such a manner.[132]

If Parliament cannot bind its successors, then later Parliaments are totally free to repeal legislation passed previously. Frequently, however, no *explicit* repeal of an existing Act will occur, but nonetheless certain provisions of later legislation may be inconsistent with wording contained in the preceding statute. In such a situation, courts will treat the earlier legislation as impliedly repealed, with the consequence that later provisions prevail over the earlier to the extent of any inconsistency. This manifestation of Parliament's continuing legislative omnicompetence has, however, been recently modified in three respects. First, the UK's membership of the European Union has necessitated revision, as will be discussed in the next section. Secondly, the Human Rights Act 1998 does not impliedly repeal earlier legislation which contains provisions which are incompatible with the 'Convention rights' which are given effect by the 1998 Act. Rather, courts are empowered to issue a declaration of incompatibility which does not affect the validity, continuing operation or enforcement of the provision in respect of which it is given.[133] Thirdly, in *Thoburn v Sunderland City Council*,[134] Laws LJ identified a class of 'constitutional statutes' – said to include the Magna Carta, the Bill of Rights 1689, the Union with Scotland Act 1706, the Representation of the People Acts 1832, 1867 and 1884, the European Communities Act 1972, the Human Rights Act 1998, the Scotland Act 1998 and the Government of Wales Act 1998 – which could only be repealed if unambiguous statutory words to that effect were employed. This judgment, which has not been followed in any subsequent case, may be seen as part of a pattern of recent judicial questioning of

---

[130] See *Madzimbamuto v Lardner-Burke* [1969] 1 AC 645.

[131] *Attorney-General for New South Wales v Trethowan* [1932] AC 526; *Harris v Minister of the Interior* 1952 (2) SA 428; *Bribery Commissioner v Ranasinghe* [1965] AC 172.

[132] *Vauxhall Estates Ltd v Liverpool Corporation* [1932] 1 KB 733; *Ellen Street Estates Ltd v Minister of Health* [1934] 1 KB 590.

[133] s. 4(6). For further discussion, see below, pp.222–25.

[134] Above p.11 (n.27).

parliamentary sovereignty, which will be explored in the final section of this chapter.

The negative limb of Dicey's account of parliamentary sovereignty states that no individual or institution can declare legislation passed by the Westminster Parliament to be invalid (that is, *primary* legislation: as previously noted, secondary legislation can be declared invalid if it goes beyond the powers delegated by the parent Act). This precludes the existence of the form of constitutional review exercised by the US Supreme Court as a consequence of *Marbury v Madison*:[135] no English court could invalidate legislation on grounds of unconstitutionality (assuming, of course, that such a phrase has any meaning in a system in which no 'higher order' constitutional law apparently exists). The point was clearly made by Lord Reid in *Madzimbamuto v Lardner-Burke*:

'It is often said that it would be unconstitutional for the United Kingdom Parliament to do certain things, meaning that the moral, political and other reasons against doing them are so strong that most people would regard it as highly improper if Parliament did those things. But that does not mean that it is beyond the power of Parliament to do such things. If Parliament chose to do any of them, the courts could not hold the Act of Parliament invalid.'[136]

Again, we shall have cause to revisit this aspect of the doctrine of parliamentary sovereignty in light of recent developments discussed in the following two sections of this chapter, as well as in chapter 5. However, Lord Reid's dictum raises an important concern in respect of Dicey's theory, as well as giving an implicit answer to that concern.

In chapter 2, we noted Dicey's strong commitment to a version of the rule of law which, while ostensibly formal in character, was rooted in an ideological preference for liberal individualism. As we have noted, he was suspicious of wide arbitrary or discretionary powers, of separate systems and principles of administrative justice, and of bills of rights. But if Parliament is omnicompetent, what or whom is to stop it legislating contrary to a Diceyan version of the rule of law? Alternatively, what constraints are there upon Parliament's capacity to pass retrospective laws, laws which are uncertain in their scope and/or application, and laws which violate human rights? To posit an even more extreme example, what or whom can stop Parliament from legislating to have all blue-eyed babies put to death?[137]

---

[135] See above, p.24.
[136] Above n.130, 723.
[137] See Dicey, above p.17 (n.47), 81 quoting L. Stephen, *Science of Ethics* (1882).

As regards legal validity, the short answer to these questions by way of strict application of the traditional Diceyan account of parliamentary sovereignty is: nothing and no one. Parliament is free to pass legislation which violates the rule of law or infringes fundamental rights – indeed it has done so on several occasions in the past (though it is yet to pass legislation authorising the type of infanticide envisaged in the last example) – and such legislation cannot be declared invalid by any institution. Indeed, the very notion of the *rule* of law, which suggests that there are fundamental principles, whether of a procedural or substantive nature, which should characterise all laws and legal systems, appears to be incompatible with the idea of an omnicompetent Parliament which can legislate as it pleases.

Dicey sought to resolve the potential tension between the two principles by referring to extra-legal constraints upon parliamentary sovereignty. In particular, he identified 'internal' and 'external' limits. The former related to the social environment which shaped the actions and beliefs of legislators, restricting the type of legislation which would, in reality, be passed (thus, only 'mad' legislators would pass laws putting blue-eyed babies to death). The latter related to public opinion, support and propensity to obey (thus, only 'idiotic' citizens would submit to such a law).[138] In a tyrannical state, laws might be passed which did not command popular support or to which obedience could not readily be expected (at least without the use of force), thus meaning that there was a divergence between the 'internal' and 'external' dimensions. However, this would not happen in a representative democracy, in which legislators reflect the will of the electorate and exercise control over executive power, thus bringing about a convergence of the 'internal' and 'external' positions. This form of 'self-correcting majoritarian democracy' would ensure compliance with the rule of law, since the preference of the electorate for that principle (and its corresponding protection of individual autonomy) would be reflected in the legislature. However, should there be any infringement of the rule of law – for example, through the exercise of wide discretionary powers by the executive – then Dicey's third limb of the rule came into play and judges would offer protection to individual rights through the principles and processes of the common law.

Dicey's attempt to resolve the principles of parliamentary sovereignty and the rule of law cannot be regarded as wholly satisfactory.[139] He undoubtedly overstated the capacity of the legislature to keep the executive in check in light of the rise to prominence of political parties which, as noted previously, contributed to a shift in the balance of power between the two branches of government. He also provided no explanation of how a sovereign legislature

---

[138] *id.*
[139] See Craig, n.108.

might be constrained from infringing the rights and interests of *minorities* in a manner which might amount to a violation of the rule of law. Furthermore (as discussed in chapter 2 and further analysed in chapter 5), the reliance upon judges to uphold individual rights may be regarded as problematic given the unrepresentative character of the judiciary.

However, it is submitted that, notwithstanding the obvious tension which may exist between parliamentary sovereignty and the rule of law, Dicey's analysis should not be altogether dismissed for two reasons. First, it serves to remind us that moral, political or practical constraints *do* exist which limit Parliament's freedom to legislate as it chooses. These constraints are, arguably, of a somewhat haphazard and unpredictable nature, which explains the concern expressed by opponents (such as Lord Hailsham) of the 'political constitution'. But they cannot be ignored and, in general, they have tended to operate to prevent an omnicompetent Parliament dominated by the executive from acting in a dictatorial or undemocratic manner.

Secondly, the role which Dicey identifies for the judges in upholding the rule of law in large part foreshadows recent developments in the judicial relationship to the legislative branch. Superficially, as Craig identifies, there appears to be a weakness in Dicey's argument here: how can the judges protect individual autonomy and rights from executive infringement if the measures which 'intrude' upon such rights take the form of statute enacted by a sovereign Parliament?[140] The answer, as Trevor Allan has noted,[141] is that the judges may use their powers of *statutory interpretation* in such a way as to uphold such rights and thus to give effect to the rule of law. Their approach in this regard has been touched upon in chapter 2 and will be further developed in the final section of this chapter, but first it is necessary to consider recent legislative changes which present a challenge to the traditional, Diceyan understanding of parliamentary sovereignty.

Challenges to parliamentary sovereignty? Legislation

i *European Communities Act 1972*

In relatively recent times, Parliament has passed a number of statutes which present, to varying degrees, a challenge to the orthodox reading of sovereignty, By far the most important of these is the European Communities Act 1972, which gave legislative effect to the UK's accession to what were then called the European Communities, now the European

---

140 *ibid*, 127.
141 Allan, above p.53 (n.134).

Union (EU). Although the British government was able to conclude the treaty which provided for the UK's membership through use of its prerogative powers alone,[142] such an action did not have any effect upon the domestic legal system. In order, therefore, for Community laws to have effect in the UK, as the Community legal order required, it was necessary to pass legislation.[143]

The problem which arises is that 'at the very heart of the Community's legal system lies the doctrine of supremacy of Community law'.[144] Jurisprudence of the European Court of Justice establishes that Community law is an autonomous legal order, distinct from the laws of member states.[145] And that law takes precedence over conflicting provisions of national law since, if it did not, the meaning and impact of Community law would differ from state to state, thus depriving it of its character as *Community* law and jeopardising the objectives of economic integration and co-operation upon which the Community was founded.[146] The difficulty is, therefore, readily apparent if not easily resolved. How (if at all) was it possible to accommodate the principle of the supremacy of Community law alongside the doctrine of the sovereignty of Parliament?

The European Communities Act 1972 provided, by way of section 2(1), that all Community law which took effect without the need for any national action to implement it ('direct applicability') and which was sufficiently clear and unconditional to be invoked by individuals seeking to enforce rights before domestic courts ('direct effect') formed part of the domestic law of the UK.[147] Section 2(2) provided powers to make delegated legislation to implement Community laws which were not of this character. Section 3(1) conferred power upon domestic courts to adjudicate upon and determine questions of Community law. Taken together, these provisions bring Community law into the domestic legal order, and make it applicable and enforceable at domestic level. But it is section 2(4) which addresses the question of the *hierarchy* of laws. The key wording here is as follows: 'any enactment passed or to be passed ... shall be construed and have effect subject to the foregoing provisions of this section'. These few words are potentially of huge constitutional significance. They indicate that courts are to interpret and to give effect to legislation – including

---

[142] For discussion of the prerogative treaty-making power, see below p.139.

[143] This section refers to 'Community law', which is the correct title at the date of the events described. As noted in chapter 6, following the Treaty of Lisbon, the correct current term is now 'European Union law'.

[144] Tomkins, above p.15 (n.39), 108.

[145] *Van Gend En Loos v Nederlandse Administratie der Belastingen* (C-26/62) [1963] ECR 1.

[146] *Costa v ENEL* (C-6/64) [1964] ECR 585.

[147] For further discussion of the types of EU law, see chapter 6.

primary Acts of Parliament – subject to the directly effective and directly applicable provisions of Community law 'brought in' by section 2(1), giving the latter precedence over contradictory provisions in domestic legislation. And, crucially, this obligation applies to enactments 'passed or *to be passed*'. The first word here creates no real difficulty: legislation passed prior to the 1972 Act would be impliedly repealed by the latter to the extent of any inconsistency. But the final three words indicate that *future* legislation is also to be interpreted and given effect subject to Community law, even if that law preceded domestic legislation. That is, the doctrine of implied repeal would not apply in such circumstances, and the Parliament of 1972 could be said to have bound its successors. If future Parliaments were to legislate in contradiction to Community law, such legislation would not be given effect.

It has been cogently argued that Parliament was not fully aware of the implications for sovereignty of the provisions contained in the 1972 Act.[148] A degree of uncertainty is also apparent in the initial reaction of the courts, although they broadly 'showed a preference for resolving potential clashes and inconsistencies by interpretation, and they were reluctant to reach the sovereignty question'.[149] Judges sought to interpret domestic legislation in such a way that it gave effect to obligations imposed by Community law, an approach which did not, in principle, conflict with orthodox notions of parliamentary sovereignty: the courts were not depriving the domestic legislation of its legal effect, but were rather interpreting its meaning in a manner which complied with the UK's treaty obligations.[150] There was, however, some judicial recognition that their task in this regard might be pushing at the boundaries of the orthodox reading of sovereignty. Thus, in *Macarthys Ltd v Smith*, Lord Denning MR held that 'in construing our statute, we are entitled to look at the Treaty [ie the EEC Treaty] as an aid to its construction, but not only as an aid but as an overriding force'.[151] Following the ruling of the European Court of Justice upon the interpretation of the relevant provisions of Community law, his Lordship stated that:

'[those] provisions ... take priority over anything in our English statute ... which is inconsistent ... That priority is given by our own law. It is given by the European Communities Act 1972 itself. Community law is now part of our law and, whenever there is any inconsistency, Community

---

[148] See D. Nicol, *EC Law and the Judicialization of British Politics* (Oxford: OUP, 2001).
[149] Bradley, n.117, 44.
[150] For further discussion of techniques of statutory interpretation, see below, pp.210–14.
[151] [1979] 3 All ER 325, 329.

law has priority. It is not supplanting English law. It is part of our law which overrides any other part which is inconsistent with it.'[152]

Similarly, in *Garland v British Rail Engineering Limited*, Lord Diplock held that statutory words should be construed, so far as they were reasonably capable of bearing such a meaning, to be consistent with Community law, 'however wide a departure from the prima facie meaning of the language of the provision might be needed in order to achieve consistency'.[153]

The implications of membership of the Community for parliamentary sovereignty became much more clearly apparent in *R v Secretary of State for Transport, ex parte Factortame Limited*. Here, the question arose as to whether the domestic courts should suspend the operation of the Merchant Shipping Act 1988 (which placed limitations upon the registration of fishing vessels owned by non-British nationals) pending determination by the European Court of Justice of the question of that statute's compatibility with Community law. The concern was that any failure to suspend the provisions of the legislation could have the consequence of depriving individuals of their rights under Community law for the period leading up to the Court's decision. The House of Lords held that no such suspension was possible under *domestic law*, on the basis that courts had no power to issue an injunction (that is, an order of the court which required government to refrain from enforcing the provisions of the 1988 Act) against the Crown.[154] However, it referred the question of whether national courts were obliged by *Community law* to secure interim protection for potential Community rights to the European Court of Justice, to which a positive response was given.[155] Consequently, when the matter returned to the House of Lords in order that the Court of Justice's ruling could be implemented in domestic law, the House issued an injunction preventing the government from exercising its powers to withhold or withdraw registration under the 1988 Act.[156] The English court had therefore 'disapplied' a statute, albeit potentially only temporarily pending the decision of the European Court of Justice on the question of the statute's compatibility with Community law.[157]

---

[152] [1981] QB 180, 200.

[153] [1983] 2 AC 751, 771.

[154] This conclusion was reached on the basis of an interpretation of Crown Proceedings Act 1947, s.21(2). For further discussion of injunctions as a remedy in judicial review cases, see below p.188.

[155] [1990] 2 AC 85. For the reference procedure, see below p.248.

[156] [1991] 1 AC 603.

[157] The European Court of Justice ruled that the 1988 Act did conflict with principles of Community law: [1992] QB 680. Parliament subsequently enacted the Merchant Shipping (Registration etc.) Act 1993 to give effect to this ruling.

Despite the claim by Lord Bridge that there was 'nothing in any way novel in according supremacy to rules of Community law in those areas to which they apply',[158] *Factortame* appears to represent a significant challenge to the Diceyan reading of parliamentary sovereignty, albeit one to which Parliament had itself (perhaps unwittingly) assented when passing the 1972 Act. Its implications were confirmed in *R v Secretary of State for Employment, ex parte Equal Opportunities Commission*,[159] when the House of Lords granted a declaration to the effect that domestic law was incompatible with Community law, without making any reference to the European Court of Justice.

As Loveland notes,[160] while these cases demonstrate *what* the impact of the 1972 Act upon parliamentary sovereignty has been, they tell us little about *how* Parliament has achieved such a result. That is, how can we explain the fact that the Parliament of 1972 apparently succeeded in binding its successors (or, to put matters differently, to entrench the 1972 Act) when this has always been thought to be a constitutional impossibility?

One possibility is that the rule of recognition has changed. The judicial acceptance of the 'political fact' of Parliament's sovereignty has been altered in the context of the UK's membership of the Community (now the EU) such that, at least in the absence of express repeal of the 1972 Act, Parliament's continuing sovereignty has been limited by the terms of the 1972 Act, whose effect is to bind successor Parliaments. This amounts to a 'constitutional revolution'.[161] The judges have accepted that a new constitutional settlement has been established which (at the least) modifies that established in the seventeenth century. An alternative view is that we are witnessing 'evolution'. It can be argued that section 2(4) of the 1972 Act merely establishes a rule of interpretation such that any later statute has to be read compatibly with rights arising in EU law, in the absence of any express statutory words indicating an intention to displace that interpretation.[162] Or – more radically – it can be contended that adherence to the principle of parliamentary sovereignty as originally understood can be explained by commitment to certain fundamental values, such as democracy and the rule of law, but that modification of the meaning of that principle may be necessary to give continued effect to such values (thus, membership of the EU and commitment to the supremacy of its laws is necessary to realise democracy and the rule of law in the conditions of contemporary politics).[163]

---

[158] Above n.156, 643.

[159] [1995] 1 AC 1.

[160] Above p.39 (n.75) 411.

[161] See W. Wade, 'Sovereignty: Revolution or Evolution?' (1996) 112 *Law Quarterly Review* 568.

[162] See J. Laws, 'Law and Democracy' [1995] *Public Law* 72, 89.

[163] See T. Allan, 'Parliamentary Sovereignty: Law, Politics and Revolution' (1997) 113 *Law Quarterly Review* 443; Loveland, above p.39 (n.75), 413–14.

Ultimately, no single one of these approaches can be said unequivocally to be 'correct', although Lord Bridge's observation that according supremacy to Community law was not 'novel' suggests that he, at least, would be inclined to reject the 'revolution' thesis. Also controversial is the (hypothetical) question of whether legislation which contains provisions which are *expressly* stated to be contrary to the laws of the European Union would be given effect by domestic courts. The 'rule of interpretation' approach would seem to suggest that a domestic court would be bound to give effect to express words which indicated an intention on the part of Parliament to legislate contrary to principles of European Union law, a position which is supported by dicta by Lords Denning[164] and Diplock.[165] The position is rather less clear if we adopt the 'revolution' thesis or the approach which explains adherence to parliamentary sovereignty as reflecting commitment to underlying values. The scenario seems somewhat fanciful: it is difficult (though perhaps not completely impossible) to imagine a UK government legislating in such a manner, especially given that to do so would prompt the commencement of infringement proceedings on the part of the European Commission with the consequent risk of a financial penalty.[166] Such legislative action would therefore seem only likely in the context of a process of UK withdrawal from the European Union. If that were to happen, it appears 'elementary that Parliament possesses the power to repeal the European Communities Act',[167] and domestic courts would, it is submitted, recognise this new 'political fact'. To that extent, Parliament retains ultimate sovereignty. However, while the UK remains a member of the European Union, that sovereignty has been limited.

ii Scotland Act 1998

Chapter 6 will analyse in greater detail the manner in which power, including in some cases legislative power, has been diffused from the three central branches of government in the British constitution. Although this is a trend which has gathered pace in recent years, the allocation of legislative power to other governmental actors is, in fact, nothing new: we have already noted above and in chapter 2 that Parliament frequently delegates law-making powers to ministers and local authorities, among others. However, the establishment of a Parliament in Scotland, sitting in Edinburgh, and Assemblies in Wales and Northern Ireland raise somewhat

---

[164] *Macarthys Ltd v Smith*, n.152, 329.
[165] *Garland v British Rail Engineering Limited*, n.153, 771.
[166] Treaty on the Functioning of the European Union, Article 258.
[167] Laws, n.162, 89.

more complex questions, especially about the relationship between political sovereignty and legal sovereignty. In view of the extent of the legislative powers which are devolved,[168] those questions are particularly acute in the case of Scotland, and it is the Scotland Act 1998 which will be the focus of attention here.

The Act confers power upon the Scottish Parliament to make laws, to be known as Acts of the Scottish Parliament.[169] Such Acts are not, however, law if they are outside the legislative competence of that Parliament.[170] The most important restrictions on competence are that Acts which are incompatible with EU law or with the rights contained in the European Convention on Human Rights are not law; nor are Acts relating to 'reserved matters'. These are listed in Schedule 5 of the Act, and include general reservations relating to aspects of the constitution, foreign affairs, defence, the armed forces *etc*,[171] and specific reservations under headings which include financial affairs (including fiscal and monetary policy), home affairs (such as the misuse of drugs, data protection, immigration and nationality), trade and industry, energy, regulation of the professions and others.[172] The consequence is, that in respect of matters which fall under the 'general' heading, or the specific matters listed in Part II of Schedule 5, the Westminster Parliament continues to legislate for Scotland (as well as for the rest of the United Kingdom), but in those areas which are not explicitly reserved, the Scottish Parliament can make law. Thus, to give just one example, the Scottish Parliament passed legislation on freedom of information in 2002, which differs from the Freedom of Information Act which is applicable to England and Wales in a number of ways.

How far do these provisions present a challenge to an orthodox, Diceyan reading of parliamentary sovereignty? Section 28(7) of the Scotland Act explicitly provides that the existence of a power for the Scottish Parliament to make laws 'does not affect the power of the Parliament of the United Kingdom to make laws for Scotland'. The Westminster Parliament therefore retains sovereignty, even over matters which the 1998 Act devolves to Edinburgh. Section 28(7) is a simple declaration of the traditional understanding of parliamentary sovereignty and serves an essentially symbolic purpose in underlining that devolution has had no impact upon this principle from a legal perspective. It is possible that it was included as a means of emphasising that the courts should

---

[168] For further discussion of the nature of devolution to Wales and Northern Ireland, see below pp.254–56.
[169] s.28(1).
[170] s.29(1).
[171] Schedule 5, Part I
[172] Schedule 5, Part II.

refrain from approaching the devolution legislation in a similar manner to that witnessed in the context of the European Communities Act 1972,[173] but its rationale would seem primarily to be political, given the concerns of some that devolution would lead to a break-up of the UK.

Yet, if *legal* sovereignty remains intact, *politically* the freedom of Westminster to legislate as it pleases has undoubtedly been constrained by devolution. Two situations may be considered here. First, while Westminster undoubtedly retains the capacity to repeal the Scotland Act 1998 and thereby to 'reclaim' those legislative powers which have been devolved, such an action would be likely to provoke significant public disquiet in Scotland and might well prove a catalyst for independence from the rest of the UK. For this reason, at least as long as the Scottish Parliament continues to retain legitimacy, such a scenario is virtually unthinkable: and it is likely to become even more so the longer that the present arrangements remain in place.

More plausible is that Westminster would legislate on matters which the 1998 Act devolves to the Scottish Parliament. This has, in fact, happened on a significant number of occasions since 1998. Once again, from a legal perspective this is unproblematic, but it might be regarded as politically controversial and as contravening at least the spirit of the devolution legislation. Accordingly, a convention has emerged whereby Westminster will not normally legislate on matters which are within the competence of the Scottish Parliament without the consent of the latter. In such situations, a 'Sewel Motion' is laid before the Scottish Parliament allowing the legislation in question to be debated and passed by the Westminster Parliament.[174] Failure to lay such a Motion and thus to secure consent would not invalidate any legislation passed by Westminster, but as a breach of convention it may be likely to attract political sanctions.[175]

iii Human Rights Act 1998

The content and operation of the Human Rights Act 1998 will be discussed in greater detail in chapter 5. Once again, the focus here is upon the implications which the legislation has for the doctrine of parliamentary sovereignty.

The movement to incorporate some form of Bill of Rights into English law provides a useful illustration of the gap between Dicey's idealised

---

[173] See Loveland, above p.39 (n.75) 441.

[174] See A. Page and A. Batey, 'Scotland's other Parliament: Westminster Legislation about Devolved Matters in Scotland since Devolution' [2002] *Public Law* 501.

[175] For discussion of the meaning and status of constitutional conventions, see below pp.168–72

version of the British constitution and the modern-day political reality. As we saw in chapter 2, Dicey was opposed to such an instrument, preferring to place faith in the mechanisms of a 'self-correcting majoritarian democracy' underpinned, where necessary, by judges applying the principles of the common law. However, many modern commentators have tended to view an omnicompetent Parliament which is dominated by the executive branch as a potential threat to human rights and civil liberties,[176] rather than as a mechanism for facilitating their realisation. Such analyses face a crucial difficulty, however. Even if we accept that some form of legal protection for individual rights is needed, a sovereign Parliament which 'can make or unmake any law whatever' can easily sweep such protections away. In the absence of the possibility of entrenchment, how far is it feasible to afford protection to fundamental human rights within the British constitution?

The proposals which the Labour Government brought forward in 1997 did not envisage any form of entrenchment of human rights. It was argued that 'an arrangement of this kind could not be reconciled with our own constitutional traditions, which allow any Act of Parliament to be amended or repealed by a subsequent Act of Parliament'.[177] Consequently, as noted above, the Human Rights Act 1998 may be repealed or amended in the same manner as any other piece of legislation.[178] This is not to say that any such change would be politically straightforward to effect. Despite widespread media criticism of certain aspects of the Act, a government which sought to remove 'rights' would be likely to confront significant political opposition. In this regard, it is notable that even the Conservative Party, which has indicated that it wishes to alter the law, recognises that the Act will have to be 'replaced by a British Bill of Rights' rather than returning to the pre-1998 position in which no legal statement of positive rights existed within the British constitution.[179] Furthermore, the impact which the Act has had upon case law cannot easily be retracted. It might therefore be argued that the principle of a codified statement of human rights has achieved a degree of *political* entrenchment, albeit that this need not necessarily take the form of the present Human Rights Act.

The Labour Government also indicated that it did not wish to grant courts the power to strike down or disapply legislation whose provisions conflict with human rights, as courts in some jurisdictions are empowered

---

[176] See Hailsham, above p.13 (n.32); L. Scarman, *English Law: the New Dimension* (London: Stevens, 1974), especially 15; but compare Griffith, above pp.12–13.

[177] *Rights Brought Home: The Human Rights Bill*, Cm 3782 (1997), [2.16].

[178] Unless it is regarded as a 'constitutional statute' which is not subject to implied repeal: above pp.103–04.

[179] Above n.119, 79.

to do.[180] This conclusion was stated to have been reached because of 'the importance which the government attaches to parliamentary sovereignty', because of the potential for conflict between the judiciary and Parliament and because there was no evidence that either judges or the public wished the courts to possess such power.[181] In consequence, the Act formally preserves parliamentary sovereignty. It provides that, while courts must interpret legislation in a manner which gives effect to the 'Convention rights' to which the Act gives effect, such interpretation 'does not affect the validity, continuing operation or enforcement' of legislation.[182] Alternatively, where it is not possible to interpret legislation in a manner which is compatible with the Convention rights, courts may issue a 'declaration of incompatibility'.[183] However, this is also expressed not to 'affect the validity, continuing operation or enforcement of the provision in respect of which it is given'.[184]

Despite these commitments to an orthodox understanding of parliamentary sovereignty, the Human Rights Act may be said to have had an impact upon the doctrine in three ways. First, as noted previously, the Act represents an exception to the principle of implied repeal: earlier legislation remains in force even if its provisions are incompatible with the rights protected by the Act. Secondly, the Act gives rise to a 'manner and form' question in so far as section 19 obliges a Minister presenting a Bill to either House of Parliament to make a statement, before Second Reading, either to the effect that, in his/her view the provisions of the Bill are compatible with the Convention rights or that, while the government is unable to make such a statement, it wishes to proceed anyway. While the second part of this provision indicates that Parliament retains sovereignty to legislate on any matter irrespective of a possible conflict with human rights, the question arises as to whether, in the event of failure to make either of the 'positive' or 'negative' statements envisaged by section 19, a court could declare the subsequent legislation to be invalid. On the basis of the arguments advanced above, the answer to such a question would appear to be 'no', but the matter has not yet been tested in court.

Thirdly, and most significantly, the task of interpretation carried out by the judiciary under section 3 appears to amount to more than ascertaining the intention of Parliament. Instead, the judges are obliged to find a meaning which is compatible with the Convention rights and, on occasion, this may result in meanings being attached to words in a manner which significantly

---

[180] See *eg* the Canadian Charter of Rights and Freedoms.
[181] Above n.177, [2.14].
[182] s.3(2).
[183] s.4(2).
[184] s.4(6).

differs from their usual definition. We shall return to this issue in greater depth in chapter 5. However, the significance of the matter for the purposes of this discussion is that, while formally the interpretative obligation imposed by the Human Rights Act is consistent with orthodox parliamentary sovereignty (especially since it was Parliament which imposed such an obligation upon the judiciary), the further the judges stray from the literal meaning of statutory words, the more questionable the 'negative' limb of Dicey's theory becomes. Although courts are not *invalidating* legislation in this context, in undertaking the task of interpretation under the Human Rights Act, they may be seen to be *refining and modifying* – perhaps even *straining* – the meaning of legislation in order to give effect to fundamental principles of human rights. This is certainly some distance from the traditional picture of a subordinate judiciary which merely respects the wishes of a sovereign Parliament as set out in statute.

Challenges to parliamentary sovereignty? The judges

The manner in which the judges have approached the interpretative obligation in section 3 of the Human Rights Act is perhaps best understood against a backdrop of growing judicial activism in recent years. A liberal, rights-conscious judiciary has exhibited an increasing tendency to seek to give effect to fundamental values and rights which might be said to be inherent in the common law, particularly through statutory interpretation. This trend, which began before the passage of the Human Rights Act 1998, has been reinforced by that legislation, which implicitly serves to identify the protection of individual rights against incursion by the executive and the legislature as a central objective for the judiciary within the British constitutional order. Its impact has been such that it may now be said to be questionable whether parliamentary sovereignty retains its place as a predominant characteristic of the British constitution or whether a 'new constitutional hypothesis', in which the rule of law is predominant, has come into existence.[185]

As noted in the preceding section, a number of judges have called for the recognition of fundamental human rights in English law for some years, with the preferred option being incorporation of the European Convention on Human Rights. Even before the Labour Government took steps to give effect to such demands by introducing legislation which became the Human Rights Act 1998, judges were using case law to advance the 'rights agenda'. Although the provisions of the Convention could not be directly enforced in domestic law until legislation had been passed to

---

[185] See Jowell, above p.61 (n.163) and the discussion of *Jackson v Attorney-General* below.

give effect to them, courts had determined that ambiguities in the meaning of statutes, or uncertainties as to the future development of the common law should be resolved in such a way as to give effect to Convention rights. In other cases, decisions or actions taken by the executive were made subject to a higher degree of scrutiny by the courts when their effect was to intrude upon fundamental rights.

None of these developments presented a direct challenge to parliamentary sovereignty. The courts were clear that unambiguous statutory words must be given their usual meaning, even if this conflicted with Convention rights. Similarly, those cases (discussed in chapter 2) in which the courts applied the 'principle of legality' to interpret legislation in a manner which gave effect to basic 'constitutional rights' which they considered to be inherent in the common law (wholly independent of the European Convention on Human Rights) can be read as consonant with traditional understandings of parliamentary sovereignty.[186]

In *Simms*, the continuing force of the traditional model of parliamentary sovereignty was acknowledged, and it is clear that Parliament retains the capacity to legislate in a manner which is *expressly* contrary to fundamental rights.[187] Yet it is no great distance from Lord Hoffman's dictum in that case to a position in which both the positive and negative limbs of Dicey's reading of the doctrine are called into question. Consider the following:

'Parliament does not legislate in a vacuum. Parliament legislates for a European liberal democracy founded on the principles and traditions of the common law, and the courts may approach legislation on this initial assumption.'[188]

'In this way the courts of the United Kingdom, though acknowledging the sovereignty of Parliament, apply principles of constitutionality little different from those which exist in countries where the power of the legislature is expressly limited by a constitutional document.'[189]

In both of these statements fidelity is being paid to orthodox readings of parliamentary sovereignty, but in both that reading is somewhat modified by the judicial role. In the first, the suggestion is made that there are limitations upon Parliament's freedom to legislate as it pleases: namely, the

---

[186] Above pp.58–59. See also *R v Lord Chancellor, ex parte Witham* [1998] QB 575 and note the closely analogous reasoning adopted in *Thoburn*, above n.134.

[187] See above p.59 (n.156).

[188] *Pierson*, above p.58 (n.155) 587 (Lord Steyn).

[189] *Simms*, above p.59 (n.156) (Lord Hoffmann).

principles and traditions of the common law (and, more broadly, the rule of law) in the context of the United Kingdom's status as a European liberal democracy, of which the courts presume Parliament has taken account. In the second it is suggested that – notwithstanding parliamentary sovereignty – courts undertake a constitutional review function of the type which they have traditionally been considered not to fulfil within the British constitutional order.

The potential of the 'principle of legality' to come into conflict with parliamentary sovereignty is made still clearer by another case which was examined in chapter 2, *Anufrijeva*.[190] There was a clear difference of opinion here between the majority judges, led by Lord Steyn, who considered that the legislation in question had not expressly displaced fundamental rights protected by way of the principle of legality (which was explicitly linked to the rule of law), and Lord Bingham in the minority, who considered that 'effect should be given to a clear and unambiguous legislative provision'.[191] It might be argued that the distinct approaches taken in this case were indicative merely of different readings of statutory wording, rather than disagreements as to the proper weight to be accorded to parliamentary sovereignty. Nevertheless, it seems apparent that the open-endedness of the principle of legality (and, still further, the related but broader notion of the rule of law) significantly enhances the capacity of judges to protect the rights of individuals *vis-a-vis* the legislature (and, by extension, the executive which dominates that branch) in such a way that the balance of power between the respective branches has shifted in the direction of the judiciary, even if there is no *outright* challenge to parliamentary sovereignty.

Perhaps unsurprisingly, liberal members of the judiciary have been more willing to express reservations as to the implications which unlimited parliamentary competence may hold for the preservation of individual rights and the rule of law *outside* of the courtroom. In a trio of articles published in the pages of *Public Law* in 1995, Lord Woolf argued that, if Parliament were to deprive the courts of their jurisdiction to review the legality of executive action, thereby repudiating the rule of law,[192] 'there are advantages in making it clear that ultimately there are even limits on the supremacy of Parliament which it is the courts' inalienable responsibility to identify and uphold';[193] Sir John Laws wrote that 'the doctrine of

---

[190] Above p.63 (n.170)

[191] *ibid*, [20].

[192] For the connection between judicial review of administrative action and the rule of law, see above pp.56–58 and below, pp.208–09.

[193] Woolf, above p.13 (n.33) 69.

Parliamentary sovereignty cannot be vouched by Parliamentary legislation; a higher-order law confers it, and must of necessity limit it';[194] and Sir Stephen Sedley expressed the view that:

> 'we have today both in this country and in those with which it shares aspects of its political and judicial culture a new and still emerging constitutional paradigm, no longer of Dicey's supreme parliament to whose will the rule of law must finally bend, but of a bi-polar sovereignty of the Crown in Parliament and the Crown in its courts, to each of which the Crown's ministers are answerable – politically to Parliament, legally to the courts.'[195]

Such views have been described as examples of 'common law radicalism'. Its exponents, who also number Trevor Allan, consider certain fundamental values – with notions of the rule of law and democracy being central – to be inherent in the common law and as placing constraints, in certain circumstances, even upon the exercise of sovereign legislative power. Critics have, however, argued that they smack of 'judicial supremacism'.[196] On such an analysis, the balance of power has tilted *too far* in favour of the judiciary and it has exceeded its proper constitutional role.

The relationship between the judiciary and parliamentary sovereignty continues to evolve and the developments outlined in this section are by no means at an end. But the most important recent expression of that relationship, and the changes which it has undergone, occurred in the judgement of the House of Lords in *Jackson v Attorney-General*, the facts of which were discussed earlier in this chapter:

> 'The classic account given by Dicey of the supremacy of Parliament, pure and absolute as it was, can now be seen to be out of place in the modern United Kingdom. Nevertheless, the supremacy of Parliament is still the *general* principle of our constitution. It is a construct of the common law. The judges created this principle. If that is so, it is not unthinkable that circumstances could arise where the courts may have to qualify a principle established on a different hypothesis of constitutionalism. In exceptional circumstances involving an attempt to abolish judicial review or the ordinary role of the courts, the Appellate Committee of the House of Lords or a new Supreme Court may have to consider whether this is a constitutional fundamental which even a

---

194   J. Laws, 'Law and Democracy' [1995] *Public Law* 72, 87.
195   S. Sedley, 'Human Rights: a Twenty-first Century Agenda' [1995] *Public Law* 386, 389.
196   Irvine, above p.13 (n.34), 77.

sovereign Parliament acting at the behest of a complaisant House of Commons cannot abolish.'[197]

'Our constitution is dominated by the sovereignty of Parliament. But Parliamentary sovereignty is no longer, if it ever was, absolute ... It is no longer right to say that its freedom to legislate admits of no qualification whatever. Step by step, gradually but surely, the English principle of the absolute legislative sovereignty of Parliament which Dicey derived from Coke and Blackstone is being qualified ... The rule of law enforced by the courts is the ultimate controlling factor on which our constitution is based.'[198]

'The courts will treat with particular suspicion (and might even reject) any attempt to subvert the rule of law by removing governmental action affecting the rights of individuals from all judicial scrutiny.'[199]

These statements suggest that, while the doctrine of parliamentary sovereignty continues to play a major role in the modern British constitutional order, its predominance is now challenged by the rule of law. The latter principle justifies judicial review not only of the legality of actions and decisions of the executive branch, but also of any legislation which seeks to subvert the rule of law (for example, by attempting to remove the courts' jurisdiction to scrutinise actions affecting the rights of individuals). On this analysis, English courts possess a constitutional review role broadly equivalent to that undertaken by courts which adjudicate upon the validity of legislative and executive acts by reference to a 'higher order' constitutional law. However, the 'higher order' law in this instance amounts to the general principle of the rule of law rather than taking the form of a constitutional text and (at least on the analysis of Lord Steyn), this review function will only be exercised in 'exceptional' circumstances.

A certain degree of caution is, perhaps, pertinent in an analysis of this case. First, the statements cited above are *obiter dicta*. Thus, while carrying more weight than the extra-judicial writings previously discussed, they do not have value as binding precedents. Secondly, the House of Lords was not unanimous on the status to be accorded to parliamentary sovereignty. Lord Bingham adhered to the orthodox Diceyan model in stating that 'the bedrock of the British constitution *is*, and in 1911 was, the supremacy of the Crown in Parliament ... Then, *as now*, the Crown in Parliament was

---

[197]   Above p.11 (n.27), [102] (Lord Steyn)
[198]   *ibid*, [104], [107] (Lord Hope).
[199]   *ibid*, [159] (Lady Hale).

unconstrained by any entrenched or codified constitution. It could make or unmake any law it wished.'[200]

For these reasons, it would seem premature to argue that the rule of recognition has changed.[201] Despite its growing importance, we cannot yet point to a general acceptance among the judges – let alone other key constitutional actors – that the rule of law is the ultimate rule within the British constitutional order, from which all other rules derive their validity. Indeed, the dicta of some of the judges present us with a problem in this regard. Lord Steyn states that parliamentary sovereignty is a 'construct of the common law', 'created' by the judges, with the consequence that it is open to the judiciary, should it wish, to create a 'new hypothesis of constitutionalism'. But, as argued above, the idea that parliamentary sovereignty as the rule of recognition emanates from the common law is as logically problematic as the idea that Parliament can confer sovereignty upon itself. This problem is only avoided if we regard the source of sovereignty as being *extra-legal*, residing for example in the general acceptance of a political reality. If that is so, then it is not open to the judges to change the rule of recognition unilaterally, as Lord Steyn appears to suggest.

D. Conclusion

The analysis offered in this chapter, both of Parliament as an institution and of the doctrine of parliamentary sovereignty, should serve to demonstrate that constitutional practice is often very different from constitutional theory. While theory (for example, that relating to the separation of powers) provides us with a valuable framework upon which we can construct an understanding of the complex network of relationships within the constitution, and offers a yardstick for evaluation of institutional arrangements, it is also important to ascertain how things actually work in reality. That is, to return to the discussion of our subject in chapter 1, we must develop both an awareness of the 'real world' context in which Parliament operates (for example, the impact upon its constitutional role of the existence of political parties), and a critical perspective upon its success – or otherwise – in discharging its functions.

When viewed in this way, we are presented with a picture of a legislative branch which is largely subordinate to the executive and whose most valuable role (which, arguably, has been performed ineffectively in recent years but which may be enhanced by recent and ongoing developments)

---

[200] *ibid*, [9]. Emphasis added.
[201] See Loveland, above p.39 (n.75), 197; Jowell, above p.61 (n.163), 563–64. But compare Lakin, above n.112.

is to act as a check and balance to that branch. We are also presented with an account of parliamentary sovereignty which differs significantly from Diceyan orthodoxy and through which we can identify an increasingly powerful judiciary which seeks to uphold individual rights and the rule of law. These themes – executive dominance and the increasing constitutional assertiveness of the judiciary – are fundamental to a comprehension of the dynamics of power in the modern British constitution. In order to understand them better, we must, of course, examine each of those other two branches of government in detail, which will be the task undertaken in the next two chapters of this book.

Chapter 4

The executive

In this chapter, we examine the most powerful and arguably most problematic branch of government in the UK, the executive. Since there are a huge number of institutions which make up this branch, there will be no attempt to describe or analyse them all in detail.[1] Instead, the primary focus will be upon the institutions at the heart of central government: Prime Minister, Cabinet and ministerial departments, although we shall also have cause briefly to consider the constitutional position and functions of the monarch and the extensive network of more or less independent governmental agencies which regulate activities of public importance. Readers should also bear in mind that regional government, discussed in chapter 6, forms part of the executive branch.

In keeping with this book's concern with power, this chapter will seek to analyse what executive power is, how it relates to powers exercised by other branches, and the mechanisms which exist both to limit its exercise and to facilitate its use. However, before considering these issues, a more obvious preliminary question presents itself: how do we define the executive branch? That is, who exercises executive power in the British constitution?

Identifying the executive

It will come as no surprise to learn that identification of the institutions and individuals which constitute the executive branch is no straightforward task. In part, this is a consequence of the lack of a codified constitutional document in the UK: in the absence of a US-style 'power map', we have no easy starting point for embarking upon such an exercise. However, the task would not necessarily be an easy one in any country, simply because the number of functions performed by modern government – and, in consequence, the range of institutions which undertake them – is vast, extending well beyond the preservation of law and order and protection

---

[1] For a scholarly analysis, see T. Daintith and A. Page, *The Executive in the Constitution: Structure, Autonomy and Internal Control* (Oxford: OUP, 1999).

from overseas threat which were the central functions of government in the early nineteenth century.[2] Notwithstanding attempts by certain political parties, especially those towards the right of the political spectrum, to reduce the role of the state, governmental intervention in economic and social activities is now commonplace, necessitating the creation of an elaborate and constantly developing machinery of agencies and officials.

Nor does case law or statute provide us with much assistance. In *Town Investments Limited v Department of the Environment*, Lord Simon commented that 'terms of political science like "the Executive" or "the Administration" or "the Government"' were 'barely known to the law',[3] while Barendt notes that key members of the executive branch are also relatively invisible: 'from a legal point of view the Prime Minister hardly appears in the constitution. His existence is mentioned in only a handful of statutes, mostly concerned with salaries and pension arrangements. If anything, the Cabinet receives even less statutory recognition'.[4] This is not to say that executive institutions or officials are absent from the law (although, as we shall see, the powers and functions of the Prime Minister are largely governed by *constitutional conventions* as distinct from legal rules): after all, legislation routinely vests powers and duties in ministers, who are also very frequently the subject of judicial review challenges in court. Rather, the terminology used in English law to refer to those institutions which we would normally regard as constituting 'government' or 'the executive' is 'the Crown', used in a metaphorical sense. We shall return to this confusing term below.

The preceding paragraphs have, of course, provided several clues as to the individuals and institutions which make up the executive branch. As noted, executive power is legally vested in the Crown and although the vast majority of executive actions and decisions are in practice taken by others, the monarch retains certain powers. Central government – consisting of the Prime Minister, Cabinet and other ministers – represents what most people consider to constitute 'the government', but we should also consider civil servants working in ministerial departments (such as the Foreign and Commonwealth Office, or the Ministry of Justice) or in executive agencies such as the National Offender Management Service (which includes the Prison Service and the Probation Service). There are also numerous public bodies and regulatory agencies exercising governmental powers within specific areas of public life, such as the Equality and Human Rights Commission, the Office of Communications and the Higher Education Funding Council for England. At local level, local education authorities and

---

[2] In 1815, there were 24,598 civil servants. By 1979, this figure had increased to 732,300. See G. Drewry and T. Butcher, *The Civil Service Today* (Oxford: Basil Blackwell, 2nd ed., 1991), 48.

[3] [1978] AC 359, 398.

[4] E. Barendt, *An Introduction to Constitutional Law* (Oxford: OUP, 1998), 113.

Primary Care Trusts are currently primarily responsible for managing, respectively, the provision of educational and health services within particular geographical areas. The armed forces and police, though clearly functioning in highly specialised areas and with very distinct powers, can also be considered to be components of the executive. This list is very far from exhaustive.

Defining executive functions

Are matters made any clearer if we attempt to identify the functions performed by the executive, as distinct from the institutions which comprise this branch of government?

As a starting point, we might return to the taxonomy of powers contained within the separation of powers doctrine, as discussed in chapter 2. Montesquieu identified the executive function as 'that of executing the public resolutions',[5] while Madison referred to the 'power to carry into effect the national laws'.[6] Similarly, Lord Templeman states that 'the executive carry the law into effect'.[7] This would appear therefore to represent something of a consensus – the function of the executive is to carry out or give effect to laws.

However, this is only one aspect of the executive's role. One problem with this analysis, as was noted in chapter 2 and as will be discussed in greater depth subsequently in this chapter is that the division of roles upon which it is premised – Parliament makes law, the executive carries that law into effect and the judiciary interprets and enforces that law – is misleading in so far as significant components of executive activity are not, in fact, authorised by Parliament at all. Furthermore, it tells us little about the *types* of function which the executive performs. Perhaps a more useful, though still incomplete list is provided by *Halsbury's Laws of England*:

> 'Executive functions may ... be said to entail the formulation or application of general policy in relation to particular situations or cases, or the making or execution of individual discretionary decisions. More specifically, they include the execution of law and policy, the maintenance of public order, the management of Crown property and nationalised industries and services, the direction of foreign policy, the conduct of military operations, and the provision, regulation, financing or supervision of such services as education, public health, transport and national insurance.'[8]

---

[5] Above p.21 (n.2).
[6] J. Madison, 'Notes of the Constitutional Convention' (June 1, 1787), available at http://www.consource.org/index.asp?bid=582&documentid=35.
[7] Above p.27 (n.20).
[8] Volume 8(2) (Reissue), [9].

From this we can see that the functions of the executive branch are extremely varied in nature: they 'range from the taking of crucial and sensitive political decisions to detailed administration involving little or no exercise of discretion'.[9] It may therefore be preferable to regard (as do a number of accounts of the British constitution)[10] executive functions as residual: that is, they comprise all those activities of government which are neither legislative nor judicial in character.

As well as analysing the functions carried out by the executive branch, we might also wish to consider the *techniques* which it uses to undertake those tasks. Daintith has outlined two ways in which government attempts to realise its policy objectives. The first he calls *imperium*: this describes a traditional form of regulation of activities through 'command and control', involving 'setting a standard or rule for the behaviour of the relevant persons and providing sanctions for non-compliance'.[11] This entails using laws, usually passed by Parliament, to order people's behaviour. He labels the second technique *dominium*, which he describes as 'the employment of the wealth of government' to achieve policy goals: for example, grants of financial assistance to individuals or groups or the award of contracts to companies.[12] He argues that there has been a shift from the first to the second of these techniques, which is reflective of the tendency of governments since the 1990s to 'steer, not row': that is, government will set the general direction of policy, establish standards and targets, allocate resources and evaluate outcomes. However, it will not deliver the service itself, relying instead upon partnerships with the private sector and other organisations within society (such as charitable bodies) and/or market-style initiatives, such as performance-related pay. We shall have cause to return to some of these notions in chapter 6, as they are indicative of changes in the location of power within the British constitution, and raise difficult questions as to the manner in which public law should respond.

A. The Crown

As was noted above, statute and case law tends to refer to 'the Crown'. What does this term in fact mean?

---

[9] Barendt, n.4, 108.

[10] Barendt, *id*; *Halsbury's Laws of England*, above n.8; A. Bradley & K. Ewing, *Constitutional and Administrative Law* (Harlow: Pearson, 15th ed., 2010), 233.

[11] T. Daintith, 'The Techniques of Government' in J. Jowell & D. Oliver (eds.), *The Changing Constitution* (Oxford: OUP, 3rd ed., 1994), 213.

[12] *id.*

Barendt has written that there exists a 'bewildering variety of usage' of the term,[13] but it is perhaps most useful to distinguish three possibilities. First, it may refer to the monarch personally or to the institution of monarchy which that person presently embodies. Secondly, it may be used to mean government or the executive: for example, in *BBC v Johns*, Diplock LJ stated that the term 'personifies the executive government of the country'.[14] Thirdly, it may be used still more broadly as 'a convenient symbol for the state'.[15] Of the three usages, it is the second which is most common. It may be explained as a simple consequence of historical development: executive power was formerly wielded by the monarch in person (and, as will be seen below, vestiges of such power remain), but gradually shifted to 'ministers of the Crown' who exercised power independently of monarchical direction and were also conferred with powers and duties by statute. However, *legally* (as distinct from politically) executive power continues to rest with the monarch: consequently, in addition to references to 'the Crown' in law, we speak of 'Her Majesty's Government' and appointment of ministers is formally undertaken by the monarch although on the advice of the Prime Minister (meaning that, in practice, it is the Prime Minster who makes the choice).

There is no doubt, however, that deployment of the terminology of 'the Crown' is apt to confuse. The point was well made by Lord Diplock in the *Town Investments* case:

'these relationships [*ie* between the monarch, ministers, government departments and civil servants] have in the course of centuries been transformed with the continuous evolution of the constitution of this country from that of personal rule by a feudal landowning monarch to the constitutional monarchy of today; but the vocabulary used by lawyers in the field of public law has not kept pace with this evolution and remains more apt to the constitutional realities of the Tudor or even the Norman monarchy than to the constitutional realities of the 20th century. To use as a metaphor the symbol of royalty, "the Crown", was no doubt a convenient way of denoting and distinguishing the monarch when doing acts of government in his political capacity from the monarch when doing private acts in his personal capacity, at a period when legislative and executive powers were exercised by him in accordance with his own will. But to continue nowadays to speak of "the Crown" as doing legislative or executive acts of government,

---

[13] Above n.4, 110.
[14] [1965] Ch. 32, 79.
[15] G. Sawar, quoted in Bradley & Ewing, above n.10, 233.

which, in reality as distinct from legal fiction, are decided on and done by human beings other than the Queen herself, involves risk of confusion.'[16]

His Lordship considered that it would be more appropriate to speak instead of "the government" – a term appropriate to embrace both collectively and individually all of the ministers of the Crown and parliamentary secretaries under whose direction the administrative work of government is carried on by the civil servants employed in the various government departments'.[17]

The difficulties are, however, not merely terminological. In *M v Home Office*,[18] the House of Lords was obliged to consider the question of whether the Home Secretary could be held in contempt for failure to comply with an order of the court which required the return of an asylum-seeker from Zaire (now, the Democratic Republic of Congo) to the UK. Although the Crown Proceedings Act 1947 had removed the immunity of the Crown from liability in tort and contract, it had not been clearly established whether the Crown itself, or ministers of the Crown acting in their official capacity, could be made subject to injunctions issued by the courts (that is, orders requiring something to be done or not to be done) or were liable for contempt for failure to comply with such injunctions. While such liability would appear to be necessary for purposes of the rule of law,[19] the difficulty arose from the fact that, as a matter of legal formality, both courts and ministers exercise powers on behalf of the Crown. The judges were therefore faced with something of a conundrum: as Tomkins puts it, 'can the Crown's courts find the Crown's ministers in contempt of the Crown's courts? Can one branch of the Crown find that another branch of the Crown is in contempt of the Crown?'[20] The court concluded that a finding of contempt could be made against a government department or a minister acting in his personal or official capacity, albeit not against the Crown itself.

There is a further difficulty, of a rather more conceptual nature. It has been argued that too great a focus upon 'the Crown' has had the consequence that little attempt has been made to define what is meant by 'the state' in the UK[21] – although there are other, related reasons for such a failure, in particular the absence of a 'power map' of the state in the form of

---

[16] Above n.3, 380–81.

[17] *ibid*, 381.

[18] [1994] 1 AC 377.

[19] See especially Lord Templeman, 395: 'the argument that there is no power to enforce law by injunction ... against a Minister in his official capacity would, if upheld, establish the proposition that the executive obey the law as a matter of grace and not as a matter of necessity, a proposition which would reverse the result of the Civil War'.

[20] Above p.15 (n.39), 53.

[21] See *eg* M. Loughlin, 'The State, the Crown and the Law', Chapter 3 in M. Sunkin and S. Payne (eds.), *The Nature of the Crown: a Legal and Political Analysis* (Oxford: OUP, 1999).

a codified constitution and the influence of Dicey's preference for private law over a separate system of public law.

Now we should, first of all, be alert to the fact that 'the state' is itself a highly ambiguous term. In political science, it generally connotes a particular form of political association, often (though not always) contiguous with a nation (for example, the UK is a state, but Scotland is a nation), but not synonymous with government (since a state – especially federal states such as Canada or Australia – may contain several governments). However, by contrast to the voluminous literature on the meaning and nature of the state in political science,[22] it has been said that 'the law of England and Wales does not know the state as a legal entity';[23] while, on the occasions on which the meaning of the term has been the subject of scrutiny in the courts, it has been generally equated with 'the Crown' in the second sense – that of the government or executive – used above.[24] This tendency to conflate the meanings of 'Crown' and 'state' is troubling for two reasons. First, an equation of government with state facilitates the labelling of opposition to particular (and transient) governmental actions or policies as not being 'in the interests of the state'. This is clearly highly problematic from a democratic perspective.[25] Secondly, the failure to properly disentangle the two terms has created difficulty in defining the boundaries of public law. As we shall see in chapter 5, the courts are obliged to determine which bodies are susceptible to judicial review and which constitute 'public authorities' for the purposes of section 6 of the Human Rights Act 1998. This task has become more awkward over the past thirty years as – consistently with the notion of 'steering not rowing' – an increasing range of functions and services which were formerly undertaken by government are performed or delivered outside of government (for example, by private companies to whom the function or service has been 'contracted out'). A broader understanding of 'the state' might lead us to conclude that such activities should remain subject to some form of public accountability through political or legal mechanisms, but it is less clear that the narrower concept of 'the Crown' is sufficient to cover them.

---

[22] A useful starting point is A. Vincent, *Theories of the State* (Oxford: Basil Blackwell, 1987).

[23] *A v Head Teacher and Governors of Lord Grey School* [2004] EWCA Civ 382, [3] (Sedley LJ).

[24] See especially Lord Devlin in *Chandler v DPP* [1964] AC 763, 807: 'the more precise use of the word "State", the use to be expected in a legal context ... is to denote the organs of government of a national community. In the United Kingdom ... that organ is the Crown'. Compare Lord Reid and Lord Hodson, who refer to 'the organised community': 790, 801. However, the judges agreed that 'the interests of the State' (for the purposes of s.1 of the Official Secrets Act 1911) were to be determined by the Crown.

[25] See *Chandler, ibid* and *R v Ponting* [1985] Crim LR 318.

The monarchy and monarchical influence and powers

The UK is a monarchy, not a republic. As such, its head of state is not an elected President, as is the case (for example) in the US, but the reigning Queen or King. However, Britain's is a *constitutional monarchy* of a type relatively common in Western Europe: a number of countries such as Belgium, Denmark, the Netherlands, Spain and Sweden have broadly similar arrangements. The powers of such a monarch are limited by constitutional rules and/or conventions with the consequence that, while the monarch is nominally the head of government (that is, the executive branch), s/he does not in practice exercise effective political power, which is instead allocated to an elected politician, usually a prime minister. The monarch, however, undertakes certain ceremonial duties and also performs a symbolic function as the embodiment of the nation.

The full range of those duties and functions will not be explored here.[26] However, prior to considering the monarch's remaining legal powers, it is useful to reflect upon the possibilities which exist for the monarch to *influence* the manner in which the Prime Minister conducts the business of government. In a famous phrase, Bagehot argued that the monarch possesses three rights: 'the right to be consulted, the right to encourage, the right to warn'.[27] Such rights are exercised primarily through the weekly audience between the monarch and the Prime Minister, which offers an opportunity both for the monarch to make her views apparent and for the Prime Minister to seek advice. It is extremely difficult to measure the degree of influence which the monarch may exercise through this channel in view of the fact that all communications with the Prime Minister are treated as confidential. However, common sense would suggest that the monarch's views may, on some occasions, have some impact given that a monarch may have reigned for a considerably longer period of time than a Prime Minister has held office.[28] Nonetheless, it is clear as a matter of democratic constitutional principle that the monarch should not publicly be seen as favouring any particular political party and that, once a decision had been reached, that she should accept and act upon the advice and decisions of the Prime Minister, whatever her personal views may be upon the merits of a particular course of action which the government proposes to take.

In addition to this somewhat intangible influence upon government, the monarch possesses a certain number of personal powers which are of

---

[26] A highly valuable discussion of constitutional monarchy in the UK is provided in R. Brazier, *Constitutional Practice* (Oxford: OUP, 3rd ed., 1999), Chapter 9.

[27] Above p.33 (n.45), 60.

[28] The present Queen has been on the throne for almost sixty years, having acceded in 1952. The longest serving Prime Minister since 1900 was Margaret Thatcher, who was in office for 11 years, 209 days.

potential constitutional significance, but which admit of little discretion in their exercise. The powers form part of the royal prerogative, a term the meaning of which will be explored in the next section, and are usually labelled 'personal prerogatives' to signify that they are exercised as a matter of the individual discretion of the monarch rather than by ministers. As we shall see, it is inherent in the nature of prerogative powers, including those exercisable personally, that their precise meaning and scope is uncertain, but the following situations are identifiable from the literature:

i Appointment of a Prime Minister

Legally, there are no constraints upon the monarch's choice of Prime Minister. However, constitutional convention prescribes that the Prime Minister should be the person best able to command the confidence of the House of Commons. In most circumstances the choice will be obvious: it will be the leader of the party with a majority of seats in the House of Commons. More difficulty arises in a situation of a 'hung' Parliament, that is, one in which no single party has an overall majority of MPs, as was the case following the general election in May 2010. In this instance, the incumbent Prime Minister, Gordon Brown, remained temporarily in office while negotiations took place between the party leaders (including Brown himself). These eventually led to the formation of a coalition between the Conservative and Liberal Democrat parties, led by the Conservative leader, David Cameron. The monarch played no part in such negotiations and was merely responsible for appointing Cameron as Prime Minister once it became clear that he could form an administration which would command the confidence of the Commons.[29]

The present Queen also exercised some discretionary power in this context in both 1957 and 1963, when Prime Ministers resigned due to ill health and no successor was readily apparent. This situation is unlikely to recur as all major political parties now have procedures for the election of leaders and, even in the event that a temporary Prime Minister is required pending the outcome of such an election, a deputy leader is usually clearly identifiable.

---

[29] This reflects the position outlined in a Cabinet Office document drafted partially before the election: above p.84 (n.59). For earlier academic debate on the monarch's role in this situation, see R. Blackburn, 'Monarchy and the personal prerogatives' [2004] *Public Law* 546. See also R. Brazier, '"Monarchy and the personal prerogatives": a personal response to Professor Blackburn' [2005] *Public Law* 45.

ii Refusal of assent to legislation

We noted in chapter 3 that the assent of the monarch is the final stage in the process of enactment of legislation. In fact, the monarch does not personally grant assent to legislation by attendance in Parliament for the purpose (although it is legally possible for her still to do so): under the Royal Assent Act 1967, the assent is signified separately to each House of Parliament by the presiding officers. However, the significant question here relates not to the procedure by which assent is given but to the possibility that such assent may be withheld by the monarch with the consequence that a Bill which has proceeded through both Houses of Parliament will not pass into law.

The last occasion on which a monarch refused assent was in 1708 and we might therefore assume that the power to refuse assent has fallen into disuse. However, given that the weight of authority suggests that a prerogative power ceases to exist only if it is abolished by statute (see further below), it remains conceivable (but perhaps only just) that a future monarch could exercise the power of veto, for example to prevent the passage of a Bill 'designed to achieve a permanent subversion of the democratic basis of the constitution'.[30] However, in view of the fact that it may not always be easy to distinguish between such 'subversion' and radical but legitimate forms of constitutional reform,[31] the monarch's powers in this regard should be exercised with circumspection and a political solution sought wherever possible.

iii Dissolution of Parliament and dismissal of ministers

Unlike the Scottish Parliament and Welsh Assembly, the Westminster Parliament has previously not been elected for a fixed term, although the maximum length of a Parliament (that is, the period between general elections) can be no longer than five years.[32] Dissolution of Parliament is carried out by way of a royal proclamation, which summons a new Parliament and requires the despatch of writs of election. The power of dissolution is, therefore, a component of the monarch's personal prerogatives, but the timing of such a dissolution has always been a matter for the judgment of the Prime Minister, albeit usually in consultation with senior party colleagues.

However, the Coalition Government has introduced a Fixed-Term Parliaments Bill which provides that elections will ordinarily take place on

---

[30] Brazier, n.26, 195.
[31] See Blackburn, n.29, 553, Brazier, n.29, 46–47.
[32] Parliament Act 1911, s.7. The length of Parliament was extended during both World Wars.

the first Thursday in May every five years, with the first such election scheduled for 7 May 2015. This date may be altered by the Prime Minister by up to two months either way, in order to respond to short-term crises. Such variation will be brought about by statutory instrument. Dissolution may occur earlier if either (a) two-thirds of the House of Commons passes a motion that there should be an election, or (b) if the House of Commons passes a motion of no confidence in the government and no alternative government is formed within 14 days.

If passed by Parliament, the Bill will remove the residual power of the monarch to dissolve Parliament against the Prime Minister's wishes, which in any case appeared only to be exercisable in highly improbable situations of 'unconstitutional' behaviour on the latter's part. [33]

It is apparent from the above discussion that the scope for any discretion in the monarch's exercise of the personal prerogative powers, which in any event was virtually nil, has been further reduced by recent developments. It is now doubtful whether any residual personal prerogatives relating to constitutional matters can be said to remain.[34] The gradual erosion of such powers serves to underline the neutrality of the monarchy, a characteristic which benefits both that institution and democratic government in general. It also corresponds to a process of displacement of executive powers from monarch to ministers which has taken place over the past three centuries. Let us now examine this development more closely.

B. Prerogative power

The powers analysed in the preceding section were described as emanating from the *royal prerogative*. We now turn to examine the meaning of this form of executive power, by whom and in what circumstances it is exercised, the constitutional problems to which it gives rise, mechanisms for control of such power and proposals for its reform. As we shall see, this is one of the most curious and controversial corners of the British constitution.

i Defining prerogative power

The royal prerogative has been described as 'a notoriously difficult concept to define adequately'.[35] In attempting to establish its meaning,

---

[33] For a discussion (which precedes the Fixed-Term Parliaments Bill), see R. Blackburn, 'The prerogative power of dissolution of Parliament: law, practice, and reform' [2009] *Public Law* 766.

[34] The monarch retains some other prerogatives such as the granting of certain honours, including the Order of the Garter and the Thistle and the Order of Merit.

[35] Public Administration Select Committee, *Taming the Prerogative: Strengthening Ministerial Accountability to Parliament* HC 422 (2003–04), [3].

we immediately encounter a controversy. Blackstone refers to 'that special pre-eminence which the King hath, over and above all other persons, and out of the ordinary course of the common law, in right of his regal dignity ... it must be in its nature singular and eccentrical, that it can only be applied to those rights and capacities which the King enjoys alone ... and not to those which he enjoys in common with any of his subjects',[36] while Dicey states that 'every act which the executive government can lawfully do without the authority of the Act of Parliament is done in virtue of this prerogative'.[37] The first of these definitions restricts prerogative powers to those which are peculiar to the Crown, with the consequence that powers which are also exercisable by ordinary citizens, such as the power to enter into contracts or to own property, are not included. Dicey's broader definition would include such powers as well, and it is this which has generally been followed,[38] although there are influential voices against such an interpretation.[39] The question is not solely one of semantics. From the perspective of the separation of powers or the rule of law, we might argue that all forms of executive power – whether equivalent to those possessed by ordinary citizens or not – should be subject to the special mechanisms of control exercised by the courts through judicial review,[40] which would lead us to favour the broader definition espoused by Dicey. On the other hand, that definition is perhaps less useful than that of Blackstone for purposes of classification of the powers possessed by the executive. For example, as was noted in chapter 1 (and consistently with Dicey's preference for private law processes and remedies), the exercise of contractual power by government is broadly regulated by private law (albeit with increasing degrees of modification, which in part reflect the impact of European Union law) and it therefore seems somewhat curious to label this as part of the prerogative.

Leaving aside this thorny issue, we may return to Dicey, who tells us also that 'the prerogative is the name for the remaining portion of the Crown's original authority, and is therefore ... the name for the residue of discretionary power left at any moment in the hands of the Crown, whether such power be in fact exercised by the Queen herself or by her ministers'.[41] If we unpack this statement further, we can better understand the character of prerogative powers.

---

[36] W. Blackstone, *Commentaries on the Laws of England* (Oxford: Clarendon Press, 1765–69), Book I, Chapter 7, 232.

[37] Above p.17 (n.47), 425.

[38] See *Attorney-General v De Keyser's Royal Hotel Ltd* [1920] AC 508, 571 (Lord Parmoor).

[39] See H. Wade, *Constitutional Fundamentals* (London: Stevens, 1980), 49.

[40] See P. Craig, 'Prerogative, Precedent and Power' in C. Forsyth and I. Hare (eds.), *The golden metwand and the crooked cord: essays on public law in honour of Sir William Wade QC* (Oxford: OUP, 1998), 88.

[41] Above p.17 (n.47), 425.

First, the prerogative forms a *portion of the Crown's original authority*. This component of Dicey's definition helps us to understand the prerogative's origin as 'attributes which of necessity inhered in kings as governors of the realm'.[42] These attributes consisted of powers (such as the power to declare war), rights (such as the right to ownership of all unmarked mute swans in open water), immunities (such as the immunity from being sued in court), and duties (such as the duty to protect subjects within the realm) which attached to the monarchy in its capacity as the executive branch of government in England and Wales prior to the Civil War in the seventeenth century. It is, however, the powers of the Crown which cause the most controversy and they will form the primary focus of the subsequent discussion.

Dicey does not specify the source of legal authority for the exercise of these powers, although it is clear from his first statement cited above that prerogative powers are not statutory in character. Since the other primary source of law (at least prior to the UK's accession to the European Community in 1973) in the English legal system is judge-made common law, it might be supposed that the prerogative is part of the latter. However, this is slightly misleading in so far as these powers were not *created* by the judges (in contrast, for example, to the principles of judicial review examined in chapter 5) but have instead been *recognised* by them. As we shall see subsequently, this characteristic may give rise to difficulty in identifying the existence and scope of certain prerogative powers.

Let us briefly pause from the task of definition to examine the relationship between prerogative and statute. The starting point here is simply to observe that, in the hierarchy of legal norms within the English legal system, statute takes precedence over common law, reflective of the sovereignty of Parliament. No problem arises where statute expressly abolishes a prerogative power, either because the power in question is no longer needed by government or because statute will in the future form the basis of those powers: although if the statute is subsequently repealed, it would appear that the prerogative will re-emerge.[43] However, if there is no such express abolition, it may be necessary to resolve the question as to whether the government can proceed under the prerogative even though it has available to it statutory powers which cover the same subject matter. In *Attorney-General v De Keyser's Royal Hotel Ltd*,[44] the House of Lords provided the answer which best accords both with constitutional principle and with the historical evolution of the relationship between Crown and Parliament which is described below: that is, that government must act in accordance

---

[42] Munro, p.25 (n.14), 257.
[43] See *Burmah Oil Co. Ltd v Lord Advocate* above p.30 (n.32), 143 (Lord Pearce).
[44] Above n.38.

with the statutory powers and the prerogative would therefore be set aside while the statute was in force. Similarly, in *Fire Brigades Union*,[45] the House of Lords held that the Home Secretary could not defeat the intentions of Parliament which had enacted a scheme – albeit one which had not been brought into force – for compensation for criminal injuries by using his prerogative powers to establish a different, cheaper scheme. However, a somewhat different result was reached in *R v Secretary of State for the Home Department, ex parte Northumbria Police Authority*,[46] in which the Court of Appeal held that a prerogative power to keep the peace co-existed with a statutory power under section 4 of the Police Act 1964. While this is a controversial decision (see further section iii below), it is possible to distinguish it from the two others discussed here on the basis that, while the Crown should not be permitted to use prerogative powers to *deprive individuals of benefits* (respectively, compensation for the requisitioning of property and a more generous scheme of compensation), it was permissible to use such powers for the *benefit of individuals* (here, maintaining peace and order), even if there was a statutory power covering the same subject matter.

Returning now to Dicey's definition, he also observes that the prerogative is the *remaining* portion of authority and *residue* of power. What this tells us is that the scope of prerogative powers is fixed. It is not possible for a 'new' prerogative power to be created, and if government wishes to exercise power in an area in which it has not previously intervened, it must seek authorisation by way of statute. The reason for this is straightforward if we briefly consider a crucial period of English history, the seventeenth century. The Stuart Kings James I and Charles I made liberal use of prerogative powers to raise money without parliamentary assent, and Charles suspended Parliament altogether from 1629 to 1640. Such actions were one of the causative factors of the Civil War, in which the parliamentarians emerged victorious over the royalists, resulting in the establishment of a republic until the monarchy was restored in 1660. However, difficulties again emerged as regards the relationship between monarchical power exercised by way of prerogative and Parliament's power to legislate, especially in the 1680s when the Catholic-leaning James II attempted to circumvent a Protestant-dominated Parliament. James was overthrown in 1688 and, in the 'Glorious Revolution', Parliament offered the throne to James's daughter Mary and her Protestant husband William of Orange. The settlement – which forms the basis of Britain's modern constitutional arrangements – included the Bill of Rights 1689, which regulates the relationship between Crown and Parliament and which contains provisions abolishing the Crown's power to suspend or dispense with laws and to levy

---

[45] Above p.14 (n.35).
[46] [1989] QB 26.

money without parliamentary consent (Articles 1 and 4). This settlement therefore functioned to fix prerogative powers in time: no new executive powers could be claimed through this mechanism since Parliament's superiority over the executive had now been clearly established. However, the Bill of Rights did not abolish all *existing* prerogative powers of the Crown, although later statutes have removed a number of the powers which William and Mary inherited. The position is well captured by a dictum of Diplock LJ in the mid-1960s when he stated that it was '350 years and a civil war too late for the Queen's courts to broaden the prerogative. The limits within which the executive government may impose obligations or restraints on citizens of the UK without any statutory authority are now well settled and incapable of extension'.[47]

We may also note that Dicey describes these powers as *discretionary*. In view of what we know of Dicey's dislike of discretion and his preference for rules (as discussed in chapter 2), we might consider this word to be more than merely descriptive. It suggests that he was – at the very least – wary of the manner in which such powers might be used by government. In particular, the word suggests that the exercise of prerogative powers may be problematic from the perspective of the rule of law, a point to which we shall return below.

Finally, Dicey informs his readers that prerogative power may be exercised *by the Queen herself or by her ministers*. We have already seen that the monarch retains certain, albeit limited, 'personal' prerogatives. Other prerogative powers – sometimes labelled 'executive' or 'ministerial' prerogatives – are exercised by the government of the day, although in formal legal terms they remain vested in the Crown (hence the label 'royal' prerogative, which is somewhat misleading in this context). In practical political terms, these are by far the most important as they are exercised relatively frequently (indeed, on a daily basis in some instances) by contrast with the highly extreme circumstances in which the personal prerogatives of the monarch might come into play. We therefore now turn to consider the areas of executive power which fall under the prerogative.

ii Principal ministerial prerogative powers

Providing a list of prerogative powers is not an easy task, given the antiquity of a number of them and their uncertain scope of application. Since the prerogative exists by virtue of recognition through the common law, it is ultimately the responsibility of the courts to determine the existence of a prerogative power. As stated by Coke CJ in the seventeenth century: 'the

---

[47] *BBC v Johns*, above p.127 (n.14), 79.

King hath no prerogative but that which the law of the land allows him'.[48] However, since prerogative powers are only intermittently the subject of litigation, the courts are not in a position to provide a complete catalogue and must proceed on an *ad hoc* basis.[49] This is problematic, since 'there are many prerogative powers for which there is no recent judicial authority and sometimes no judicial authority at all. In such circumstances, the Government, Parliament and the wider public are left relying on statements of previous Government practice and legal textbooks, the most comprehensive of which is now nearly 200 years old'.[50] As we shall see in the next section, there are good reasons to be concerned about this situation from the perspective of fundamental constitutional principle.

The position has been ameliorated somewhat by recent work on the prerogative conducted by the House of Commons Public Administration Select Committee[51] and by the Ministry of Justice.[52] While the lists of prerogative powers which have been drawn up are not exhaustive and cannot be regarded as binding statements of the legal position given that determination of the existence of a prerogative power is a matter for the courts alone, they nonetheless offer some assistance to us in building an understanding of the areas of modern government which are regulated by way of the prerogative.

The Public Administration Select Committee divides prerogative powers into three broad categories: the Queen's constitutional prerogatives (the 'personal prerogatives' previously discussed); legal prerogatives of the Crown, which include important principles such as the Crown not being bound by statute except by express wording or necessary implication – however, such powers are not exercised by ministers; and prerogative executive powers (or ministerial prerogative powers) with which we are concerned here.[53] The latter category may be further broken down in a number of ways. One possibility is to divide prerogative powers into those which relate to domestic issues and those which relate to foreign affairs. However, the Ministry of Justice has adopted a different classification,[54] as follows:

---

[48] *Case of Proclamations* (1611) 12 Co Rep 74.

[49] 'It has not at any stage in our history been practicable to identify all the prerogative powers of the Crown. It is only by a process of piecemeal decision over a period of centuries that particular powers are seen to exist or not to exist, as the case may be': *Northumbria Police Authority*, above n.46, 56 (Nourse LJ).

[50] Ministry of Justice, *Review of the Executive Royal Prerogative Powers: Final Report* (2009), [27]. The reference to the leading textbook is to J. Chitty, *A Treatise on the Law of the Prerogatives of the Crown* (London: Butterworths, 1820).

[51] Above n.35.

[52] Above n.50.

[53] Above n.35 [5]–[8].

[54] Above n.50, 31–34.

- Powers relating to government and the civil service. This category includes powers to set up ministerial departments and non-departmental public bodies; powers to appoint civil servants and to manage the civil service (the latter is now enshrined in statute, see below).
- Powers relating to the justice system and law and order, including powers to appoint Queen's Counsel (senior barristers); the prerogative of mercy (relating to the issuing of pardons and the reduction of sentences); the power to keep the peace.
- Powers relating to foreign affairs. This category comprises a number of important powers, including recognition of states; governance of British Overseas Territories; making and ratification of treaties; conducting diplomacy; acquiring and ceding territory; issuing, refusing or withdrawing passports.
- Powers related to armed forces, war and emergency situations. Another important category, this includes making war or peace or engaging in hostilities short of war; deployment and use of armed forces overseas; use of the armed forces in the UK to keep the peace; control and organisation of the armed forces; powers in the event of an emergency including entering, requisitioning and destruction of property.
- Miscellaneous powers. These include powers to establish corporations (such as the BBC) by royal Charter; power to hold public inquiries not covered by the Inquiries Act 2005; right of printing or licensing the printing of the Authorised Version of the Bible, the Book of Common Prayer, state papers and Acts of Parliament.

Two observations may be made about this list. First, it can be seen that the scope of prerogative powers is extremely broad. It ranges over all aspects of executive activity, from foreign policy and diplomacy to management of the civil service. Secondly, these are not unimportant powers. They include some of the most significant decisions or actions which a government may undertake, including declarations of war, deploying armed forces and keeping the peace. In view of this fact, we might wish to be reassured that the powers accord with the fundamental constitutional values identified in chapters 2 and 3 of this book. Let us now examine whether this is the case.

iii Prerogative powers and constitutional principles

The extent and significance of executive powers which are exercised by means of the prerogative is likely to surprise most observers of the British constitutional order. But, as public lawyers, our critical analysis of this area of government should be rooted in more than mere curiosity. Rather, we should seek to evaluate prerogative powers against the underlying principles of the separation of powers, parliamentary sovereignty and the rule of law in order to ascertain how comfortably this form of power fits with our constitutional arrangements.

The incompatibility of prerogative powers with the separation of powers is relatively straightforward to establish. Under that principle, there should be a functional separation between the tasks performed by the legislative and executive branches. However, when the executive is acting through prerogative powers, it is doing more than simply giving effect to the law made by Parliament: it is – at least in some instances – in effect making law itself. Similar arguments apply to the principle of parliamentary sovereignty. Dicey's account of this principle regarded Parliament as the *sole* source of legislative power. Prerogative powers clearly constitute a challenge to such a reading of the constitution since there is no obligation upon government even to consult the legislature prior to the exercise of such powers albeit, as will be noted in the next section, that ministers are accountable to the legislature for the decisions and actions they have taken by way of the prerogative.

As an illustration of these issues, we might consider the recent case of *R (on the application of Bancoult) v Secretary of State for Foreign and Commonwealth Affairs*.[55] This case involved the validity of a prerogative Order in Council issued by the Crown in respect of the British Indian Ocean Territory. This purported to remove the right of abode of the residents of the Chagos Islands, who had been removed and resettled by the British government so as to enable the US to establish a military base there. The islanders lost the case, on the basis that the exercise of the prerogative power by the government was not irrational or an abuse of power, given the unfeasibility and expense of resettlement and the UK's security and diplomatic interests. However, most pertinent to analysis here is the view of the House of Lords on the nature of the prerogative power at issue in this case and the reasons why it might be subject to judicial control. In response to counsel for the Crown's contention that the Order in Council could not be subject to review in the court as it was 'primary legislation having unquestionable validity comparable with that of an Act of Parliament', Lord Hoffmann observed:

'the fact that such Orders in Council in certain important respects resemble Acts of Parliament does not mean that they share all their characteristics. The principle of the sovereignty of Parliament, as it has been developed by the courts over the past 350 years, is founded upon the unique authority Parliament derives from its representative character. An exercise of the prerogative lacks this quality; although it may be

---

[55] [2008] UKHL 61.

legislative in character, it is still an exercise of power by the executive alone.'[56]

It is apparent from this dictum that at least some types of prerogative power are of a legislative type, thus violating the principle of the separation of powers, and that these represent a challenge to traditional understandings of parliamentary sovereignty. On the latter point, the preparedness of the House of Lords to expose the Order in Council to scrutiny by way of judicial review does at least signal a willingness to look beyond the legislative form of the prerogative power in this case and to hold such exercises of power to legal account, given that they lack the democratic character inherent in Parliament's expression of its sovereign will.

Bancoult also serves to illustrate how the prerogative may give rise to rule of law concerns. In powerful dissenting judgments, Lords Bingham and Mance observed that there was no precedent for the existence of a power to exile an indigenous population from its homeland.[57] The absence of such precedent seems highly problematic. We noted in chapter 2 that, on the most straightforward conception of the rule of law, the executive must have lawful authority for all of its actions: as expressed by Lord Camden CJ in *Entick v Carrington*: 'if it is law, it will be found in our books. If it is not to be found there, it is not law'.[58] It is undoubtedly the case that it will always be harder for the executive to point to lawful authority (by way of judicial precedent or commentary in textbooks) for the exercise of prerogative powers than will be the case where power is exercised by virtue of statute, but it can be argued that the majority in *Bancoult* are too ready to concede that such a power exists and are insufficiently alert to key rule of law values such as certainty and accessibility of laws.

This difficulty is perhaps even more starkly illustrated by the *Northumbria Police Authority* case.[59] This concerned the question of whether the Home Secretary could utilise powers under the prerogative to provide equipment such as CS gas and plastic baton rounds to police forces for use in instances of serious public disorder. The Court of Appeal was of the opinion that a prerogative power to keep the peace existed, but was very hazy upon its origins and provenance. Croom-Johnson LJ stated that he had 'no doubt that the Crown does have a prerogative power to keep the peace, which is bound up with its undoubted right to see that crime is

---

[56] *ibid*, [35].

[57] *ibid*, [70], [150].

[58] Above p.43 (n.90). Lord Camden's dictum was cited by Lord Bingham in *Bancoult*: *ibid*, [69].

[59] Above n.46.

prevented and justice administered',[60] while Purchas LJ referred to Chitty,[61] whose work does not in fact specifically identify such a prerogative, although it does discuss the Crown's duty of protection. Most controversially of all, Nourse LJ considered that the prerogative of making war and peace (which clearly exists) 'must have extended as much to unlawful acts within the realm as to the menaces of a foreign power', and contended that the 'scarcity of references in the books to the prerogative of keeping the peace within the realm does not disprove that it exists. Rather it may point to an unspoken assumption that it does'.[62]

Nourse LJ's dictum is quite startling from a rule of law perspective. The judge appears to be indicating that the *absence* of clear authority for a particular prerogative power is evidence *in favour* of its existence in so far as the power is so self-evident as to not require committing to paper. This seems totally to contradict the values of certainty and predictability which lie at the heart of accounts of the rule of law, particularly the formal version of that principle. Furthermore, it calls into question the maxim that no new prerogatives can be created, as articulated by Lord Diplock in *BBC v Johns*.[63] Nourse LJ maintained that he was not seeking to establish a new power, but merely to give more 'exact definition' to one which already existed but which had not been the subject of previous judicial consideration in view of the fact that the factual situation prevailing in the case was 'a phenomenon which has been observed only in recent times'.[64] Yet it is a very small step from the claim that 'there has probably never been a comparable occasion for investigating a prerogative of keeping the peace within the realm'[65] to an acknowledgment that the power in question broke new ground.

It is tempting to dismiss *Northumbria Police Authority* as simply having been wrongly decided.[66] However, the case does afford an excellent demonstration of why we might consider the unclear, archaic and wide-ranging powers which make up the prerogative to be constitutionally problematic, especially if we are concerned about the propensity of the executive to abuse such powers. In view of such worries, it is important that adequate mechanisms through which the government may be held accountable for its use of prerogative powers. It is to these that we next turn.

---

[60]   *ibid*, 44.
[61]   Above n.50.
[62]   Above n.46, 58.
[63]   Above n.47.
[64]   Above n.46, 56.
[65]   *id*.
[66]   See C. Vincenzi, *Crown Powers, Subjects and Citizens* (London: Continuum, 1998), 121.

iv Accountability for the exercise of prerogative powers

The prerogative is problematic, at least in part, because it is an undemocratic source of power. There is no requirement for government, when exercising such powers, to gain the approval of Parliament prior to so doing. In practice, government may, on occasion, consult Parliament first. The most notable recent example of this was the decision of Tony Blair's government to send troops to Iraq in 2003, which was put to parliamentary vote. But it is important to note that this was a political gesture designed to secure some degree of democratic legitimacy for a controversial decision, rather than a constitutional obligation placed upon the Prime Minister.[67] Furthermore, it has been observed that this was the first instance in which Parliament had voted on a motion to deploy armed forces in conflict before the commencement of hostilities since the Korean War in 1950.[68]

There are other means by which Parliament can scrutinise and control the executive's use of prerogative powers. As noted in section i, legislation may be enacted which abolishes or restricts the prerogative or which places it on a statutory basis. We shall note in the next section recent reforms which place management of the civil service on a statutory footing, and another example is afforded by the Civil Contingencies Act 2004 which covers much of the ground relating to the Crown's power to act in emergency situations (for example, by requisitioning property). The approval of Parliament is also necessary when the exercise of prerogative powers requires spending money.

However, these forms of parliamentary control are somewhat weak and haphazard: certainly not every exercise of prerogative power will be subject to them. In practice, Parliament's primary opportunity for holding government to account for the exercise of prerogative powers occurs *after* they have been used, through mechanisms such as select committees and parliamentary questions which were described in chapter 3. Ministers are accountable to Parliament for the exercise of prerogative powers just as they are accountable for the exercise of statutory or other common law powers. Nonetheless, if we are concerned as to the potential for the executive to exceed or abuse its power, we might not be satisfied with this situation. We observed in chapter 3 (and the matter will be returned to below) that these mechanisms tend not to be highly effective means of scrutiny

---

[67] It has been argued that this action established a constitutional convention that government must seek parliamentary consent for deployment of troops: see *eg* Public Administration Select Committee, above n.35, [25]. It is almost certainly too early to conclude whether such a convention does indeed exist. For discussion of the nature of constitutional conventions, see below.

[68] Constitution Committee, *Waging War: Parliament's Role and Responsibility*, HL 236-I (2005–06), [16].

of the executive generally, given the realities of modern party politics. Furthermore, there are particular difficulties with regard to parliamentary scrutiny of prerogative powers. In particular, there is a disparity of information between Parliament and government. As noted in section i, it is only in recent years that attempts have been made to list prerogative powers. This has at least provided Parliament with some knowledge of the powers which exist, but there remain problems in holding particular exercises of power to account given the view, expressed by a former Prime Minister, that 'it is for individual ministers to decide on a particular occasion whether and how to report to Parliament on the exercise of prerogative powers'.[69] This is especially the case for those powers on the exercise of which the government may decline to answer questions, such as the disposition of the armed forces (which raises issues of national security) or the dissolution of Parliament (which is regarded as a political decision solely within the remit of the Prime Minister).[70]

This brings us to legal forms of accountability via the mechanism of judicial review of administrative action. In this context, the prerogative offers an excellent illustration of the trend (noted in chapter 1) of increasing judicial activism in the review of executive power as a means of redressing the apparent imbalance between the executive and the other two branches of government – the 'elective dictatorship' identified by Lord Hailsham[71] – which has been exacerbated by the relative inadequacy of legislative checks over the executive branch. Indeed, it should be recalled that the most comprehensive judicial account of this development comes, in fact, from a judgment concerning the exercise of prerogative powers, the *Fire Brigades Union* case,[72] albeit that the judge responsible for the statement, Lord Mustill, dissented from the majority as to the unlawfulness of the Home Secretary's use of such powers.

This trend may be said to have commenced with the leading decision in the modern law of judicial review, *Council of Civil Service Unions v Minister for the Civil Service* (also referred to as the *GCHQ* case), decided in 1984.[73] Prior to this case, it was clear that the courts could adjudicate upon whether a prerogative power existed or not, since it was necessary for government to demonstrate that it had a source of legal authority for its actions to comply with the principle articulated in *Entick v Carrington*, and it was impossible for new prerogative powers to come into existence. However, it appeared that once this had been established, and in contrast

---

[69] *House of Commons Debates*, 1 Mar 1993, col. 19W (J. Major).
[70] But see now above, p.133.
[71] Above p.13 (n.32).
[72] Above pp.13–14, 27–28.
[73] [1985] AC 374.

to the position regarding statutory powers, they could not review the *manner* in which the power had been exercised in order to ascertain whether the executive had abused its powers by acting in an unreasonable manner or violating principles of fair procedure.[74] However, in *GCHQ*, which involved the prerogative power of management of the civil service, the House of Lords established that the fact that powers were derived from the prerogative did not in itself preclude review by courts, Lord Roskill commenting that he was:

> 'unable to see ... that there is any logical reason why the fact that the source of the power is the prerogative and not statute should today deprive the citizen of that right of challenge to the manner of its exercise which he would possess were the source of the power statutory. In either case the act in question is the act of the executive. To talk of that act as the act of the sovereign savours of the archaism of past centuries.'[75]

Underpinning this passage we may detect judicial concerns as to the executive's compliance with the rule of law and the inadequacy of other checks and balances relating to the exercise of prerogative powers, coupled with a perception that the previous stance of limited judicial review did not properly reflect the constitutional subservience of the Crown which was confirmed in the settlement of 1688–89.

GCHQ establishes that prerogative powers are, in principle, reviewable in the same manner as any other form of executive power. However, not every decision or action based upon the prerogative will, in practice, be reviewed by the courts. This was made clear subsequently in Lord Roskill's judgment, when he stated that:

> 'I do not think that that right of challenge can be unqualified. It must, I think, depend upon the subject matter of the prerogative power which is exercised. Many examples were given during the argument of prerogative powers which as at present advised I do not think could properly be made the subject of judicial review. Prerogative powers such as those relating to the making of treaties, the defence of the realm, the prerogative of mercy, the grant of honours, the dissolution of Parliament and the appointment of ministers as well as others are not, I think suscepti-ble to judicial review because their nature and subject matter are such

---

[74] There were some exceptions to this general position. See especially *R v Criminal Injuries Compensation Board, ex parte Lain* [1967] 2 QB 864 and *Laker Airways Ltd v Department of Trade and Industry* [1977] QB 643.

[75] Above n.73, 417.

as not to be amenable to the judicial process. The courts are not the place wherein to determine whether a treaty should be concluded or the armed forces disposed in a particular manner or Parliament dissolved on one date rather than another.'[76]

The decisive question for the courts when confronted with a challenge to the manner in which an executive power has been exercised is not, therefore, the *source* of the power but the *nature of the subject matter*. Certain subjects are inherently less susceptible to judicial review than others and may be regarded as *non-justiciable*, that is inappropriate for adjudication in a court of law. In such cases, the 'political' branches of government (Parliament and the executive) are considered to have greater expertise, information and democratic legitimacy than the courts, and/or the adversarial style of legal process may be ill-suited to the consideration and weighing of the numerous competing considerations which arise in such areas of government.[77] Non-justiciable matters could arise in the context of the review of statutory powers (for example, the courts have traditionally been reluctant to determine questions relating to the allocation of resources in public services such as the National Health Service),[78] but they are particularly characteristic of the prerogative. Such was the case in *GCHQ*, where the subject matter (a ban on membership of trade unions in the organisation responsible for the monitoring of overseas communications) was considered to be an issue of national security, which was 'par excellence a non-justiciable question',[79] with the consequence that the House of Lords reached the conclusion that the exercise of the prerogative power in this instance could not be categorised as unlawful.

Since the decision in this case, the courts have shown a willingness to review the manner of exercise of prerogative powers in certain areas, and continued reluctance in others. Within the former category falls the *Fire Brigades Union* case, *R v Secretary of State for Foreign and Commonwealth Affairs, ex parte Everett*,[80] relating to the prerogative power to issue passports, and *R v Secretary of State for the Home Department, ex parte Bentley*,[81] in which certain aspects of the prerogative of mercy – one of the categories of subject matter which had been excluded from review by Lord Roskill in *GCHQ* – were held to be reviewable. Against this trend of expansion of judicial scrutiny of the prerogative, one might cite a number of cases

---

[76] *ibid*, 418.

[77] For a valuable discussion of some of these issues, see J. Jowell, 'Of vires and vacuums: the constitutional context of judicial review' [1999] *Public Law* 448.

[78] See especially *R v Cambridge Health Authority, ex parte B* [1995] 1 WLR 898.

[79] Above n.73, 412 (Lord Diplock).

[80] [1989] QB 811.

[81] [1994] QB 349.

concerning the exercise of foreign policy and defence powers in the context of the 'war' against terrorism and UK military action in Iraq.[82] *Bancoult* is somewhat more difficult to categorise: here, the two dissenting judges regarded the prerogative power as justiciable,[83] while two of the majority judges did not;[84] the third, Lord Hoffmann made no direct statement in this regard, although he did favour a restrictive approach to review on the basis that the case involved 'policy as to the expenditure of public resources and the security and diplomatic interests of the Crown'.[85] However, the case is authority for the proposition that prerogative powers of a legislative nature (rather than, as was the case in *GCHQ*, executive actions which derive their authority from the prerogative) are, in principle, reviewable by a court.

What are we to make of the position reached by the courts in respect of the review of prerogative powers? It is clear that the scope for control of the executive's use of such powers is much wider than was the case before the *GCHQ* decision in 1984. It is no longer the case that these powers are not subject to review simply because they emanate from the prerogative. If there are concerns as to the propensity for the executive to abuse such powers and, in the process, to violate fundamental constitutional principles (and section iii has suggested that such concerns are justified), then such a development is clearly welcome, especially given the relative weakness of parliamentary forms of control. However, judicial intervention only extends so far and there remain significant areas of the prerogative – especially those concerned with foreign policy, defence and national security – in which the freedom of action of the executive remains relatively unconstrained. This provokes a final question with regard to this controversial and wide-ranging form of executive power and the limits upon it: what prospects exist for future development?

v Reform?

It is clear from the above discussion that prerogative power poses a number of controversial questions for public lawyers and, indeed, for anyone concerned as to the democratic quality of British constitutional

---

[82] *R (on the application of Campaign for Nuclear Disarmament) v Prime Minister* [2002] EWHC 2777 (Admin); *R (on the application of Abbasi) v Secretary of State for Foreign and Commonwealth Affairs* [2002] EWCA Civ 1598; *R. v Jones* [2006] UKHL 16; *R (on the application of Gentle) v Prime Minister* [2006] EWCA Civ 1689.

[83] Above n.55, [72] (Lord Bingham); [159] (Lord Mance).

[84] *ibid*, [109] (Lord Rodger); [130] (Lord Carswell).

[85] *ibid*, [58]. For critical analysis of the House of Lords decision, see M. Elliott and A. Perreau-Saussine, 'Pyrrhic public law: *Bancoult* and the sources, status and content of common law limitations on prerogative power' [2009] *Public Law* 697.

arrangements. It is not surprising, therefore, that there have been frequent calls for reform: for example, in 1988 and 1999 Tony Benn MP introduced unsuccessful Private Member's Bills which would have placed the prerogatives on a statutory basis.[86] In recent years, the movement for reform has gained greater momentum. In 2003, the Public Administration Select Committee called upon government to put forward proposals for legislation to provide for greater parliamentary control over prerogative powers, expressing particular concern as to decisions on armed conflict, the making and ratifying of treaties and issuing of passports.[87] This was followed by a report on the war prerogative issued by the Select Committee on the Constitution in the House of Lords, which recommended establishment of a constitutional convention requiring government normally to seek approval of Parliament prior to deployment of British forces outside the UK in actual or potential armed conflict.[88]

Partly in response to these developments, the Labour Government issued proposals for the reform of prerogative powers in a consultation document issued shortly after Gordon Brown became Prime Minister in 2007. Stating that 'the Government believes that in general the prerogative powers should be put onto a statutory basis and brought under stronger parliamentary scrutiny and control',[89] it was proposed that the approval of Parliament of exercise of the power to deploy troops should be formalised by way of a parliamentary resolution, that the existing convention whereby treaties which require ratification are laid before Parliament for 21 days should be placed on a statutory basis,[90] that a convention should be developed obliging the Prime Minister to seek the approval of the House of Commons before requesting a dissolution of Parliament, that management of the civil service should be governed by statute, and that remaining prerogative powers be reviewed to establish if they could be abolished, transferred elsewhere or placed on a statutory basis.

However, subsequent developments indicated that the government of Gordon Brown had developed a case of cold feet. While the Constitutional Reform and Governance Act 2010 gives effect to the proposal on treaties and places the core values of the civil service and the principle of appoint-

---

[86] Crown Prerogatives (House of Commons Control) Bill 1988, HC Bill 117 (1988–89); Crown Prerogatives (Parliamentary Control) Bill 1999, HC Bill 55 (1998–99). See also Constitutional Reform (Prerogative Powers and Civil Service etc.) Bill 2006, HL Bill 222 (2005–06).

[87] Above n.35.

[88] Above n.68.

[89] Ministry of Justice, *The Governance of Britain*, Cm 7170 (2007), [24].

[90] This convention is known as the 'Ponsonby Rule'. 'Laying before Parliament' merely provides Parliament with information as to the content of the treaty and does not trigger a debate. Government has undertaken to provide the opportunity for parliamentary debate of any treaty involving significant political, diplomatic or military issues upon request: *ibid* [33].

ment by merit on a statutory footing,[91] and the Government indicated that it was continuing to prepare a draft resolution of the House of Commons to provide for approval by the latter before deployment of troops overseas,[92] other reforms (such as placing the power to issue passports on a statutory basis) were postponed.[93] More controversially still, other areas of the prerogative – including those relating to the organisation and control of the armed forces, the prerogative of mercy, powers in the event of a grave national emergency and powers to keep the peace – were considered not to warrant reform. The government's conclusions were as follows:

'Some of the remaining prerogative powers could be candidates for abolition or reform, but their continued existence has – at the minimum – no significant negative effects. In many cases it is positively useful. Legislation to replace some of them could itself give rise to new risks: of unnecessary incursions into civil liberties on the one hand, or of dangerously weakening the state's ability to respond to unforeseen circumstances on the other ... The Government has concluded that it is unnecessary, and would be inappropriate, to propose further major reform at present. Our constitution has developed organically over many centuries and change should not be proposed for change's sake. Without ruling out further changes aimed at increasing Parliamentary oversight of the prerogative powers exercised by Ministers, the Government believes that any further reforms in this area should be considered on a case-by-case basis, in the light of changing circumstances.'[94]

While it remains to be seen if the present or future governments will take a different view, the prospects for further reform do not appear rosy at present.[95] As the Brown Government admitted, 'prerogative powers can provide flexibility in dealing with specific or exceptional circumstances that are not covered by statutory provisions'.[96] This makes them difficult to express in statute in anything other than very wide terms, with the consequence that mechanisms for parliamentary and judicial control will always be limited by the sheer breadth of discretion enjoyed by government. Alternatively, a more cynical reading of recent events would point to the breadth and lack of clarity of these powers and the relative weakness

---

[91] Parts 1 and 2.
[92] Above n.50, [37].
[93] *ibid*, [38].
[94] *ibid*, [111]–[112].
[95] The proposals relating to dissolution of Parliament have been superseded by the Fixed-Term Parliaments Bill, above p.132.
[96] Above n.50, [109].

of control mechanisms (particularly those of a political nature) which place the executive branch in a very strong position. When coupled with the relatively invisibility of prerogative powers to the public, this means that it is unlikely to be in the interest of a government to use its dominance over the legislature to secure reform. It seems likely, therefore, that prerogative power will continue to remain a thorny problem for public lawyers for some time to come.

C. Prime Minister, Cabinet and government departments

Let us return now to our task of mapping the key power-wielding institutions within the executive branch. Most powerful of all, of course, is the **Prime Minister**, the UK's head of government. One might reasonably expect, therefore, that the powers, functions and responsibilities of this individual would be set out clearly in law but in fact, as noted above, there is scant reference to the office of Prime Minister in statute.[97] Rather, the office has evolved primarily as a matter of practical politics and the 'rules' which regulate the exercise of prime ministerial power are expressed almost exclusively by way of constitutional convention. We shall explore the meaning of this important source of public law at the end of this chapter.

We noted earlier that appointment of the Prime Minister strictly falls within the personal prerogatives of the monarch, but that convention requires that the person selected is the person best able to command the confidence of the House of Commons. This will normally be the leader of the party which wins a majority of seats at a general election, or an individual succeeding such a person to the leadership of the party in circumstances where the previous leader has resigned.[98] In light of the emphasis upon the Commons' confidence, it is understandable that the person appointed should be a member of that House of Parliament, rather than the House of Lords, and although members of the upper House have served as Prime Ministers in the past,[99] it would appear that convention now precludes this. The consequence is that the Prime Minister is accountable and responsible to the electorate in two ways. First, through general elections at which s/he seeks a *mandate* from the public for the policies carried out by his/her party while in government; and secondly (and, arguably, more importantly) on a day-to-day basis to the representatives of the elec-

---

[97] Above n.4.

[98] As occurred in the cases of John Major (succeeding Margaret Thatcher) in 1990 and Gordon Brown (succeeding Tony Blair) in 2007.

[99] The last Prime Minister who was a member of the House of Lords was Lord Salisbury, who held office until 1902.

torate – that is, other members of Parliament – through the conventions of individual and collective responsibility which will be discussed shortly.

In the absence of a codified statement to this effect, the precise extent of prime ministerial powers cannot be easily specified: moreover, much depends upon the 'style' adopted by the individual concerned, as will be noted below. However, a number of key functions may be identified. First, the Prime Minister appoints other ministers, either at Cabinet level or not: similarly, s/he may dismiss them or move them to other portfolios of responsibilities (this often occurs through the process known as a 'Cabinet reshuffle'). Relatedly, the Prime Minister determines the 'architecture' of central government. That is, s/he determines which ministerial depart- ments should exist and the extent of the responsibilities which they should undertake. The Prime Minister is also Minister for the Civil Service and as such is responsible for the manner in which it is organised and managed. The Prime Minister chairs meetings of the Cabinet, decides upon its agenda and controls the numbers and functions of Cabinet committees (see below). S/he is particularly visible in relation to foreign affairs, exercis- ing prerogative powers to declare war, to make peace, to deploy troops and to enter into treaties: additionally, the Prime Minister takes part in meet- ings of the European Council (see further chapter 6). As we have seen, the Prime Minister has weekly audiences with the monarch and has previously determined the date of a general election by requesting a dissolution of Parliament. Finally, the Prime Minister is the most visible manifestation of the principle of responsible government, to which we shall return below, notably through weekly question and answer sessions in the House of Commons at Prime Minister's Questions (which receive widespread media coverage), but also by way of an annual appearance in front of the House of Commons Liaison Committee, which has heard evidence from the Prime Minister on matters of general public policy since 1992.[100]

In recent years, there has been considerable discussion of an apparent move towards a 'presidential' style of government by the Prime Minister and a consequent diminution in the power of the **Cabinet**.[101] We noted in chapter 2 that Bagehot regarded the latter as the key institution linking executive and legislative branches,[102] but it should be remembered that executive functions are much more extensive today than was the case in the Victorian era and this fact, coupled with the tendency of the modern

---

[100] The Liaison Committee is made up of the chairs of all of the other Commons select committees and is responsible for considering the overall work of the select committees in the House.

[101] See eg M. Foley, *The British Presidency* (Manchester: Manchester University Press, 2000); R. Heffernan, 'Prime Ministerial predominance? Core executive politics in the UK' (2003) 5 *British Journal of Politics and International Relations* 347.

[102] Above p.33.

media to personalise politics, has arguably rendered collective decision-making by the Cabinet less feasible. Nonetheless, the trend is not necessarily irreversible. In part, a more collegiate, collective approach to decision-making is a function of the personality and preferences of a particular Prime Minister, but it also reflects the degree of support which s/he enjoys in the party and country as a whole, and the size of the governmental majority in the House of Commons. Deficiencies in any of these respects may be fatal even to an otherwise strong Prime Minister, as was most visibly demonstrated by the fall of Margaret Thatcher in 1990 when she lost the support of significant number of her Cabinet colleagues.[103]

Like the Prime Minister, the existence and function of the Cabinet is not enshrined in legal rules. In principle, the Prime Minister has entirely free rein as to which ministers sit in Cabinet, but in practice it would be impossible to exclude key offices such as Chancellor of the Exchequer, Home Secretary and Foreign Secretary. Statute does, however, prescribe an upper limit to the numbers who may sit since, by virtue of Schedule 1 of the Ministerial and Other Salaries Act 1975, no more than twenty salaries may be paid to Cabinet ministers, apart from the Prime Minister and Lord Chancellor, at any given time.

In the absence of a clear legal statement to this effect, it is difficult to give a precise account of the role of the Cabinet. In any event, that role will change according to the propensity of the Prime Minister to make use of the body for the purpose of decision-making. In principle, the Cabinet is the central co-ordinating body of government, offering ministers an opportunity to bring particular departmental policies and problems to the attention of their colleagues, and formulating and initiating the government's overall policy programme. This is reflected in the *Ministerial Code* (the status of which will be considered later in this chapter), which provides that the business of Cabinet consists mainly of 'questions which significantly engage the collective responsibility of the Government because they raise major issues of policy or because they are of critical importance to the public' and 'questions on which there is an unresolved argument between departments'.[104] However, despite recent attempts to foster 'joined-up government',[105] many decisions are in fact not taken by the full Cabinet but within one of a series of committees, the number and scope of which

---

[103] See R. Brazier, 'The downfall of Margaret Thatcher' (1991) 54 *Modern Law Review* 471.

[104] Cabinet Office, *Ministerial Code* (2010), [2.2].

[105] This phrase refers to the notion that 'all or many parts of executive government should interconnect, complement one another, and pool related information. The aim is for the various units of government to present a single face to those they are dealing with and operate as a unit on problems that are interrelated': C. Hood, 'The Idea of Joined-Up Government: a Historical Perspective' in V. Bogdanor (ed.), *Joined-Up Government* (Oxford: OUP, 2005), 19.

are established by the Prime Minister, acting on a permanent or *ad hoc* basis.[106] Some of these committees also have sub-committees.

The work of the Cabinet is assisted by the Cabinet Office, whose functions also include providing support to the Prime Minister and ensuring that the civil service is organised effectively. Given the usual predominance of the Prime Minister over Cabinet, it has been argued that the Cabinet Office functions in practice, if not in name, as the Prime Minister's own ministerial department.[107]

Turning now to such ministerial or non-ministerial **departments**, the realities of modern government – especially the breadth of activities which it undertakes – mean that it is here where most key decisions are taken. This fact is reflected in the *Ministerial Code*, which states that 'matters wholly within the responsibility of a single Minister and which do not significantly engage collective responsibility need not be brought to the Cabinet or to a Ministerial Committee unless the Minister wishes to inform his colleagues or to have their advice'.[108] As noted above, the Prime Minister determines which departments shall exist and what are their responsibilities, and in consequence some departments have a very brief lifespan, reflecting particular interests of the government of the time.[109] Others, however – notably the Home and Foreign Offices – have existed for centuries.

The departments are usually headed by ministers,[110] most of whom will sit in Cabinet. They are supported by junior ministers who assume responsibility for particular areas of policy within the department's overall remit: for example, there are currently four junior ministers in the Department of Health, who respectively cover performance; health services and patient safety; care services and quality; and public health. Each department is otherwise staffed by civil servants.

It is within departments that most government policies or legislative proposals are initiated and such departments are also responsible for the implementation of policies: though, as we shall see shortly, an important

---

[106] For example, the Parliamentary Business and Legislation Committee (permanent) and the Olympics sub-committee (*ad hoc*).

[107] See Heffernan, n.101, 360–64.

[108] Above n.104, [2.4]. The notions of individual and collective responsibility are discussed in detail below.

[109] For example, Harold Wilson's Labour Government established a Ministry of Technology in 1964. This department was merged with the Board of Trade to form the Department of Trade and Industry by Wilson's Conservative successor, Edward Heath, in 1970. That Department then became the Department for Business, Enterprise and Regulatory Reform in 2007, and it is currently known as the Department for Business, Innovation and Skills.

[110] Some departments, such as the Office of Fair Trading are non-ministerial, headed by a senior civil servant rather than a minister. For a full discussion of the office of government minister, see R. Brazier, *Ministers of the Crown* (Oxford: OUP, 1997).

distinction is drawn between the strategic policy-making role and the day-to-day carrying out of such policy. Departments also manage the budget allocated annually to them by the Treasury under the terms of the Finance Act and have oversight of the work of executive agencies which fall within their remit (see below).

Ministerial departments are not defined in law, although lists of such departments (which can be revised as necessary) are maintained under the provisions of certain statutes.[111] However, it is almost always to such departments that statute (and prerogative) allocates functions, powers and duties, rather than to government as a whole. The general practice is for statute to vest the powers in question upon 'the Secretary of State' rather than a named minister,[112] which reflects the fact that legally the powers of ministers are interchangeable, although it will usually be readily apparent which minister is, in fact, responsible. Transferral of ministerial functions is, of course, sometimes necessary if the departmental structure is changed, and this is normally achieved by way of the Ministers of the Crown Act 1975 which authorises the Crown to make delegated legislation to this effect, which is subject to parliamentary scrutiny. Prerogative powers are also available for this purpose.[113]

D. The Civil Service, executive agencies and non-departmental public bodies

In the preceding section, our focus was upon the political arm of the executive. The offices of minister and Prime Minister are occupied by politicians, generally those elected by the public as MPs. The Cabinet is also a political body, made up as it is by ministers, although it should be noted that there is a system of committees staffed by civil servants and running in parallel to Cabinet committees to assist the latter in their work.

We now turn to consider those working in central government who are not politicians. Our starting point is the **civil service**, an organisation which describes its function as to 'help the government of the day to develop and deliver its policies as effectively as possible'.[114] There are, in fact, two administratively separate services, comprising the Home Civil

---

[111] See eg Parliamentary Commissioner Act 1967, Schedule 2: though note that this does not distinguish between government departments and other authorities subject to the Act.

[112] The office of 'Secretary of State' dates back many centuries, but is today the title given to the ministerial head of most departments, with a few exceptions (notably the Treasury, which is headed by the Chancellor of the Exchequer).

[113] s.5(5).

[114] See http://www.civilservice.gov.uk/about/index.aspx.

Service and the Diplomatic Service, while Northern Ireland has an entirely separate structure.

Civil servants are employees of the Crown, not including those holding political or judicial offices, members of the armed forces, employees of the National Health Service and employees of state-owned industries. In mid-2009 there were 492,000 such employees, a significant reduction from the peak of 1.16 million in 1944, but more than five times as many as were employed in 1902.[115] Sections 3(1) and (2) of the Constitutional Reform and Governance Act 2010 vest the power of appointment to the Home Civil Service and the Diplomatic Service respectively in the Minister for the Civil Service (*ie* the Prime Minister) and the Foreign Secretary, while section 10(2) provides that appointment must be on merit on the basis of fair and open competition, overseen by a Civil Service Commission.

One of the central characteristics of the civil service in the UK is its permanence: as distinct from other countries where senior appointments in the civil service will alter in accordance with changes in government, British civil servants remain in place (subject, of course, to the normal processes of retirement, resignation or transfer) irrespective of which political party is in power. This principle is reflected in the title of the most senior civil servant within a government department, the Permanent Secretary. In addition to oversight of the running of the department on a day-to-day basis and acting as the most senior adviser to the minister, the Permanent Secretary also acts as 'accounting officer' for the department, in which capacity s/he has personal responsibility for the organisation, management and staffing of the department and for departmental procedures in financial and other matters.

The characteristic of permanence connects to other key values upon which the civil service has traditionally been regarded as being founded. These values are stated in the *Civil Service Code*, which was introduced in 1996 and which forms part of the terms and conditions of employment of all civil servants. The Code states that the 'core values' of the civil service are integrity (acting in a professional manner, using resources properly and efficiently, not misusing one's official position, accepting benefits which might be seen to compromise one's judgment or disclosing official information without authority); honesty (setting out facts and issues truthfully, not deceiving or knowingly misleading ministers or Parliament); objectivity (providing information and advice on the basis of evidence, not ignoring inconvenient facts or relevant factors when providing advice); and impartiality ('acting solely according to the merits of the

---

[115] See http://www.civilservice.gov.uk/about/facts/statistics/index.aspx#.

case and serving equally well Governments of different political persuasions').[116] Of these, it is the last-mentioned which is of the greatest significance for an analysis of the British constitution. The civil service is expected to maintain a stance of political neutrality, and advice offered by civil servants to ministers should not be influenced by the ideological or political preferences of the individual. There are restrictions upon the involvement of civil servants in political activities, especially those working in senior grades, and, as noted in chapter 2, civil servants are ineligible for membership of the House of Commons. It is clear therefore that the primary duty of the civil servant is to the government of the day and this is reflected in the principle that civil servants are accountable *to ministers* (the executive), not to Parliament (the legislature). This constitutional relationship is further buttressed by the doctrine that the civil service should be anonymous, meaning that the minister is the visible focus for all departmental policies and decisions while the civil servant, protected by anonymity from direct public and media criticism, can maintain impartiality and political neutrality.

A number of recent developments have, however, served to call into question the centrality of some of these traditional values. Of relevance here is the desire of select committees to call civil servants to give evidence when conducting an inquiry into aspects of a department's work. Written rules now provide that a minister should normally agree to a request from a committee to interview a named civil servant,[117] and it is possible for the committee to order attendance if the minister refuses.[118] However, it remains the case that civil servants who provide evidence to a select committee do so *on behalf of the minister*,[119] and to this extent the traditional pattern of accountability, and the principle of neutrality, is – at least in principle – maintained.

A further challenge to the long-standing values of the civil service has been posed by the recent tendency of governments to employ special advisers. Such advisers, who are recruited from outside the departmental structure, are appointed to provide advice in the development and presentation of government policy, to provide expert opinion on particular policy areas, to act as a link between government, party and outside interests and to offer an alternative perspective to the view taken within the department itself. The advisers – whose appointment must be approved by the Prime Minister and whose number is limited to two (paid or unpaid) per Cabinet minister, with the exception of the Prime

---

[116] *Civil Service Code* (2010), [3], [6–15].
[117] Cabinet Office, *Departmental Evidence and Response to Select Committees* (2005), [44].
[118] *ibid*, [47].
[119] *ibid*, [40].

Minister[120] – are subject to the provisions of a *Model Contract* and *Code of Conduct*. These documents provide that the status of a special adviser is as temporary civil servant, but that they are exempt from the obligations of impartiality and objectivity contained in the *Civil Service Code*.[121] Hence, special advisers are viewed 'as an additional resource for the Minister, providing assistance from a standpoint that is more politically committed and politically aware than would be available to a Minister from the permanent civil service'.[122] There now appears to be a general recognition that such advisers play an important and necessary role in modern government,[123] but concerns remain that, notwithstanding the provisions of the *Code of Conduct* which set strict limits on the relationship between such individuals and permanent civil servants, the existence of special advisers imperils the core civil service principles of objectivity and impartiality.

It is in part as a response to worries of this nature that the Constitutional Reform and Governance Act 2010 establishes a statutory basis for the management of the civil service. In essence, this places the values of integrity, honesty, objectivity and impartiality which characterise the permanent civil service on a statutory footing, the objective being that these values should not be subject to change or erosion without any prior discussion in Parliament. The Act also imposes an obligation upon the Minister for the Civil Service to publish codes of conduct for the Home Civil Service and for special advisers.[124] Such codes, as noted, already exist in practice.

A further illustration of the constitutional problems generated as a consequence of the management of the civil service having previously been a matter for prerogative, not statute, is provided by the initiation some twenty years ago of a programme for the creation of a system of **executive agencies** with only limited opportunities for parliamentary debate and no need for legislative authorisation. The reform, which, when taken together with other changes in the public sector which are examined at greater length in chapter 6, has been described as a 'fundamental revolution in public administration',[125] sprang from the desire of the government of Margaret Thatcher to make the civil service operate in a more efficient manner. The primary component of the reform was to separate

---

[120] *Ministerial Code*, above n.104, [3.2].

[121] Cabinet Office, *Code of Conduct for Special Advisers* (2007), [4].

[122] *ibid*, [2].

[123] See *eg* Public Administration Select Committee, *A Draft Civil Service Bill: Completing the Reform*, HC 128-I (2003–04), [8]. The Constitutional Reform and Governance Act 2010, s.15 gives statutory recognition to the existence of such advisers.

[124] ss.5, 8. It is the responsibility of the Foreign Secretary to publish a code of conduct for the Diplomatic Service: s.6.

[125] Select Committee on Public Service, *Public Service*, HL 55 (1997–98), [152].

central government's executive functions in the purest sense – the day-to-day delivery of services – from the policy advice function carried out by senior civil servants. The 'core' of the civil service would be relatively small and would consist of ministers and senior civil servants within departments, who would be responsible for setting policies, managing and allocating resources, establishing objectives and targets and reviewing performance. Working within this framework would be a number of agencies undertaking executive functions which fall within the remit of the department (thus, for example, agencies for which the Ministry of Justice is responsible include Her Majesty's Courts Service, the National Offender Management Service (including Her Majesty's Prison Service) and the Tribunals Service). These would possess significant degrees of independence from departmental control in carrying out operational and administrative tasks, and the respective responsibilities of, and relationship between, the minister and the chief executive would be clearly defined. The latter was to be a publicly visible head of the agency, thus further undermining the principle of anonymity. There are currently 65 executive agencies in England,[126] employing well over half of all civil servants, with similar agencies responding to the devolved regional governments elsewhere in the UK.

It was intended that this restructuring would provide civil servants with a clearer specification of their roles and expected outputs in a manner comparable to organisations operating within the private sector. However, the reform is premised upon a division between 'policy' and 'operations' and consequent responsibility and accountability for each which may be difficult to draw in practice, particularly where an agency is involved in high-profile, politically controversial work as has been the case with agencies such as the Prison Service or the Child Support Agency. As will be discussed in the next section, this has given rise to some significant constitutional problems.

Executive agencies operate within the civil service, and are staffed by civil servants (although chief executives may on occasion be appointed from outside of government). By contrast, **non-departmental public bodies** do not fall within the civil service. However, their importance to modern government should not be underestimated. There are significant numbers of such bodies: in March 2009, there were 766 bodies sponsored by the UK Government (separate bodies exist for each of the devolved administrations), employing over 110,000 people, spending £46.5 billion and covering a hugely diverse range of subject matters, from those which are high-profile (such as the Competition Commission, the Environment

---

[126] See http://webarchive.nationalarchives.gov.uk/+/http://www.cabinetoffice.gov.uk/ministerial_responsibilities/executive_agencies.aspx

Agency and the Independent Police Complaints Commission) to those which are less publicly visible (for example, the Reviewing Committee on the Export of Works of Art and Objects of Cultural Interest and the Northern Lighthouse Board).[127] Broadly, the bodies may be classified into two primary types: executive bodies carrying out administrative and regulatory functions; and advisory bodies, which offer expert advice to government on a range of issues. There are also tribunal bodies, which will be considered in more detail in chapter 6, and independent monitoring boards for prisons.[128]

A non-departmental public body may be defined as a 'body which has a role in the processes of national government, but is not a government department or part of one, and which accordingly operates to a greater or lesser extent at arm's length from ministers'.[129] This definition provides an insight into why such bodies may present constitutional difficulties. The bodies have considerable autonomy from ministerial control – deliberately so, since their tasks are often highly specialised or technical, and excessive political involvement in their work might cast doubt upon the legitimacy of their decisions. But the greater the degree of independence such bodies enjoy, the less democratic control over their work there is. This is especially the case given that those serving on such bodies are appointed by government, not elected. Ministers are required to answer to Parliament for the overall performance of bodies operating within the remit of their departments, but not for their day-to-day activities. Select committees may also review their work, and the bodies are subject to mechanisms explored in chapters 5 and 6 – judicial review, freedom of information and the Parliamentary Ombudsman. Nonetheless, concerns are frequently expressed about the degree to which such bodies are accountable, and politicians frequently make promises to review the system of non-departmental public bodies if they are elected to government.[130]

The institutions of government discussed in this section frequently give rise to particularly awkward questions of accountability. We have come across this central principle of public law on a number of previous occasions in this text. Now, however, we need to explore in greater depth what is meant by the concept of accountable government – and its close relative, responsible government – and the manner in which it is realised in the British constitution. The discussion here will be focused mainly upon

---

[127] See Cabinet Office, *Public Bodies 2009*.

[128] *ibid*, 5.

[129] *id*.

[130] The Coalition Government has announced plans to abolish significant numbers of such bodies in order to achieve savings, to which end it has introduced a Public Bodies Bill to confer powers upon Ministers to abolish, merge or transfer the powers of such bodies: HL Bill 25 (2010–11).

constitutional theory and principle. For the political *mechanisms* through which accountable and responsible government is realised, you should refer to the discussion of parliamentary scrutiny of the executive in chapter 3; while legal mechanisms for securing the accountability of government are examined in more depth in the next chapter.

E. Accountable and responsible government

In chapter 2, we noted that the executive does not have total freedom to act in whichever manner it sees fit, in spite of the absence of a higher-order constitution which might set legal limits to its powers. The constitutional principle of the rule of law operates to ensure that government is not above the law, while the notion of the separation of powers provides that the legislature and the judiciary each possess checks and balances which function to limit the potential for the executive to abuse its powers. Here, we might also consider the even broader notion of democracy, which, at the most fundamental level, expresses the idea of 'rule by the people'.[131] While pragmatic considerations dictate that the people must elect representatives to carry out the government of a state, such representatives may continue to govern only while the people express their consent to this being the case, either by way of occasional elections or – on a less intermittent basis – through mechanisms which enable the actions and decisions of those governing to be scrutinised and explained to the people between such elections.

These considerations point to the centrality of the *accountability* of government within a system of democracy. Accountability may be defined as answering for, explaining or justifying one's actions or decisions, usually to some external body which is independent of the original decision-maker/actor. This can take varying forms, some of which may be pursued concurrently. It may be legal in nature (in which case the focus is upon explaining that the action or decision is in compliance with the law); it may be financial (government is called upon to demonstrate that it has complied with principles of financial probity); it may be administrative (justification of actions or decisions in terms of principles of good administration such as timeliness, fair process, impartiality, availability of appeals *etc*); it may be managerial (exceptionally, an internal form of accountability based upon quality assurance within the organisation and aiming at securing improvement in levels of performance); or it may relate to values such as efficiency (demonstrating that resources have been spent in a

---

[131] See D. Held, *Models of Democracy* (Cambridge: Polity, 3rd ed., 2006), 1–2.

manner which offers 'value for money' to the public). This list is not exhaustive and other typologies of accountability may be developed.[132] Our focus in this section, however, is upon *political* accountability. The word 'political' here may be understood in two senses. First, it expresses the nature of the external body to which the government owes a duty to account – Parliament (as distinct from, say, the courts); and second, it expresses the character of the explanatory obligation placed upon government – that is, to account for the manner in which it has pursued the public good by way of its conduct of national and international affairs and its evolution and implementation of policies. The primary mechanism through which this form of accountability is realised in the British constitution is by way of the doctrine of ministerial responsibility to Parliament.

We are already presented with a difficulty. Is there a difference between 'responsibility' and 'accountability'? The matter is not one of mere semantics. We saw in the preceding section that the establishment of executive agencies in the civil service was founded upon a division between matters which were operational in character and those which were matters of policy. This created significant difficulties in 1995 when the then Home Secretary, Michael Howard, responded to an independent inquiry into prison security in England and Wales which had been established in response to a number of lapses including escapes from high-security institutions, by sacking the Chief Executive of the Prison Service, Derek Lewis.[133] When questioned in the House of Commons, Howard accepted that he had an obligation to *account* to Parliament (that is, to explain the situation and how he proposed to address it), but he did not accept that he was *responsible* for the failures which had been identified by the inquiry, since (on his analysis) those failures were operational matters for which the Chief Executive was responsible, as distinct from policy failures which would be the responsibility of the minister. Consequently, Howard refused to *accept the blame* for what had happened and, with the support of the Prime Minister and backbench government MPs, was able to keep hold of his job.[134]

This episode demonstrates that any distinctions between the concepts of 'responsibility' and 'accountability' can be readily exploited by a tenacious minister in order to limit his/her liability for departmental failures, particularly when they are of an operational character. This places the executive in a strong position *vis-a-vis* Parliament and it is therefore not

---

[132] See *eg* J. Greenwood, R. Pyper and D.Wilson, *New Public Administration in Britain* (Abingdon: Routledge, 3rd ed., 2002), 228–32.

[133] *Review of Prison Service Security in England and Wales and the Escape from Parkhurst Prison*, Cm. 3020 (1995) (the 'Learmont Report').

[134] For his account of the episode, see D. Lewis, *Hidden Agendas* (London: Hamish Hamilton, 1997).

surprising that the latter has taken steps to reassert its authority. The Public Service Select Committee of the House of Commons, in an important report issued in 1996, rejected the distinction, stating that 'it is not possible absolutely to distinguish an area in which a minister is personally responsible, and liable to take blame, from one in which he is constitutionally accountable. Ministerial responsibility is not composed of two elements with a clear break between the two'.[135] Subsequently, the House of Commons passed a resolution setting out its understanding of the meaning of the constitutional principle of ministerial responsibility,[136] which is now repeated in the *Ministerial Code* issued by the Cabinet Office, a document which sets out the duties and responsibilities of ministers. This draws no distinction between 'accountability' and 'responsibility', providing that 'ministers have a duty to account, and to be held to account, for the policies, decisions and actions of their departments and agencies'.[137] In this sense, the Commons resolution and *Ministerial Code* appear to endorse the position adopted by the Public Service Committee, that 'proper and rigorous scrutiny and accountability' is more significant than the capacity of Parliament to enforce a sanction of resignation against a blameworthy minister.[138] However, as Tomkins observes, these developments were nonetheless important in establishing parliamentary 'ownership' of the principle of ministerial responsibility – and thus strengthening the checks and balances available to the legislature – in so far as they establish that government cannot redefine the meaning of the principle to its own advantage.[139]

Let us turn now to explore the meaning of this constitutional principle in more depth, retaining the phraseology 'ministerial responsibility' by which it is most commonly known, while acknowledging that its central component now consists of an obligation upon government to *explain its actions and decisions* to Parliament.

Ministerial responsibility has two facets, which are outlined in the *Ministerial Code*. The first is *collective* responsibility, which 'requires that ministers should be able to express their views frankly in the expectation that they can argue freely in private while maintaining a united front when decisions have been reached ... Decisions reached by the Cabinet or Ministerial Committees are binding on all members of the

---

[135] Public Service Committee, *Ministerial Accountability and Responsibility*, HC 313 (1995–96), [21].

[136] *House of Commons Debates*, 19 March 1997, col. 1046.

[137] Above n.104, [1.2(b)].

[138] Above n.135, xvii.

[139] Above p.15 (n.39), 158–59. Resolutions of the House of Commons may only be amended by a Commons vote to that effect.

Government'.[140] This principle therefore preserves the unity of government in front of Parliament and the public. Viewed from a different perspective, the Prime Minister and other ministers are answerable to Parliament, and by extension to the public, for their overall programme of government. If the government loses the confidence of the House of Commons (as indicated by defeat in a vote of confidence), the Prime Minister will be expected to resign or to seek a dissolution of Parliament, the latter triggering a general election.[141] This is, in fact, a very rare occurrence: while government defeats on other matters are not uncommon, only three governments were defeated on a vote of confidence in the entire course of the twentieth century.[142] On this basis, it might be contended that collective responsibility has dwindled in significance as bonds of party loyalty – which were weaker in the eighteenth and nineteenth centuries – have strengthened, making it possible for all but minority governments to survive a vote of confidence. Certainly, it is true that a combination of the greater coherence of political parties and the increasing workload of modern government (which means that relatively few decisions are actually made on a collective basis) has shifted the emphasis of parliamentary control towards individual ministerial responsibility, which will be considered below.

Nonetheless, it would be a mistake to dismiss this aspect of the principle of ministerial responsibility as largely irrelevant to modern conditions. Most broadly, and to speak in somewhat abstract terms, it expresses the relative positions of legislature and executive in the constitutional hierarchy established after 1688–89. The Crown is inferior to Parliament and the theoretical ability of the latter to dismiss the government is a reflection of this fact. More pragmatically, the obligation upon ministers to present a united front 'enables Parliament to identify exactly what the government's position is on any given issue',[143] thus facilitating the task of scrutiny of government policies. Furthermore, it limits the propensity for individual ministers to 'pass the buck', claiming that an unpopular decision or policy was, in fact, initiated in a different department: again, this facilitates Parliament's work in holding government to account. More troublesome, however, are two other implications of collective responsibility. First, it tends to strengthen prime ministerial power. Since the Prime Minister ultimately determines what the government's policy is on any given matter, s/he can employ the united front which arises from the doctrine of collective responsibility as a way of bolstering her/his position, thereby exercising

---

[140] Above n.104, [2.1], [2.3].
[141] See now the Fixed-Term Parliaments Bill, discussed above pp.132–33.
[142] In January and October 1924 and March 1979.
[143] Tomkins, above p.15 (n.39), 136.

control over other ministers both in the Cabinet and elsewhere.[144] The doctrine thus tends to reinforce the trend towards a 'presidential' rather than collective style of government. Secondly, the doctrine serves to exacerbate the secretive nature of British government, in so far as public and Parliament will be unaware of discussions leading to the formulation of policy, or disagreements which exist between ministers. The *Ministerial Code* underlines this point, providing that 'the privacy of opinions expressed in Cabinet and Ministerial committees, including in correspondence, should be maintained'.[145] This acts as a limitation upon the capacity of Parliament effectively to scrutinise executive policies and decisions, and might be seen as contrary to a general trend towards greater openness in government.[146]

The second dimension of this constitutional principle is the *individual* responsibility of ministers to Parliament. As noted above, the *Ministerial Code* provides that ministers have a duty to account to Parliament, and to be held to account, for the policies, decisions and activities of their departments and agencies. This expresses clearly the key notion that a minister is obliged to answer to Parliament for what takes place in the department in which s/he works, including the executive agencies which fall within the remit of that department. Not surprisingly, this covers decisions, policies or actions personally taken by the minister, but more difficult questions arise in relation to failures at departmental level which cannot be attributed directly to any action on her/his part. It was noted previously that the impartial and anonymous civil servant is 'shielded' by the minister: civil servants are accountable to the minister and the minister is accountable to Parliament (meaning, of course, that the minister accepts praise for departmental work in which s/he may have had little personal involvement, as well as blame for what has gone wrong). The implications of this were fleshed out in a statement to Parliament by the Home Secretary in 1954, following an inquiry into the 'Crichel Down affair', relating to alleged instances of maladministration in the management and sale of agricultural land by government.[147] The minister argued that it was 'quite wrong' to view the principle of individual ministerial responsibility as meaning that 'civil servants cannot be called to account and are effectively responsible to no one'. Instead, he emphasised that the responsibility of the civil servant

---

[144] On a small number of occasions, most notably in relation to the referendum on remaining in the European Community in 1975, collective responsibility has been waived, permitting 'agreements to differ' amongst Cabinet ministers.

[145] Above n.104, [2.1].

[146] For discussion of the role of the Freedom of Information Act 2000 in securing the accountability of the executive, see chapter 6.

[147] See I. Nicolson, *The Mystery of Crichel Down* (Oxford: OUP, 1986). A clear, brief account is offered in Tomkins, above p.15 (n.39), 145–48.

was owed to the minister. This meant that the minister should protect and defend a civil servant who had carried out a ministerial instruction, and one who had acted in accordance with a ministerial policy. It also meant that:

> 'where an official makes a mistake or causes some delay, but not on an important issue of policy and not where a claim to individual rights is seriously involved, the minister acknowledges the mistake and he accepts the responsibility, although he is not personally involved. He states that he will take corrective action in the department ... [and] where action has been taken by a civil servant of which the minister disapproves and has no prior knowledge, and the conduct of the official is reprehensible, then there is no obligation on the part of the minister to endorse what he believes to be wrong, or to defend what are clearly shown to be the errors of his officers ... But, of course, he remains constitutionally responsible to Parliament for the fact that something has gone wrong, and he alone can tell Parliament what has occurred and render an account of his stewardship.'[148]

There are, however, two factors which complicate the apparently straightforward principle that ministers are answerable for everything which takes place in their departments, whether personally implicated or not. First, it is unclear whether any sanction attaches to the obligation of accountability: that is, is a minister expected to resign if serious departmental failures come to light? The belief that this was the case springs largely from the Crichel Down affair itself, in view of the resignation of the then Minister of Agriculture, Sir Thomas Dugdale. However, later investigation has demonstrated both that the minister did have some personal involvement in the matter and that he opposed a change of policy on state ownership of agricultural land, and that this was why he resigned.[149] As Tomkins notes, in the latter respect this was an instance of the operation of collective rather than individual ministerial responsibility.[150] There is little subsequent evidence to support the existence of an obligation of resignation. Although a considerable number of ministers have resigned since 1954, such resignations have, in most cases, related to issues of personal (mis)conduct, rather than departmental failures. The major exception was the resignation of the Foreign Secretary, Lord Carrington, in 1982 following the Argentine invasion of the Falkland Islands, but on other occasions – notably in respect of the inquiry into 'Arms to Iraq' which found that

---

[148] *House of Commons Debates*, 20 July 1954, cols. 1286–7 (Sir David Maxwell-Fyfe).
[149] Nicolson, n.147.
[150] Above p.15 (n.39), 147.

ministers had given misleading information to Parliament on a number of occasions[151] – no resignations ensued.

The second complicating factor has already been touched upon. The principle of answerability for departmental failures is difficult to square with the significant restructuring of the civil service in recent years through the creation of executive agencies. A central feature of such agencies is that they possess a high degree of operational independence from the 'sponsoring' department. Such independence does not sit happily with the traditional model of individual ministerial responsibility which is premised upon a hierarchical model of ministerial control over, and knowledge of what takes place in, the department. We might express this problem as follows. The 'traditional' model of individual ministerial responsibility expresses a vertical series of relationships, with the minister accounting upwards to Parliament for all that goes on 'beneath' her/him, and delegating responsibilities and powers downwards first to senior civil servants and then onwards to those in more junior grades. However, the relationship between agencies and the 'core' department is a more horizontal one, with each having a large degree of autonomy over, respectively, operational and policy matters. In consequence, it is relatively easy for a minister to escape responsibility, as the Prison Service example demonstrates. And if this is true for agencies – which exist within the civil service and accountability for which the *Ministerial Code* indicates *ought* to rest with the minister – then it is even more the case for non-departmental public bodies which are not staffed by civil servants and which operate at even greater distance from ministerial influence.

Problems such as these have led a number of leading commentators to conclude that individual ministerial responsibility is too weak to act as an effective means of control over the executive branch: indeed, it has been described as a 'merely mythic principle of the constitution'.[152] Moreover, this is not a view which is exclusive to academics. In chapters 1 and 2, we noted that the powerful dissent of Lord Mustill in the *Fire Brigades Union* case offers an incisive analysis of a recent shift from a legal to a political constitution. His Lordship noted that the employment of 'Parliamentary remedies' had frequently proved inadequate to secure accountability for the use of executive powers, with the consequence that the courts had had to step in to fill the vacuum.

However, there are others – notably Adam Tomkins – who take a much

---

[151] The 'Scott Report': above p.31 (n.37).

[152] C. Turpin, 'Ministerial Responsibility' in Jowell and Oliver (eds.), above n.11, 111. This chapter was removed from the fourth edition of the book, the editors arguing that 'the doctrine of individual ministerial responsibility has been significantly weakened over the last ten years or so, so that it can no longer be said, in our view, that it is a fundamental doctrine of the constitution': 4th ed., 2000, viii.

more positive view of ministerial responsibility. Emphasising in particular the report of the Public Service Committee in 1996 and the Resolution of the House of Commons in 1997, the author argues that 'it is premature to have written the obituary of ministerial responsibility' and claims that 'the political constitution is alive and well'.[153]

As is often the case, the truth probably lies somewhere between these opposing positions. Parliament does possess mechanisms – the most valuable of which appears to be the select committee system examined in chapter 3 – which at least possess the potential to effectively scrutinise the activities of government and to call individual ministers to account. As Tomkins argues, there is some evidence in recent years of a determination by the House of Commons to take this function more seriously. Moreover, we should not forget the increasing willingness of the House of Lords, which is not dominated by a single political party and which has acquired greater legitimacy as a parliamentary chamber since the removal of most hereditary peers in 1999, to perform a 'constitutional watchdog' role, especially in respect of human rights matters, powers delegated by the legislature to the executive, and laws emanating from the European Union. This work exposes government policies in general to parliamentary scrutiny, albeit that the smaller numbers of ministers sitting in the House of Lords sets limits on the capacity of that institution to enforce *individual* ministerial responsibility.

However, there remain significant obstacles which serve to impede Parliament's ability to hold ministers collectively and individually to account. In addition to the structural factors discussed above, there is disparity in the availability of information: while the *Ministerial Code* provides that 'ministers should be as open as possible with Parliament',[154] they nonetheless retain control over *which* information, and *how much* of it, to disclose when being questioned on a policy or decision. This undoubtedly limits Parliament's capacity to hold ministers to account, especially – though not exclusively – in respect of the exercise of the very indistinct powers which derive from the royal prerogative. But the most prominent impediment to effective ministerial responsibility arises from the partial fusion of executive and legislative branches noted in chapter 2. The Prime Minister and most senior ministers sit in the House of Commons and, by enforcing party loyalty, can exercise a significant degree of control over what takes place in the chamber. This is especially true when the governing party possesses a significant majority of MPs. This is problematic because 'what we mean when we come to say that the government is accountable to Parliament is that the government is accountable to a group of politi-

---

153 Above p.15 (n.39), 134, 169.
154 Above n.104, [1.2(d)].

cians the majority of whom are members of the same political party as that which forms the government'.[155] The consequence is that the strength of parliamentary scrutiny of ministerial actions, policies and decisions, and especially the degree to which sanctions for failure are enforced, tends to be dependent upon a combination of unpredictable variables of a political character such as the support of the Prime Minister and backbench MPs, the reaction of the media, the mood of the wider party in the country and the size of the governing party's majority in the House of Commons. For a public lawyer committed to the separation of powers and the rule of law, this is not an especially satisfactory state of affairs. Accountability of the executive should not be contingent upon random political factors, but should instead be a permanent feature of the relationship between the branches of government, independent of transient considerations of party and personality.

F. Conventions of the constitution

Much of what has been discussed in this chapter does not take the form of 'law', as we normally understand it. The circumstances in which the monarch may personally exercise her prerogative powers, the choice of the person who is to be Prime Minister, the response of the Prime Minister to a defeat in an election or a vote of confidence, the doctrine that ministers must sit in one of the Houses of Parliament (and that the Prime Minister must be a member of the House of Commons) and – still more broadly – the system of Prime Ministerial and Cabinet government and the principles of collective and individual ministerial responsibility (to list but a few) are largely regulated by constitutional convention, rather than by statute or common law.

Various definitions of the term 'convention' are provided in the public law literature.[156] Perhaps the most straightforward is that offered by Tomkins, who states that 'a constitutional convention is a non-legal, but nonetheless binding, rule of constitutional behaviour'.[157] This expresses the notion, traceable to Dicey, that conventions and laws (whether originating in statute or common law) are to be distinguished in so far as the former 'are not enforced by the courts'.[158] We might usefully add to this the idea, derived from the work of Jennings, that there should be a 'reason'

---

[155] Tomkins, above p.15 (n.39), 164.

[156] For analysis, see J. Jaconelli, 'The nature of constitutional convention' (1999) 19 *Legal Studies* 24.

[157] Above p.15 (n.39), 10.

[158] Above p.17 (n.47), 24.

for the existence of the rule.[159] Thus, conventions have a normative quality: there is a justification for obeying them. If we consider the examples
of conventions within the British constitution which were listed above, we
can readily identify fundamental values such as the separation of powers,
the rule of law or democracy which provide the rationale for the existence
of such rules. It is helpful also to refer to the definition offered by Barendt:
'non-legal rules stating the powers and obligations of the branches of
government, in particular the executive, and their relations with each
other',[160] since this places an appropriate emphasis upon the centrality of
conventions as a means of regulating the relationship between Crown and
Parliament, especially the principles of accountability.[161]

If conventions are non-legal in character, then why do public lawyers
care about them? Two answers might be given to this question. First, any
account of the British constitution – or, for that matter, many other constitutions[162] – would be incomplete without an analysis of this source of obligation. As Jennings writes, conventions 'provide the flesh which clothes
the dry bones of the law; they make the legal constitution work'.[163] An
understanding of conventions is especially important given the traditionally *political* character of the British constitution, but even the recent shift
towards legal constitutionalism has not deprived them of their importance. Secondly, while not *legally* binding, conventions are still rules, and
violation of them is a matter of constitutional significance. Lawyers are not
simply concerned with laws: they are also interested in other means by
which binding obligations may be created.[164]

How do conventions come into existence? For Jennings, there were
three decisive factors:[165] the existence of precedents – the 'idea that events
which occurred in the past exert a 'binding' influence on the political

---

[159] Above p.25 (n.12), 136.

[160] Above n.4, 42.

[161] See also G. Marshall, *Constitutional Conventions: the rules and forms of political accountability* (Oxford: Clarendon, 1984), 18: 'the major purpose of the domestic conventions is to give
effect to the principles of governmental accountability that constitute the structure of responsible government'.

[162] See Barendt, n.4, 40–41.

[163] I. Jennings, *Cabinet Government* (Cambridge: CUP, 3rd ed., 1959), 81–82.

[164] Note especially the concept of 'soft law', which can be defined as 'rules of conduct that,
in principle, have no legally binding force but which nevertheless may have practical effects': F.
Snyder, 'Soft law and institutional practice in the European Community' in S. Martin (ed.), *The
Construction of Europe: Essays in Honour of Emile Noel* (Dordrecht: Kluwer, 1994), 197. Although
mainly deployed in the context of international and European law, this concept appears to have
increasing relevance to English public law: see *eg* Jowell and Oliver (eds.), above p.39 (n.75), xiv.
For discussion of soft law in the context of constitutional conventions, see A. McHarg,
'Reforming the United Kingdom Constitution: Law, Convention, Soft Law' (2008) 71 *Modern
Law Review* 853.

[165] Above n.163.

actors of today';[166] whether those affected by the convention consider themselves bound by it; and, as we have seen, whether there is a reason for the existence of the convention. A convention is thus a product of a process of evolution over time, whereby a particular practice or manner of behaving in given circumstances gradually hardens into an obligation to continue behaving in that way. This gives rise to two further issues.

First, can a convention be created merely by declaration – that is, can a convention be *made* rather than *develop*? It has been argued by some commentators that conventions may come into existence by express agreement of those affected,[167] while others argue that a declaration that something is a convention does not make it so: instead, a 'chain of actions' and expectations based on observance is necessary.[168] This is not merely an abstract question. Earlier in this chapter, we noted proposals for the reform of certain prerogative powers. The intention was that two of these – the proposal that Parliament's approval should be obtained prior to a decision to deploy troops and that the Prime Minister should not dissolve Parliament without first seeking its consent (the latter now superseded by the Fixed-Term Parliaments Bill) – would be formalised by way of constitutional convention rather than in statutory form, although in the case of the first, it was intended that the convention thereby created would be translated in due course into a parliamentary resolution. McHarg argues that statements of this nature cannot in themselves create conventions, at least until 'a consistent and reasonably persistent constitutional practice' to this effect has developed.[169] She contends instead that these represent attempts to influence constitutional behaviour, without enacting formal laws which might offer greater constraints upon the executive's freedom of action.

Secondly, it is frequently difficult to determine the point at which a mere practice becomes a convention. To take an example from the issues discussed in this chapter, at what date subsequent to 1708 can it be said that there was now a convention that the monarch should not refuse assent to legislation (except, possibly, in extreme constitutional circumstances)? A short answer might be to say that the practice crystallised into a convention at the point when the monarch regarded her/himself bound by it: but this moment in time, too, is not easy to pinpoint with precision. This is really an aspect of a broader characteristic of conventions which is that their scope and meaning, as well as their existence, is often uncertain. Again, the monarch's personal prerogatives afford a useful illustration of

---

[166] Jaconelli, n.156, 28.
[167] Jennings, n.163, 81; Barendt, n.4, 43–44; Marshall, n.161, 8–9.
[168] Jaconelli, n.163, 39–42.
[169] Above n.164, 861.

this point. There is debate between commentators as to the scope of discretion which the monarch retains in the exercise of these powers, some considering it to be more limited than do others.[170] This reflects uncertainty in the extent and content of the conventions which govern the exercise of such powers. From a rule of law perspective, this is problematic since the rules (though they are not 'rules of *law*') may be said to lack the clarity which is a central dimension of that principle.

It might be supposed from this that conventions are inherently flexible in a way which legal rules are not. This is, indeed, often regarded as being a characteristic of these types of rule. However, this quality may be overstated. The very fact that, to come into existence, a convention requires a consistent pattern of observance on the part of actors affected by it suggests that conventions are not as flexible as is sometimes supposed. This is not to say that conventions cannot change. As noted previously, there have been a number of adaptations in the understanding of what is meant by the conventions of collective and individual ministerial responsibility over the course of time. However, that change is also characterised by a process of evolution rather than the more decisive and immediate alterations which tend to characterise legislation, although perhaps not common law.

It would also be mistaken to assume that conventions are necessarily unwritten rules. It is true that many important conventions, such as those regulating the monarch's use of personal prerogatives, are not expressed in written form (save in the work of commentators upon the British constitution). Others, however, are: the most notable example being the *Ministerial Code* which, as well as other matters, seeks to codify the conventional rules of collective and individual ministerial responsibility. Commitment of conventions to paper serves to enhance their clarity, although there remains considerable scope for interpretation of the precise meaning of the broad statements which the *Code* contains. The same could, however, be said of many statutes.

The chief distinction between conventions and legal rules is, of course, that the former are not *legally* binding. A constitutional convention cannot be enforced by a court. For example, in *Madzimbamuto v Lardner-Burke*, in which the question arose whether the UK Parliament could legislate for the colony of Southern Rhodesia in light of a convention that it would not do so without the consent of the colony's government, the Privy Council ruled that this 'very important convention ... had no legal effect in limiting the legal power of Parliament', Lord Reid observing that 'their Lordships in declaring the law are not concerned with these matters'.[171] However, this is not to say that conventions are ignored altogether by the

---

[170] See above n.29.
[171] Above p.103 (n.130).

courts. They may recognise their existence, even if they cannot adjudicate directly upon disputes arising from them (that is, they are non-justiciable). Thus, in *Attorney-General v Jonathan Cape*, the court took notice of the convention of collective responsibility in assessing whether an injunction should be issued to prevent publication of the diaries of a former Cabinet minister.[172]

If conventions are not enforceable by a court, why do affected political actors obey them? To pose such a question is to touch upon one of the primary issues in legal philosophy: the nature of legal, moral and other forms of obligation. However, to restrict ourselves to the context being examined here, we might postulate two responses. First, while breach of a constitutional convention does not attract any legal sanction, it will produce political consequences. For example, a failure by a monarch to give royal assent to (non-extreme) legislation would not be unlawful, but it would undoubtedly be regarded as unacceptable – and, more strongly, as 'unconstitutional' – in so far as it would violate the accepted rules upon which the British constitution is based. At the very least, it would provoke strong criticism in Parliament and in the media. More seriously, it might trigger a chain of events which could lead to abolition of the monarchy.

Secondly, conventions are obeyed because political actors consider themselves to be bound by them. This observation might appear to be somewhat circular, but it expresses an important truth about the nature of obligation. Not all rules are obeyed simply because there is a threat of legal sanction attached to their non-observance. In his seminal work of legal philosophy, Hart writes of 'social rules', giving as a (slightly dated) example the removal of hats by men in church,[173] a standard of behaviour which people (including those wearing hats) consider should be followed and the non-observance of which will attract criticism (even if such criticism amounts to no more than withering glances from other churchgoers). Conventions may be seen as 'social rules' in a similar manner.[174] They are obeyed because those affected by them are aware that these are the 'rules of the game' and that other political actors will hold them in low regard if those rules are not followed.

---

[172] [1976] QB 752.

[173] Above p.98 (n.109), 9–10. The 'social rule' thesis is not uncontroversial: see especially R. Dworkin, *Taking Rights Seriously* (London: Duckworth, 1978), 49–58.

[174] Jaconelli, n.156, 28–31; see also J. Jaconelli, 'Do conventions bind?' (2005) 64 *Cambridge Law Journal* 149.

G. Conclusion

Having reached the end of this chapter, a reader might be forgiven for feeling a slight sense of unease. Notwithstanding the primacy of Parliament over the Crown which was the consequence of the Civil War and which was given effect in the constitutional settlement of 1688–89, the executive branch remains, in reality, the most powerful branch of government within the British constitution. Indeed, its powers are in many respects greater than was the case prior to 1688 simply because government undertakes such an extensive range of activities within the modern state, notwithstanding a recent tendency to reduce the scope of the public sector and to introduce market principles into the delivery of public services.

The principle of the separation of powers is premised upon the need to avoid the concentration of excessive power in one branch of government. From this perspective, it is important to ensure that checks and balances exist to enable the legislative and judicial branches to keep the executive in check. However, it is questionable whether the 'check' of ministerial responsibility is sufficiently powerful for this purpose and more generally, whether a relationship between Crown and Parliament which rests primarily upon conventions which cannot be legally enforced adequately conforms to notions of constitutionalism. Equally, the prevalence of non-legal rules of uncertain scope in this area, coupled with the lack of clarity inherent in the royal prerogative, serves to cast doubt upon compliance with the rule of law which, as we have seen, operates to ensure that government is carried out under the law.

We might see the increasing importance of legal mechanisms of accountability, particularly judicial review – which will be explored in the next chapter – as being, at least in part, a response to concerns of this type. However, before we move on to a consideration of the constitutional role of the judicial branch, we should recall that there is an alternative reading of the issues summarised in the preceding paragraph. If we adopt a more 'green light' approach to public law, regarding the function of public law as being to facilitate the discharge by government of its duties and responsibilities in the interests of society as a whole, then mechanisms for securing accountability are of less value than a framework which enables the executive to undertake its tasks expeditiously and effectively. The principles and powers described in this chapter, which accord the executive considerable scope for acting in a manner which it judges to be in the best interests of the public, might be said to meet this requirement. Moreover, even if we accept that some means of restraining potential excesses of executive power is necessary, we might prefer to rely upon political forms of accountability, which – being activated by elected representatives sitting in

Parliament – might be regarded as more democratic in character than mechanisms which are operated by unelected judges. If that view is taken, then the emphasis should lie upon reinforcement and reinvigoration of the principles outlined here, rather than relying upon the courts to assume responsibility for the task. As ever in public law, neither of these positions can be described as 'correct' in an absolute sense, but it is important to be fully critically attuned to the various possibilities.

Chapter 5

The judiciary

It is often claimed that the third branch of government, the judiciary, exercises less power within the constitutional order than do either the legislature or the executive. Alexander Hamilton, one of the Founding Fathers of the United States, wrote that:

'Whoever attentively considers the different departments of power must perceive, that, in a government in which they are separated from each other, the judiciary, from the nature of its functions, will always be the least dangerous to the political rights of the Constitution; because it will be least in a capacity to annoy or injure them. The Executive not only dispenses the honours, but holds the sword of the community. The legislature not only commands the purse, but prescribes the rules by which the duties and rights of every citizen are to be regulated. The judiciary, on the contrary, has no influence over either the sword or the purse; no direction either of the strength or of the wealth of the society; and can take no active resolution whatever. It may truly be said to have neither force nor will, but merely judgment; and must ultimately depend upon the aid of the executive arm even for the efficacy of its judgments.'[1]

This view has been endorsed by senior members of the judiciary, both in the US[2] and in the UK.[3]

Yet even a cursory reading of the preceding chapters of this book should indicate that such evaluations are, at best, incomplete accounts of the role which judges in fact play within the modern British constitution. In chapters 1 and 2, we noted Lord Mustill's important dictum in the *Fire Brigades Union* case, in which he outlines the need for the judiciary to act

---

[1] A. Hamilton, *Federalist*, No.78, 'The Judiciary Department' (1788).
[2] See Bickel, above p.24 (n.10).
[3] See J. Steyn, 'The weakest and least dangerous department of government' [1997] *Public Law* 84.

to fill the 'vacuum' created by the inadequacies of legislative checks upon the executive branch. In chapters 2 and 3, we saw how the judges have recently deployed the open-ended principle of the rule of law to such an extent that it challenges the primacy of the doctrine of parliamentary sovereignty, on one account at least amounting to 'the ultimate controlling factor on which our constitution is based'.[4] And in chapter 4, we observed the contemporary evolution of judicial control over the prerogative, which, while not complete, nonetheless ensures a degree of accountability for the exercise by the executive of these wide-ranging and constitutionally significant powers.

These developments, manifestations of the broader shift from a political to a legal constitution which was identified in chapter 1, may be considered by some to be cause for concern. The judiciary is unelected and therefore not democratically accountable, although the fact that hearings take place in open court, where decisions (and reasons for them) are also provided, does facilitate a degree of public scrutiny.[5] Furthermore, judges appear unrepresentative of British society as a whole, as a consequence of which their political beliefs may differ significantly from the majority of the electors, or from those in government or Parliament. Such factors might not matter if the judiciary could somehow be detached from politics – and, indeed, as will be seen, constitutional conventions exist which seek to preserve the neutrality of judges by isolating them from *party* politics. But, as noted in chapter 1, the interpenetration of public law and politics in a broader sense is such that it is unrealistic to conceive of the judiciary being somehow 'above' politics, especially in light of recent constitutional developments such as the rise of judicial review and the enactment of the Human Rights Act 1998, which have had the effect of propelling decision-making which might formerly have been political in character into the courtroom.[6] In such circumstances, the democratic credentials of the judiciary are likely, on occasion, to be called into question.

This chapter will offer a discussion of three functions performed by the judiciary which have a significant constitutional impact: judicial review of administrative action, statutory interpretation, and adjudication under the Human Rights Act 1998. The objective is not to provide an exhaustive account of the extensive law in these three fields, but rather to explore the role played by the judiciary within the modern British constitutional order, and the problems created by the exercise of this role. However, as a precursor to this analysis, it is necessary first to consider the extent to which

---

[4] *Jackson*, above p.11 (n.26), [107] (Lord Hope).
[5] Steyn, n.3, 84.
[6] See Nicol, above p.16 (n.46)

constitutional rules serve to protect the independence of the judiciary, regarded as a fundamental component of the rule of law.[7]

A. Judicial independence

Protection of the principle of judicial independence within the British constitution is afforded by way of a mixture of statutory provisions and conventions relating to the judiciary. The principle itself was not, however, given statutory expression until 2005, when (as noted in chapter 2) the Constitutional Reform Act imposed a duty upon the Lord Chancellor, ministers and others involved in the administration of justice to uphold the continued independence of the judiciary.[8] This raises the theoretical prospect of the Lord Chancellor or others being held to account by a court for failure to discharge this obligation, although the very open-ended nature of the duty might lead such a court to the conclusion that the primary mode of enforcement should remain political, for example through mechanisms of ministerial responsibility, rather than legal. A more specific obligation is imposed by section 3(5) upon the Lord Chancellor and other ministers not to seek to influence particular judicial decisions through special access to the judiciary, although it will be noted that this stops short of protecting the judges from all forms of political criticism which might also serve to undermine their independence. The value of the statutory protection afforded by these provisions is therefore a matter of some debate. Woodhouse has observed that their 'vagueness', while understandable in light of the fluidity of meaning of judicial independence beyond certain core components, means that they are of 'little practical use'.[9] By contrast, Lord Woolf, speaking in parliamentary debate during the passage of the Bill, took a much more optimistic view of the Act's potential to underpin judicial independence:

'The future independence of the judiciary will be safer than it has ever been. That independence will no longer be dependent on the hope that there will be in the future, as there has been in the past, a benevolent Lord Chancellor or Prime Minister who is prepared to mount his steed and ride to the rescue of the judiciary.'[10]

---

[7] See *eg* Raz, above p.42 (n.89), pp.200–01; Bingham, above p.56 (n.145) (2007), 80; (2010), Chapter 9.

[8] s.3(1).

[9] D. Woodhouse, 'The Constitutional Reform Act 2005 – defending judicial independence the English way' (2007) 5 *International Journal of Constitutional Law* 153, 164.

[10] *House of Lords Debates*, 7 December 2004, col. 758.

In chapter 2 it was also noted that the previous system of judicial appointment, in which the Lord Chancellor played the decisive role in making recommendations, had been overhauled by the 2005 Act, which establishes an independent Judicial Appointments Commission. While appointments are still formally made by the monarch or by the Lord Chancellor (the latter in the case of lay magistrates and certain other junior appointments) and in that respect may be regarded as a function of the executive, the scope for departure from the recommendations of the Commission is extremely limited. In particular, the Lord Chancellor (to whom the Commission will submit the name of one preferred candidate) cannot put forward an alternative, although he can reject a nomination or refer it back for reconsideration by the Commission on one occasion only. Although these reforms were considered to amount to 'a significant improvement' upon the previous position, minimising the possibility of patronage and the risk of damage to judicial independence,[11] the government of Gordon Brown nonetheless consulted on the possibility of further reducing the executive's role in appointment, including removal of any role for the Prime Minister in recommending appointment of Supreme Court justices to the monarch,[12] and upon involvement of Parliament in the appointment process. However, no such further reform has yet reached the statute book.

The Appointments Commission is obliged to 'have regard to the need to encourage diversity in the range of persons available for selection for appointments'.[13] Diversity in membership of the judicial branch is valuable for a number of reasons. While the main criterion for appointment remains merit,[14] drawing judges from a relatively narrow pool of candidates may have the consequence that highly able individuals are ignored. Furthermore, public confidence in the judiciary may be weakened if there is a perception that the judge will favour or disfavour a particular sector of society, such as an ethnic minority or social class, in cases which come before him or her:

> 'Society must have confidence that the judiciary has a real understanding of the problems facing people from all sectors of society with whom they come into contact. However, if the make-up of the judiciary as a whole is not reflective of the diversity of the nation, people may ques-

---

[11] *The Governance of Britain: Judicial Appointments*, Cm 7210 (2007), [4.10].

[12] *ibid*. In practice, the Prime Minister is required to nominate the person recommended to him by the Lord Chancellor following the convening of an *ad hoc* Supreme Court Selection Commission: Constitutional Reform Act 2005, s.26(3).

[13] Constitutional Reform Act 2005, s.64(1).

[14] Constitutional Reform Act 2005, s.63. For critical discussion of the principle, see K. Malleson, 'Rethinking the Merit Principle in Judicial Selection' (2006) *Journal of Law and Society* 126.

tion whether judges are able fully to appreciate the circumstances in which people of different backgrounds find themselves.'[15]

While such concerns are, perhaps, especially pertinent as regards criminal trials, a lack of judicial diversity may also be problematic in the public law context. Here, the key issue is likely to be the social class and educational background of the judges[16] – which may lead them to adopt a particular political perspective – rather than gender or ethnicity, which have tended to be the factors upon which attempts to enhance the diversity of the judiciary have primarily focused to date.

The difficulties may be illustrated by the startling 1925 case of *Roberts v Hopwood*, in which a local authority which paid equal minimum wages to male and female council workers was held to have acted unlawfully, on the basis that it had failed to give proper effect to the duty which it owed to the local ratepayers whose taxes funded the payments. The judgment – especially Lord Atkinson's dictum that the councillors had 'allowed themselves to be guided in preference by some eccentric principles of socialistic philanthropy, or by a feminist ambition to secure the equality of the sexes in the matter of wages in the world of labour'[17] – has been seen as politically motivated, rather than an instance of the application of objective legal principle.[18] If that analysis is accepted, it is not difficult to reach the conclusion that the social and educational background of the judges was a key factor in inclining them to adopt a particular ideological perspective which, in turn, shaped the decision. The danger, therefore, is that public law adjudication – whether through judicial review or, more recently, under the Human Rights Act 1998 – functions not only as a legitimate control mechanism *vis-a-vis* an over-mighty executive branch but also as a political tool whereby unelected judges who are unrepresentative of society as a whole can further their socially-determined political preferences: favouring the executive when its actions and decisions correspond with their views, and ruling against it when they do not.[19] This is a key reason

---

[15] Department for Constitutional Affairs, *Increasing Diversity in the Judiciary*, CP 25/04 (2004), [1.2].

[16] See P. Darbyshire, 'Where do English and Welsh Judges come from?' (2007) 66 *Cambridge Law Journal* 365.

[17] [1925] AC 578, 594.

[18] See P. Fennel, '*Roberts v Hopwood:* The Rule against Socialism' (1986) 13 *Journal of Law and Society* 401.

[19] For an illustration of this, see Sedley, above p.12 (n.30), 280, arguing that the rather passive attitude of the judiciary towards the executive in the period between the two World Wars can be explained by the fact that 'all the upper echelons of the civil service were populated by men, a remarkable proportion of them with firsts and double firsts, who had shared their schools, universities and clubs with the barristers who became the judiciary of the interwar years. With such a background, a new sense of mutual confidence shared by judiciary and executive was not surprising'.

why scholars who have adopted a functional approach to public law, and who favour a 'green light' perspective upon the role of state, tend to distrust the judiciary and to prefer political forms of accountability.[20] In the view of such analysts, the judiciary will generally tend to favour individual freedom against state intervention, which may be regarded as especially problematic because the executive is democratically accountable in a way which the judiciary is not.

Efforts to introduce greater diversity into the judicial branch have not yet been wholly successful. In 2008, the then Lord Chancellor, Jack Straw, admitted that expectations that the new system of judicial appointments would result in a more diverse judiciary had not been fulfilled. Subsequently, an Advisory Panel on Judicial Diversity was established. The Panel produced a series of recommendations in February 2010.[21] It rejected the idea of implementing diversity quotas or specific targets for judicial appointments, emphasising instead the need to encourage diversity from the time in a legal career when an individual might first consider becoming a judge, as distinct from focusing solely upon the appointments process. As the Panel acknowledged in stating that there was 'no quick fix to moving towards a more diverse judiciary',[22] such change would be unlikely to occur rapidly.

While addressing any judicial predispositions which may result from educational and social background has proved a tricky constitutional problem, there are a series of somewhat clearer legal rules and conventions which govern more overt manifestations of political preference. Hence, as noted in chapter 2, senior judges are disqualified from membership of the House of Commons, while the establishment of the Supreme Court by the Constitutional Reform Act 2005 has effected a greater degree of separation between the judiciary and the upper House. Judges are also expected to avoid partisan political controversy and party political activity is accordingly regarded as unacceptable. Previous restrictions upon judicial appearances in the media have been relaxed, although, as Brazier notes, judges are still 'expected to be careful not to say anything extra-judicially which might damage their authority as judges or prejudice the performance of their judicial work'.[23]

Nevertheless, judges have frequently expressed strong views as to government policy. A notable instance of this occurred in 2004, when government sought to implement severe restrictions on the availability of

---

[20] See especially Griffith, above p.13 (n.31); and *The Politics of the Judiciary* (London: Fontana, 5th ed., 1997).

[21] *The Report of the Advisory Panel on Judicial Diversity 2010.*

[22] *ibid*, 4.

[23] Brazier, above p.153 (n.110), 177.

judicial review in asylum and immigration cases. The proposal generated widespread judicial criticism, including a claim that it was 'fundamentally in conflict with the rule of law and should not be contemplated by any government if it had respect for the rule of law',[24] and it was eventually dropped. Correspondingly, while rules of parliamentary practice preclude members of Parliament from commenting directly upon a judge's character or motives, ministers have often been highly critical of judges in general or of particular judicial decisions. Again, the asylum and immigration context provides a useful illustration. In 2003, the then Home Secretary, David Blunkett, responded to an Administrative Court decision[25] by arguing that 'if public policy can always be overridden by individual challenge through the courts, then democracy itself is under threat', and claimed that it was 'time for judges to learn their place'.[26] These exchanges suggest that the relationship between the executive and the judiciary has come under some strain in recent years,[27] a state of affairs which is reflective of the more assertive constitutional role which the judiciary has assumed. While such tension is not necessarily problematic and, indeed, is arguably inevitable given the checking and balancing function performed by the judiciary over the executive branch,[28] it is clearly important for both the rule of law and the separation of powers that critical reactions to judicial decisions do not constitute a form of political pressure upon judges to reach a particular conclusion in future cases. To this end, it has been recommended that explicit guidelines should be inserted in the *Ministerial Code* governing public comment by ministers on individual judges.[29] However, such a step has not yet been taken.

Judicial independence is secured by a number of other means. As noted in chapter 2, the senior judiciary enjoys a substantial degree of security of tenure and salaries are not subject to review by the legislature. Judges are also immune from legal proceedings in respect of anything said or done in the exercise of judicial functions.[30] They are also obliged, both at common

---

[21] Lord Woolf, 'The Rule of Law and a Change in the Constitution' (2004) 63 *Cambridge Law Journal* 317, 328; and see, for further discussion, R. Rawlings, 'Review, Revenge and Retreat' (2005) 68 *Modern Law Review* 378.

[25] *R (on the application of Q) v Secretary of State for the Home Department* [2003] EWHC (Admin) 195.

[26] Cited in A. Bradley, 'Judicial independence under attack' [2003] *Public Law* 397, 402.

[27] For discussion, see Constitution Committee, *Relations between the Executive, the Judiciary and Parliament*, HL 151 (2006–07), [34]–[53].

[28] See Bingham, above p.56 (n.145) (2007), 79: 'there is an inevitable, and in my view entirely proper, tension between the [executive and the judiciary]. There are countries in the world where all judicial decisions find favour with the government, but they are not places where one would wish to live.'

[29] Constitution Committee, n.27, [51].

[30] *Sirros v Moore* [1975] QB 118.

law and under Article 6 of the European Convention on Human Rights (as given effect by the Human Rights Act 1998) to be impartial as between the parties to legal proceedings: of course, in public law cases one such party will, in practice, be an organ of government (although not necessarily a central government body). Judicial impartiality is considered further below.

This area of the constitution therefore offers an instructive illustration of the manner in which a variety of conventions, statutory provisions and case law interact to give effect to a fundamental value in the absence of a codified constitutional document. However, it is also demonstrative of the recent trend towards formalising these disparate sources in written form and rendering them (at least in principle) enforceable through the courts. The 'formalisation' of key aspects of judicial independence through the Constitutional Reform Act 2005 may have come about, as suggested in chapter 2, as a consequence of a mixture of pragmatic concerns (in particular, possible violation of Article 6 of the European Convention on Human Rights) and principled constitutional thinking, but its longer-term impact is likely to be to render the delineation between the judiciary and the other branches of government more clear-cut and less susceptible to future erosion, as Lord Woolf has suggested.[31] In view of the increasingly active and often politically contentious role which it has played in recent years, the degree of insulation from governmental pressure which the 2005 Act provides is imperative if the judiciary is to continue to fulfil its function as a counterbalance to executive power.

B. Judicial review of administrative action

The judicial review jurisdiction represents the primary means through which the judicial branch may exercise scrutiny of the actions and decisions of the executive branch within the British constitutional order. In this sense, 'judicial review' has a more limited meaning than in countries, such as the US, where a court may be empowered to strike down legislation which violates constitutional provisions. As we saw in chapter 3, English courts do not, in general, possess a power to invalidate primary legislation because of the doctrine of parliamentary sovereignty, except in the context of legislation which conflicts with European Union law. It is

---

[31] Above n.10. See also Constitution Committee, n.27, Appendix 3 (K. Malleson): 'The provisions of the Constitutional Reform Act have an important role to play in establishing clearer boundaries between the branches of government and taking the negotiations, tensions and conflicts between them from the private corridors of power into the public arena'.

also possible for the executive branch to utilise its control over the legislature to secure the passage of legislation which has the effect of reversing the impact of a legal judgment, with the consequence that the courts are bound to give effect to that legislation.[32] Indeed, it would be theoretically possible for Parliament, prompted by the executive, to legislate to abolish the judicial review jurisdiction altogether, although (as was also noted in chapter 3) a number of judges have recently expressed doubt as to whether they would honour the principle of parliamentary sovereignty in this, admittedly extreme, scenario.[33]

It is important also to note at the outset that judicial review is not an *appeal* process. Appeals may be distinguished from judicial review in so far as the former exist only if there is specific provision for them, usually in the form of statutory provision. By contrast, judicial review is an inherent supervisory jurisdiction residing in the superior courts to restrain excess of power, which even relatively clear statutory words may be insufficient to displace.[34] Furthermore, when a decision reached by an administrative body (or, for that matter, a judicial body such as a court) is appealed, the claim is being made that the decision was wrong: that is, the claimant is concerned with the *merits or demerits* of the original decision. When a decision is judicially reviewed, the claim is that the original decision, although it may have been correct, was somehow *unlawful*. The focus is not upon the outcome, but upon the process by which decisions are made and the powers which the body has purported to exercise. In consequence, courts in judicial review cases are not empowered to substitute their view of what is the 'correct' outcome for that of the original decision-maker, as is normally possible on appeal. Rather, the court generally remits (sends back) the decision to the decision-maker, with its judgment forming an explanation of the manner in which the first decision was unlawful. It is therefore quite possible for the decision-maker to reach the same conclusion again (that is, to decide the same way as to the merits and demerits), provided that it does so in accordance with the standards of lawfulness set out by the court.

All of this might suggest that judicial review is, at most, an inconvenience for an executive branch which ultimately occupies the dominant position in the British constitution. Indeed, it has famously been described in a leading account as 'sporadic and peripheral'.[35] Such an assessment

---

[32] See above p.30 (n.32).

[33] See above pp.118–120 (n.197, 199).

[34] See especially *Anisminic Ltd v Foreign Compensation Commission* [1969] 2 AC 147, discussed further below, pp.195, 207.

[35] S. de Smith, *Judicial Review of Administrative Action* (London: Stevens & Sons, 4th ed., 1980), 3. In the most recent edition of this text, the authors acknowledge that 'caution is now needed before relegating judicial review to a minor role in the control of official power' (London: Sweet & Maxwell, 5th ed., 1995), [1-033].

points to the difficulty in assessing the degree to which judicial review has an impact upon administrative decision-making, especially in disassociating it from other factors which may have a bearing.[36] But, while it is difficult to quantify the precise effect of judicial review, to regard it as being of peripheral significance is misleading for a number of reasons.

First, we should recall that 'the executive' is not simply comprised of Cabinet and Prime Minister, nor even of central government departments, but instead encompasses a huge number of public bodies which exercise functions of an administrative nature. The range of actions and decisions which might, therefore, give rise to a judicial review claim (and, correspondingly, the variety of defendants to such a claim) is very broad indeed, and administrative officials at every level, not just those in central government, must accordingly be conscious of the need to act within the law. Secondly, judicial review cases frequently provoke media comment and this form of scrutiny serves as an additional source of pressure upon a public body to reverse its decision or act in a particular way.[37] For this reason, judicial review is a useful means by which groups and others may pursue a political campaign against government policies or decisions, especially because (as will subsequently be discussed) the rules as to who may bring a claim in judicial review are relatively liberal. Thirdly, the grounds upon which courts base determinations of whether an executive action or decision is unlawful are very open-ended and in an ongoing state of evolution: as Lord Donaldson MR has observed, 'judicial review is a jurisdiction which has been developed and is still being developed by the judges.'[38] This characteristic affords judges considerable discretion, both as regards whether and how to apply the ground to the facts of the case and also as to the intensity of review which is exercised,[39] the consequence being that administrative officials need to exhibit considerable care in decision-making in order to avoid falling foul of the courts. Fourthly, the number of judicial review cases has grown significantly over the past few decades. In 1974, 160 claims were filed, whereas in 2008 the figure was 7,169.[40] Statistically, therefore, the likelihood that a public body will encounter

---

[36] See *eg* G. Richardson, 'Impact Studies in the United Kingdom' in M. Hertogh and S. Halliday (eds.), *Judicial Review and Bureaucratic Impact: International and Interdisciplinary Perspectives* (Cambridge: CUP, 2004).

[37] For discussion, see C. Harlow and R. Rawlings, *Pressure through Law* (Abingdon: Routledge, 1992), especially Chapter 5.

[38] *R v Secretary of State for the Home Department, ex parte Brind* [1991] 1 AC 696, 722.

[39] Thus certain types of decision, such as those involving 'high policy' or allocation of scarce resources, will be subject to a lower level of judicial scrutiny as to their lawfulness than others, for example those which impact upon individual rights. For further discussion, see below pp.232–234.

[40] Ministry of Justice, *Judicial and Court Statistics 2008*, Cm 7697 (2009),16.

judicial review has significantly increased,[41] especially when we consider that these figures do not include instances in which a lawyer 'threatens' the body with judicial review but stops short of filing a claim (perhaps because the body revisits the decision or action in question in response to the threat). Finally, we should note that the 'raw' figures on the incidence of judicial review do not tell the full story of its impact. The judgment of a court will have a 'ripple' effect upon other public bodies which are not parties to the case, in so far as these bodies will be prompted to alter their administrative practices or decision-making procedures in order to comply with the law as articulated by the court and thus avoid being subjected to judicial review themselves in the future.

It would be impractical, in a book of this length, to attempt to offer a full account of the law relating to judicial review of administrative action. Specialist texts on administrative law[42] – of which judicial review is a major component – can offer such discussion. However, a knowledge both of the procedure by which claims are brought and of the grounds upon which courts determine cases is imperative if we are to comprehend the role played by judicial review in the modern British constitutional order and, more broadly, the meaning and function of public law.

Judicial review procedure and remedies

The rules of procedure which govern how a legal claim may be brought to court are frequently of a somewhat technical nature and are usually studied in more depth in the 'professional' stage of legal training, rather than on academic courses at university. However, judicial review affords an exception to this general position for the reason that an understanding of the procedure casts light on a key question posed at the beginning of this book: what is public law for?

In chapter 2, we noted Dicey's opposition to the existence of a specialised system of administrative law along the lines of the model used in France, on the basis that such a system would, in his view, be likely to favour the state over the individual. Prior to 1977, the influence of Dicey's distaste could be detected in the absence of a coherent, unified procedure

---

[41] It should, however, be noted that the percentage of cases which proceed to a full hearing has declined over the same period: see V. Bondy and M. Sunkin, *The Dynamics of Judicial Review Litigation: the Resolution of Public Law before final hearing* (Margate: Public Law Project, 2009), 2–3. For further discussion, see below, p.187. Note also that the number of cases heard by tribunals annually significantly exceeds judicial review cases. Tribunals are discussed further below, chapter 6.

[42] See *eg* P. Craig, *Administrative Law* (London: Sweet & Maxwell 6th ed., 2008); P. Cane, *Administrative Law* (Oxford: OUP, 4th ed., 2004); T. Endicott, *Administrative Law* (Oxford: OUP, 2009).

for judicial review: rather, different rules applied depending upon the remedy which was being sought. The process was substantially simplified in that year, and is now governed by section 31 of the Senior Courts Act 1981 and Part 54 of the Civil Procedure Rules 1998. This provides a single 'umbrella' procedure through which all of the remedies described later in this section may be obtained. Key elements of this process differ from procedural requirements in private law cases and claims are made to a specialist section of the High Court (the Administrative Court), while the grounds of review (described in the following section) are specific to public law. This would suggest that, contrary to Dicey's prescription, English law *does* now distinguish between claims in administrative law and other types of legal claim. Furthermore, in so doing, the law recognises that protection of individual autonomy against the state, which underpinned Dicey's version of the rule of law, is not necessarily the overriding objective in this field. In order to understand this, we need to explore aspects of the judicial review procedure in more depth.

First, the law imposes restrictions upon *who may bring a claim in judicial review*, that is, there is a test of *standing* (sometimes labelled with the Latin phrase *locus standi*). The claimant must demonstrate that they have a 'sufficient interest in the matter to which the application relates'.[43] The existence of such a restriction indicates that not everyone will be able to bring a judicial review claim. Of course, not everyone is entitled to bring a claim in private law proceedings either, but the distinction here lies in the fact that in private law, the cause of action itself serves to define who can bring the case. For example, in the tort of negligence, an individual must demonstrate that a duty of care is owed to them: thus, if there is no such duty, then there can be no liability. By contrast, in judicial review, the test of 'sufficient interest' is, in principle, independent of the question of whether there has been unlawful action. A decision-maker might (to take one example) have exceeded the powers allocated to it by Parliament, but if the court takes the view that the person(s) bringing the claim do not have 'sufficient interest' in the manner in which those powers are exercised, the claim will fail.

In practice, judicial interpretation of the meaning of 'sufficient interest' (which is not further defined in statute) is not as clear-cut as this discussion would suggest. In the leading case of *IRC v National Federation of Self-Employed and Small Businesses Ltd*,[44] the House of Lords suggested that assessment of whether a 'sufficient interest' existed required the court to consider the substance of the case. To an extent, therefore, the question of

---

[43] Senior Courts Act 1981, s.31(3).
[44] [1982] AC 617.

standing is fused with the merits of the claim: the stronger the argument that there has been unlawful action, the more likely it is that the court will consider the 'sufficient interest' test to have been made out, irrespective of the identity of the claimant.[45] This has had the consequence that a relatively generous approach to access has been taken by the courts, with a broad range of individuals and pressure groups being granted standing and only a very limited class of 'busybodies' being excluded, whose motivation, in essence, is merely to create trouble for the public body in question in situations where no serious unlawfulness has occurred.[46]

Secondly, and again in contrast to private law proceedings, judicial review contains a 'filter' mechanism in the form of an obligation to obtain permission from a judge to bring a claim, normally in the absence of an oral hearing. Only if such permission is granted will the case proceed to a hearing at which the court will determine whether one or more of the grounds described in the next section has been made out on the facts of the case. The claimant must demonstrate 'an arguable ground for judicial review having a realistic prospect of success ... it is not enough that a case is potentially arguable'.[47] Figures demonstrate that only 22 per cent of applications for permission which were considered by the courts in 2006 were granted.[48]

Thirdly, there is a time limit for the bringing of a judicial review claim. Claims must be made promptly and in any event within three months of the date on which the grounds for the application arose.[49] The court may extend this period, but equally it may determine that an application brought within the three-month period is not 'prompt' and may refuse permission or may refuse the remedy sought on the ground that there has been 'undue delay'.[50] This deadline appears strict when contrasted with the normal limitation period of six years in private law proceedings, or three for personal injury actions.

Fourthly, since the function of judicial review is to consider the lawfulness of a decision, rather than to revisit the merits, disputes of fact tend to be of less relevance than legal arguments. Partly for this reason, the disclosure of documents held by the parties is less important in judicial review cases than in other proceedings, and is not required unless the court orders otherwise.[51] However, while disclosure of documents is likely to remain

---

[45] For discussion, see P. Cane, 'Standing, Legality and the Limits of Public Law' [1981] *Public Law* 332.

[46] See *eg R v Somerset County Council, ex parte Dixon* [1998] Env LR 111, 121.

[47] *Sharma v Brown-Antoine* [2007] 1 WLR 780, [14] (Lord Bingham and Lord Walker).

[48] Bondy and Sunkin, n.41, Table 4.1.

[49] *Civil Procedure Rules*, Rule 54.5(1).

[50] Senior Courts Act, s.31(6).

[51] *Civil Procedure Rules*, Practice Direction 54A, Rule 54.16.

exceptional, courts will approach the matter flexibly and will 'judge the need for disclosure in accordance with the requirements of the particular case, taking into account the facts and circumstances'.[52]

Finally, the remedies which a court may grant in judicial review are discretionary in nature. There are two categories of remedy: the 'prerogative' orders (so called because they are associated with the right of the Crown to ensure that justice is done), which are exclusive to public law, and remedies which are also available in private law proceedings. The former comprise the quashing order, which deprives a decision of its legal effect; the prohibiting order, which prevents a body from doing something which would be unlawful; and the mandatory order, which compels a body to act. The latter comprise injunctions, which restrain someone from doing something unlawful; declarations, which state the legal rights of the parties; and (in conjunction with a claim for one of the other remedies) damages. It is important to note that, unlike the other remedies, damages are not available merely because a public body has acted unlawfully, but only when there has also been a private law 'wrong' such as commission of the torts of negligence or breach of statutory duty, or where there has been a failure to give effect to a directive in European Union law.[53]

The discretionary character of the remedies means that a claimant may succeed in demonstrating that the public body has acted in an unlawful manner, but the court may still refuse to grant the relief which is being sought. Such refusal may be justified on a number of bases, including prejudicial delay in bringing the case, the conduct and motives of the claimant (for example, suppression or misrepresentation of material facts), absence of any practical effect, or absence of any substantial hardship to the claimant.[54] A distinction may again be drawn here with private law proceedings in which compensation is sought where, if the court holds that a legal wrong has been committed, then damages are awarded as of right (although the amount awarded may be nominal). It should be noted, however, that *equitable* remedies in private law proceedings, such as specific enforcement of a contract, are also of a discretionary character.

Additionally, it is important to note the general principle that judicial review is regarded as a remedy of last resort. The consequence of this is that a court may refuse to award the relief sought (or to grant permission to proceed) if it considers that the claimant has not exhausted all alternative processes for resolution of the dispute (such as an internal complaints process) which are at least equally appropriate as judicial review.

---

[52] *Tweed v Parades Commission for Northern Ireland* [2006] UKHL 53, [32] (Lord Carswell).

[53] *Francovich and Bonifaci v Italy*, (C-6,9/90) [1991] ECR I-5357. Damages are also available under the Human Rights Act 1998, for which see further below.

[54] For discussion, see T. Bingham, 'Should public law remedies be discretionary?' [1991] *Public Law* 64.

There are, therefore, a number of significant differences between procedural aspects of judicial review and proceedings in private law, for example claims in tort or contract. This underlines the point made previously, that notwithstanding Dicey's model of the rule of law, English law now treats public law matters differently from private law questions. But what is the rationale for doing so?

In order to answer this question, it is helpful to turn to two judgments issued by Lord Diplock in the early years of the newly-reformed procedure for application for judicial review. In the *National Federation for Self-Employed* case, his Lordship said of the requirement to obtain permission that:

> 'its purpose is to prevent the time of the court being wasted by busybodies with misguided or trivial complaints of administrative error, and to remove the uncertainty in which public officers and authorities might be left as to whether they could safely proceed with administrative action while proceedings for judicial review of it were actually pending even though misconceived.'[55]

Subsequently, in *O'Reilly v Mackman*, he provided a more comprehensive analysis of the rationale for different procedural rules in judicial review cases brought under Order 53 of the Rules of the Supreme Court (the predecessor of Part 54 of the Civil Procedure Rules):

> 'The public interest in good administration requires that public authorities and third parties should not be kept in suspense as to the legal validity of a decision the authority has reached in purported exercise of decision-making powers for any longer period than is absolutely necessary in fairness to the person affected by the decision ... [the] public policy that underlies the grant of those protections [is] the need, in the interests of good administration and of third parties who may be indirectly affected by the decision, for speedy certainty as to whether it has the effect of a decision that is valid in public law ... it would in my view as a general rule be contrary to public policy, and as such an abuse of the process of the court, to permit a person seeking to establish that a decision of a public authority infringed rights to which he was entitled to protection under public law to proceed by way of an ordinary action and by this means to evade the provisions of Order 53 for the protection of such authorities.'[56]

---

55 Above n.44, 642–43.
56 [1983] 2 AC 237, 280–81, 284.

These dicta indicate that the judicial review procedure is designed to afford a degree of protection to public bodies which might be confronted with a judicial review challenge. Such protection is justified because there is a 'public interest in good administration', especially in timely and certain decision-making upon which public bodies and third parties may rely. To put matters somewhat differently, and to adopt a metaphor used in chapter 1,[57] a 'red light' reading of the function of judicial review, in which the role of the court is simply to protect individual autonomy from encroachment by controlling the activities of the state, is incomplete. Although the individual is not overlooked – note that Lord Diplock refers to Order 53 in *O'Reilly* as a 'procedure by which every type of remedy for *infringement of the rights of individuals* that are entitled to protection in public law'[58] – the need to protect his or her interests is balanced against a broader public interest in good administrative decision-making. On such analysis, governmental actions and decisions should not necessarily be viewed negatively, since government seeks to act for the good of the population as a whole. The protections for public bodies which are contained in the judicial review procedure thus function to give effect to a more 'green light' perspective on the role of law *vis-a-vis* the state. In principle, they operate to reduce the frequency of judicial review, enabling bodies to discharge their public functions relatively free from the prospect of having to divert scarce time and resources to litigation and in the knowledge that their decisions can be acted upon after the lapse of a relatively short period of time. This is beneficial not only to such bodies, but also to the broader public in whose interests those bodies act.

However, while the protections inherent in the judicial review process may be viewed as legitimately limiting litigation in the public interest, the courts are not wholly denied a role (though certain of the 'green light' theorists would prefer to minimise the role of the courts as far as possible, especially in view of the undemocratic and unrepresentative nature of the judiciary, as previously discussed). In addition to giving effect to a continued concern for the position of the individual, the courts can facilitate good administrative practice by articulating standards of decision-making in their judgments, especially in respect of procedural fairness (discussed in the next section). These standards will assist both the body in question when it reconsiders the original decision, as well as other public bodies tasked with making comparable choices in the future. The public will also gain from fairer, speedier, more open and certain administrative decision-making by bodies which do not misuse the powers allotted to them.

---

[57] Above pp.5–6.
[58] Emphasis added.

Contrary to Dicey, therefore, public law can and should be distinguished from private law, because it serves a different purpose:

'I regard public law as being the system which enforces the proper performance by public bodies of the duties which they owe to the public. I regard private law as being the system which protects the private rights of private individuals or the private rights of public bodies. The critical distinction arises out of the fact that it is the public as a whole, or in the case of local government the public in the locality, who are the beneficiaries of what is protected by public law and it is the individuals or bodies entitled to the rights who are the beneficiaries of the protection provided by private law ... In considering whether these features of the application for judicial review, which ... restrict access to the courts, are justified, it is essential to bear in mind that the application is designed to enforce public law duties and that, therefore, it is not only the interests of the parties to the application who have to be considered. The position of the public in general must be taken into account, since ... public law is designed to protect the public as a whole as well as any individual applicant. The public has a very real interest in seeing that litigation does not necessarily and unduly interfere with the process of government both at a national and local level.'[59]

We might be a little wary of drawing the conclusion that the 'public interest in good administration' is the only rationale for the existence of the restrictions contained within the judicial review procedure. Lord Diplock admits that the permission stage also reduces the workload of the courts;[60] the short time limit, the exclusion of 'busybodies' by the 'sufficient interest' test and the obligation first to exhaust alternative remedies can also be viewed in this light.[61] Furthermore, it might be argued that the courts are not consistent in the manner in which they approach the procedural protections. In particular, the relatively liberal approach adopted to the standing requirement appears to go against the grain of making sure that 'litigation does not necessarily and unduly interfere with the process of government', since this *increases* the number of claimants who can be admitted to the process, and hence the frequency of judicial review. A somewhat different reading of the function of public law appears to be at work in this instance. The courts appear primarily to be concerned that the rule of law is upheld by ensuring that unlawful action does not go

---

[59] H. Woolf, 'Public law – private law: why the divide? A personal view' [1986] *Public Law* 220, 221, 230.

[60] See above n.55.

[61] See also Harlow and Rawlings, above p.5 (n.7), 687–694.

unchecked, whoever brings the case. For example, Sedley J argues that 'public law is not at base about rights, even though abuses of power may and often do invade private rights; it is about wrongs – that is to say misuses of public power'.[62]

Nonetheless, if it is accepted that there is justification for offering a greater degree of protection to public bodies performing public functions than to those (whether private individuals, companies or public bodies) who are seeking to assert private rights, we might want to ensure that the judicial review process, which provides such protection, is the *only* process used in the case of disputes which relate to public bodies exercising public functions. This is the logic underlying the principle of *procedural exclusivity* which was introduced by Lord Diplock in the *O'Reilly* case. His Lordship indicated that it would be an 'abuse of the process of the court' to litigate a public law matter against a public body through any mechanism other than the Order 53 process for application for judicial review, since this would allow the claimant to circumvent the protections for public bodies laid out in that process. Such a claim would be struck out by the court. This was so even though the procedural changes instigated in 1977 did not appear to rule out the possibility of obtaining the 'private law' remedies of declaration and injunction outside of Order 53.

While the rationale for existence of the principle of procedural exclusivity was relatively clear-cut, application of the principle in practice gave rise to considerable difficulty. Putting aside the details of the manner in which the courts approached exceptions to the principle, two broad problems may be identified. First, there was a danger that an individual or group who had suffered some degree of harm to their interests would be denied a remedy in law 'on the technicality' that they had chosen to pursue the claim through the wrong process.[63] Secondly, the principle, which formalises the distinction between private and public law, was particularly badly-timed in so far as it was articulated at a period in political history when the boundaries between 'public' and 'private' were becoming increasingly blurred as a result of the policies adopted by successive British governments from 1979 onwards, which privatised industries and services and sought to expose those activities which were still conducted by the state to a greater degree of competitive pressure.[64] In such a situation, it became difficult to establish what was a 'public' matter and thus susceptible to judicial review.

---

[62] *Dixon*, above n.46, 121.

[63] See W. Wade, 'Procedure and Prerogative in Public Law' (1985) 101 *Law Quarterly Review* 180, 187–88.

[64] See S. Fredman and G. Morris, 'The Costs of Exclusivity: Public and Private Re-examined' [1994] *Public Law* 69.

Recent developments in civil justice have effectively rendered the principle of procedural exclusivity obsolete. It remains the case that it is only the exercise of 'public functions' which may be challenged by way of the Part 54 procedure,[65] but the courts now take a more flexible approach to a claimant's choice of procedure. Cases may be transferred to and from the Administrative Court at any stage, and courts will not generally strike out claims because the wrong procedure has been chosen.[66] This flexibility is reflective of the overriding objective of the Civil Procedure Rules, which is to enable 'the court to deal with cases justly'.[67]

Judicial review grounds

In the next section of this chapter, we shall explore the question of how the judicial review jurisdiction can be constitutionally justified in more depth. However, one important point to note at this stage is that (with the exception of incompatibility with the rights protected under the European Convention on Human Rights, which is considered in section D below), the grounds which courts apply in order to determine whether a public body's action or decision is unlawful have been created by the judges. There is no statute which lays out the bases upon which an individual or group may bring an action in judicial review and, in consequence, it is necessary to look to decided cases in order to establish these. This, however, is problematic for the simple reason that judges do not always agree about what the grounds are, or what they should be labelled, creating difficulties for students and litigants alike. The most commonly-used modern classification is that employed by Lord Diplock in *Council of Civil Service Unions v Minister for the Civil Service ('GCHQ')*, a case which we also encountered in our analysis of the prerogative in chapter 4.[68] But it should be noted that, as his Lordship himself acknowledged in that case, new grounds may emerge which cannot easily be fitted into these headings: we shall have cause to consider one of these (legitimate expectations) in this section and another (proportionality) in section D. Furthermore, even the categories which Lord Diplock does identify are not clear-cut. As Lord Irvine stated in *Boddington v British Transport Police*, 'categorisation of types of challenge assists in an orderly exposition of the principles underlying our developing public law. But these are not watertight compartments because the various grounds for judicial review run together'.[69]

---

[65] *Civil Procedure Rules*, Rule 54.1. For discussion of the meaning of 'public function', see *R v Panel on Takeovers and Mergers, ex parte Datafin plc* [1987] QB 815.
[66] See *Clark v University of Lincolnshire and Humberside* [2000] 1 WLR 1988.
[67] *Civil Procedure Rules*, Rule 1.1(1).
[68] Above p.144 (n.73).
[69] [1999] 2 AC 143, 152.

As noted previously, the highly pliable nature of the judicial review grounds is, in large part, what gives them their strength *vis-a-vis* the executive: the latter must exercise considerable caution in reaching decisions or taking actions because it is impossible to predict with any degree of certainty how the courts will respond. Yet the extent of judicial discretion which is inherent in the grounds of review may be said to conflict with the principle of the rule of law which, as noted in chapter 2, requires certainty and predictability in application of the law. This is somewhat paradoxical since, as discussed below, the function of judicial review may be said to give effect to the rule of law within the constitutional order.

i Illegality

Lord Diplock described this ground as meaning that 'the decision-maker must understand correctly the law that regulates his decision-making power and must give effect to it'.[70] At its most straightforward, this means that a public body in which legal power is vested must act within the scope of the power allocated to it. For example, if a statute establishes a tribunal to provide compensation for accidents which occur in the workplace and limits the amounts which may be awarded to £500,000, the tribunal will be acting unlawfully either if it awards compensation of £600,000 or if it awards compensation to a victim of some other form of accident (for example, one taking place in the home). Since the scope of powers in such a situation appears clear, it might be expected that few public bodies would act in such a manner. However, (and as section C below will explore) the meaning of statutes is not always as readily apparent as the preceding example suggests. Furthermore, as established in the *GCHQ* case itself, powers deriving from the royal prerogative are also susceptible to judicial review and (as noted in chapter 4), the scope of these powers is often highly uncertain.

Additionally, while public bodies are permitted to do that which is 'reasonably incidental' to their allotted powers, a court may consider that certain actions are not incidental. For example, in *Hazell v Hammersmith and Fulham London Borough Council*,[71] a local authority which established a fund to enable it to speculate upon future changes in interest rates (hoping to benefit from a fall in those rates) was held to have acted unlawfully since this form of speculation could not be said to be incidental to the council's statutory powers to borrow money.

---

[70] Above p.144 (n.73), 410.
[71] [1992] 2 AC 1

The reference in Lord Diplock's dictum to the need for correct understanding of the law which regulates a body's power raises the question of the scope of judicial review of mistakes of fact or law. It was noted in the previous section that the judicial review jurisdiction is not primarily concerned with issues of fact: if the court were to re-open factual disputes, it would run the risk of substituting its view on the merits of the case for that of the original decision-maker. Such errors are therefore not normally reviewable, although a decision which has no basis in evidence at all, or in which an established and relevant fact has been misunderstood or ignored, may be quashed.[72] By contrast, a reviewing court is clearly constitutionally empowered to scrutinise decisions which may be based upon errors of law, given that determination of the meaning of the law is the fundamental role of the judiciary. The key case here is *Anisminic*,[73] in which the House of Lords determined that a misunderstanding of the meaning of secondary legislation which governed the compensation tribunal's powers rendered the decision which it reached unlawful. It was to be assumed that Parliament had only conferred the decision-making powers on the premise that these were to be exercised on the correct legal basis. Thus, a misdirection in law would take the decision-maker outside of the scope of its powers.[74]

In chapter 1 of this book, we noted that decision-makers can be afforded power in the form of duties or discretion, the former connoting an obligation to act in a certain way, the latter a choice of actions. In fact, the dividing line between these two concepts is less clear-cut than may appear at first sight. It is possible for a duty to be phrased in such a broad way that the decision-maker has virtually unlimited choice in how to go about fulfilling it, such as the duty to uphold the independence of the judiciary under section 3(1) of the Constitutional Reform Act 2005 which was discussed previously in this chapter. In other situations, no specific obligation at all is imposed upon the public body, which is apparently conferred with total freedom of action. In such circumstances, when can a reviewing court justifiably intervene?

Two broad situations may be identified. First, if discretionary powers are conferred upon a body or individual, then *that body or individual* must *actually exercise discretion*. Consequently, it is in principle unlawful for the body to which power is allocated to assign the decision-making power to someone else, or for a body to act or decide in a certain way because another

---

[72] See *R v Criminal Injuries Compensation Board, ex parte A* [1999] 2 AC 330, 344–45 (Lord Slynn).
[73] Above n.34.
[74] See also *R v Lord President of the Privy Council, ex parte Page* [1993] AC 682, 701 (Lord Browne-Wilkinson).

body has instructed it to do so, although statute or common law may allow for exceptions in the interests of administrative convenience.[75] Additionally, a public body may 'fetter' its discretion by sticking too rigidly to a policy or guideline which it has adopted in order to assist its decision-making process. Courts will recognise that it is administratively expedient to operate such policies and guidelines (since they speed up the decision-making process and ensure that cases are treated in a consistent manner), but will not permit the decision-maker totally to 'shut its ears' to an application.[76] Consequently, it is necessary always to consider whether an exception should be made to the general policy on the basis of the individual circumstances presented.

In these situations, there is a failure to exercise discretion. However, a public body may also act unlawfully by *abusing the discretionary power* with which it is conferred by statute or prerogative. Perhaps self-evidently, this will be the case if the body acts maliciously or in bad faith, but more frequently a reviewing court will be called upon to intervene in instances where it is alleged that the decision-maker has acted in a pursuit of an improper objective, that it has taken irrelevant factors into account in reaching its decision, or that it has failed to take relevant factors into account. These bases for review, which are closely related to each other, can best be illustrated by reference to relevant case law.

Thus, in *Porter v Magill*,[77] a local authority which had sold council houses was held to have acted improperly as regards its statutory powers to dispose of land because it had done so in order to enhance the electoral chances of a political party. In *R v Secretary of State for the Home Department, ex parte Venables*,[78] the Home Secretary was held to have acted unlawfully in reaching a decision upon a minimum sentence period for a youth because he had taken account of a newspaper campaign through which the public had expressed the view that detention should be for life: this was considered by the court to be irrelevant to the minister's exercise of independent judgment in the exercise of a function which was judicial in character. And in *R v Somerset County Council, ex parte Fewings*, the decision of a council which banned stag hunting on land which it owned was declared unlawful. In the High Court, Laws J held that the language of the relevant statutory provision, which allowed the authority to make decisions relating to the 'benefit,

---

[75] See Local Government Act 1972, s. 101(1) (permitting local authorities to delegate discharge of functions to committees, sub-committees or officers); *Carltona Ltd v Commissioner of Works* [1943] 2 All ER 560 (Minister permitted to delegate to civil servants).

[76] See *British Oxygen Co. Ltd v Minister of Technology* [1971] AC 610.

[77] [2001] UKHL 67.

[78] [1998] AC 407.

improvement or development' of the area,[79] was not sufficiently broad to allow councillors to make decisions 'based upon freestanding moral perceptions' as to the ethical acceptability of hunting.[80]

Cases which fall under the heading of improper purposes/irrelevant/relevant considerations are constitutionally more problematic than those examined at the beginning of this section since statute (and still less, prerogative) may not make clear exactly *which factors* a body is permitted to take into account or *which objectives* it should pursue. Consequently, there may be space for the courts to 'read in' to the grant of power to the public body factors or purposes *which they consider* must be relevant or proper to the exercise of its discretion. The implications of this will be explored further below.

ii Irrationality

Lord Diplock stated that the second ground of review which he enumerated in the *GCHQ* case could be 'succinctly referred to as "*Wednesbury* unreasonableness"'.[81] As a starting point, therefore, it is important to consider the case of *Associated Provincial Picture Houses Ltd v Wednesbury Corporation*, in which licensees of a cinema sought to challenge a condition imposed by the local authority, that children under 15 should not be admitted on a Sunday. The Court of Appeal found in favour of the council on the basis that the moral welfare of children was a relevant factor to the exercise of its licensing powers and that the condition imposed was not unreasonably wide. The case is, however, less important for its result than for the test of 'unreasonableness' which was articulated by Lord Greene MR: 'It is true to say that, if a decision on a competent matter is so unreasonable that no reasonable authority could ever have come to it, then the courts can interfere'.[82] By way of illustration of the application of this principle, he cited the case of *Short v Poole Corporation*,[83] in which the judge had given an example of a teacher sacked because she had red hair. This formulation suggests that judicial intervention is only permissible in the most extreme of cases, a view which is supported by Lord Diplock's further explanation of the test of irrationality (his preferred terminology) as being 'a decision which is so outrageous in its defiance of logic or of accepted moral standards that no sensible person who had applied his mind to the question to be decided could have arrived at it'.[84]

---

[79] Local Government Act 1972, s.120(1)(b).
[80] Above p.4 (n.6), 529–30. The Court of Appeal upheld the decision, albeit on somewhat different grounds: [1995] 1 WLR 1037.
[81] Above p.144 (n.73), 410.
[82] [1948] 1 KB 223, 230.
[83] [1926] Ch. 66, 91.
[84] Above p.144 (n.73), 410.

It might therefore be assumed that very few decisions would fall foul of this test. The rationale for adopting this seemingly high hurdle of review is to preclude the courts from being drawn into evaluating the merits of a decision. Note that this head of judicial review is concerned with the decision itself (or, to put matters another way, with the *output* of the decision-making process) and, if courts were regularly to intervene on this basis, they would be substituting their view for that of the original decision-maker. Consequently, as Lord Greene MR pointed out in *Wednesbury*, the test is not satisfied by what *the court* considers to be unreasonable.[85] The rationale for the strict standard was clearly expressed by Lord Ackner in *Brind*:

> 'The standard of unreasonableness ... has to be expressed in terms that confine the jurisdiction exercised by the judiciary to a supervisory, as opposed to an appellate, jurisdiction ... To seek the court's intervention on the basis that the correct or objectively reasonable decision is other than the decision which the minister [or other public body] has made is to invite the court to adjudicate as if Parliament had provided a right of appeal against the decision – that is, to invite an abuse of power by the judiciary.'[86]

However, the irrationality test is not always applied in this strict manner. Rather, it is applied more or less intensively according to the context. It is therefore 'a sliding scale of review, more or less intrusive according to the nature and gravity of what is at stake'.[87] In some instances, the standard will be lowered and the court will demonstrate a greater willingness to hold the decision or action unlawful. For example, in cases involving the alleged violation of 'constitutional rights', the court will adopt an approach of 'anxious scrutiny' and the onus will, in effect, be placed upon the public body to justify that its decision is within the 'range of responses open to a reasonable decision-maker'.[88] Conversely, where the subject matter being challenged is one for which the court lacks constitutional or institutional capacity (or 'competence') to resolve the dispute – for example, because the question is one of high policy, involves the allocation of scarce resources, or the exercise of expert technical judgment – the court is likely to apply the *Wednesbury* test in its strictest sense. The court will reserve for itself only the faintest possibility of review in a case where the

---

85 Above n.82, 230.

86 Above n.38, 757–58.

87 *R v Secretary of State for Education and Employment, ex parte Begbie* [2000] 1 WLR 1115, 1130 (Laws LJ).

88 *R v Ministry of Defence, ex parte Smith* [1996] QB 517, 554 (Sir Thomas Bingham MR). Many such rights will now be protected by the Human Rights Act 1998 and subject to the standard of review applied by the courts in that context, for which see further section D below.

outcome might be regarded as utterly absurd but, to all intents and purposes, the decision will be rendered immune from review. Indeed, as *GCHQ* itself indicates and as was discussed in chapter 4,[89] some decisions may be wholly non-justiciable, although the courts are generally reluctant *completely* to exclude any possibility of review.

The irrationality ground has been subjected to criticism. Lord Cooke described *Wednesbury* as 'an unfortunately retrogressive decision in English administrative law' which, if applied strictly, justified too high a level of judicial restraint in reviewing executive action.[90] Other eminent academic commentators have argued that the test is tautologous: 'it allows the courts to interfere with decisions that are unreasonable, and then defines an unreasonable decision as one which no reasonable authority would take'.[91] Furthermore, application of the test does not offer the claimant (or the wider public) a structured explanation of *why* the decision in question is unlawful or not: irrationality/unreasonableness is too open-ended a concept to provide adequate explanation for often controversial judicial intervention. Relatedly, the breadth of the principle raises questions as to its acceptability for rule of law purposes. While the adoption of a 'sliding scale' approach allows a more nuanced judicial response in differing contexts, it might also be seen as conferring unacceptably wide discretion on the judiciary and thus as violating notions of certainty and predictability.

In part for these reasons, some judges have advocated replacement of the irrationality standard by the test of proportionality, which is used in European Union law and in the jurisprudence of the European Court of Human Rights.[92] This test has been adopted by English courts in those contexts, and its meaning will be considered in relation to judicial review under the Human Rights Act 1998, discussed in section D of this chapter. Outside of those areas, the irrationality standard appears to be moving closer to the proportionality test (not least because significant number of applications for judicial review will now in practice combine arguments based upon the 'ordinary' grounds of judicial review and claims of violations of rights given effect by the Human Rights Act).[93] But it appears that the tests have not yet been totally assimilated.[94]

---

[89] Above pp.145–47.

[90] *R (on the application of Daly) v Secretary of State for the Home Department* [2001] UKHL 26, [32].

[91] J. Jowell and A. Lester, 'Beyond *Wednesbury*: Substantive Principles of Administrative Law' [1987] *Public Law* 368, 372.

[92] See especially J. Laws, 'Is the High Court the Guardian of Fundamental Constitutional Rights?' [1993] *Public Law* 59; Lord Cooke, n.90 above.

[93] See *eg Alconbury*, above p.58 (n.154), [51] (Lord Slynn), *R (on the application of Association of British Civilian Internees: Far East Region) v Secretary of State for Defence* [2003] EWCA Civ 473, [34] (Dyson LJ).

[94] See *Doherty v Birmingham City Council* [2008] UKHL 57, [135] (Lord Mance).

iii Procedural impropriety

The third of the grounds identified by Lord Diplock in *GCHQ* relates to the procedures employed by public bodies in making decisions. In some instances, procedural requirements may be laid down in legislation. For example, a body may be required to consult interested persons prior to reaching a decision, or to provide a process whereby its decisions may be appealed. If the body fails to comply with those requirements, it can be said to be acting unlawfully in a manner which is comparable to the most straightforward meaning of 'illegality' identified above: the decision-maker is not giving proper effect to the law which regulates its decision-making power. However, the courts will not invalidate every decision in which there is a failure to comply with a statutory procedural requirement. A distinction is drawn between requirements which are 'mandatory' and those which are 'directory', in the latter case enabling the courts to give effect to a 'green light' perspective by allowing governmental decisions to stand if no serious harm to the claimants will accrue as a consequence.

The other components of procedural impropriety derive from the common law. The notion of 'natural justice' can be tracked back through several centuries of case law, with *Bagg's Case* in 1615 demonstrating that an individual could not lawfully be removed from office without first affording him a hearing.[95] By the late nineteenth century, natural justice had become a standard ground of review,[96] but for a long period until the 1960s, the principles described below – in particular, those relating to hearings – were given restrictive application and applied only to situations in which the decision was 'judicial' or 'quasi-judicial' in nature. From a 'green light' perspective, this could be seen as beneficial, since it enabled a significant number of executive actions and decisions to proceed without the delay and expense which the grant of a hearing would entail. However, the distinctions between 'judicial' and other types of decision were not easy to draw and this form of classification was rejected by the House of Lords in the key decision of *Ridge v Baldwin*,[97] a case which was largely responsible for stimulating the modern development of the law of judicial review. Subsequently, the courts have tended to reject the label 'natural justice' in favour of a more broadly-stated 'duty to act fairly', which is viewed as a more appropriate description in cases where the decision cannot readily be regarded as being judicial in character.[98] Indeed, in *GCHQ*, Lord Roskill

---

[95] (1615) 11 Co. Rep. 936.

[96] See D. Galligan, *Due Process and Fair Procedures: a study of administrative procedures* (Oxford: OUP, 1996), 183.

[97] Above p.12 (n.30).

[98] See especially *McInnes v Onslow-Fane* [1978] 1 WLR 1520, 1530 (Megarry VC).

expressed the view that the phrase 'natural justice' 'might now be allowed to find a permanent resting place'.[99]

Natural justice as traditionally understood encompasses two principles. The first is that a decision-maker should be independent and impartial. It is not necessary that a judge should actually show favour towards one party or another: it is enough that there is an appearance of bias which might damage public confidence in the integrity of the decision-making process. That is, 'it is of fundamental importance that justice should not only be done but must manifestly and undoubtedly be seen to be done'.[100]

Any direct financial interest which a decision-maker has in the outcome of the case will result in automatic disqualification,[101] and in *R v Bow Street Stipendiary Magistrate, ex parte Pinochet Ugarte*, the House of Lords controversially extended automatic disqualification to situations in which a judge was ideologically involved in 'promoting the same causes in the same organisation as is a party to the suit'.[102] In other instances judges are not automatically disqualified. Instead, the courts apply a test of 'whether the fair-minded and informed observer, having considered the facts, would conclude that there was a real possibility that the [decision-maker] was biased'.[103] This test was introduced to bring the common law into line with Article 6 of the European Convention on Human Rights (as given effect by the Human Rights Act 1998), which provides a right to an 'independent and impartial tribunal' in determination of 'civil rights and obligations'. However, Article 6 has created further difficulty in cases in which administrative decisions, such as those relating to planning or allocation of housing,[104] are reached by ministers or officials of the local authority concerned who might be argued not to be independent or impartial. The English courts have so far resisted claims that such activities should become more judicialised through the imposition of full procedural protections, but this is an evolving area of law and more cases can be expected.

The second principle is that there is a right to a fair hearing. This is not as absolute as the first, and while an individual will generally be entitled to know of the case against him or her and to have an opportunity to provide a response, the precise requirements which the reviewing court will impose will depend upon the context of the case,[105] including the

---

[99] Above p.144 (n.73), 414.

[100] *R v Sussex Justices, ex parte McCarthy* [1924] 1 KB 256, 259 (Lord Hewart CJ).

[101] See *Dimes v Grand Junction Canal Proprietors* (1852) 10 ER 301.

[102] [2000] 1 AC 119, 135 (Lord Browne-Wilkinson).

[103] *Porter v Magill*, above n.77, [103] (Lord Hope).

[104] See *Alconbury*, above p.58 (n.154), *Runa Begum v Tower Hamlets London Borough Council* [2003] UKHL 5.

[105] *R v Secretary of State for the Home Department, ex parte Doody* [1994] 1 AC 531.

importance of the matter and the consequences to the individual, the relevant statutory framework and the nature of the decision-making body.
Thus, there may – or may not – be an oral hearing, legal representation,
cross-examination of witnesses and so on. The prime consideration is to
ensure that there is no 'unfairness amounting to abuse of power'.[106] Once
again, we can see here the degree of discretion which the grounds of judicial review accord to the judiciary.

The more flexible conceptualisation of natural justice as a duty to act
fairly has provided an impetus to courts to develop procedural protections
in situations in which they would not previously have intervened. Two of
these are particularly worthy of comment here. First, the courts have
shown an increasing willingness to require that a decision-maker must
provide reasons for the decision. In principle, there remains no general
obligation of this type in common law (in part, at least, because the courts
have been concerned at the administrative inconvenience, delay and
expense which might result),[107] but the circumstances in which such a
duty will be imposed by the court are now so numerous that it has been
stated that 'what were once seen as exceptions to a rule may now be
becoming examples of the norm, and the cases where reasons are not
required may be taking on the appearance of exceptions'.[108] This development may be read in conjunction with statutory provision of a right to
access information (discussed in chapter 6) and has clear benefits as regards
accountability and the legitimacy of decision-making, both on an individual and systemic level.[109]

Secondly, where a process of consultation upon a particular decision or
policy choice has taken place, whether as a result of a statutory requirement or because the government has indicated that it will consult (see
further section iv below), the courts have shown preparedness to intervene
to ensure that the process is meaningful. Thus, they seek to ensure that
sufficient information and time to comment is provided to consultees, that
consultation takes place at a time when the proposals are at a formative
stage and that the outcome of consultation should be considered when the
final decision is taken (although a decision-maker is not bound by any
views expressed).[110] In *R (on the application of Greenpeace) v Secretary of State
for Trade and Industry*, it was acknowledged that a decision-maker had wide
discretion on how to carry out a consultation exercise, especially where it

---

[106] See *R v North and East Devon Health Authority, ex parte Coughlan* [2001] QB 213, discussed
further below, pp.203–04.
[107] See *Doody*, n.105.
[108] *Stefan v General Medical Council* [1999] 1 WLR 1293, 1301 (Lord Clyde).
[109] For a general discussion of the value of reason-giving, see F. Schauer, 'Giving Reasons'
(1995) 47 *Stanford Law Review* 633.
[110] See *R v Brent London Borough Council, ex parte Gunning* (1985) 84 LGR 168.

was aimed at the entire adult population of the UK, but that the court could declare the process unlawful on the ground of unfairness if something had gone 'clearly and radically wrong'.[111]

iv Legitimate expectations

It was noted above that a public body may act unlawfully if it fails to exercise discretion by fettering itself by too rigid an adherence to a policy or guideline. But there are also factors pulling in the opposite direction: consistency and certainty in decision-making are values which the courts will also seek to uphold. These tensions are apparent in the concept of 'legitimate expectations', a principle which exists in European Union law and which was first articulated in English law by Lord Denning in *Schmidt v Secretary of State for Home Affairs* in 1969.[112] This was not one of the grounds of review identified by Lord Diplock in *GCHQ*, but it should be recalled that his Lordship envisaged that new grounds of review would emerge, and it can be argued that this principle is now sufficiently well developed that it can be regarded as a head of review in its own right.

The basic rationale underlying this concept is relatively straightforward to understand. If public bodies indicate that they are going to act in a certain manner – for example, by making a promise or representation, declaring a policy or through consistent past practice to that effect – it might be regarded as an abuse of power if they were subsequently to go back on such assurances and to act differently. The principle therefore gives effect to the values of predictability and certainty, but it cannot be absolute and permanent since public bodies must have freedom to react to new or changing circumstances which might necessitate a revision of the policy or a change in practice (as the rule against the fettering of discretion acknowledges). In effect, therefore, the courts are required to strike a balance between the interests of an individual (or group of individuals) who may be harmed by the frustration of what they expected to happen, and the public interest that governmental bodies should have freedom to adapt to changing circumstances. As we have seen previously in this chapter, this type of balancing process is especially characteristic of public law.

The courts have had relatively little difficulty in upholding expectations which are of a *procedural* nature. For example, in *Attorney-General of Hong Kong v Ng Yuen Shiu*,[113] a failure to honour a promise to illegal immigrants that they would not be deported without first being interviewed was held

---

[111] [2007] EWHC 311.
[112] [1969] 2 Ch. 149.
[113] [1983] 2 AC 629.

to be unlawful. Similarly, in the *GCHQ* case,[114] a past practice of consultation with trade unions about changes in terms and conditions of employees generated an expectation of a procedural nature which might have been upheld if national security considerations had not 'trumped' it. In such cases, the reviewing court is not obliging the original decision-maker to change its mind (for example upon whether the illegal immigrant should be deported). It is simply requiring that body to implement a particular procedure before the decision in question is taken.

But where the expectation is of a *substantive* nature, the constitutional problems are greater. In such instances, the individual has been led to expect that they will receive a particular benefit, such as early release from prison on parole,[115] or that they will be able to remain in a residential care home for the rest of their life.[116] Although some protection can be afforded to the frustrated claimant(s) in such cases by affording them a hearing to explain why the promise should not be retracted or the policy altered, what they actually expect to receive is 'the thing itself'. This is problematic because if a court obliges (say) a health authority to keep a residential care facility open because of the promise which has been made, notwithstanding that the facility has become too costly to operate, it is effectively stepping into the shoes of the original decision-maker and substituting its view on what public interest requires in a given case. It is, however, now established that a court may uphold an expectation of this type in situations in which there has been 'unfairness amounting to an abuse of power' and, in so doing, it will 'weigh ... the requirements of fairness against any overriding interest relied upon for the change of policy'.[117] Nonetheless, the situations in which the courts will intervene on this ground are limited. In particular, a substantive expectation will normally only be upheld where the undertaking in question is specific in nature and those holding the expectation are few in number.[118] Conversely, promises of a general, political nature – such as those made in an election campaign[119] – will be enforceable (if at all) only through the political process, not in court. There are, therefore, limits to the extent to which legal forms of accountability can be said to have superseded political forms.

---

[114] Above p.144 (n.73).

[115] *Re Findlay* [1985] AC 318.

[116] *Coughlan*, n.106.

[117] *ibid*, [57]

[118] *ibid*, [60]; see also *R (on the application of Bhatt Murphy) v Independent Assessor* [2008] EWCA Civ 755, [46] (Laws LJ).

[119] See *Begbie*, n.87; also *R (on the application of Wheeler) v Office of the Prime Minister* [2008] EWHC 1409 (Admin) (ratification of Lisbon Treaty without holding referendum).

Judicial review: constitutional role and justification

The increasing incidence of challenges, the liberal approach taken to the requirement of standing, the open-textured nature of the grounds of review and the evolution of new grounds such as legitimate expectations all point towards the growing significance of judicial review within the British constitutional order. But it is important to tease out the nature of the role of judicial review and the justification for it with a little more precision, not least because it is controversial from the perspective of democratic theory.

As was noted in chapter 2,[120] the existence of judicial review gives rise to a 'counter-majoritarian difficulty' in so far as it entails the invalidation, by an unelected and largely unaccountable judiciary, of decisions and actions taken by elected officials, or officials who are accountable to those who are elected. And while the problem may be more acute in a system in which it is open to judges to invalidate legislation rather than one in which, as is generally the case in the UK, they merely review *administrative* action, it is nonetheless apparent that judicial review can frequently come into conflict with democratically expressed preferences. For example, in addition to *Roberts v Hopwood*, which was noted above, we might consider *Bromley London Borough Council v Greater London Council*.[121] Here, the House of Lords held that implementation of a cheap transport fares policy, which had been promised in an election manifesto, was unlawful because the council's statutory obligation to provide an 'economic' transport system did not permit it to offer a long-term subsidy from local taxation to cover a deficit incurred as a result of the pursuit of a social policy. While Loveland may be correct to argue that it is overly simplistic to view this case as illustrative of a conservative judiciary seeking to undermine left-of-centre policies,[122] the decision nevertheless demonstrates that judicial review can, on occasion, intervene in democratic politics in a dramatic and highly contentious manner. The enactment of the Human Rights Act, discussed later in this chapter, has only increased this possibility as judges are now obliged to determine what is 'necessary in a democratic society'.

In order to evaluate the constitutional role of judicial review and how it may best be justified, it is helpful to consider how it connects to the three major constitutional principles identified in chapters 2 and 3. Of these, the relationship to the separation of powers doctrine can be addressed most briefly since this has, to a large extent, been covered previously in this

---

[120] Above p.24 (n.10).

[121] [1983] 1 AC 768.

[122] Above p.39 (n.75), 332. For analysis of the case, see P. McAuslan, 'Administrative law, collective consumption and judicial policy' (1983) 46 *Modern Law Review* 1; J. Griffith, 'Judicial decision-making in public law' [1985] *Public Law* 564.

book. As is perhaps most clear from Lord Mustill's speech in the *Fire Brigades Union* case,[123] judicial review can be viewed as a check and balance operated by the judicial branch over the executive. Accordingly, if we take the view (suggested in chapter 4) that executive power within the British constitution is excessive, the growth of judicial review as a counterbalance is to be welcomed, especially if we share Lord Mustill's belief that Parliamentary mechanisms for the scrutiny of the activities of the executive (discussed in chapter 3) are inadequate. However, as his Lordship also reminds us, there are limits to this role, since 'the judges are not appointed to administer the country'. These limitations are apparent in various aspects of judicial review, including the preclusion from intrusion upon the merits of the decision which underpins the high hurdle established in the *Wednesbury* case, and the supervisory nature of the jurisdiction which prevents substitution of the original decision. We have also noted that certain exercises of executive power are more susceptible to review than others. The flexible nature of the judicial review grounds and the variable intensity with which they – especially irrationality – can be applied, enables the courts to exercise a degree of *deference* to the administrative decision-maker, respecting the fact that it, and not the court, has been allocated power (usually, by Parliament) to make the decision in question, and that it may well be better equipped than the court to do so. We shall return to the concept of deference in discussion of proportionality, in section D below.

This brings us to the question of the relationship between judicial review and parliamentary sovereignty. In the most obvious sense, judicial review may be seen as respectful of the sovereignty of Parliament in so far as courts are not constitutionally empowered to subject primary legislation to review, at least outside of the context of conflict with the law of the European Union. However, the relationship is more complex than this. One way of conceptualising judicial review is to regard the function of the courts as being to give effect to the sovereignty of Parliament by ensuring that bodies to which the legislature allocates powers do not exceed those powers. Courts 'police the boundaries' of executive power, scrutinising actions and decisions in order to establish that these are not *ultra vires* (beyond the powers) which Parliament has conferred. Performance of this role can most easily be detected in the context of 'illegality', especially the most straightforward reading of that ground identified above. It might also be noted that the *ultra vires* approach connects to the separation of powers, in that a governmental body which exceeds the powers allocated to it by Parliament may be said to be acting in a 'law-making' capacity by award-

---

[123] Above pp.14. 27–28.

ing itself legal powers which the legislature did not intend that it should possess.[124]

For many years, this reading dominated analyses of how judicial review could best be constitutionally justified. If courts are simply giving effect to Parliament's intention, then no real 'counter-majoritarian difficulty' can be said to arise. It is, however, problematic for a number of reasons. First, with the exception of certain elements of procedure which are given statutory effect in the Senior Courts Act 1981, judicial review is a judge-made creation. Is it therefore realistic to talk of giving effect to Parliament's intention as being the underlying rationale for judicial review? Secondly, the *ultra vires* reading becomes less convincing the further we move away from the most straightforward understanding of illegality and try to account for judicial review of the exercise of discretionary power. Hence, while certain statutes do indeed specify factors which are to be considered or purposes which are to be pursued when a public body undertakes its tasks, many do not. And how can we justify judicial review of discretionary powers which appear to be totally open-ended? For example, in *Padfield v Minister of Agriculture*, where there was power to refer complaints as to the operation of a milk marketing scheme to a committee of investigation 'if the Minister in any case so directs',[125] does it make sense to speak of confining the minister to the powers conferred by Parliament, given that Parliament apparently intended a totally free choice to be exercised? Similarly, how can we account for judicial review on the basis of a 'duty to act fairly' in situations where the statutory power in question contains no specified procedural requirements? Thirdly, and relatedly, what of the situation in *Anisminic*,[126] in which the decision was held to be subject to review on the grounds that the body had committed an error of law which took it outside of its jurisdiction? Here, Parliament had seemingly indicated in express words (by stating that a determination by the Foreign Compensation Commission 'shall not be called in question in any court of law') that judicial review was not to apply to decisions reached by this body. And finally, how can the *ultra vires* approach justify review of the exercise of prerogative power or of bodies which are not statutory in origin?

Some of these questions can, of course, be answered. For example, it is possible to argue that the existence of judicial review in general, and the application of particular grounds such as review for irrelevant considerations/improper purposes or the duty to act fairly can be justified on the basis of an imputed or implicit parliamentary intention. Thus (for example)

---

[124] For discussion of this aspect, see Craig, above p.98 (n.108), especially 113.
[125] [1968] AC 997.
[126] Above n.34.

it is *assumed by the courts that Parliament intends* that administrative bodies should operate fair decision-making procedures, even though there may be no specific statutory requirements to that effect in the case in question. Similarly, the 'reading in' of considerations and purposes may be seen as part of the normal process of judicial interpretation of statutory provisions, discussed in the next section of this chapter, which frequently involves the application of presumptions as to what Parliament intends.

Nonetheless, it has been contended that *ultra vires* is a 'fig leaf to cover the true origins' of judicial review,[127] which lie not in parliamentary intention but in the common law. According to this view,

> 'the legislature will rarely provide any indication as to the content and limits of what constitutes judicial review. When legislation is passed the courts will impose the controls which constitute judicial review *which they believe are normatively justified* on the grounds of justice, the rule of law, etc ... The courts will decide on the appropriate procedural and substantive principles of judicial review which should apply to statutory and non-statutory bodies alike. Agency action which infringes these principles will be unlawful. A finding of legislative intent is not necessary for the creation or general application of these principles.'[128]

This view, which is said to present a more realistic picture of the manner in which the courts operate within this field, is not *inconsistent* with parliamentary sovereignty. Its proponents argue that Parliament can displace the 'controls' which the courts exercise by way of judicial review through clear statutory words, which courts are bound to follow, and that it can legislate to overturn judicial decisions. However, the foundation of judicial review is not parliamentary intention. Rather, 'the principles of judicial review are developed by the courts pursuant to the rule of law. These principles are used to control public power and some species of quasi-public power.'[129]

What, then, is the relationship between judicial review and the rule of law? First, under the heading of illegality, partial effect is given to a Diceyan reading of the rule, which seeks to exclude 'wide discretionary power' which it is feared may be exercised in arbitrary fashion. While the courts, recognising the need for the existence of discretionary power in a modern welfare state, do not wholly exclude this form of power (as Dicey and Hayek might have wished), they will seek to ensure that discretion is

---

[127] Laws, above p.110 (n.162), 79.

[128] N. Bamforth and P. Craig, 'Constitutional analysis, constitutional principle and judicial review' [2001] *Public Law* 763, 767. Emphasis added.

[129] *ibid*, 773. Much of the debate between the *ultra vires* and common law theorists is usefully collected in C. Forsyth (ed.), *Judicial Review and the Constitution* (Oxford: Hart, 2000).

not misused or abused to the detriment of the individual. Secondly, the ground of procedural impropriety gives 'concrete expression' to the 'notion contained in the rule of law that no person should be condemned unheard'.[130] Similarly, as noted earlier in this chapter, judicial independence and impartiality, as given effect by the rule against bias, are central facets of the rule of law and in so far as judges are precluded from favouring government as against individuals, are also broadly consonant with Dicey's second meaning of the rule. Thirdly, the protection of legitimate expectations enables the courts to uphold values of predictability and certainty of decision-making, which we have seen to be fundamental to the formal version of the rule of law. Finally, although it has been argued that irrationality is more difficult to fit into the rule, a decision which lacks any rational basis (such as sacking a teacher because she has red hair) can be regarded as arbitrary and thus as offensive to the rule of law. Furthermore, in so far as this ground (at least, if applied in a relatively intensive fashion as in cases such as *ex parte Smith*) tends to draw the courts into an evaluation of the merits of a decision, it may be seen as a means of giving effect to substantive approaches to the rule of law, such as those which are focused upon rights.[131]

There are, therefore strong arguments for the view that 'the principles of judicial review give effect to the rule of law'.[132] We might also note a further point made previously: that a broad approach to the standing requirement, in which the identity of the party bringing the action is considered of lesser concern than ensuring that unlawful actions or decisions are quashed, also points towards a rule of law justification.

It might therefore plausibly be contended that the rule of law, rather than the *ultra vires* principle, offers the conceptual basis for judicial control of government within the British constitutional order, and that judicial review represents the main practical means for achieving that control. It does not necessarily follow from this that we must subscribe to the radical view (articulated in *Jackson* and discussed in chapter 3) that a 'new hypothesis of constitutionalism' has been created, in which the rule of law now operates as the ultimate constitutional rule, trumping parliamentary sovereignty.[133] Nonetheless, the willingness with which certain judges in that case articulated their opinions in terms of the rule of law would surely have been unthinkable in the absence of the dramatic evolution of judicial review over the past forty years or so.

---

[130] Jowell, above p.39 (n.75), 19.
[131] See also the discussion of the 'principle of legality', above pp.58–59.
[132] *Alconbury*, above p.58 (n.154), [73] (Lord Hoffmann).
[133] Above, pp.119–121.

C. Statutory interpretation

On a conventional reading of the British constitutional order, Parliament is the supreme law-maker. Of course, in effect, judges also make law through development of the common law in decided cases: the principles of judicial review, discussed in the preceding section of this chapter, provide a striking example of 'judge-made' law. However, within the hierarchy of legal norms, legislation clearly takes precedence over common law.

But this does not tell the full story. Statutory provisions need to be *interpreted* so that it can be determined whether they apply to given factual situations. While the formal version of the rule of law specifies that laws should be clear and accessible, the inherent uncertainty of linguistic expression sometimes renders this impossible. In fact, words employed in statutes may be unclear for a number of reasons.[134] They may simply be ambiguous in that they possess two or more distinct meanings without clear evidence from the context as to which is to apply. There may be a mistake in the drafting: for example, there may be an erroneous reference to another statute. The wording may be broad in that the word or phrase used is of wide meaning (consider, for example, the word 'vehicle'). Technological, scientific or social changes may not have been foreseen when a particular statute was drafted, leading to questions as to whether the legislation can be extended to cover these. Or the lack of clarity may be deliberate on Parliament's part. It may be that certain words or principles were omitted because they are regarded as being included by necessary implication (as was noted previously, some commentators argue that this applies to the grounds of judicial review: for example, the duty to act fairly may not be explicitly stated within a statute but might be considered implicit in every grant of power). Alternatively, the wording may be unclear because the matter is politically contentious – in such a case the use of ambiguous language serves to 'disguise' the controversial nature of the provision.

Interpretation of statutes is a matter for the judiciary. This is consonant with the judiciary's role under the separation of powers doctrine as articulated by Lord Diplock in *Duport Steels v Sirs*.[135] Although Parliament has enacted legislation, such as the Interpretation Act 1978, which provides standard definition of certain commonly-used terms or phrases (thus enabling statutes to be shorter), it has not indicated to the judges how they should go about fulfilling the interpretative task. Commentators have

---

[134] F. Bennion, *Bennion on Statute Law* (London: Longman, 3rd ed., 1990), Chapters 15–19.
[135] Above, p.26 (n.19).

traditionally suggested that three approaches (or 'rules') may be identified, although case law rarely refers to any of these by name. These are:

(a) *The literal rule*. This approach simply involves attaching the normal meaning to statutory words: 'if the words of the statute are in themselves precise and unambiguous, then no more can be necessary than to expound those words in their natural and ordinary sense'.[136] This approach therefore gives clear expression to the doctrine of the sovereignty of Parliament, but is of limited value where the words are ambiguous or broad.

(b) *The golden rule*. This approach takes a literal reading of statutory words as a starting point, but modifies this in a situation where such a reading would produce an absurdity or inconsistency with the rest of the statute. In such a case, the court can modify the grammatical and ordinary meaning in order to avoid such an absurdity or inconsistency.[137]

(c) *The mischief rule*. On this approach, a court will identify the deficiency ('mischief') in the existing law (whether common law or statute) which the statutory provision was intended to remedy and will interpret ambiguous wording in such a manner that the deficiency would be prevented from recurring.

However, while these three historical approaches are not irrelevant to the modern practice of the courts, the contemporary approach to statutory interpretation in cases in which wording is unclear is normally described as *purposive* in character. A clear explanation of the meaning of this has been provided by Lord Bingham:

> 'The basic task of the court is to ascertain and give effect to the true meaning of what Parliament has said in the enactment to be construed. But this is not to say that attention should be confined and a literal interpretation given to the particular provisions which give rise to difficulty ... The court's task, within the permissible bounds of interpretation, is to give effect to Parliament's purpose. So the controversial provisions should be read in the context of the statute as a whole, and the statute as a whole should be read in the historical context of the situation which led to its enactment.'[138]

---

[136] The *Sussex Peerage* case (1844) 11 Cl. & Fin. 84, 143 (Tindal CJ).

[137] See *Grey v Pearson* (1857) 6 HL Cas. 61; *River Wear Commissioners v Adamson* (1877) 2 App. Cas 743.

[138] *R (on the application of Quintavalle) v Secretary of State for Health* [2003] 2 AC 687, [8].

Of course, in many cases adoption of a literal approach which focuses upon the normal meaning of words will enable a court to ascertain what Parliament's purpose was in enacting the legislation. But what other aids may courts employ in order to establish Parliament's intention? In some instances, assistance may be found within the statute itself: for example, in the long title or preamble to the legislation in question.[139] Elsewhere, related statutes dealing with the same subject matter,[140] dictionaries and legal textbooks,[141] and Law Commission reports which form the basis of a legislative provision,[142] have been held, among other materials, to be relevant as guides for the court. Courts also operate a number of *presumptions* when interpreting legislation, including the 'principle of legality' which was considered in chapter 2 and which, at its broadest, means that 'unless there is the clearest provision to the contrary, Parliament must be presumed not to legislate contrary to the rule of law'.

However, it was previously the case that a court might not employ parliamentary materials for any purpose connected to the interpretation of statutes.[143] Most significantly, this excluded the official record of parliamentary proceedings, *Hansard*, from being used as an aid to ascertaining the intention of Parliament where statutory words were unclear or ambiguous. There were both constitutional and practical rationales for this stance. From the former perspective, it was argued that ascertaining parliamentary intention by reference to statements made by ministers (who, as we have seen in chapter 3, are effectively in control of the legislative process) would accord sovereignty to the executive rather than to the legislature. This might be seen as especially problematic when we consider the party political nature of much legislative debate, especially in the Commons. Pragmatically, there was thought to be a danger that judicial reference to *Hansard* would both lengthen and increase the cost of litigation as lawyers would 'trawl' through the reports of debates in order to find a statement which supported their client's case.

---

[139] As an illustration of these components of legislation, consider the Parliament Act 1911. The long title is 'An Act to make provision with respect to the powers of the House of Lords in relation to the House of Commons, and to limit the duration of Parliament', This is followed by the preamble, which commences 'Whereas it is expedient that provision should be made for regulating the relations between the two Houses of Parliament. And whereas it is intended to substitute for the House of Lords as it at present exists a Second Chamber constituted on a popular instead of hereditary basis, but such substitution cannot be immediately brought into operation ...'. In *Jackson*, above p.11 (n.27) [89], Lord Steyn indicated that words in the preamble to this legislation could not prevail over clear statutory words.

[140] *Attorney-General v Prince Ernest Augustus of Hanover* [1957] AC 436.

[141] See *eg White and Collins v Minister of Health* [1939] 2 KB 838; *Re Castioni* [1891] 1 QB 149.

[142] *I v Director of Public Prosecutions* [2001] 2 All ER 583.

[143] See *Davis v Johnson* [1979] AC 264.

This position was substantially relaxed by the House of Lords in *Pepper (Inspector of Taxes) v Hart*. Lord Browne-Wilkinson stated that reference to parliamentary materials should be permitted, albeit in limited circumstances namely where (a) legislation was ambiguous or obscure or led to an absurdity; (b) the material relied upon consisted of one or more statements by a minister or other promoter of the Bill (as well as such other parliamentary material as was necessary to understand such statements and their effect); and (c) the statements relied upon were clear.[144] This relaxation meant that the courts would no longer be 'cut ... off from the one source in which may be found an authoritative statement of the intention with which the legislation is placed before Parliament',[145] and would minimise the risk of subjecting the individual to a law which Parliament did not intend to enact. Practical concerns were dismissed by reference to jurisdictions (such as Canada and New Zealand) in which use of parliamentary materials as aids to interpretation was permitted but where the length and cost of litigation was said not to have greatly increased.[146]

Pepper v Hart has been subjected to widespread judicial and academic criticism from both practical and constitutional standpoints, as a consequence of which it has been held that the limitations laid down by Lord Browne-Wilkinson should be 'strictly insisted upon'.[147] As for the practical arguments, it has been argued that, notwithstanding views to the contrary expressed in the case itself, '*Pepper v Hart* has substantially increased the cost of litigation to very little advantage',[148] the latter point reflecting the fact that reference to parliamentary materials has rarely made a difference to the outcome of litigation. In constitutional terms, it is contended that reference to ministerial statements is problematic from a separation of powers perspective and does not necessarily assist in ascertaining Parliament's intention (assuming, in any event, that it makes sense to speak of a multi-member body as having an 'intention'):

'Under our constitution Parliament enacts legislation, the courts interpret and apply the enacted laws and the executive act in conformity with the law as interpreted by the courts. The executive is enormously powerful in getting its proposals enacted. But it has no law-making function and it has no authority to declare what the law is or will be if a Bill is enacted ... In truth a minister speaks for the government and

---

[144] [1993] AC 593, 640.

[145] *ibid*, 617 (Lord Griffiths).

[146] *ibid*, 633 (Lord Browne-Wilkinson). A contrary opinion was expressed by Lord Mackay, 615.

[147] *R (on the application of Spath Holme Ltd) v Secretary of State for Environment, Transport and the Regions* [2001] 2 AC 349, 393 (Lord Bingham).

[148] J. Steyn, '*Pepper v Hart*: a re-examination' (2001) 21 *Oxford Journal of Legal Studies* 59, 64.

not for Parliament. The statements of a minister are no more than indi-
cations of what the government would like the law to be. In any event,
it is not discoverable from the printed record whether individual
members of the legislature, let alone a plurality in each chamber, understood and accepted a ministerial explanation of the suggested meaning
of the words.'[149]

Kavanagh further argues that the decision not only undermines the separation of powers between executive and legislature but also that between
judiciary and the executive, as it effectively confers an interpretative role
upon members of the executive (sitting in the legislature). It thus nullifies
the role of courts as mediators between the state and the individual and
increases the risk of the abuse of legislative authority by government.[150]

It is possible to construct a contrary argument, which would view *Pepper
v Hart* as representing a pragmatic acceptance by the courts of the reality
of the modern British constitutional order, in which the executive dominates the legislature. On this analysis, it may be seen as another example
of a shift away from an orthodox but outdated Diceyan perspective on the
constitution (for, as we noted in chapter 3, Dicey overstated the capacity
of the legislative branch to restrain the executive especially given the existence of political parties). In so far as this constitutes a more accurate reading of the current political context in which the law operates, this view has
some merit. However, it does appear to go against the grain of most of the
constitutional developments outlined in the pages of this book. We have
noted a recurring theme of judicial disquiet at the consequences of executive dominance, coupled with a perception of the need to fashion mechanisms to redress the balance of power between the branches of
government, especially through invocation of the rule of law. In that
sense, the subsequent reining back of *Pepper v Hart* in *Wilson v First County
Trust Limited (No. 2)*, in which it was stated that courts should regard a clear
and unambiguous ministerial statement merely as 'part of the background
to the legislation' and not as determinative of the meaning of an Act of
Parliament,[151] was neither unexpected nor unwelcome.

D. The Human Rights Act 1998

The Human Rights Act 1998 is undoubtedly the most important piece of

---

[149] *ibid*, 61, 65.
[150] A. Kavanagh, '*Pepper v Hart* and Matters of Constitutional Principle' (2005) 121 *Law
Quarterly Review* 98.
[151] [2004] 1 AC 816, [58–59] (Lord Nicholls).

legislation in the field of public law since the European Communities Act 1972. Indeed, its significance extends well beyond the public law arena to numerous areas of private and public law. Although the Act has only been in force for just over a decade, since October 2000, it can be argued that the government's prediction in the White Paper which preceded the introduction of the legislation to Parliament, that 'rights will be brought much more fully into the jurisprudence of the courts throughout the United Kingdom, and their interpretation will thus be far more subtly and powerfully woven into our law'[152] has now been fully realised. This is so both as regards the specific rights which are given effect within the Act and, more broadly, in that there is an underlying commitment by the judiciary to the protection of human rights as a central facet of the judicial role in mediating between the individual and the state.

The sheer breadth of its impact renders it impossible to cover all of the implications of the Human Rights Act in a text such as this. Even within the field of public law, the Act has had an effect upon substantive law – for example, that relating to privacy, police powers and public order – which is well beyond the scope of this book's primary focus upon the nature of the modern British constitutional order. The intention, therefore, is the more modest, albeit still significant, one of examining how far the mechanisms contained within the Act may be said to affect the balance of power between the judicial and other two branches of government, which, it has been claimed, has been unaffected by the legislation.[153] In that respect, the discussion which follows should be read alongside references to the Act elsewhere in this book, notably in chapter 3.

i Background

The 1998 Act gives further effect to the rights and freedoms guaranteed under the European Convention on Human Rights. This international treaty, which the UK ratified in 1951 and which came into force in 1953, derives from the Council of Europe, an international organisation founded after the Second World War (and not to be confused with the European Community, which later became the European Union) whose current primary aim is stated to be 'to create a common democratic and legal area throughout the whole of the continent, ensuring respect for its fundamental values: human rights, democracy and the rule of law.'[154] To that end, the Convention confers rights which may be enforced by individuals

---

[152] *Rights Brought Home*, above p.114 (n.177), [1.14].
[153] See Department for Constitutional Affairs, *Review of the Implementation of the Human Rights Act* (2006), 9.
[154] http://www.coe.int/aboutCoe/index.asp?page=nosObjectifs&l=en

against member states of the Council, or by one state against another, through the European Court of Human Rights which sits in Strasbourg (France). The Convention protects rights of a civil and political nature, including the right to life, a prohibition of torture, the right to liberty and security of the person, the right to a fair trial, the right to respect for private and family life, freedom of thought, conscience and religion, freedom of expression, freedom of assembly and association and so on.

Citizens of other member states of the Council of Europe could also enforce rights protected by the Convention in *domestic* courts within the jurisdiction in question. However, this was not possible in the UK since ratification of an international treaty (an act of the prerogative) did not itself effect a change in domestic law, for which legislation would be needed. This is not to say that the Convention had no effect upon English law.[155] Cases in which the European Court of Human Rights determined that the UK was in breach of the Convention would trigger legislative or administrative change.[156] Furthermore, since the courts operate a presumption of statutory interpretation that Parliament does not intend to legislate in a manner which would result in the UK being in breach of its international obligations, any ambiguity in the meaning of a statutory provision would be interpreted in such a way that compliance with the Convention was achieved;[157] while if there was uncertainty in the manner in which the common law might develop, the courts should choose the path which was Convention compliant.[158] But, in addition to the fact that the latter avenues were only open when the law was uncertain,[159] the fact that the Convention gave rise to legal obligations only at an international level meant that individuals could not base an action in an English court *directly* upon an alleged violation of a Convention right. Instead, some pre-existing legal cause of action would form the basis of challenge, with counsel attempting to persuade the court to develop the law in that field in the direction of the Convention. The consequence of this was, as the Labour Government observed in the White Paper which formed the precursor to the Human Rights Bill, that individuals who wished to assert their Convention rights would frequently incur 'inordinate delay and cost',[160]

---

[155] For a full discussion of the pre-Act impact of the Convention, see M. Hunt, *Using Human Rights Law in English Courts* (Oxford: Hart, 1997).

[156] See *eg Malone v UK* (1987) 7 EHRR 14, resulting in Interception of Telecommunications Act 1985.

[157] See *eg R v Chief Immigration Officer, ex parte Salamat Bibi* [1976] 1 WLR 979, 984 (Lord Denning MR).

[158] See *eg Attorney-General v Guardian Newspapers Ltd (No. 2)* [1990] 1 AC 109, especially Lord Goff: 203; *Derbyshire County Council v Times Newspapers Ltd* [1992] QB 770 (CA).

[159] For a case in which there was no statutory ambiguity, see *Brind*, n.38.

[160] Above p.114 (n.177), [1.14].

given that cases were only admissible in the European Court of Human Rights *after* all domestic mechanisms for challenging the decision in question had first been exhausted.

The Act therefore gives *further* effect to Convention rights which may previously have some impact upon the development of English law, making these directly enforceable in domestic courts in the first instance, although the possibility remains of bringing a case before the European Court of Human Rights once all domestic avenues have been exhausted. It should be noted that not all of the rights protected by the Convention are given effect by, and listed in Schedule 1 to, the Human Rights Act. Most importantly, Article 13 (the right to an effective remedy) is omitted, the argument being that this was not needed since the Act itself afforded the necessary remedies.[161] Furthermore, it is important to understand that the Act does not 'incorporate' the body of European Convention law into domestic law in the same manner that the European Communities Act 1972 does for what is now EU law. This is so in two senses. First, the Act gives 'further effect' only to the Articles of the Convention, not to the case law which has evolved in interpretation of those Articles. Although section 2 of the 1998 Act obliges domestic courts to 'take account' of the case law developed by the European Court of Human Rights, they are not required to follow it.[162] Secondly, as discussed in chapter 3, the Convention is not accorded 'higher-order' legal status in English law in the manner enjoyed by EU law. As will be explored below, legislation passed both before and after 1998 is to be interpreted in accordance with the Convention rights but, if the courts are unable to find an interpretation which accords with those rights, the legislation is not to be 'disapplied' as happened in the context of EU law in the *Factortame* case.

With this background in mind, let us now move on to examine the relationship between the judiciary and the legislative and executive branches respectively through consideration of three key sections of the 1998 Act.[163]

---

[161] See *K v Camden and Islington Health Authority* [2002] QB 198, [54] (Sedley J).

[162] However, in *Secretary of State for the Home Department v AF* [2009] UKHL 28, the House of Lords considered itself obliged to follow a decision of the European Court of Human Rights. Lord Hoffmann opined that 'the United Kingdom is bound by the Convention, as a matter of international law, to accept the decisions of the European Court of Human Rights on its interpretation. To reject such a decision would almost certainly put this country in breach of the international obligation which it accepted when it acceded to the Convention. I can see no advantage in your Lordships doing so': [70].

[163] See also above p.115 for brief discussion of section 19 of the Act.

ii Judiciary and legislature: section 3

Section 3 of the Human Rights Act 1998 has been described as 'pivotal'.[164] It imposes an interpretative obligation, 'so far as it is possible to do so' to read and give effect to primary and secondary legislation (whether passed before or after 1998) in a manner which is compatible with Convention rights. This is unusual in view of the fact that, as was indicated in the preceding section of this chapter, statutory interpretation is normally a matter for the judiciary alone: Parliament does not generally provide guidance on the approach to be taken when courts are construing the meaning of statutory provisions. It should also be noted that section 3 is not specifically addressed to courts and/or tribunals, but applies universally – thus, public bodies such as local authorities or central government departments are expected to read legislation governing their powers in a manner which is compatible with the Convention rights, and a failure of such bodies to do so may give rise to a challenge under section 6 of the Act as considered below.

However, the key to understanding section 3 and the impact which it has upon the balance between the three branches of government lies in an analysis of the manner in which the courts approach the task of interpreting statutes under this section. In particular, it is important to establish what is understood by the word 'possible', since it is this which determines the limits of interpretation and the boundaries between this section and section 4 (the declaration of incompatibility). As a starting point, the traditional approaches to statutory interpretation, as described in the preceding section, remain open to the courts,[165] but it is equally apparent that section 3 authorises the judiciary to go beyond both these and the modern, purposive approach. This was made clear by Lord Steyn in *R v A*, who observed that:

> 'The interpretative obligation under section 3 of the 1998 Act is a strong one. It applies even if there is no ambiguity in the language in the sense of the language being capable of two different meanings ... Section 3 places a duty on the court to strive to find a possible interpretation compatible with Convention rights. Under ordinary methods of interpretation a court may depart from the language of the statute to avoid absurd consequences: section 3 goes much further. Undoubtedly, a court must always look for a contextual and purposive interpretation: section 3 is more radical in its effect. In accordance with the will of

---

[164] A. Lester and K. Beattie, 'Human Rights and the British Constitution', in Jowell and Oliver (eds.), above p.39 (n.75), 69.

[165] See *R v A* [2001] UKHL 25, [39] (Lord Steyn).

Parliament as reflected in section 3 it will sometimes be necessary to adopt an interpretation which linguistically may appear strained. The techniques to be used will not only involve the reading down of express language in a statute but also the implication of provisions. A declaration of incompatibility is a measure of last resort. It must be avoided unless it is plainly impossible to do so. If a *clear* limitation on Convention rights is stated *in terms,* such an impossibility will arise.'[166]

It is readily apparent from this statement that 'special principles of interpretation ... need to be used in interpreting legislation under the Act'.[167] The courts will 'read up' or 'read down' legislation (that is, interpret it broadly or narrowly) and may read words into or out of a statute in order to render it compatible with Convention rights. Furthermore, the 'strong' interpretative obligation which arises under section 3 is triggered even when the statutory wording is unambiguous, by contrast with the purposive approach described in section C. According to Lord Steyn, the only situation in which section 3 does not apply, and recourse, as a 'last resort', must be had to the issuing of a declaration of incompatibility under section 4, is where the statute in question *explicitly* sets out to restrict Convention rights. In all other instances, even where the wording is clear, the courts must strive (if necessary, by straining the language in question) to achieve a Convention-compliant interpretation.

The breadth of 'possible' interpretations under section 3 can be illustrated by the facts of *Ghaidan v Godin-Mendoza,*[168] which raised the question of whether the same-sex partner of a person holding a statutory tenancy under the Rent Act 1977 (as amended) could succeed to the tenancy after the tenant's death. The case turned upon whether the phrase 'surviving spouse', defined by the Act as 'a person who was living with the original tenant as his or her wife or husband', could be rendered compliant with Article 14 of the Convention (prohibition on discrimination in respect of enjoyment of the Convention rights), taken together with Article 8 (right to respect for private and family life, home and correspondence). By a majority of 4 to 1, the House of Lords considered that the statutory provision could be read in a manner which was compatible with the Convention rights so as to cover a same-sex partnership. In reaching this conclusion, Lord Nicholls expressed the view that:

---

[166] *ibid*, [44]. Emphasis in original.
[167] Lord Lester of Herne Hill, 'The art of the possible – interpreting statutes under the Human Rights Act' (1998) 6 *European Human Rights Law Review* 665, 669.
[168] [2004] UKHL 30.

'The interpretative obligation decreed by section 3 is of an unusual and far-reaching character. Section 3 may require a court to depart from the unambiguous meaning the legislation would otherwise bear. In the ordinary course the interpretation of legislation involves seeking the intention reasonably to be attributed to Parliament in using the language in question. Section 3 may require the court to depart from this legislative intention, that is, depart from the intention of the Parliament which enacted the legislation ... Section 3 enables language to be interpreted restrictively or expansively. But section 3 goes further than this. It is also apt to require a court to read in words which change the meaning of the enacted legislation, so as to make it Convention-compliant. In other words, the intention of Parliament in enacting section 3 was that, to an extent bounded only by what is "possible", a court can modify the meaning, and hence the effect, of primary and secondary legislation.'[169]

Academic commentators have expressed reservations as to the wide reading of what is interpretatively possible under section 3 which emerges from these two dicta. Nicol describes Lord Steyn's approach in *R v A* as 'far-fetched' and 'over-zealous',[170] while the decision of the majority in *Ghaidan* has been characterised as 'open to serious criticism for its lack of attention to the words of the statute, which endangers both legal certainty and ... constitutional legitimacy'.[171] Furthermore, in each of the two cases cited above, narrower approaches to the task of interpretation were taken by other judges. In *R v A*, Lord Hope, while agreeing that section 3 operated in a manner which was 'quite unlike any previous rule of statutory interpretation [in that] there is no need to identify an ambiguity or absurdity', reminded the House that it was 'only a rule of interpretation'.[172] Similarly, in *Ghaidan*, Lord Millet stated that 'it must ... be possible, *by a process of interpretation alone*, to read the offending statute in a way which is compatible with the Convention'.[173]

Underlying these latter statements are concerns that too broad an approach to the obligation under section 3 risks violating the fundamental principles of parliamentary sovereignty and the separation of powers by shifting the courts' role from a constitutionally permissible one of *interpreting* legislation to an impermissible one of *rewriting* legislation. Hence, Lord

---

[169] *ibid*, [30], [32].

[170] D. Nicol, 'Statutory interpretation and human rights after *Anderson*' [2004] *Public Law* 274, 280–81.

[171] J. van Zyl Smit, 'The new purposive interpretation of statutes: HRA section 3 after *Ghaidan v Godin-Mendoza*' (2007) 70 *Modern Law Review* 294, 306.

[172] Above n.165, [108].

[173] Above n.168, [66]. Emphasis added.

Hope stated that section 3 'does not entitle the judges to act as legislators',[174] while Lord Millett considered that extension of the provisions of the Rent Act to encompass same-sex relationships was a matter of social policy which, if addressed by the court under the guise of interpretation through section 3, would entail 'usurping the function of Parliament'.[175] Elsewhere, Lord Woolf cj has stated, obiter, that 'section 3 does not entitle the court to *legislate* (its task is still one of *interpretation*, but interpretation in accordance with the direction contained in section 3)',[176] while Lord Bingham has warned against using section 3 in a manner which 'would not be judicial interpretation but judicial vandalism'.[177]

As Kavanagh states, the location of the dividing line between 'interpretation' and 'legislation' in this context is 'elusive'.[178] One key question is whether ascertainment of Parliament's intention remains central to the courts' interpretative role under section 3. In *Ghaidan*, Lord Nicholls indicated that 'section 3 may require the court to depart from this legislative intention, that is, depart from the intention of the Parliament which enacted the legislation' (in this case, the Rent Act 1977, as amended in 1988).[179] But he also expressed the view that the court should give effect to the *wishes of the Parliament which enacted the Human Rights Act*, and that this Parliament had not intended a court to focus upon the precise wording of legislation at issue in any case, but rather upon the 'concept expressed in that language'.[180] On this approach, the House of Lords was able to interpret the legislation in such a way that it referred to 'a relationship of social and sexual intimacy exemplified by, but not limited to, the heterosexual relationship of husband and wife'.[181] However, there are limits to how far the courts may go in this respect. Lord Nicholls suggests that, when enacting the Human Rights Act, Parliament:

'cannot have intended that in the discharge of this extended interpretative function the courts should adopt a meaning inconsistent with a fundamental feature of legislation. That would be to cross the constitutional boundary section 3 seeks to demarcate and preserve. Parliament has retained the right to enact legislation in terms which are not

---

[174] Above n.165, [108].

[175] Above n.168, [99].

[176] *Donoghue v Poplar Housing and Regeneration Community Association Limited* [2001] EWCA Civ 595, [75]. Emphasis in original.

[177] *R (on the application of Anderson) v Secretary of State for the Home Department* [2002] UKHL 46, [30].

[178] A. Kavanagh, 'The elusive divide between interpretation and legislation under the Human Rights Act 1998' (2004) 24 *Oxford Journal of Legal Studies* 259.

[179] Above n.168, [30].

[180] *ibid*, [31].

[181] *R (on the application of Wilkinson) v IRC* [2005] UKHL 30, [18] (Lord Hoffmann).

Convention-compliant. The meaning imported by application of section 3 must be compatible with the underlying thrust of the legislation being construed ... . Nor can Parliament have intended that section 3 should require courts to make decisions for which they are not equipped.'[182]

While there is intuitive attraction in the notion that the court's interpretative function under section 3 is limited to matters which are not 'fundamental' to the policy objectives being pursued by Parliament when the legislation in question was enacted (not least because it preserves some degree of fidelity to the principles of parliamentary sovereignty and the separation of powers), this approach does not necessarily establish any more clearly where the appropriate dividing line between interpretation and legislation lies. After all, in the same case, Lord Millett dissented from the majority on the basis that 'the essential feature of the relationship which Parliament had in contemplation was an open relationship between persons of the opposite sex'.[183] Section 3, which 'shifts the interpretative focus from what Parliament originally intended, towards fulfilling the overriding goal of achieving compatibility with the Convention', therefore enables judges to 'detach legislative meaning from its original contextual setting'.[184] This endows the judiciary with significant discretion.

Of course, the task of statutory interpretation prior to the Human Rights Act was also not a straightforward matter of the application of clear 'rules'.[185] Nevertheless, it might be argued that the extended nature of the interpretative obligation under section 3 has strengthened the position of the judiciary relative to the other two branches of government. On occasion, however, this may have come at the cost of clarity and predictability and may therefore be to the detriment of the rule of law.

iii Judiciary and legislature: section 4

Where it is not possible to interpret legislation in a manner which is compatible with the Convention rights under section 3, section 4 empowers specified higher courts (in England and Wales, from the level of High Court upwards),[186] to issue a declaration of incompatibility. As noted in chapter 3, the issuing of such a declaration does not have any effect on the

---

[182] Above, n.168, [33].

[183] *ibid*, [78].

[184] A. Kavanagh,'The role of parliamentary intention in adjudication under the Human Rights Act 1998' (2006) 26 *Oxford Journal of Legal Studies* 179, 205.

[185] *ibid*, 205–06.

[186] s. 4(5).

validity, continuing operation or enforcement of the statutory provision which forms the subject matter of the case. Furthermore, it is not binding upon the parties to the proceedings.[187] This has the consequence that an individual whose rights have been violated through application of a statutory provision which a court has determined to be incompatible with the Convention may remain in the same position subsequent to the issuing of a declaration, at least until the provision is amended by Parliament.[188] However, the Act does provide a 'fast-track' process for amendment of legislation which a court (whether a domestic one, or the European Court of Human Rights) has declared to be incompatible, by way of secondary legislation under section 10.[189]

Declarations of incompatibility have been relatively rare. As of January 2009, 17 declarations had become final (*ie* were not subject to further appeal).[190] Undoubtedly the most striking instance in which such a declaration was issued was *A v Secretary of State for the Home Department.*[191] Here, the House of Lords issued a declaration that section 23 of the Anti-Terrorism, Crime and Security Act 2001, which authorised the indefinite detention without charge of non-British nationals who had been certified by the Secretary of State as suspected terrorists but who could lawfully not be deported,[192] was incompatible with Articles 5 (the right to liberty and security of the person) and 14 (prohibition of discrimination in respect of enjoyment of any of the rights). This result was achieved even though the government had sought to 'derogate' from Article 5 (that is, in effect, to 'opt out' of the protection which it afforded) on the basis that the post 9/11 security situation constituted a 'public emergency threatening the life of the nation'.[193] Although the majority of their Lordships were prepared to accept (or 'defer' to) the government's assessment of the security situation

---

[187] s. 4(6)(b).

[188] For this reason, and because a minister is not *obliged* to amend offending legislation, a declaration may not amount to an 'effective remedy' for the purposes of Article 13 of the Convention (which, as noted, has not been given further effect by the 1998 Act): see C. Neenan, 'Is the Declaration of Incompatibiity an Effective Remedy?' [2000] *Judicial Review* 247. In *Hobbs v UK,* App. No. 63684/00 (2002), the European Court of Human Rights held that the requirement to exhaust domestic remedies before a case was admitted did not oblige the applicant to seek a declaration, since the latter was not an 'effective remedy' for that purpose.

[189] This provision is controversial as it effectively enables the executive branch to amend primary legislation without proper parliamentary scrutiny: see above, p.34 (n.49). It is rarely used: as of January 2009, only one remedial order under section 10 had been issued: *Responding to Human Rights Judgments: Government Response to the Joint Committee on Human Rights' Thirty-First Report of Session 2007–08*, Cm 7254 (2009), 41.

[190] *id.*

[191] Above p.62 (n.165).

[192] As a consequence of the decision of the European Court of Human Rights in *Chahal v UK* (1996) 23 EHRR 413.

[193] Human Rights Act 1998, s.14 permits derogations, which are governed by Article 15 of the Convention.

and the consequent need to derogate, they did not consider that the measures taken in response to the emergency were, as it was necessary to show, 'strictly required by the exigencies of the situation'. In particular, it was not clear that discriminating between British and non-British nationals could be viewed as 'strictly required'. Accordingly, the court declared the derogation to be invalid, thus clearing the way for it to issue a declaration of incompatibility in respect of the statutory provision which authorised indefinite detention without charge. The government's response was to secure the passage of the Prevention of Terrorism Act 2005, which replaced indefinite detention by a system of 'control orders' restricting the movement and activities of terrorist suspects.[194]

The scarcity of declarations of incompatibility may be explained by a number of factors. It is possible that the courts consider that the absence of a directly enforceable remedy which immediately impacts upon the individual's circumstances to render section 4 of limited use. The fact that the declaration very publicly proclaims a 'failure' by Parliament (and, by extension, the executive) to give effect to human rights may also be a factor militating against it: the judiciary may prefer to avoid the visible controversy which a declaration is likely to generate. However, the most significant explanation would appear to be that the courts are seeking to give effect to the original intentions of the framers of the Human Rights Act. This is most readily apparent in the judgements of Lord Steyn in *R v A* and *Ghaidan*. In the first of these cases, citing statements made by the Lord Chancellor and the Home Secretary in Parliament during the passage of the Human Rights Bill,[195] his Lordship described a declaration of incompatibility as 'a measure of last resort'.[196] In the latter, he expanded upon this view, arguing that section 3 must be regarded as the 'principal remedial measure', since 'the mischief to be addressed was the fact that Convention rights as set out in the European Convention on Human Rights, which Britain ratified in 1951, could not be vindicated in our courts'.[197]

Notwithstanding Lord Steyn's concerns, it can be argued that greater use of declarations of incompatibility would be more consonant with fundamental constitutional and democratic principles. Since such declarations operate, in effect, merely as means of 'bringing the problem to the

---

[194] These have also proved to be controversial from a human rights perspective: see *eg AF*, n.162. For a general discussion, see E. Bates, 'Anti-terrorism control orders: liberty and security still in the balance' (2009) 29 *Legal Studies* 99.

[195] These were, respectively, that 'in 99% of the cases that will arise, there will be no need for judicial declarations of incompatibility' and that 'We expect that, in almost all cases, the courts will be able to interpret the legislation compatibility with the Convention.'

[196] Above, n.165, [44].

[197] Above, n.168, [39], [42].

attention of the executive and the legislature, and acting as a trigger for amending legislation',[198] the problem of judicial intrusion upon the legislative function and conflict with parliamentary intention does not arise as it does under section 3. It has further been argued that a rehabilitation of section 4 would be beneficial because it would facilitate a 'dialogic' approach to the protection of rights.[199] This theory, which has been especially influential in Canada,[200] assumes that courts do not have the 'last word' on human rights issues. Instead, it envisages that their judgments – or, in the case of the Human Rights Act, the issuing of a declaration of incompatibility – stimulate a process of debate, in which all three branches of government are engaged, as to how rights might best be upheld and upon the circumstances in which they may legitimately be limited. Under this approach, amendment of the legislation which has been declared incompatible would not necessarily occur if the process of political debate which follows the court's ruling suggests that there are good reasons to leave the law as it is. This might be viewed as more 'democratic' than a situation in which unelected and unaccountable judges frequently 'depart from the intention of the Parliament which enacted the legislation'.[201] Nevertheless, despite the view that sections 3 and 4 were designed to create this 'new dynamic',[202] it would appear from the statements made in Parliament, and cited by Lord Steyn in *R v A*, that section 3 was envisaged as taking precedence over section 4.

iv Judiciary and executive: section 6

Section 6(1) of the 1998 Act provides that 'It is unlawful for a public body to act in a way which is incompatible with a Convention right'. This provision represents the primary mechanism through which individuals may challenge an alleged violation of a right protected under the Act. The Act establishes no specialised legal procedure by means of which an individual may bring an action to enforce their Convention rights: section 7(1) of the Act provides that a claim under section 6 may be brought 'in the appropriate court or tribunal' and that the right(s) may be relied upon 'in any legal proceedings'. It might, for example, be possible for an individual to mount

---

[198] Lester and Beattie, n.164, 74.

[199] F. Klug, 'Judicial deference under the Human Rights Act 1998' [2003] *European Human Rights Law Review* 125, 131. See also R. Clayton, 'Judicial deference and "democratic dialogue": the legitimacy of judicial intervention under the Human Rights Act 1998' [2004] *Public Law* 33.

[200] See especially P. Hogg and A. Bushell, 'The Charter Dialogue between Courts and Legislatures (or perhaps the Charter isn't such a bad thing after all)' (1997) 35 *Osgoode Hall Law Journal* 75.

[201] Lord Nicholls, n.179.

[202] Klug, n.199, 130.

a defence to a criminal charge on the basis of an alleged violation of a right by the public body (*eg* the police) in question.

For the purposes of this book, however, the main point of interest lies in the manner in which section 6 may be used in judicial review proceedings.[203] Two procedural matters will briefly be addressed first. Section 7(5) states that proceedings must be brought before the end of a period of one year,[204] commencing on the date on which the alleged action took place, but specifies that this is 'subject to any rule imposing a stricter time limit in relation to the procedure in question'. The consequence of this is that if a claim that a right has been violated is brought by way of proceedings in judicial review, the shorter period (which, as seen above, is normally three months) will apply. Secondly, section 7(1) provides that proceedings may only be brought by a 'victim' of the unlawful act, a term which, as indicated in section 7(7), is to be accorded the same meaning as that used by the European Court of Human Rights in interpreting the Convention. It is clear from that court's jurisprudence that the concept of 'victim' is defined more narrowly than 'sufficient interest' for the purposes of judicial review. In particular, it excludes pressure groups which are bringing legal actions on questions of general public interest. This seems unsatisfactory both from a procedural and conceptual perspective. Procedurally, it is awkward for the courts to operate two distinct tests of standing, especially when Convention arguments are often combined with 'standard' grounds of judicial review in the same proceedings. Conceptually, it is difficult to square with the view that public law proceedings are, in essence, concerned with the primary rule of law objective of ensuring that wrongful actions and decisions are quashed and subsequently corrected,[205] rather than the vindication of personal rights.[206]

An even more contentious question has been what constitutes a 'public authority' for the purposes of section 6. The Act offers no comprehensive definition of this term, although section 6(3) specifies that it includes a court or tribunal and any person 'certain of whose functions are functions

---

[203] Section 8(1) provides that a court may award such remedies 'within its powers as it considers just and appropriate'. Consequently, in judicial review proceedings, all of the remedies identified in section B above are available. Damages may also be awarded if the court considers that this is necessary to accord 'just satisfaction' to the parties, having regard to the European Court of Human Rights' jurisprudence on the award of compensation: s.8(4). In practice, damages are awarded rarely, the primary remedy being a declaration that the right has been violated.

[204] Although this period may be extended where the court or tribunal considers it equitable to do so, having regard to all the circumstances: s.7(5)(b).

[205] See especially Sedley J in *Dixon*, n.62.

[206] For a comprehensive critical discussion of the nature and implications of the 'victim' test, see J. Miles, 'Standing Under the Human Rights Act 1998: Theories of Rights Enforcement and the Nature of Public Law Adjudication' (2000) 59 *Cambridge Law Journal* 133

of a public nature', but that it does not include Parliament (except the House of Lords acting in its (now former) judicial capacity). The exclusion of Parliament serves to preserve sovereignty by enabling it to legislate, should it choose to do so, in contravention of the Convention rights. However, the absence of further definition – for example, in the form of a list of public authorities annexed to the legislation, as exists under the Freedom of Information Act 2000 – has the consequence that the courts have had to determine the parameters of section 6.

In *Aston Cantlow and Wilmcote with Billesley Parochial Church Council v Wallbank*, the House of Lords sought to draw a distinction between 'core' and 'hybrid' public authorities. Lord Nicholls considered that the former category referred to 'a body whose nature is governmental in a broad sense of that expression', a classification which was underpinned by factors such as 'the possession of special powers, democratic accountability, public funding in whole or in part, an obligation to act only in the public interest, and a statutory constitution'. He gave as examples government departments, local authorities, the police and the armed forces, and noted that 'a body of this nature is required to act compatibly with Convention rights in respect of everything that it does'.[207] By contrast, 'hybrid' public authorities, that is those 'certain of whose functions are functions of a public nature' are not liable under section 6 in respect of activities or decisions which are private in character.

Underlying the relatively restrictive definition of a 'core' public authority adopted in *Aston Cantlow* was the consideration that section 7(7) of the Act provides that a 'victim' of an alleged violation of human rights is to be defined by reference to Article 34 of the Convention. Under the latter, claims cannot be brought by governmental organisations. Consequently, if the category of 'core' public authority (*ie* governmental organisation) were to be expanded too broadly, significant numbers of bodies would be excluded from bringing cases as 'victims' under the Act. Given this approach, it is inevitable that difficult questions will arise within the category of 'hybrid' authorities, as to whether such a body is nonetheless exercising functions of a public nature, making it potentially liable under section 6. This has been particularly problematic in respect of functions, such as those relating to housing or residential care, which local authorities have 'contracted out' to private sector or charitable organisations. In two cases, *R (on the application of Heather v Leonard Cheshire Foundation)*[208] and *YL v Birmingham City Council and Others*,[209] the courts took a restrictive approach to the scope of section 6, holding that (respectively) a charity and

---

[207] [2003] UKHL 37, [7].
[208] [2002] EWCA Civ 366.
[209] [2007] UKHL 27.

a private company which provided residential care facilities on behalf of local authorities, were not exercising public functions and thus were not subject to section 6. The primary concern, most clearly expressed by Lord Scott in YL,[210] appears to have been of a 'green light' nature. A broad reading of what constitutes a 'public function' would give rise to almost unlimited potential liability under the Act. But a contrary view is easily stated. Should public bodies be able to circumvent their human rights obligations simply by 'contracting out' services to the private sector, especially where the victims of the alleged violation are (as they were in these cases) vulnerable individuals? This might be thought to be especially pertinent in so far as one of the stated aims of government when introducing the legislation which became the 1998 Act was to 'bring about the creation of a human rights culture in Britain'.[211] It scarcely seems consonant with such an aim to render it straightforward for a body such as a local authority to evade its responsibilities through a process of 'contracting out'. Perhaps unsurprisingly, therefore, the decision in YL generated widespread criticism,[212] and legislation was enacted reversing the decision in respect of care homes, provision of accommodation in which is now stated to be a public function.[213] It should be noted, however, that the issue of what constitutes a 'public function' may still arise in other fields.[214]

While a restricted approach to the meaning of 'public authority' under section 6 may have the consequence of limiting the reach of the Human Rights Act, a trend which pulls in the other direction is to give the Act some degree of 'horizontal' effect. That is, it is rendered applicable as between private individuals or companies (as distinct from 'vertically', that is against organs of the state). Although a private body which is not performing public functions is not subject to section 6, section 6(3) does define courts and tribunals as public authorities. The consequence of this is that, when adjudicating upon a legal dispute – even where none of the parties are public authorities for the purposes of section 6 – the court or tribunal will be obliged to carry out *its* functions in a manner which is compatible with the Convention rights. This is relevant in two situations. As we have already seen in the *Ghaidan* case, section 3 of the Act obliges courts to interpret statutes so far as possible to give effect to Convention rights, notwithstanding that (as was so in that case) neither party is a

---

[210] *ibid*, [30].

[211] *House of Commons Debates*, 21 October 1998, col.1358 (J. Straw).

[212] See *eg* S. Palmer, 'Public, private and the Human Rights Act 1998: an ideological divide' (2007) 66 *Cambridge Law Journal* 559; Joint Committee on Human Rights, 'Legislative Scrutiny: Health and Social Care Bill', HL 46/HC 303 (2007–08), [1.6]–[1.21].

[213] Health and Social Care Act 2008, s.145.

[214] See *eg R (on the application of Weaver) v London and Quadrant Housing Trust* [2009] EWCA Civ 587.

public body. More controversially, a court may give 'indirect horizontal effect' to the Convention by developing the common law as it applies between two private parties in such a manner that it gives effect to rights. This is 'indirect' in so far as the claimant in such a case cannot base the legal claim upon a violation of a Convention right (as they might if the other party was a public authority), but must find some pre-existing cause of action in English law.[215] Nonetheless, as demonstrated by a number of cases in which the existing tort of breach of confidence has been developed in a manner which gives effect to Article 8 (the right to respect for private and family life), balanced against Article 10 (the right to freedom of expression), the judicial function in this regard can have a significant impact upon the evolution of the common law.[216]

Let us turn now to examine the standard of review applied by the courts in cases in which a victim challenges an alleged violation of Convention rights in judicial review proceedings. As a starting point, it may be helpful to conceive of section 6(1) of the Act as affording an additional ground of review to those outlined in section B of this chapter. Alternatively, we might think of the provision as connected to the 'illegality' ground. That is, the 'boundaries' of a public body's lawful authority are constituted not only by the statute (or other source, such as prerogative) which establishes it and which grants it powers, but also by the Convention rights given effect by the Human Rights Act 1998. If the body acts in a manner which is incompatible with those rights, then such an action takes it outside of the scope of its lawful power and its decisions or actions may be quashed in judicial review proceedings.

Certain of the rights protected by the Convention and given further effect by the 1998 Act are *absolute*, or unqualified, in character. This means that there can be no lawful justification for their infringement by a public body. For example, Article 3 of the Convention simply provides that 'No one shall be subjected to torture or to inhuman or degrading treatment or punishment'. In such a situation, a court will still have a role in identifying whether the action being challenged falls within the scope of the Article. For example, does the withdrawal of financial support and accommodation to an asylum-seeker with the consequence that he is forced to spend two nights sleeping rough with no access to food, washing facilities or money amount to treatment of such severity that it can be characterised as 'inhuman or degrading'?[217] However, once it has been established that

---

[215] See *Venables v News Group Newspapers Ltd* [2001] 2 WLR 1038, [27].

[216] For a useful discussion, see D. Sherborne, M. Thomson and H. Tomlinson, *The Law of Personal Privacy* (Oxford: Hart, 2011).

[217] See *R (on the application of Limbuela) v Secretary of State for the Home Department* [2005] UKHL 66.

the factual circumstances fall within the scope of the Article in question, a public body cannot lawfully infringe such a right.[218]

Other rights are *limited* in ways which are specified in the Article in question. The most obvious example of this is Article 5, the right to liberty and security of the person, which specifies six situations in which deprivation of liberty, in accordance with a procedure prescribed by law, is permissible. These include the 'lawful detention of a person after conviction by a competent court' and the 'lawful detention of persons for the prevention of the spreading of infectious diseases, of persons of unsound mind, alcoholics or drug addicts or vagrants'.

Another set of rights, exemplified by Articles 8–11 of the Convention, may be described as *qualified*. In these instances, restriction of the rights in question is permissible if (a) the restriction is prescribed by law; (b) it is 'necessary in a democratic society'; and (c) the restriction is imposed in pursuit of one of the legitimate aims specified in each of the Articles, which include objectives such as national security, public safety, prevention of disorder or crime and protection of the rights of others. The second of these requirements is assessed by reference to the test of proportionality, which was touched upon briefly in section B of this chapter. This was confirmed in *R (on the application of Daly) v Secretary of State for the Home Department*,[219] in which Lord Steyn set out the test of review to be adopted in cases involving violation of Convention rights as having three elements. In order to ascertain whether a limitation of a right (in this case, under Article 8) was 'necessary in a democratic society', the court will ask whether (i) the objective being pursued is sufficiently important to justify limiting a fundamental right; (ii) the measures designed to meet the objective are rationally connected to it; and (iii) the means used to impair the right are no more than necessary to accomplish the objective.

The key question for present purposes is whether this test is more or less intensive than the irrationality/*Wednesbury* unreasonableness standard of review examined in section B. This is important for two reasons. First, if the test *is* of a more searching nature, then it would appear that the judiciary has enhanced its capacity to exercise oversight of executive actions and decisions: the 'check and balance' of judicial review has been strengthened, at least in the human rights context. Secondly, the more intensive the test is, the more likely it is that a court may be drawn into a review of

---

[218] Such rights may also give rise to a *positive* obligation on the part of a public body to take action to ensure the right is not violated. In such situations the right is not absolute, but is to be 'interpeted in a way which does not impose an impossible or disproportionate burden on the authorities': *R (on the application of Pretty) v Director of Public Prosecutions* [2001] UKHL 61, [90] (Lord Hope). In such a situation, the test of proportionality, discussed below, is relevant.

[219] Above n.90.

the merits of the decision or action which might be regarded as constitutionally problematic from a separation of powers perspective.

In *Daly*, Lord Steyn makes a number of points which are relevant in this regard. First, he states that the 'criteria are more precise and more sophisticated than the traditional grounds of review'.[220] It was noted above that the irrationality/unreasonableness test could be viewed as inadequate in that it fails to provide an explanation of *why* the decision in question is unlawful. The three-stage test articulated in *Daly*, by contrast, offers a much more structured explanation of 'what went wrong' with the decision in question. This is beneficial not only to the 'victim', but also from a systemic perspective, both because it is likely to enhance public understanding of, and confidence in, the court's judgment and because it makes it clearer both to the public body involved and to other such bodies how they might best avoid acting unlawfully in future cases.

Secondly, Lord Steyn argues that, while the application of proportionality and 'standard' grounds of judicial review (ie, those outlined in section B) may result in the same outcome in 'most cases', the two approaches may 'sometimes yield different results'. In particular, this is because

'the doctrine of proportionality may require the reviewing court to assess the balance which the decision maker has struck, not merely whether it is within the range of rational or reasonable decisions [and] ... the proportionality test may go further than the traditional grounds of review inasmuch as it may require attention to be directed to the relative weight accorded to interests and considerations.'[221]

Thus, under the irrationality/unreasonableness test (at least, in principle), only the most extreme of decisions or actions which are beyond the range of rational decisions can be declared unlawful. However, proportionality requires the court to assess whether the decision-maker has *appropriately balanced the objective being pursued on the one hand with individual rights on the other*, and the *relative weight which is attached to the various factors having a bearing upon the decision*. If the 'balance' is 'tilted' too far away from the victim's right, the decision or action will be disproportionate. Of course, we have seen that irrationality/unreasonableness is, in reality, applied on a sliding scale which ranges from effective non-justiciability to 'anxious scrutiny'. Nonetheless, it does indeed appear, as Lord Steyn acknowledges, that 'the intensity of review is somewhat greater under the proportionality

---

[220] *ibid*, [27].
[221] *ibid*, [27], [28].

approach'.[222] Most notably, it places a burden upon the public body to *justify* the actions which it has taken and to indicate what alternative measures were considered as a means of pursuing an objective, in a manner which irrationality/unreasonableness does not.

Thirdly, Lord Steyn contends that the adoption of proportionality 'does not mean that there has been a shift to merits review'. This argument is perhaps harder to grasp. Like irrationality/unreasonableness, proportionality review focuses upon the outcome of the decision,[223] but since it requires an evaluation of the balance which has been struck, it seems to bring the court much closer than does the former test to an assessment of whether the original decision was right or wrong, as distinct from lawful or unlawful. This concern underpinned the refusal of the House of Lords to extend the proportionality test to the common law in the pre-Human Rights Act case of *Brind*.[224] However, Jowell has argued that there is a distinction. Proportionality entails an assessment by the court of the justification offered by the public body for infringing the right (including the extent to which it has considered less intrusive means of achieving the objective) and, more broadly, of whether the limitation may be justified overall in light of the values inherent in a modern democratic society.[225] This latter question is, of course, a profoundly *political* one, underlining the interpenetration of law and politics which was noted both in chapter 1 and earlier in this chapter. But it is not the same as the question of whether the decision or action is *desirable*, which merits review would entail.

For these reasons, judicial scrutiny of the executive in cases involving an alleged violation of a Convention right is likely to be more intense than in cases where such rights are not at issue. However, there remain situations in which the courts will still adopt a restrained approach to their task of oversight. The 1998 Act effectively imposes a constitutional obligation upon courts to adjudicate upon alleged violations of Convention rights. This means that the subject matter of such a claim (assuming that the factual situation falls within the scope of one of the rights) cannot properly be described as wholly non-justiciable: the court cannot completely refuse to entertain the case. But courts may still accord the decision-maker a substantial 'discretionary area of judgment within which policy choices

---

[222] *ibid*, [27]. Note that Lord Steyn indicated that the test of 'anxious scrutiny' applied in *Smith*, n.88 would not be appropriate for the protection of human rights under the 1998 Act.

[223] 'What matters in any case is the practical outcome, not the quality of the decision-making process that led to it': *Belfast City Council v Miss Behavin' Ltd* [2006] UKHL 15, [31] (Lord Bingham).

[224] Above n.38, 762 (Lord Ackner), 767 (Lord Lowry)

[225] Above p.11 (n.26), 681–82.

may legitimately be made'.[226] Within this area judges will be most unlikely to rule that an action or decision is unlawful. In such situations, it is often said that the court will *defer* to the decision-maker, allowing certain questions to be settled by government or Parliament without intrusion, or with a minimal level of intrusion, by the court.

In *International Transport Roth GmbH v Home Secretary*,[227] Laws LJ identified four principles which were relevant to the issue of whether, and to what extent, a court should defer to a decision-maker: (1) greater deference should be paid to Parliament than to secondary legislative or executive acts; (2) there is less scope for deference in the case of unqualified, or apparently unqualified, rights; (3) greater deference should be paid when a matter lies within the constitutional responsibility of the executive (such as defence of the realm) than within the constitutional responsibility of the courts (such as criminal justice); (4) greater deference should be paid where the question turns on matters of executive expertise (such as macroeconomic policy). It appears that deference is not a free-standing general legal principle which is to be applied automatically in certain situations, but instead is a matter for judicial discretion according to all of the circumstances of the case.[228]

As an illustration of the application of this approach, we may consider two cases. In *A v Secretary of State for the Home Department*, discussed above,[229] a majority of the House of Lords considered that it should defer to the executive's judgment on the question, which was one of national security, on whether there was a 'threat to the life of the nation' which justified derogation from Article 5 of the Convention. This was pre-eminently a political matter to be determined by the executive and legislature on the basis of information which was available to them. However, this did not render the subject matter non-justiciable. The court was still obliged to assess whether the interference with rights was 'strictly required' (which assessment required a proportionality-style analysis). The measures which government had taken (authorised by Parliament) restricted the right to liberty, an area in which the courts could be described as having specialist expertise. The court was therefore much less inclined to defer to the executive and the legislature on the question of whether indefinite detention without trial was a measure which was 'necessary' to respond to what it acknowledged was an emergency situation. By contrast, in *R (on the*

---

[226] *R v A*, n.165, [36] (Lord Steyn).

[227] [2002] EWCA Civ 158, [83]–[87]. See also J. Rivers, 'Proportionality and Variable Intensity of Review' (2006) 63 *Cambridge Law Journal* 174, 204.

[228] See *Huang v Secretary of State for the Home Department* [2007] UKHL 11 and further Lord Steyn, 'Deference: a Tangled Story' [2005] *Public Law* 346, criticising the reasoning of Lord Hoffmann in *R (on the application of Prolife Alliance) v BBC* [2003] UKHL 23, [75]–[76].

[229] Above, p.223.

application of Prolife Alliance) v BBC,[230] the House of Lords concluded that it should defer to the broadcaster on its assessment of whether material contained in a party election broadcast was such that its broadcast would contravene the obligation not to offend against 'good taste and decency'. In this instance, the right (Article 10: freedom of expression) was of a qualified character and the broadcasters could be said to have a degree of expertise, which was not possessed by the court, in determining matters of taste and decency.

The notion of deference therefore gives effect to ideas of the relative institutional capacity (or 'competence') of the judiciary to adjudicate upon particular issues upon which it may or may not have expertise, and to the principle of the separation of powers.[231] In this sense, the label 'deference' is perhaps an unnecessarily confusing means of describing a relatively familiar task for the courts in public law cases,[232] that is of determining how far it is constitutionally and institutionally proper for them to intervene. Hence, in *Prolife Alliance*, Lord Hoffmann criticised the word 'deference' for its 'overtones of servility, or perhaps gracious concession', noting that 'what was happening' was that 'in a society based upon the rule of law and the separation of powers, it is necessary to decide which branch of government has in any particular instance the decision-making power and what the legal limits of that power are'.[233] Similarly, in *A v Secretary of State for the Home Department,* Lord Bingham indicated that it was

'perhaps preferable to approach this question as one of demarcation of functions or ... "relative institutional competence". The more purely political (in a broad or narrow sense) a question is, the more appropriate it will be for political resolution and the less likely it is to be an appropriate matter for judicial decision. The smaller, therefore, will be the potential role of the court. It is the function of political and not judicial bodies to resolve political questions. Conversely, the greater the legal content of any issue, the greater the potential role of the court, because under our constitution and subject to the sovereign power of Parliament it is the function of the courts and not of political bodies to resolve legal questions.'[234]

---

[230] Above, n.228.

[231] See Steyn, n.228, especially 352 ('The true justification for a court exceptionally declining to decide an issue, which is within its jurisdiction, is the relative institutional competence or capacity of the branches of government '); also J. Jowell, 'Judicial deference, servility, civility or institutional capacity?' [2003] *Public Law* 592.

[232] See *Huang*, n.228, [14]: 'We think, with respect, that there has been a tendency, both in the arguments addressed to the courts and in the judgments of the courts, to complicate and mystify what is not, in principle, a hard task to define, however difficult the task is, in practice, to perform.'

[233] Above n.228, [75].

[234] Above, p.62 (n.165), [29].

E. Conclusion

The existence of a notion of deference under the Human Rights Act demonstrates that in this context, as also in judicial review, the courts are aware of the need to demonstrate what Lord Mustill describes in the *Fire Brigades Union* case as 'sensitivity' in preserving the 'delicate balance' between the branches of government within the British constitutional order.[235] Yet, as his Lordship also acknowledges, there is no doubt that we have witnessed an 'unprecedented judicial role' over recent years,[236] in light of the rapid evolution of judicial review and, subsequently, the enactment of the Human Rights Act. This enhancement of the power of the judiciary might be viewed as a necessary 'rebalancing' of a constitution which was previously tilted too far in favour of the executive branch. Certainly it is likely to be welcomed by those who value the primacy of the rule of law as a constitutional value, especially since this principle may be seen as underlying much recent case law as well as legislative activity, in the form of the Constitutional Reform Act 2005 (in respect of the independence of the judiciary) and the Human Rights Act 1998 (as giving effect to a substantive conception of the rule of law).

For others, however, the expanded judicial role which is evident from the developments considered in this chapter is a matter for considerable concern. In part, such disquiet connects to the unrepresentative and democratically unaccountable nature of the judiciary, matters which have always troubled advocates of a 'political constitution'.[237] Additionally, those in government (or those whose ambition is to attain governmental office) have, in recent years, been increasingly prone to view a more assertive judiciary as interfering with their capacity to act in the public interest, not as exhibiting sensitivity to constitutional balance. For example, earlier in this chapter we noted the then Home Secretary David Blunkett's angry response to a judicial review case relating to the refusal to provide welfare support for certain categories of asylum-seekers. His statement makes it quite clear that he considered that the judiciary was improperly intruding upon the work of the executive and legislature:

'Frankly, I'm personally fed up with having to deal with a situation where Parliament debates issues and the judges then overturn them. I

---

[235] Above, p.28 (n.26).

[236] Above, p.28 (n.25).

[237] See *eg* K. Ewing, 'The Human Rights Act and Parliamentary Democracy' (1999) 62 *Modern Law Review* 79, 79: 'the [Human Rights] Act ... represents an unprecedented transfer of political power from the executive and legislature to the judiciary, and a fundamental re-structuring of our "political constitution".'

don't want any mixed messages going out so I am making it absolutely clear that we don't accept what Justice Collins has said ... . I also have the right to say Parliament did debate this, we were aware of the circumstances, we did mean what we said and, on behalf of the British people, we are going to implement it.'[238]

Nowhere is this tension more apparent than in the context of the Human Rights Act. Speaking while in opposition in 2006, future Prime Minister David Cameron argued that 'the Human Rights Act ... has had a damaging impact on our ability to protect our society against terrorism' and called for its replacement with a 'modern British Bill of Rights' which would enable 'a British Home Secretary to strike a common-sense balance between civil liberties and the protection of public security'.[239] Two years later, the Conservative Party's spokesperson on justice issues, Nick Herbert, argued that the Act had undermined parliamentary sovereignty, had 'propelled judges into the political arena and, in so doing, has eroded the principle of the separation of powers' and had 'transferred significant power out of the hands of elected politicians and into the hands of unelected judges'.[240] It was therefore not surprising that the party's manifesto for the May 2010 general election contained a commitment to 'replace the Human Rights Act with a UK Bill of Rights'.[241] However, in view of the support of the Conservatives' partners in the subsequent Coalition Government, the Liberal Democrats, for the Act, this promise was later amended to one to 'establish a Commission to investigate the creation of a British Bill of Rights that incorporates and builds on all our obligations under the European Convention on Human Rights, ensures that these rights continue to be enshrined in British law, and protects and extends British liberties'.[242]

It therefore seems probable at present that the core of the Human Rights Act will remain intact, although the precise form which any expanded 'British Bill' might take remains a matter for speculation. However, it is unlikely that any such reform, if implemented, would in fact result in a significant diminution of the constitutional role which the judiciary has acquired in recent years. It is certainly possible that such a document will seek to adjust the balance between individual rights and what government (assisted by the legislature, where relevant) defines as the 'public interest'

---

[238] Cited in Bradley, n.26, 400.

[239] 'Balancing freedom and security – a modern British Bill of Rights', Speech to Centre for Policy Studies, 26 June 2006.

[240] 'Rights without responsibilities – a decade of the Human Rights Act', British Institute for Human Rights lecture, 24 November 2008.

[241] Conservative Party, above p.100 (n.119), 79.

[242] HM Government, above p.71 (n.12), 11.

in favour of the latter, especially on matters pertaining to national security. But the fact that a set of codified, positive and legally enforceable rights appears likely to continue to exist means that the judiciary will retain its clear and powerful constitutional role as mediator between the state and the individual. The scope of that role certainly could not have been envisaged forty years ago.

Undoubtedly, this will create tension between the judiciary and the other branches on future occasions, as it has in the past. Rather than being a symptom of a breakdown of the constitutional order, however, such tension might be regarded as the sign of a properly functioning and healthy democracy: one in which even a dominant executive branch is subjected to critical scrutiny and accountability through law.[243]

---

[243] See above n.28.

Chapter 6

Shifting patterns of power in the modern British constitution

As discussed in chapter 2, the separation of powers doctrine is a long-established means of classifying the primary forms of governmental power which exist within a constitutional order, and is very helpful in constructing a map of where power lies, by whom it is exercised and how it is controlled. It is hoped that the discussion in the preceding three chapters, which has been based around this classification (albeit that it has necessarily ranged quite widely at times), has provided readers of this book with a sound working knowledge of key institutional arrangements in the British state and of the relationship between that state and the individual.

However, while a map based upon the separation of powers provides us with an immensely valuable starting point for navigation through the complexities of the British constitution, it does not reveal all and it is therefore important not to be wholly constrained by it. We have, for example, already noted the view that the separation of powers – at least, the 'pure' variant of that doctrine – is emphatically not realised within the British constitution, given the numerous overlaps between the branches which were outlined in chapter 2 and which have been explored in more depth in the three chapters which followed. Now, as the organisation of this book suggests, this does not preclude the employment of the categories of legislature, executive and judiciary as organising concepts which can assist in building understanding of how the constitutional order is constructed and how the various institutions relate to each other. Nevertheless, it does signal to us that we should retain a somewhat critical approach to this categorisation. We should accordingly acknowledge that certain powers or institutions are not easily accommodated within the separation of powers in so far as this provides an explanatory model, although (assuming that we believe that the principle also has normative value in that it offers an account of what the constitutional order *should* look like) we might also wish to argue that change is required. Consider, for example, the prerogative powers discussed in chapter 4. By their very nature, these violate the separation of powers, but this also provides a good reason for their reform.

A further reason to look beyond the threefold categorisation offered in chapters 3–5 is that this map may not offer a wholly clear delineation of the manner in which the location and balance of power in the modern British constitution has shifted, and is continuing to shift. It is true that certain aspects of the evolution of the constitutional order can be analysed on the basis of such a classification. For example, we have had cause to remark upon the move from a 'political' towards a 'legal' constitution on numerous occasions, notably in chapter 5. But other developments may be less well captured, for example, those relating to the *diffusion* of power away from the centralised institutions of Parliament, central government and the judiciary. Such diffusion, while not new (in particular, power has been exercised by institutions of government at a local level for centuries), has been a particular feature of changes in the constitution which have occurred in recent years. In some instances the diffusion takes a 'geographical' form such that power has shifted from its former location in London to centres of power in Europe and in the constituent countries of the United Kingdom. Additionally, or alternatively, the diffusion might be viewed as 'functional' in that power which might broadly be described as being of a legislative, executive or judicial type is exercised by institutions other than those described in the previous three chapters. And thirdly, power, or the means of controlling that power, may be removed altogether from the state and placed in the hands of private bodies or groups. This last form of diffusion takes us to the very boundaries of public law.

Although a number of these developments have been touched upon earlier in this book, this chapter considers some of the most significant changes at greater length. The purpose is not to offer an exhaustive account of each but rather to provide an overview, to enable development of a better appreciation of the diverse and shifting nature of power within the modern British constitutional order. As noted in chapter 1, such adjustments are relatively easily achieved in view of the uncodified and unentrenched character of the constitution. The relative ease with which such changes may be brought about is not, however, without its problems. Transfer of power away from Parliament, central government and/or the judiciary may have the consequence that the checks and balances which exist to ensure that each branch exercises some degree of institutional oversight over the others are evaded. If this is the case, the principle of accountability may be said to have been weakened, a development which is likely to be regarded as bad for democracy. On the other hand, certain of the shifts described in this chapter may be seen as enhancing democracy by bringing government closer to those upon whom it most directly impacts, thereby affording the public a greater degree of control of, and involvement in, the exercise of power.

A. The European Union

The most striking and significant power shift which has occurred in the modern British constitution has resulted from membership of what is now the European Union (EU) from 1973 onwards.[1] We have already had occasion to address one of the major constitutional implications of membership, the impact upon parliamentary sovereignty, in chapter 3, and that aspect will not be further developed here. Rather, the discussion will centre upon two issues: first, the structure of European governmental institutions; and secondly, the law made by those institutions, its reception in the domestic legal system, and the extent to which such law is subject to scrutiny by the Westminster Parliament. While this necessarily offers only an outline of this highly complex area of law, it will nonetheless provide a foundation for better understanding of the manner in which executive, legislative and judicial power has partially been displaced from the branches of UK government described in chapters 3–5, and to where it has moved. Since the present chapter seeks especially to consider the impact of *recent* developments upon the relationships of power within the constitutional order, a particular focus of the discussion will be upon changes introduced by the Lisbon Treaty, which amends the existing Treaty on European Union (TEU) and the Treaty Establishing the European Community, which is renamed the Treaty on the Functioning of the European Union (TFEU), and which became law on 1 December 2009.[2]

Institutions of the European Union

Craig has argued that 'classical ideas of the separation of powers are not ... central to the institutional ordering' within the EU: rather, the concern is with 'institutional balance' between the different organs.[3] It might, of course, be possible to make the same argument about the British constitution. The significant overlap between the executive and the legislature certainly renders a 'pure' reading of the separation of powers inapplicable, and much of the preceding discussion in this book has been concerned with the checks and balances which exist to ensure that no single branch accrues too much power. However, in the EU context, the focus upon balance rather than separation helps us to comprehend that – even more than is the case in the British constitutional order – the institutions cannot

---

[1] Following the Lisbon Treaty, the European Community has been replaced and succeeded by the European Union: see Article 1, TEU.

[2] For an excellent analysis of the implications of the Treaty, see House of Lords European Union Committee, *The Treaty of Lisbon: an impact assessment*, HL 62-I (2007–08).

[3] P. Craig, 'Britain in the European Union', in Jowell and Oliver (eds.), p.39 (n.75), 89.

straightforwardly be categorised according to the familiar threefold division between the branches of government, and that the executive and legislative functions (in particular) are exercised on a shared basis by several institutions. It also points to the fact that the institutional architecture is designed in such a way as to allow for the articulation of different interests, specifically those of the Union itself, the member states (as represented by heads of government and other ministers) and the citizens of the EU (via political parties). The Lisbon Treaty has had an impact upon this balance, as will be discussed subsequently.

The institutional architecture of the EU reflects the inherent tension between supranationalism and intergovermentalism which lies at the heart of the Union: that is, between pursuit of the goals of the Union as a distinct entity in which the sovereignty of member states has been pooled and to which certain decision-making powers have been delegated, and advancement of the interests of member state governments exercising their sovereign power, albeit in co-operation with other sovereign states. Article 13 of the TEU sets out an 'institutional framework which shall aim to promote its [ie the Union's] values, advance its objectives, serve its interests, those of its citizens and those of the Member states, and ensure the consistency, effectiveness and continuity of its policies and actions.' To this end, it establishes seven institutions.[4] Two of these, the European Central Bank (which maintains price stability in the euro and conducts European monetary policy) and the European Court of Auditors (which ensures that the EU budget is correctly implemented) will not be considered further here. The others are:

i The European Council

The European Council's role is to 'provide the Union with the necessary impetus for its development and [to] define the general political directions and priorities thereof'.[5] It meets twice every six months,[6] and consists of the heads of state or government of the member states, the President of the Commission, and the President of the European Council.[7] The European

---

[4] Various other institutions exist, including the Committee of the Regions, which articulates local and regional views on EU legislation, and the European Ombudsman, who investigates complaints of maladministration in EU institutions and bodies. For a full description, see European Commission, *How the European Union works: Your Guide to the EU Institutions* (Brussels: European Commission, 2007), though note that this publication predates the Lisbon Treaty.

[5] Article 15(1), TEU.

[6] Article 15(3), TEU. The President of the European Council may also convene special meetings.

[7] Article 15(2), TEU, which also specifies that the High Representative of the Union for Foreign Affairs and Security Policy may be involved in its work. Members may be assisted by a minister, while the President of the Commission may be assisted by a member of the Commission: article 15(3), TEU.

Council has no legislative power, but in view of its membership, it plays a key role in setting the strategic agenda and priorities of the Union and in resolving disputes and disagreements within other institutions.[8] Its procedure is relatively informal and it proceeds by consensus.[9]

The office of President of the European Council was established by the Lisbon Treaty, replacing the previous system in which the presidency rotated between the member states on a six-monthly basis. The President's role is defined as chairing the Council and driving forward its work, ensuring the preparation and continuity of its work in co-operation with the President of the Commission, endeavouring to facilitate cohesion and consensus within the European Council, presenting a report to the European Parliament after each meeting, and ensuring the external representation of the Union on issues relating to its common foreign and security policy.[10] The President is elected by the European Council for a term of two and a half years, which is renewable once.[11] It remains to be seen what long-term impact the creation of the office of President will have, but Craig has speculated that:

'it is very likely that the enhanced position of Presidency of the European Council will alter the power dynamics within the European Union, since the incumbent will have two-and-a-half or five years in which to develop a vision for the European Union, in a way that was simply not plausible under the regime of six-monthly rotating Presidencies that operated hitherto.'[12]

ii The Council

The TEU defines the role of the Council as being 'legislative and budgetary', in conjunction with the European Parliament. It is to 'carry out policy-making and co-ordinating functions'.[13] Its membership consists of a ministerial representative from each member state.[14] This is not fixed, but rather meets 'in different configurations' according to the particular

---

[8] See *eg* Article 31(2), TEU, which allows referral of a matter from the Council where a member state opposes the adoption of a decision 'for vital and stated reasons of national policy'.

[9] Article 15(4), TEU.

[10] Article 15(6), TEU.

[11] Article 15(5), TEU.

[12] P. Craig, 'The Lisbon Treaty: process, architecture and substance' (2008) 33 *European Law Review* 137, 152. Note, however, that the election as first President of a relatively low-profile politician, Herman Van Rompuy (formerly Belgian Prime Minister) rather than other better-known candidates such as Tony Blair suggests that intergovernmental, not supranational, interests will continue to prevail.

[13] Article 16(1), TEU.

[14] Article 16(2), TEU.

matter being discussed (thus, if the agenda concerns the environment, the membership will consist of environment ministers of the member states).[15] The Council's work is prepared by a Committee of Permanent Representatives,[16] which consists of the heads of each member state's representation to the EU (effectively, a country's 'ambassador' to the Union).

The Council has been described as 'the EU's main decision-making body'.[17] Its members (the ministers) are empowered to commit the government of the member state in question,[18] and are accountable for their actions in that regard to their national legislatures. It is generally regarded as functioning in an intergovernmental manner. In respect of common foreign and security policy, it does not act as a law-maker,[19] but rather is responsible for framing the policy and making the decisions necessary for defining and implementing it on the basis of guidelines and strategy set by the European Council.[20] Elsewhere, it passes legislation (normally jointly with the Parliament on the basis of a proposal by the Commission), co-ordinates economic policies of member states, concludes international agreements between the EU and international organisations or non-EU states, and (with the Parliament) approves the Union's annual budget. In most instances, it will reach decisions by way of qualified majority voting (which involves states being allocated votes broadly in accordance with its population (meaning that Germany, France, Italy and the UK have the most votes, and Malta the fewest)).[21] In some areas, however, the Council continues to make decisions on the basis of unanimity, reflecting the retention by member states of sovereignty over these fields: this applies generally to decisions on foreign and security policy,[22] and to a number of issues relating to freedom, security and justice.[23]

---

[15] Article 16(6), TEU.
[16] Article 16(7), TEU.
[17] European Commission, n.4, 15.
[18] Article 16(2), TEU.
[19] Article 31(1), TEU.
[20] Article 26, TEU.
[21] Article 16(3), TEU. The Lisbon Treaty amends the requirements for qualified majority voting, introducing (from November 2014 onwards, although not exclusively until April 2017) a 'double majority' system whereby a proposal will be passed if 55 per cent of the members of the Council (presently, at least 15 of the 27 member states) representing 65 per cent of the population of the Union, support the proposal. For a proposal to be blocked, at least four member states must oppose it: Article 16(4), TEU.
[22] Article 31(1), TEU.
[23] Title V, TFEU.

iii The Commission

Together with the European Council, the Commission provides the impetus for driving the Union forward, reflected in Article 17(1) TEU, which identifies its function as being 'to promote the general interest of the Union and take appropriate initiatives to that end.' Unlike the previous two institutions, it is independent of national governments and therefore has a clear supranational role.[24] The names of commissioners are put forward by member states and are selected by the Council in consultation with the President-elect of the Commission (who is proposed by the European Council – thus preserving a degree of control over the choice to the member states which are represented thereon – and then approved by the European Parliament). The European Parliament then approves the team as a whole, which is then appointed by the European Council.[25] At present, there is one Commissioner for each member state serving a term of office of five years,[26] but the Lisbon Treaty provides that, from November 2014, the Commission will consist of members corresponding to two-thirds of the number of member states, chosen on a rotation basis, unless the European Council decides to alter this number.[27] The Commission is responsible to the European Parliament and the latter may pass a motion of censure (with a two-thirds majority) requiring the entire Commission to resign.[28] The Commission is also represented at each session of the Parliament so that it can clarify and justify its policies.

The Commission is staffed by civil servants, of whom there are presently some 23,000.[29] It is divided into Directorates General and Services, which are roughly equivalent to governmental departments with responsibility for particular policy areas. Legislative proposals emanate from these 'departments' (although the original suggestion may have come from the Council, the European Parliament or a member state) and are passed to the Commissioners for approval by a majority. The TEU provides that legislative acts of the Union shall normally only be adopted on the basis of a Commission proposal.[30]

In addition to this law-initiating function, which broadly corresponds to that exercised by the 'core executive' of Cabinet and ministers in the British constitution, the Commission fulfils other executive functions.

---

[24] Article 17(3), TEU.

[25] Article 7(7), TEU.

[26] Article 17(4), TEU.

[27] Article 17(5), TEU. This change appears unlikely to come into effect: following the initial rejection of the Lisbon Treaty by Irish voters in a referendum, each member state was promised a commissioner.

[28] Article 17(8), TEU.

[29] European Commission, n.4, 21.

[30] Article 17(2), TEU.

With the assistance of the Court of Auditors, it is responsible for supervision of expenditure, it implements policy decisions, it enforces EU law (referring matters to the Court of Justice where necessary), and it has a role in representing the Union internationally, the key player being the High Representative of the Union for Foreign Affairs and Security Policy (popularly viewed as the EU's 'Foreign Minister'), who sits on the Commission.

iv The European Parliament

The European Parliament has been described as the 'institutional winner' in the Lisbon Treaty.[31] Article 14(1) provides that it exercises legislative and budgetary functions jointly with the Council, and the Treaty significantly extends the areas in which the 'ordinary legislative procedure' (formerly known as the co-decision procedure) is applicable. This involves both the Council and Parliament considering and adopting a proposal from the Commission, but confers significant powers upon Parliament to amend, and a power of veto.[32]

The Parliament is directly elected by votes cast in each member state. These 'elected representatives of the Union's citizens' sit in loose coalitions of political groups arranged along broad ideological lines, rather than on a national basis. Under the Lisbon Treaty, the Parliament is to number no more than 750 members, with the number of members being determined by population and with no state having more than 96 members.[33]

In addition to its legislative role, the Parliament has shared responsibility with the Council for the Union's budget.[34] The budget does not come into force until it has been declared as adopted by the President of the Parliament. As noted previously, Parliament also exercises supervision of the Commission by way of its approval of the appointment of Commissioners, by questioning Commissioners and considering Commission reports. Members also ask questions of the Council.

v The Court of Justice of the European Union

The Lisbon Treaty has had relatively little effect upon the EU's judicial organs.[35] Article 19(1) specifies that the Court of Justice of the European Union consists of the 'Court of Justice, the General Court and specialised courts.' The first of these, commonly referred to as the European Court of

---

[31] Above n.12, 157.
[32] Articles 289, 294, TFEU.
[33] Article 14(2), TEU.
[34] Article 314, TFEU.
[35] Craig, n.12, 157.

Justice (ECJ), consists of one judge from each member state, nominated by the governments for a six-year renewable term,[36] and now (under the Lisbon Treaty) assessed for suitability by a panel consisting of former members of the Court, members of national supreme courts and lawyers of recognised competence.[37] The Court is assisted by eight Advocates General,[38] who assist the ECJ in providing a (non-binding) opinion on the case before it. Pressure upon the ECJ's workload led to the establishment of a Court of First Instance (now called the General Court) in 1989, from which there is appeal to the ECJ. The 'specialised courts' referred to in Article 19(1) TEU allow judicial bodies with specific, limited jurisdiction to be created:[39] there is presently a European Union Civil Service Tribunal which adjudicates upon disputes between EU institutions as employers and their employees.

The Court's functions are described very broadly in Article 19(1) TEU as 'ensur[ing] that in the interpretation and application of the Treaties the law is observed'. Article 19(3) expands slightly upon this in stating that the Court may rule on actions 'brought by a Member State, an institution or a natural or legal person', that it may give preliminary rulings at the request of courts of the member states on interpretation of Union law or the validity of acts of institutions, and that it may rule in other cases provided for in the Treaties. In practice, the most important forms of proceedings brought before the Court will be actions brought by the Commission or a member state for failure to comply with EU law,[40] judicial review of the legality of actions and decisions by EU institutions (for which purpose member states and EU institutions have standing, but the standing of individuals is limited),[41] and the preliminary reference procedure,[42] which is described in the next section.

EU law in the UK

The law of the European Union, like that made by the Westminster Parliament, may be classified as either primary or secondary. Primary law consists of the Treaties. These establish the institutional architecture of the Union, set out the powers of the various institutions and their relationship with one another (and, crucially, with member states), provide for interpretation of the meaning of the provisions through the ECJ, and enumerate

---

[36] Article 253, TFEU.
[37] Article 255, TFEU.
[38] Article 252, TFEU.
[39] Article 257, TFEU.
[40] Articles 258 and 259, TFEU.
[41] Article 263, TFEU.
[42] Article 267, TFEU.

substantive rights and freedoms, both in the familiar form of human rights,[43] and in the more specific context of freedoms relating to the operation of an internal market within the Union.[44] In many respects, therefore, the principal Treaties under which the EU operates, the TEU and the TFEU, are 'constitutional' documents, although the provisions relating to the operation of the internal market go beyond that which one would normally expect to find in a constitution.[45]

Secondary legislation is that which is made by the institutions established under the Treaties. The forms of such law are specified in Article 288 TFEU as regulations, directives, decisions, recommendations and opinions, the latter two being non-binding. Regulations are binding in their entirety and are 'directly applicable' in member states, meaning that no action upon the part of the legislature in the member state is required to render them enforceable in domestic law once they have been approved by the EU institutions. Directives are 'binding as to the result to be achieved ... but shall leave to the national authorities the choice of form and methods'. Consequently, the member state will be required to enact law to implement the directive, within a specified time limit. Decisions (such as those issued by the ECJ) are also binding in their entirety, but only upon those to whom they are addressed.

In chapter 3, we noted that the ECJ expressed the view in the *Van Gend en Loos* case that what was then the European Community constituted a 'new legal order of international law, for the benefit of which the states have limited their sovereign rights'. The court went on to state that:

'the subjects [of this legal order] ... comprise not only member states but also their nationals. Independently of the legislation of member states, Community law therefore not only imposes obligations on individuals but is also intended to confer upon them rights which become part of their legal heritage. These rights arise not only where they are expressly granted by the Treaty, but also by reason of obligations which the Treaty imposes in a clearly defined way upon individuals as well as upon the member states and the institutions of the Community.'[46]

---

[43] As a consequence of the Lisbon Treaty, the Charter of Fundamental Rights of the European Union, which dates from 2000, is to have the 'same legal status as the Treaties', and the Union will accede to the European Convention on Human Rights: Article 6(1), (2), TEU.

[44] The core principles of the operation of the internal market are the free movement of goods, the free movement of persons, the free movement of services and the free movement of capital.

[45] See *Parti Ecologiste Les Verts v European Parliament* (C-294/83) [1986] ECR 1339, [23] describing the Treaty establishing the European Economic Community as 'the basic constitutional charter'.

[46] Above p.107 (n.145), 12.

This laid the foundations for the doctrine of 'direct effect', which enables rights established in primary or secondary legislation of the European Union to be claimed and enforced in domestic courts, including – under section 2(1) of the European Communities Act 1972 – courts in the UK.[47] As Craig observes, this has 'national constitutional significance' in that 'law derived from sources other than Parliament and the common law will avail individuals before their own national courts in a way which has not been the case on this scale hitherto'.[48] The significance is, of course, heightened by the principle of the supremacy of EU law, which was discussed in chapter 3. Direct effect enables rights granted under EU law to be enforced in domestic courts, and supremacy means that these take precedence over any domestic legal provisions to contrary effect. Thus, not only does law emanating from the Treaties and institutions constitute a source of law which is additional to that made by Parliament and the courts, it is a form of law which is superior in the hierarchy of norms to domestic law, in instances where the two are in conflict. Additionally, the doctrine of direct effect places domestic courts in a position where they have central responsibility for the interpretation and enforcement of EU law. It remains open for a domestic court to request a preliminary ruling from the ECJ under Article 267 TFEU on the interpretation of the Treaties and the validity and interpretation of acts of the Union's institutions, bodies, offices or agencies – as happened in the *Factortame* case – but such reference is only required where the court considers it 'necessary to enable it to give judgment'. In many instances, the domestic court may understand the law well enough to avoid the need to seek a preliminary ruling,[49] but even if reference takes place, it will be necessary for the domestic court to implement the ECJ's ruling on the question of the meaning of EU law in the context of the case before it.

Membership of the EU has, therefore, had the consequence that laws which are not made by any of the three branches of government analysed in chapters 3–5 can generate rights and be legally enforced in the UK. From a democratic perspective and from a standpoint of constitutionalism, it would therefore seem to be important that such laws should be subject to a degree of scrutiny by institutions which are accountable to the British public, whose legal position and relationships such laws will affect. It is for

---

[47] It should be noted that there are preconditions for applicability of the doctrine of direct effect, meaning that it will not apply to all forms of EU law, and that directives are only effective vertically (that is, against the state or an 'emanation of the state') while Treaty provisions and regulations are also effective against private parties. For discussion, see Craig, n.3, 99–103.

[48] *ibid*, 103.

[49] See *eg Equal Opportunities Commission*, above p.110 (n.159), and for discussion of the circumstances in which reference to the ECJ should and should not be made, see *R v International Stock Exchange Ltd, ex parte Else (1982) Ltd* [1993] QB 534, 545 (Sir Thomas Bingham MR).

each member state to determine how scrutiny of such laws will take place. At Westminster, various possibilities exist.

First, legislation may be necessary, with the attendant potential for debate upon the proposals. We have already seen that passage of the European Communities Act 1972 was necessary in order to give domestic legal effect to Community law.[50] In addition, the European Parliamentary Elections Act 2002 provides that any treaty which increases the powers of the European Parliament must be approved by Parliament in the form of primary legislation,[51] while the European Union (Amendment) Act 2008 provides that any treaty amending the TFEU and TEU will also require primary legislation.[52] Directives also need legislative action, since they are not directly applicable. However, most Directives are transposed into domestic law by way of secondary legislation, under the general power granted to ministers by section 2(2) of the European Communities Act 1972. As noted in chapter 3, such legislation is subject to limited parliamentary scrutiny and even less opportunity for debate.

Secondly, select committees in both Houses of Parliament have been established to scrutinise legislation emanating from, and other issues pertaining to the EU. In the Commons, the European Scrutiny Committee assesses the legal and/or political importance of EU documents (which term is defined to include draft Regulations, Directives and Decisions) together with explanatory memoranda produced by government upon these, and decides which are to be debated, whether in committee or on the floor of the House. The Committee also monitors Council meetings and the actions of UK ministers in these. In the Lords, the European Union Committee considers EU documents and other EU-related matters before decisions are taken upon them, so as to 'influence the Government's position in negotiations in Brussels, and to hold them to account for their actions at EU level'.[53] In order to carry out this work, it has established seven sub-committees dealing with specific policy areas. It considers fewer documents than the Commons committee, but in more depth. Importantly, both committees benefit from a 'scrutiny reserve resolution', which constrains ministers from agreeing to legislative proposals and certain other measures in the European Council or Council which have

---

[50] See also European Union (Amendment) Act 2008, s.2, which gave domestic effect to the Lisbon Treaty, by adding it to the list of Treaties specified in European Communities Act 1972, s.1(2).

[51] s.12.

[52] s.5. Note also s.6, which provides that the approval of Parliament is required prior to a favourable UK vote in European Council or Council in relation to a number of provisions of TEU and TFEU.

[53] See http://www.parliament.uk/business/committees/committees-a-z/lords-select/eu-select-committee-/role/

not completed scrutiny in the committees or which have been recommended for debate but not yet been debated. This requirement may be waived if the minister considers that an EU proposal is confidential, routine or trivial, substantially the same as one on which scrutiny has already been completed or if s/he provides 'special reasons'. The scrutiny reserve is not legally binding upon ministers, but the committees will call for evidence from ministers who override it without good cause.[54]

Thirdly (and more broadly) there are opportunities to question ministers, whether in relation to proposed EU legislation or other matters, in debates or parliamentary question time. This form of accountability is somewhat constrained by two factors. First (and in contrast to some European nations), there is no government department dedicated solely to EU issues, although a junior minister in the Foreign Office has responsibility for European matters. In practice, this means that questions relating to the EU dimension of a particular department's work are taken alongside (and may be subsumed by) questions on their national-level responsibilities. Secondly, the existence of qualified majority voting in Council means that the Union may adopt a measure which has been opposed by the UK. In such circumstances, the national Parliament in Westminster has little scope to exercise a meaningful check upon what happens at EU level.

From a UK perspective, the concern is that these mechanisms for scrutiny and accountability are insufficiently powerful to afford adequate democratic control over the significant legislative, executive and judicial powers which have been transferred to the EU. That concern is strengthened by perceptions of a 'democratic deficit' at the heart of the EU. Of the three institutions involved in the process of making legislation, only the Parliament is a directly elected institution at *European* level, and it suffers from a lack of public visibility and apathy, reflected in low turnouts at European parliamentary elections.[55]

It is interesting to note that the Lisbon Treaty has made attempts to address the problem of democracy. The establishment of the office of President of the European Council can be seen as a means of personalising the Union, and therefore making it more accessible to European citizens. As noted above, the Treaty has also strengthened the powers of the Parliament, which is proclaimed by Article 10(2) TEU to be the institution which directly represents citizens at Union level. Elsewhere in the TEU, Article 10(1) states that the functioning of the Union shall be founded on participatory democracy, Article 10(3) provides that 'every citizen shall

---

[54] See Department of the Clerk of the House of Commons, *The European Scrutiny System in the House of Commons* (2009), 11.

[55] The turnout across the Union in 2009 was 43 per cent of voters: see http://www.europarl.europa.eu/parliament/archive/elections2009/en/turnout_en.html

have the right to participate in the democratic life of the Union' and that 'decisions shall be taken as openly and as closely as possible to the citizen', Article 11(2) provides that the institutions 'shall maintain an open, transparent and regular dialogue with representative associations and civil society', and Article 11(4) provides for a 'citizens' initiative' process whereby no less than one million citizens who are nationals of a significant number of member states may call upon the Commission to bring forward new policy proposals. Provisions of the TFEU and TEU also seek to enhance the transparency of the decision-making process of EU institutions.[56] Additionally, Article 12 stresses the means by which *national* parliaments may actively contribute to the functioning of the Union, for example, by having draft legislation forwarded to them and co-operating with other parliaments and with the European Parliament. National parliaments are also empowered to ensure that EU institutions respect the principle of 'subsidiarity', which means that the Union should only act if it is better placed to achieve objectives than institutions in the member states. Protocol 2, annexed to the Treaties, provides for a 'yellow' and 'orange card' system whereby national parliaments may express concern as to the compliance of a proposal with the principle of subsidiarity.[57]

Two views may be taken as to the significance of these provisions. On the one hand, they may be viewed as serious efforts to address the EU's 'democratic deficit'. As such, they might function to reconnect the Westminster Parliament and (by extension) the British public to institutions to whom significant powers have been transferred with limited scope for democratic control over, or participation in their exercise. On the other hand, they might be seen as little more than 'rhetorical flourishes, with little or any substance'.[58] Only time will tell which of these evaluations proves to be correct.

B. Devolution

The UK has often been described as possessing a unitary constitutional structure. Such a description serves to distinguish it from nations, such as the United States, Germany or Australia, which are organised in the form of a federation. In that type of arrangement, power – including, but not restricted to, legislative power – is distributed by a constitutional instrument between central (or federal) institutions and those operating at state

---

[56] See *eg* Article 15, TFEU, Article 16(8), TEU.
[57] Articles 7(2), (3), Protocol 2. See also Protocol 1 on the role of national Parliaments in the European Union.
[58] Craig, n.12, 160.

or provincial level, and the respective institutions have particular areas of competence into which the other bodies are not permitted to intrude. Federalism might be said to be more responsive to differences in culture, political outlook, economic development, social values and religious preference (among other factors) which may exist within the boundaries of the broader nation state. It also serves a purpose in limiting power, as Barendt makes clear:

> 'A federal constitution, like the separation of powers principle, reduces the risk of a concentration of power and the danger of arbitrary government. The former distributes authority vertically between the centre and the states or regions, while the separation principle operates on the horizontal level to allocate powers between different institutions or organs of government. Both therefore serve the value of constitutionalism in similar ways.'[59]

By contrast, power in the UK has traditionally tended to be highly centralised, notwithstanding the existence of local government which has powers to raise revenue and to make 'byelaws' which apply within the locality in question. This state of affairs is underpinned by the doctrine of parliamentary sovereignty, under which the omnicompetent legislature at Westminster may legislate on any matter which it chooses – including those which are within the competence of a local or regional institution which has been accorded legislative and/or executive authority – or may abolish local or regional structures of government altogether. It should of course be noted that, while the Westminster Parliament may legislate for the entire UK, there are three separate legal systems within the boundaries of the nation state, with separate courts and legal professions: namely, those of England and Wales; Scotland; and Northern Ireland. However, as Munro observes, 'the existence of different legal systems is not a consequence of a federal system. It is a consequence of our political history, including the arrangements made when unions were agreed and the arrangements made since for different parts of the state'.[60]

This state of affairs has altered significantly in recent years as a consequence of the devolution legislation enacted in the late 1990s. Devolution was defined by the Royal Commission on the Constitution, which was established in 1969 to examine the functions of central government and legislature in relation to the countries, regions and nations of the United Kingdom, as 'the delegation of central governmental powers without the

---

[59] Barendt, above p.124 (n.4), 58.
[60] Munro, above p.25 (n.14), 16.

relinquishment of sovereignty'.[61] The Commission identified three forms of devolution: legislative (entailing the devolution of certain law-making powers to regional assemblies); executive (regional policy-making and administration); and administrative (no new regional institutions of government, but some aspects of central government to be carried out in a regional setting).[62] The latter form of devolution already existed, with departments of central government in London assuming responsibility for dealing with Welsh, Scottish and Northern Irish issues. However, the government of Tony Blair wished to go much further, and secured the passage of the Scotland Act 1998 and the Government of Wales Act 1998, in each case following positive votes in referendums of the affected populations. In the same year, the Northern Ireland Act was also passed following the 'Good Friday Agreement' between the major political actors in the province.

i Scotland

The forms of devolution to these three constituent parts of the United Kingdom differ from each other in important respects. Devolution to Scotland takes both legislative and executive forms, with the establishment of a unicameral Scottish Parliament under the Scotland Act 1998.[63] This body is empowered to make legislation within broad areas of competence which are not reserved to the Westminster Parliament. This issue is discussed in more depth in chapter 3, and readers are invited to return to that analysis to gain a fuller picture of the nature of legislative devolution to Scotland.

In addition, and importantly, the Scottish Parliament possesses the power to vary the basic rate of UK income tax by up to 3 pence in the pound, potentially giving it a limited degree of financial independence from the rest of the UK.[64] Questions as to whether the Parliament has competence to legislate upon particular issues, or whether it has acted compatibly (as it is obliged to do)[65] with European Union law or the Convention rights given further effect by the Human Rights Act 1998, may arise in the course of any legal proceedings whether in Scotland or elsewhere in the UK. Such a 'devolution issue' may be referred by the court or tribunal in question to a superior court and ultimately to the Supreme

---

[61] *Royal Commission on the Constitution 1969–1973*, Volume I, Report Cmnd 5460 (1973), [543].
[62] *ibid*, [546]
[63] s.1.
[64] Part IV of the 1998 Act. The power has not, to date, been used.
[65] s.29(2)(d).

Court for resolution. A Scottish Executive is also established by the 1998 Act,[66] comprising a First Minister (who is nominated by the Parliament and appointed by the Queen), ministers appointed by the First Minister, and the Scottish Law Officers. Members of the Executive (except for the Law Officers) are required to sit in Parliament and, as such, are accountable to it in a manner comparable to that which applies in the Westminster Parliament.

ii Wales

Devolution to Wales is more limited in scope. No transfer of primary law-making powers has yet taken place, nor does power exist to raise revenue by varying the rate of taxation. Rather, the legislation enacted in 1998 gave effect to a form of executive devolution, in which the functions previously performed by the Welsh Office within central government, and various non-departmental public bodies dealing with Welsh matters, were transferred to an elected Welsh Assembly.[67] This is a unicameral body with power to make delegated legislation within certain fields, including education and training, the environment, health and health services, housing, social services, transport and the Welsh language. Initially, no separate executive was established, although a form of Cabinet-style government evolved in practice.

This position was changed by the Government of Wales Act 2006, which establishes a Welsh Assembly Government consisting of a First Minister (nominated by the Assembly and appointed by the Queen), ministers appointed by the First Minster from Assembly members, deputy ministers and a Counsel General who provides legal advice on matters relating to devolved functions.[68] The 2006 Act also enhances the Assembly's legislative powers in so far as the Westminster Parliament may grant powers, via a 'Legislative Competence Order', to the Assembly to pass 'Assembly Measures' which have legal effect in Wales in relation to particular subject matters within specified fields,[69] subject to various general restrictions (eg those precluding incompatibility with Convention rights or European Union law).[70] The Act also contains provisions which will enable

---

[66] s.44.

[67] Government of Wales Act 1998, s.1.

[68] s.45.

[69] s.93. The subject matters and exceptions are listed in Schedule 5.

[70] See, eg, NHS Redress (Wales) Measure 2008, competence for the making of which was conferred by the National Assembly for Wales (Legislative Competence) (Conversion of Framework Powers) Order 2007. The Order inserted the power to make 'Provision for and in connection with the provision of redress without recourse to civil proceedings in circumstances in which, under the law of England and Wales, qualifying liability in tort arises in connection with the provision of services (in Wales or elsewhere) as part of the health service in Wales' into the field of health and health services specified by Schedule 5, Part 1 of the 2006 Act.

the Assembly to pass primary legislation, although unlike in Scotland there is no general power to legislate on all issues except those which are reserved to Westminster. Rather, legislation may occur only within the specified fields.[71] This power to enact primary legislation (to be known as 'Assembly Acts') will only be triggered if approved in a future referendum of the Welsh people.[72]

iii Northern Ireland

Arrangements for devolution to Northern Ireland are complicated by the difficult nature of the political situation there. Northern Ireland had a system of devolved government from 1922 onwards, but in the wake of escalating violence and disorder between nationalist supporters of union with the Republic of Ireland and those ('Unionists') who wished to remain part of the UK, this was suspended in 1972 and 'direct rule' from London re-established. Following the political agreement reached in 1998, and subsequent to a referendum endorsing that agreement, the Northern Ireland Act of that year laid the framework for devolution, although the process has been suspended on a number of occasions in response to political problems, most notably from October 2002 to May 2007, during which period direct rule from London recommenced.[73]

The 1998 Act provided that Northern Ireland should remain part of the UK and should not cease to be so without the consent of a majority of its population voting in a poll held for that purpose.[74] The Act also established legislative and executive institutions, but within a framework of power-sharing and cross-community support. Thus, the First Minister and Deputy First Minister were originally elected by the members of the Northern Ireland Assembly on the basis of 'parallel consent', which entailed achieving a majority of all voting members *and* a majority of those members who had designated themselves as Nationalists and those who had designated themselves as Unionists.[75] Further ministers are allocated in accordance with the size of parties in the Assembly. The Assembly has primary legislative powers in respect of matters which have been *transferred*

---

[71] ss.107–109. Matters within the legislative competence of the Assembly are listed in Schedule 7.

[72] s.103. The Coalition Government promises to 'introduce a referendum on further Welsh devolution': HM Government, above p.71 (n.12), 28.

[73] See Northern Ireland Act 2000.

[74] s.1.

[75] See now Northern Ireland (St. Andrews Agreement) Act 2006, s.8 which provides that the leader of the largest party in one designation (in practice, the Unionists) shall nominate the First Minister, and the leader of the largest party in the other designation (in practice, the Nationalists) shall nominate the Deputy Minister.

to it. These are listed in Schedule 4 of the Act and include education, the environment, health and social services. Matters which are *excepted*, listed in Schedule 2, are outside the competence of the Assembly and can only therefore be legislated upon by the Westminster Parliament. These include international relations, defence, national security and taxation. *Reserved* matters, which include public order, firearms and explosives, consumer safety and telecommunications and broadcasting,[76] can be transferred to the Assembly by an Order in Council approved in draft by both Houses of Parliament following a resolution requesting the transfer which has been passed by the Assembly with cross-community support. This occurred in respect of policing and justice powers in March 2010. The Assembly may also legislate on reserved matters in specific instances with the consent of the Secretary of State for Northern Ireland.

iv England

Where does this leave England, which is by far the largest of the constituent elements of the UK, with well over 80 per cent of the total population? It has been argued that 'England is the gaping hole in the devolution settlement'.[77] In so far as any decentralisation of power has taken place at all, it has taken the form of regionalism, rather than devolution. No legislative or significant executive powers have been conferred upon institutions which represent the nation as a whole, and the steps which have been proposed and/or taken have been succinctly described as a form of 'super-local government'.[78] The most comprehensive developments have taken place in London, which has a directly elected mayor and assembly, whose principal purposes relate to the promotion of economic development and wealth creation, social development and improvement of the environment.[79] Elsewhere, no elected bodies exist at regional level,[80] although in nine English regions (including London), Government Offices exist to co-ordinate and input into the work of central government at local level, Regional Development Agencies exercise statutory powers

---

[76] Schedule 3.

[77] R. Hazell, 'Introduction: What is the English Question?' in R. Hazell (ed.) *The English Question* (Manchester: Manchester University Press, 2006), 1.

[78] B. Hadfield, 'Devolution in the United Kingdom and the English and Welsh Questions' in Jowell and Oliver (eds.), above p.37 (n.62), 249.

[79] See Greater London Authority Act 1999.

[80] The Labour Government made an attempt to introduce elected regional assemblies: see *Your Region, Your Choice: Revitalising the English Regions*, Cm 5511 (2002) and Regional Assemblies (Preparations Act) 2003, which enabled regional referendums to be held to determine whether an assembly should be established. Only one such referendum was held, in the North East in November 2004, and the weight of the majority vote against the proposal persuaded the Government to abandon its plans.

relating to economic development,[81] and non-statutory regional assemblies (consisting of representatives of local authorities and social, economic and environmental organisations) were established to liaise with the Regional Development Agencies and central government. The assemblies (but not the London Assembly) were abolished between 2008 and 2010, and the Coalition Government announced in June 2010 that Regional Development Agencies were to be phased out by 2012. It would therefore appear that progress towards regional government in England has fizzled out, at least for the present.

Still less have any of the major political parties demonstrated enthusiasm for the creation of an English Parliament, which would complement those in Scotland, Wales and Northern Ireland.[82] The absence of any momentum in this direction would seem to be a reflection of public apathy, perhaps grounded in the relative lack of a distinctly *English* identity by comparison with those in Scotland, Wales and Northern Ireland whose identities, at least in part, are shaped by *not* being English. But, while such inaction is politically understandable, it is constitutionally problematic. The particular difficulty relates to what has been dubbed the 'West Lothian Question'.[83] While English MPs cannot participate in debates or vote upon matters which have been devolved to the Parliament in Edinburgh, or the Assemblies in Cardiff and Belfast, Scottish, Welsh and Northern Irish MPs continue to sit in the Westminster Parliament and can participate in debates and legislation on issues which solely affect England. In consequence, England is 'the only UK nation *all* of whose laws are made and *all* of whose policies are formulated by a UK body and *never* by a solely English-elected body'.[84] No easy solution to this problem has been identified.[85] 'Withdrawal' of non-English MPs from matters which are solely English cannot necessarily resolve the conundrum as it might well mean that a government which possesses a parliamentary majority on matters affecting the whole of the UK would no longer possess a majority on English matters once the other MPs were removed. But the creation of an English Parliament – even if there were the political will for it – would run the risk of sidelining the UK Parliament at Westminster and might raise

---

[81] See Regional Development Agencies Act 1998.

[82] But note the existence of a single-issue political group, the Campaign for an English Parliament.

[83] The issue is so called because the question was raised in 1978 by the MP for the Westminster constituency of West Lothian, Tam Dalyell. See further *The West Lothian Question*, House of Commons Research Paper 95/58 (1995).

[84] B. Hadfield, 'Devolution, Westminster and the English question' [2005] *Public Law* 286, 291. Emphases in original.

[85] The Coalition Government has announced that it will establish a Commission to investigate the question: HM Government, above p.71 (n.12), 27.

difficult constitutional questions as regards the doctrine of parliamentary sovereignty.

vi Conclusion

The West Lothian Question neatly demonstrates the asymmetrical character of devolution in the UK. Different models apply in the different parts of the nation, and legislative and executive powers are far from equally distributed. In large part, this represents a pragmatic response to differing historical, political and cultural factors. For example, the relative weakness of the Welsh model by comparison with that which exists in Scotland reflects the lower levels of support for devolution in Wales which, in turn, may be explained by the fact that Wales has been administratively and legally united to England since the thirteenth century. The consequence of such pragmatism is that constitutional principle is relegated to a secondary consideration, as the West Lothian Question again illustrates.

But, while no clear thread of constitutional principle can be said to underpin the devolution 'settlement', the process of reform does, of course, have significant constitutional implications. We have already noted, in chapter 3, the challenge which it presents to the traditional understanding of parliamentary sovereignty notwithstanding that the devolution legislation explicitly preserves the omnicompetence of the Westminster Parliament, even over matters which are devolved. Relatedly, the major pieces of devolution legislation – the Scotland Act 1998, the Government of Wales Act 2006, and the Northern Ireland Act 1998 – might be regarded as broadly equivalent to constitutional instruments: for example, Lord Bingham expressed the view that while the Northern Ireland Act 1998 'does not set out all the constitutional provisions applicable to Northern Ireland ... it is, in effect a constitution'.[86] A number of consequences follow from this. First, in the same case, it was indicated that a 'generous and purposive' approach, which sought to give effect to the underlying values of the constitution rather than to the specific words used, should be taken to interpretation of the statutory provisions.[87] Secondly, in *Thoburn*, Laws LJ indicated that the Scotland and Government of Wales Acts 1998 fell within the category of 'constitutional statutes' to which the principle of implied repeal did not apply.[88] Thirdly, and some-

---

[86] *Robinson v Secretary of State for Northern Ireland* [2002] UKHL 32, [11].

[87] *id.*

[88] Above p.103 (n.134). Note that this case was decided before the enactment of the Government of Wales Act 2006, while the Northern Ireland Act 1998 was not specifically included in the category, perhaps because the devolved institutions were suspended at that time, casting doubt upon the long-term stability of the devolution arrangement.

what less tangibly, it can be argued that the absence of such a constitutional document in the English case means that the trend in the direction of a 'legal' rather than a 'political' constitution is somewhat less strong there than is the case in the other three constituent parts of the UK, where relationships between governmental institutions are now prescribed by statute and subject to interpretation and adjudication by courts.[89]

Another, more subtle way in which devolution may have a long-term impact upon power relations within the UK constitutional order arises from its role as a 'constant, indigenous source of comparison'.[90] While there are points of similarity between London on the one hand and Edinburgh, Cardiff and Belfast on the other: notably, a prime ministerial/Cabinet style of government in which ministers are drawn from the legislature and are responsible to it, there are also significant variations. The electoral systems differ from that presently used in Westminster, with those in Scotland and Wales being based upon the additional member system and that in Northern Ireland upon the single transferable vote. In turn, this has tended to produce minority or coalition governments: necessarily so in the power-sharing context of Northern Ireland. A significant amount of the work of the legislature takes place in committees, rather than in plenary session. Furthermore, each legislature sits for a fixed four-year term.

The existence of these points of difference assists those who argue for reform at Westminster. Provided that the devolved institutional arrangements are seen to be working well, a strong argument can be made that these alternative ways of doing things should be 'transferred across'. There is some indication that this is happening at present. While the election of a Coalition Government for the UK in 2010 cannot be said to have been directly linked to the frequency of such governments under devolution, the experiences of Scotland, Wales and Northern Ireland may have rendered the notion of coalition more familiar to the British public. That government has subsequently announced both that Parliament will sit for a fixed term of five years,[91] and that there will be a referendum on reform to the electoral system for the UK. We have also noted in chapter 3 that there has been a recent resurgence in the power of select committees in Westminster, although this would appear to be attributable more to the scandal on MPs' expenses than to a comparison with the devolved institutions. All of these developments, if carried through, will tend to limit the power of the executive to exercise control over the legislative branch.

---

[89] See Hadfield, n.84, 254.
[90] Loveland, above p.39 (n.75), 451.
[91] Above p.132.

Devolution may therefore have multiple impacts upon the balance of power between executive, legislature and judiciary, and between the state and the individual. Most obviously, it reduces the power of both Westminster (notwithstanding the formal preservation of parliamentary sovereignty) and of central government *vis-a-vis* these constituent parts of the UK. Correspondingly, the power of the judiciary is somewhat increased, especially as it is called upon to resolve 'constitutional' disputes as to the competences of the devolved institutions. In Scotland, Wales and Northern Ireland, devolution has brought the institutions of government closer to the public, which should result in enhanced accountability and participation. Yet, in the longer term, the impact may be an enhancement of the position of the legislature relative to the executive in the UK as a whole, as the previously-discussed 'experiments' (in voting systems, coalition governments, parliamentary committees and fixed-term governments) which have been trialled under devolution become a permanent feature of the British constitutional landscape.

C. Administrative justice

As chapter 5 indicates, the recent growth in judicial review of administrative action, both as regards the frequency of its use and the scope of its subject matter, is a startling feature of the modern British constitutional order. But the picture which this paints is slightly misleading, for the vast majority of disputes between individuals and the executive branch of government are not, in fact, resolved in the courtroom but rather through one of the other mechanisms of administrative justice. To give an example, the Tribunals Service dealt with 568,153 cases between April 2008 and March 2009,[92] compared with the 7,169 applications for judicial review which were lodged in 2008.

It is common to refer to a 'system' of administrative justice, which embraces the various mechanisms which exist for resolving disputes and airing grievances relating to executive decisions which are made in relation to particular persons.[93] But this overstates the degree of rationality which went into creation of the various institutions. As an important government policy document puts it, 'administrative justice can be described as a system but it was not created as a system and no coherent design or design principle has ever been applied systematically to it. It is a patchwork.'[94] This state

---

[92] Tribunals Service, *Annual Report and Accounts*, HC 599 (2009), 8.

[93] See, for example, Tribunals, Courts and Enforcement Act 2007, Schedule 7, [13(4)].

[94] Department for Constitutional Affairs, *Transforming Public Services: Complaints, Redress and Tribunals*, Cm 6243 (2004), [4.21].

of affairs is perhaps unsurprising given that, in the absence of a codified constitutional document, theorising about institutional structures in general has taken a largely academic rather than practical political form in the UK. The consequence has been that mechanisms have tended to spring up in an *ad hoc* manner as the state has assumed new responsibilities in areas of the economy and society, with the attendant possibility of disputes arising from governmental decisions as to the rights and obligations of individuals. Furthermore, Dicey's opposition to 'French-style' specialist institutions and processes for the resolution of individual grievances against the state has also been highly influential in retarding the development of administrative justice, at least until recently. However, the 'patchwork' nature of the 'system' may be regarded as problematic from the perspective of the rule of law if we read the latter as emphasising the need for clarity and access to justice. As the same policy document continues, 'the existing landscape of dispute resolution options is confused and confusing with many variations in name, style and technique'.[95]

The institutional landscape of administrative justice has been undergoing a process of evolution in recent years.[96] That process commenced with a review of the tribunal system conducted in 2001, which recommended that the haphazard structure – which consisted of seventy different jurisdictions over various areas of government established at different times and with different procedures, powers and workloads – should be unified, simplified and rendered more clearly independent from the executive branch.[97] The proposals were taken forward in *Transforming Public Services: Complaints, Redress and Tribunals*,[98] published in 2004, which set out the government's proposals for reform and focused in particular upon the notion of 'proportionate dispute resolution', which entailed matching a dispute, and the individual's objective in pursuing it, with the most appropriate mechanism for resolution. Subsequently, the Tribunals, Courts and Enforcement Act 2007 gave effect to the proposals. That legislation focused primarily upon the tribunal system, but it also established a non-departmental public body, the Administrative Justice and Tribunals Council, to provide oversight of administrative justice as a whole. In principle, this body had the potential to sit at the apex of a coherent system of administrative justice operating alongside the judicial review jurisdiction, managing the relationships between the various mechanisms in the interests of those who use them. In practice, its capacity to fulfil this role was always

---

[95] *ibid*, [2.8].
[96] For a valuable recent discussion of various aspects of administrative justice, see M. Adler (ed.), *Administrative Justice in Context* (Oxford: Hart, 2010).
[97] *Tribunals for Users: One System, One Service* (2001) (the 'Leggatt Report').
[98] Above n.94.

likely to be limited by its small size (it consists of up to fifteen appointed members) and budget (£1 million per year).[99] The fact that there still remains considerable scope for rationalisation and simplification of administrative justice has been indicated by the Council, which acknowledges that 'there is at present no coherent system of administrative justice. Rather, the "system" comprises a large number of disparate elements that have to a great extent developed separately to perform different functions'.[100] These will now be described. Most attention will be given to tribunals, since the most important recent reforms have been in this field, but the other mechanisms will also be outlined.

i Tribunals

The modern system of tribunals emerged in the wake of the development of the welfare state in the twentieth century. Once the state begin to confer benefits upon and provide services to individuals, it became inevitable that disputes as to entitlement would arise. Such disputes could have been allocated to the courts, but influenced by 'green light' theorists who viewed the ideological preferences of judges with suspicion and who sought to devise mechanisms which were accessible to users but compatible with efficient administration,[101] decisions were generally taken to establish specialised statutory tribunals to resolve disputes within a particular field of administration. Such bodies were perceived as being speedier, cheaper, more informal and hence more accessible than the ordinary courts, and were also considered useful as a means of reducing the judicial burden. There has therefore been a tendency to regard tribunals as 'court substitutes'. This perception was underpinned by the *Report of the Committee on Administrative Tribunals and Enquiries*, which put forward the view that 'tribunals should properly be regarded as machinery provided by Parliament for adjudication rather than as part of the machinery of administration'.[102] Accordingly, within the threefold classification adopted in chapters 3–5, tribunals sit most happily alongside the judiciary, their role being to hear appeals – usually, on issues of fact – against administrative decisions. As such, it is felt that they should embody rule of law-type values of 'openness, fairness and impartiality',[103] with consequent judicial-style procedural characteristics, albeit within a more informal and accessi-

---

[99] The Council will be abolished in line with proposals for savings in expenditure on non-departmental public bodies outlined by the Coalition Government: see above p.159 (n.130).

[100] Administrative Justice and Tribunals Council, *The Developing Administrative Justice Landscape* (2009), [11].

[101] See Harlow and Rawlings, above p.5 (n.7), 440–43.

[102] Cmnd 218 (1957), [40].

[103] *ibid*, [41].

ble framework. These might include a legally qualified chairperson, public hearings, the right to legal representation, the giving of reasons and provision of a right of appeal to a court (though it should be noted that there was considerable variability in the approach taken to these matters across different tribunals).

In one particular respect, however, tribunals did not resemble courts. Notwithstanding the importance attached to impartiality, tribunals were dependent for administrative support, resources, (some) staffing and specification of procedures upon the department with responsibility for decision-making in the area of government which was being challenged. This created the perception of a lack of independence or, as the Leggatt Report succinctly put matters, 'for users, as has been said, "Every appeal is an away game"'.[104] The response to this concern (which, as noted in chapter 2, connects to Article 6 of the European Convention on Human Rights) was the establishment of a single Tribunals Service in April 2006. This is an executive agency of the Ministry of Justice but is otherwise independent of government. The Service's primary tasks are 'to provide a responsive and efficient tribunals administration; to promote and protect the independence of the (tribunals) judiciary; to contribute to the improvement of the quality of decision-making across government; and to reform the tribunals' justice system for the benefit of its customers and the wider public.'[105]

Alongside this development, the enactment of the Tribunals, Courts and Enforcement Act 2007 brought about the simplification of the 'patchwork' structure of tribunals. The Act established a two-tier system consisting of a First-Tier and Upper Tribunal, divided into Chambers which cover similar types of jurisdiction.[106] Most appeals are brought in the first instance to the First-Tier Tribunal; the Upper Tribunal primarily hears appeals from the First-Tier, although certain cases go directly to it and it also exercises a limited judicial review jurisdiction. An appeal from a decision of the Upper Tribunal on a point of law may lie, with permission, to the Court of Appeal.[107] The Act establishes a new post, Senior President of Tribunals,[108] whose responsibilities for oversight of the system and communication to ministers are broadly comparable to those of the Lord Chief Justice in relation to the 'ordinary' judiciary: he is also a judge in the Court of Appeal. Legal members of tribunals (many of which also contain

---

[104] Above n.97, Overview, [3].

[105] Tribunals Service, *Annual Report and Accounts 2009–10*, HC 239 (2010), 6.

[106] For example, the Social Entitlement Chamber, which is part of the First-Tier Tribunal, hears appeals on social security and child support, criminal injuries compensation and asylum support.

[107] s.13.

[108] s.2.

non-legal or 'lay' panel members with expertise in the particular subject matter) are given the title 'judge',[109] and the guarantee of continued judicial independence provided by section 3 of the Constitutional Reform Act 2005 is extended to them.[110] A Tribunal Procedure Committee is established to make rules which will apply at First-Tier and Upper Tribunal level.[111]

It is apparent that the 2007 Act strengthens the trend for tribunals to be regarded as adjuncts to the judicial branch. As Harlow and Rawlings state, the Act 'will, as was intended, push tribunals into the ambit of courts: in future they are likely to be less court substitutes and more quasi-courts.'[112] There is, however, something of a tension here.[113] The government's preference for proportionate dispute resolution envisages that disputes should be resolved without recourse to formal mechanisms of adjudication where this is appropriate in the circumstances of the case, which points us towards cheap, speedy and user-friendly mechanisms. On the other hand, the reforms to tribunals push them further in the direction of the most formalised mechanism for adjudication, courts, a trend which is consistent with the attention recently directed to constitutional principles in respect of the judiciary, most notably evident in the Constitutional Reform Act 2005. In effect, we see here a classic clash between a 'red light' perspective, which would seek to protect individual rights against state intrusion via formalised mechanisms which give effect to rule of law values, and the 'green light' approach which is sympathetic to the state's pursuit of its goals and seeks to ensure that law works with, not against the state: for example, in its pursuit of efficiency and value for money. The 2007 Act seems to place tribunals, together with courts, squarely in the former camp. The danger is that this will result in an enduring division between more and less formal mechanisms. This is scarcely conducive to the development of a coherent and unified system of administrative justice. Rather, it looks like a split between two distinct systems, the one modelled upon judicial adjudication and the other upon other modes of dispute resolution.

---

[109] ss.3–4.

[110] s.1.

[111] s.22.

[112] Above p.5 (n.7), 522. See also G. Richardson and H. Genn, 'Tribunals in transition: resolution or adjudication?' [2007] *Public Law* 116; R. Carnwath, 'Tribunal justice: a new start' [2009] *Public Law* 48, especially, 50: '[the Act] confirms the place of the tribunal judiciary as part of the judicial system, rather than as an appendage of the administration'.

[113] See further LeSueur, above p.37 (n.62); Richardson and Genn, *id.*

ii Inquiries

The need for inquiries arose as government acquired powers to plan, purchase and develop land for public purposes, such as the construction of roads, power stations or airports. In such circumstances, the government's objectives might conflict with the rights of affected individuals including – but not restricted to – property rights. This having been said, inquiries may cover a wide range of subject matters ranging from accidents and natural disasters to allegations of child abuse or neglect.[114] This indicates that there are two broad uses for inquiries: first as part of the 'normal' decision-making process in government, especially in relation to planning decisions, and secondly as a means of responding to public concern as to 'out of the ordinary' events, with a view to ensuring that mistakes made are identified and are not repeated in the future.

Inquiries may be set up under subject-specific legislation, for example that which relates to planning (cg the Planning Act 2008) or the Health and Safety at Work Act 1974. In addition, the Inquiries Act 2005 confers a general power upon a minister (including those in the devolved administrations) to cause an inquiry to be held where it appears to him or her that 'particular events have caused, or are capable of causing, public concern or there is public concern that particular events may have occurred'.[115] It is also possible for inquiries to be set up in the absence of any statutory basis, either simply as part of the process of administration or as an exercise of the royal prerogative, as is the case with Royal Commissions, which are often (although not exclusively) established to investigate major constitutional questions.[116]

The *Report of the Committee on Administrative Tribunals and Enquiries* saw the inquiry process as serving the twin purposes of ensuring procedural protection for the interests of those most affected by a government proposal by way of a right to be heard and of ensuring that government was better informed in reaching its final decision.[117] The consequence was that the inquiry could be viewed as a hybrid mechanism, partly administrative and partly judicial in character. However, while rules or procedure in relation to specific types of inquiry may incorporate judicial-style procedural protections such as notice and a right to appear and be represented, and are enforceable in the courts, the House of Lords has made clear that an inquiry, such as that into construction of a motorway, 'is quite unlike any civil litigation'.[118] Thus, while the procedure has to be fair, it need not

---

[114] For illustrations, see above p.31.
[115] s.1(1)
[116] See *eg* above n.61.
[117] Above n.102, [269].
[118] *Bushell v Secretary of State for the Environment* [1981] AC 75, 96 (Lord Diplock).

entail all of the procedural protections which would be applicable in a court setting, such as cross-examination. This is important in respect of compliance with Article 6 of the European Convention on Human Rights. In the *Alconbury* case,[119] the House of Lords held that, although a minister who determined planning appeals could not be regarded as 'independent and impartial' for the purposes of that Article (since the state had an interest in the outcome of the appeals), there was no violation of the Convention because the decision-making process was administrative in character and involved the formation and application of policy. In such circumstances, the possibility that the decision could, if necessary, be judicially reviewed (even though this did not permit appeal on the merits) was sufficient to meet the requirements of fairness imposed by the Article.

The potential for tension between the interests of affected individuals and those of government which arises as a consequence of the dual functions performed by inquiries is perhaps most apparent in respect of 'big inquiries' such as that into Terminal 5 at Heathrow Airport, which may take several years and cost millions of pounds. Perhaps understandably, governments have sought to streamline such processes in order that policy decisions may be implemented more quickly: but this is likely to entail limitations upon the rights of affected individuals and groups to participate in the decision-making process. The Planning Act 2008, which was designed to facilitate decisions on 'nationally significant infrastructure projects',[120] was criticised for replacing the inquiry process with examination of an application, normally to be conducted on the basis of written representations, by an appointed Infrastructure Planning Commission.[121] The Coalition Government has announced the abolition of this body and its replacement with 'an efficient and democratically accountable system that provides a fast-track process for major infrastructure projects.'[122] It remains to be seen whether the goal of efficient decision-making can be satisfactorily combined with procedures which enable affected interests to voice their views on such projects, or whether an irreconcilable and permanent conflict of values exists here.

iii Ombudsmen

Perhaps no better illustration could be provided of the difficulty which is sometimes encountered in allocating institutions and mechanisms within the British constitution to one of the three branches of government than

---

[119] Above p.58, (n.154).
[120] s.14.
[121] See Harlow and Rawlings, above p.5 (n.7), 587.
[122] HM Government, above p.71 (n.12), 11.

the office of Ombudsman. Writing in 1984, the then incumbent of the post of Parliamentary Commissioner for Administration (now known as the Parliamentary Ombudsman (PO)) commented that 'the office ... stands curiously poised between the legislature and the executive, while discharging an almost judicial function in the citizen's dispute with his government; and yet it forms no part of the judiciary'.[123] The Ombudsman, whose existence derives from the Parliamentary Commissioner Act 1967, is an officer of the House of Commons who is appointed by the Crown on the advice of the Prime Minister, but who (like judges) holds office during good behaviour subject to removal on a vote of both Houses. The role complements – and is, in principle, subordinate to – that of Parliament as a mechanism for the redress of grievances in that a matter can only be investigated if it is referred by an MP (the so-called 'MP filter').[124] However (and in contrast to tribunals), the PO cannot be seen as a 'court substitute' given that the Act specifically excludes from his or her jurisdiction actions in respect of which the individual could bring a claim in a court or tribunal,[125] unless it would not be reasonable to expect the individual to pursue a claim in such manner.[126]

Instead, the PO performs a role within the administrative justice 'system' which is distinct from the adjudicative functions undertaken by courts and tribunals. The PO's task is to 'investigate any action taken by or on behalf of a government department or other authority to which this Act applies' in relation to the exercise of administrative functions where a member of the public 'claims to have sustained injustice in consequence of maladministration'.[127] The word 'investigate' indicates that the ombudsmen are to take an inquisitorial approach – actively investigating the facts of the case by calling for and examining evidence – as distinct from judicial-style adversarial proceedings in which two opposing parties seek to persuade a neutral judge to accept their version of events on the basis of evidence which they select to support it. Although an attempt may first be made to settle the matter without investigation, the PO may subsequently compel witnesses to give evidence and to produce documents. However, oral hearings are not generally held and there are no fixed rules of evidence applicable to the investigation. If the matter has not previously been settled or otherwise concluded, a report will be sent to the referring MP (and may, although it need not, be sent to the individual who made

---

[123] *Annual Report 1983*, HC 322 (1983–4), 1.
[124] s.5(1)(a).
[125] s.5(2).
[126] But note that s.5(5) confers wide discretion upon the PO to determine whether to initiate, continue or discontinue an investigation.
[127] s.5(1).

the complaint) and to the department or authority against whom the complaint is made.[128] The PO has no formal powers of enforcement but recommendations – which may include the making of compensatory payment, an apology or a reversal of the decision in question – normally secure compliance. In extreme circumstances, a report may be laid before Parliament,[129] but this power is very infrequently used.

The concept of 'maladministration' is not defined in the 1967 Act, but this flexible concept has been explained by a former PO as including such matters as rudeness, refusal to answer reasonable questions, knowingly giving misleading or inadequate advice, showing bias, failure to notify a right of appeal and failure by management to monitor compliance with procedures.[130] It will be noted that this includes some of the procedural defects which may be challenged in judicial review proceedings, but that it extends more widely than these.[131] However, and comparably to judicial review, the PO is precluded by the 1967 Act from questioning the merits of a decision taken without maladministration.[132]

The ombudsman concept has proved popular. In addition to the original PO, there are public sector ombudsmen for the Health Service (in practice, the same person), local government in England, and for Scotland, Wales and Northern Ireland. There are also numerous ombudsmen in the private sector, including those for housing, legal services, pensions and estate agency.[133] Such a proliferation would suggest that ombudsmen are regarded as an effective means by which 'justice' may be obtained and the imbalance of power between the individual and the state (in the case of public sector ombudsmen) or commercial concerns (in the case of private sector ombudsmen) may, at least partly, be redressed. Of course, deficiencies in the mechanism should not be overlooked: the MP filter (which only applies to the PO) limits accessibility (albeit that the service is free to the individual), the process of full investigation can be lengthy, ombudsmen continue to lack a degree of public visibility, and the division of roles (for example, between health and local government) does not properly reflect the integrated manner in which modern government tends to be conducted.

---

[128] ss.10(1), (2).

[129] s.10(3).

[130] *Annual Report 1993*, HC 290 (1993–4), [7].

[131] 'Maladministration comes in many guises, and while there is a substantial element of overlap between maladministration and unlawful conduct by councils or officers or councillors in local government, they are not synonymous': *R v Local Commissioner for Administration in North and North East England, ex parte Liverpool City Council* [2001] 1 All ER 462, [17] (Henry LJ).

[132] s.12(3)

[133] On the latter, see S. Brooker, *Lessons from Ombudsmania* (London, National Consumer Council, 2008).

Nevertheless, the existence of ombudsmen allows for a form of account-ability of – or, to put matters differently, a 'check and balance' upon – the executive which is wholly distinct from the political and legal forms exam-ined in chapters 3 and 5 and which therefore carries the potential to add something of genuine value to constitutional arrangements. In that regard, the key would appear to be the capacity of the work of an ombudsman to contribute to realising the 'green light' goal of improving the quality of administrative decision-making and encouraging enhancements in stan-dards of service to ensure that individuals do not suffer injustice in the first place. As the present PO puts it: 'whilst righting individual wrongs is the core of our work, my Office also has a wider "public benefit" role. One of my Office's key priorities is therefore to capture and share the learning from our casework in order to drive improvements in public services and to inform public policy'.[134] To this end, the publication of three sets of principles, of good administration, good complaints handling and for remedy[135] may prove to be highly valuable in the long term. It is notable that the Administrative Justice and Tribunals Council has drawn upon these in seeking to discharge its statutory obligation to consider ways to make the administrative justice system 'accessible, fair and efficient'.[136]

iv Internal review

The mechanisms discussed above, as well as the judicial review jurisdiction of the courts, are *external* to the organisation making the original decision which is subject to complaint. From a rule of law perspective, this is impor-tant in so far as it ensures that the issue is resolved by an independent and impartial 'judge'. Indeed, as we have noted in the context of both tribunals and the 'ordinary' judiciary, the recent trend has been to strengthen such independence, at least in part because of the obligation imposed by Article 6 of the European Convention on Human Rights.

But the independent judicial model of adjudication, or the investigatory approach taken by ombudsmen, is not appropriate in every instance. In many cases, an individual who is adversely affected by a decision or action of a governmental body may be satisfied with an apology, or an indication that comparable mistakes will not be made in the future. In such situations, fairness and independence are less crucial than the speed, informality,

---

[134] Parliamentary and Health Service Ombudsman, *Every Complaint Matters: Annual Report 2008–09*, HC 786 (2008–09), 6.

[135] Available at http://www.ombudsman.org.uk/improving-public-service/ombudsmansprin-ciples.

[136] Tribunals, Courts and Enforcement Act 2007, Schedule 7, [13(1)(b)]. See Administrative Justice and Tribunals Council, *Principles for Administrative Justice* (2010), [1].

cheapness and responsiveness of the process for resolution of the complaint. This points to an internal rather than external mechanism. Furthermore, complaints made by individuals have value to the organisation as they are a means of identifying where mistakes are being made so that performance and standards of service may be improved in the future. While external resolution does not preclude such lesson-learning, the time and expense which is required in order to respond to a court case, tribunal hearing or ombudsman investigation will necessarily interfere with and impede the body's discharge of its governmental functions. It may therefore be preferable to resolve matters internally, especially as the speed with which the matter can be resolved means that any necessary changes to working practices can be made almost immediately. Such an approach also chimes well with the commitment to proportionate dispute resolution, which seeks to resolve disputes 'fairly, quickly, efficiently and effectively' without recourse to more formal mechanisms where this is not necessary.[137]

Internal review of the initial decision and procedures for making complaints within the organisation in question are therefore important dimensions of administrative justice, albeit that they are often overlooked by lawyers who are more familiar – and comfortable with – the formal mode of adjudication exemplified by courts. In some instances, there is a statutory obligation imposed upon the decision-maker to provide for revision and substitution of the original decision where necessary. More commonly, where an individual questions a decision which has been reached, the decision-maker – or someone more senior in the organisation – may reconsider it as a part of normal administrative practice. In other situations, an informal internal process may be combined with a more formal, independent and external mode of dispute resolution. For example, in the National Health Service, the first stage of the complaints process consists of 'local resolution', in which the complaint is made to the practitioner concerned, or to a designated complaints manager within the organisation. Should this fail to resolve the matter in a satisfactory manner, the individual may refer the issue to the Health Ombudsman.

v Conclusion

The existence of a diversity of mechanisms for an individual who wishes to question or challenge a decision reached by government demonstrates that a narrow focus upon judicial review (including challenges under the Human Rights Act 1998) as a check on executive power is misplaced. While the authority of a court judgment and the media interest which it tends to

---

[137] Department for Constitutional Affairs, n.94, [2.3].

generate renders judicial review the most high-profile means of securing administrative justice, the resolution of a dispute is more likely to be achieved through one of the means described here.

The recent reforms to the tribunal system are not as constitutionally dramatic as most of the other developments described in this chapter. Nonetheless, they also effect a subtle rebalancing of power. If successful (and it is arguably too early at this stage to form a judgment on this), they will offer a fully accessible and independent means for the individual to resolve grievances against the state, partially redressing the inevitable imbalance which exists in that relationship. Another way of reading the recent changes is to regard tribunals as, in effect, now part of the judicial branch discussed in chapter 5: as courts in all but name. If that view is accepted, then the position of the judiciary relative to government has surely been enhanced as a consequence of the additional legitimacy which the tribunal system is likely to attain in light of its greater independence and more coherent structure. That coherence remains somewhat lacking in respect of the remaining mechanisms described here. The abolition of the Administrative Justice and Tribunals Council will scarcely assist in the quest for a greater degree of rationality in the administrative justice 'system', which might further enhance the capability of these processes to act as effective means for securing the accountability of the executive.

D. Freedom of information

One characteristic of British government which has tended to reinforce the dominant position of the executive within the constitutional order is its propensity to secrecy. The most obvious manifestation of this is the breadth of the protection given to classes of information in the Official Secrets Act 1989, the consequence of which is that the executive branch has very considerable discretion over the information which it makes available to the public. This is problematic from the standpoint of democracy and the separation of powers, as it impedes the capacity of the public to participate in the process of government and hinders the process of holding government to account. The concerns were eloquently expressed by Lord Bingham in *R v Shayler*:

'There can be no government by the people if they are ignorant of the issues to be resolved, the arguments for and against different solutions and the facts underlying those arguments. The business of government is not an activity about which only those professionally engaged are entitled to receive information and express opinions. It is, or should be, a participatory process. But there can be no assurance that government is carried out for the people unless the facts are made known, the issues publicly ventilated. Sometimes, inevitably, those involved in the conduct of government, as in any other walk of life, are guilty of error, incompetence, misbehaviour, dereliction of duty, even dishonesty and malpractice. Those concerned may very strongly wish that the facts relating to such matters are not made public. Publicity may reflect discredit on them or their predecessors. It may embarrass the authorities. It may impede the process of administration. Experience however shows, in this country and elsewhere, that publicity is a powerful disinfectant. Where abuses are exposed, they can be remedied. Even where abuses have already been remedied, the public may be entitled to know that they occurred. The role of the press in exposing abuses and miscarriages of justice has been a potent and honourable one. But the press cannot expose that of which it is denied knowledge.'[138]

It might be added that it is not simply the media which encounters difficulty in obtaining sufficient information on government's activities to be able to discharge its functions. As noted in chapters 3 and 4, an imbalance of information between the legislature and the executive – created, at least in part by the conventions of individual and collective ministerial responsibility which allow government to control the amount of information passed to Parliament – can act as a significant impediment to the former's ability to hold the latter to account, especially in matters which have security implications or which involve the exercise of prerogative powers.

Once again, however, the traditional constitutional position is in a process of evolution as a consequence of recent developments. The enactment of the Freedom of Information Act 2000, which came into force in 2005, has – at least, in principle – shifted the focus from an essentially negative, executive-favouring approach of categorising information which it is unlawful to disclose,[139] to a positive, individual-oriented right of access to information held by government. Section 1 of the Act provides, for the first time, a legally enforceable right (a) to know whether a public authority[140] holds particular information and (b) to have this information communicated. This right is underpinned by a supervisory and enforcement mechanism consisting initially of a process of internal review within the public authority concerned, followed by complaint to an Information

---

[138] [2002] UKHL 11, [21].

[139] This somewhat understates the value of initiatives taken in the first half of the 1990s, notably the introduction of a code of practice on access to government information in 1993 which, while not legally enforceable, was overseen by the Parliamentary Ombudsman.

[140] Public authorities which are subject to the Act are listed in Schedule 1: note the distinction from the Human Rights Act 1998, which contains no such list of authorities.

Commissioner who is appointed by, but independent of, government and who is accountable to Parliament (by way of the laying of an annual report).[141] This may be followed by appeal to an Information Tribunal from where there may be further appeal to a court on a point of law.[142] The Commissioner has powers to secure compliance with decisions by issuing an enforcement notice,[143] failure to follow which is punishable as a contempt of court. It should be noted that access to information does not come about solely through individual applications: section 19 obliges public authorities which are subject to the Act to issue 'publication schemes' specifying, in broad terms, the classes of information which they intend to make available and how such publication will take place (for example, on a webpage). The Commissioner is required to approve such schemes and has power to issue models for them,[144] together with general rule-making powers to issue codes of practice.[145]

The Act suffers from a number of weaknesses. First, it should be noted that the right conferred upon the individual is of access to *information*, not to the actual documents held by the public authority. Although the public authority is obliged, 'so far as is reasonably practicable' to give effect to the preference of the applicant for the form in which the information is communicated, there is no obligation to provide the information in permanent form, and the authority may choose to provide a summary or digest,[146] raising the possibility of 'selective editing'. Secondly, a public authority is not obliged to comply with an application if it estimates that the cost of compliance (taking into account the time spent in identifying, locating and extracting the information) would exceed the 'appropriate limit'.[147] This limit is established by secondary legislation: it presently stands at £600 for requests to central government bodies and £450 for other public authorities. Thirdly – and significantly – while the Information Commissioner is empowered to issue a 'decision notice' obliging a public authority to disclose information when it has refused to do so, this notice may be overridden by a certificate issued by government (normally, by a minister) specifying that, upon reasonable grounds, the opinion has been formed that there was no breach of the obligation to

---

[141] s.49.

[142] s.59. If the address of the public authority is in England and Wales, the appropriate court is the High Court.

[143] s.52.

[144] s.20. The Commissioner has issued a generic model, which all public authorities are expected to adopt, and sector-specific variants *eg* for the police, health authorities *etc.* See http://www.ico.gov.uk/what_we_cover/freedom_of_information/publication_schemes.aspx

[145] s.45.

[146] s.11.

[147] s.12.

disclose information. A copy of such a certificate must be laid before both Houses of Parliament.[148] It has been argued that this 'executive override' 'undermines any credibility to the claim that the Act creates a legally enforceable individual right of access',[149] the argument being that the breadth of the power is such that disclosure of information is better viewed as a matter of governmental discretion rather than as a legal obligation. This having been said, the controversial nature of the section 53 power is such that it is unlikely to be frequently used.[150]

The most obvious manner in which the right of access to information conferred by the Act has been restricted is by way of the various exemptions to the obligation to disclose which are listed in Part II of the Act. It would, of course, have been naïve to assume that *all* information held by government would be made available to the public upon application: there are good reasons why certain categories of information – for example, that relating to national security or economically sensitive material – should be protected. Nonetheless, the extent of the exemptions is striking. Twenty-three categories of information are specified, protected from disclosure to varying degrees. In some instances, such as information supplied by, or relating to, bodies dealing with security matters,[151] or information provided in confidence,[152] the exemption is absolute with the consequence that there is no duty to disclose at all (and, in some instances, even to confirm or deny that the information exists). In other cases, the public authority is not obliged to disclose any information falling within a certain class where it considers that 'the public interest in maintaining the exemption outweighs the public interest in disclosing the information'.[153] This applies to a number of categories, including information required for the purpose of safeguarding national security,[154] information held for the purposes of criminal or certain other investigations,[155] and information the disclosure of which would or would be likely to endanger the physical or mental health or safety of any individual.[156] The final

---

[148] s.53.

[149] R. Austin, 'The Freedom of Information Act 2000 – a Sheep in Wolf's Clothing?' in Jowell and Oliver (eds.) above p.39 (n.75), 399.

[150] Section 53 has, to date, only been used on two occasions: in February 2009 in relation to minutes of Cabinet meetings at which ministers took the decision to commit troops to Iraq, and in December 2009 in relation to disclosure of the minutes of the Cabinet Ministerial Committee on devolution to Scotland, Wales and the English regions. It will be noted that both of these relate to confidentiality of proceedings in Cabinet, underlining the continuing strength of collective responsibility as a justification for secrecy.

[151] s.23.

[152] s.41.

[153] s.2(2)(b).

[154] s.24.

[155] s.30.

[156] s.38.

group of exemptions are those in which the public authority may with-hold the information – having first taken the view that the public interest in maintaining an exemption outweighs the public interest in disclosure – only where disclosure would 'prejudice' the interest in question. These include information which would be likely to prejudice international rela-tions,[157] relations between administrations (that is, the devolved govern-ments) in the UK,[158] or the economic interests of the UK, among others.[159]

A number of further observations may be made about these exemp-tions. First, it should be noted that it is the responsibility of the public authority in the first instance to determine the balance between the public interest in disclosure and the public interest in maintaining an exemption, albeit that its decision on where the balance lies may be subject to internal review and subsequent appeal to the Information Commissioner. Secondly, the wording of section 2 suggests that the balance is weighted in favour of non-disclosure rather than access to information. Thirdly, the test of 'prej-udice' is relatively easy to satisfy, meaning that non-disclosure is more likely than would have been the case if a test of 'substantial prejudice' or 'substantial harm' had been adopted.[160] Finally, certain of the exemptions are extremely broad in scope. In particular, we might note sections 35 and 36. The former exempts information relating to the 'formulation or devel-opment of government policy',[161] although once a decision on such policy has been taken, the exemption is not to apply to statistical information used as a background to the decision.[162] The latter exempts, among other types of information, that which 'in the reasonable opinion of a qualified person' (normally, a minister) would, or would be likely to prejudice 'the effective conduct of public affairs'.[163] Such wording appears to confer almost unlimited discretion upon government to exempt all manner of information from disclosure, albeit subject to oversight by the Information Commissioner.

In view of these many limitations upon the right of access to informa-tion, it is tempting to conclude that the Freedom of Information Act does little to alter the balance of power between the branches of government or between the individual and the state. Rather, it might be seen as a means by which the executive branch continues to exercise substantial control

---

[157] s.27.

[158] s.28.

[159] s.29.

[160] The policy document preceding the legislation, *Your Right to Know* (Cm 3818, 1997) had proposed a test of 'substantial harm'. The test used in the equivalent Scottish legislation is one of 'substantial prejudice': see *eg* Freedom of Information (Scotland) Act 2002, s.30.

[161] s.35(1)(a).

[162] s.35(2).

[163] s.36(2)(c).

over the information which is publicly available, thereby restricting the extent to which it is obliged to offer the explanations and justifications which lie at the heart of accountability. This is the view of Austin who, in a powerful critique, has argued that 'what the government has enshrined in this Act is a discretionary power to choose what information to disclose ... We have returned ... to an all-pervasive culture of secrecy and of seeking to find reason for not disclosing, rather than a culture of openness'.[164]

Yet notwithstanding the Act's obvious limitations and some initial practical problems with its application, the legislation has proved to be of much greater value than was anticipated. Indeed, it serves as a useful reminder that the constitutional significance of a piece of legislation cannot be measured simply through analysis of provisions as they appear on paper, but must be assessed in the political context in which it is actually employed on a day-to-day basis. The utility of the Act has been commended by the pressure group the Campaign for Freedom of Information, which has published a summary of more than a thousand stories appearing in national and regional newspapers during 2006 and 2007 as a result of disclosures under the Act and its Scottish equivalent. The Campaign emphasises the wide range of issues upon which information has been obtained and reaches a positive conclusion upon the impact of the Act:

> 'They include significant disclosures about the Iraq conflict, the possible cause of gulf war syndrome, assaults on public service staff, the state of civil service morale, compensation paid to victims of medical accidents, schools' efforts to inflate their exam results, hospital techniques for deflating waiting lists, the universities teetering on the edge of financial collapse, police officers with criminal records, government efforts to encourage gambling, lobbying by multinational oil, pharmaceutical and food companies, nuclear safety and other hazards, crimes committed by offenders on parole, unpublicised prison escapes, the expansion of the national DNA database and innumerable reports about high expenses claims and dubious public spending.
>
> These disclosures throw new light on the government's approach to many issues, identify shortcomings in public service delivery, highlight other problems which have not been addressed and show where policies have succeeded. They reveal the substantial contribution to accountability made by the Freedom of Information Act.'[165]

---

[164] Above n.149, 405.
[165] Campaign for Freedom of Information, *1000 FoI Stories from 2006 and 2007* (London: Campaign for Freedom of Information, 2008).

However, the most momentous use of the Act has occurred in relation to disclosure of expense claims made by members of Parliament. In fact, the information in question was obtained by the *Daily Telegraph* newspaper as a consequence of unauthorised disclosure by a parliamentary employee, rather than directly through the Act. Nonetheless, the disclosures would not have taken place in the absence of the legislation. Anticipating the coming into force of the Act, the House of Commons had issued a publication scheme in 2002 covering the total sums paid to MPs in respect of the Additional Costs Allowance which may be claimed by MPs who need a second home to enable them to combine work at Westminster with constituency responsibilities outside London. Seeking further details of the allowance claims, three journalists had made applications under the Act in 2005 and 2006, but these were refused. However, following appeal to the Information Commissioner, Tribunal and High Court,[166] disclosure was ordered in relation to the fourteen MPs who were the subjects of the original application. This success was, in the long run, sufficient to breach the dam of parliamentary secrecy on the issue and full details of the 'creative' uses being made by some MPs of the allowance scheme emerged in the media in May 2009, prior to the date when official publication was scheduled to occur. The scandal resulted in a number of ministerial resignations and that of the Speaker of the House of Commons, while other MPs chose to stand down at the subsequent general election. An Independent Parliamentary Standards Authority was established to administer the payment of salaries and allowances,[167] and knowingly providing false or misleading information in making an expenses claim was made a criminal offence.[168] The Authority has appointed a Compliance Officer who is responsible for investigating claims of misuse of allowances.[169]

This dramatic episode, in which freedom of information legislation played a key role, suggests that the pessimism of commentators such as Austin may have been misplaced. Far from being weak, the Act has proved to be a valuable addition to the existing range of mechanisms, both political and legal, through which accountability for the exercise of public power (or, in this instance, the expenditure of public funds) may be achieved. Although deployed here against members of the legislative branch (some of whom, of course, were also government ministers), the primary use of the Act, as the report produced by the Campaign for Freedom of Information indicates, is likely to be against government. In that respect, the Act represents another

---

[166] *Corporate Officer of the House of Commons v Information Commissioner* [2008] EWHC 1084 (Admin).
[167] Parliamentary Standards Act 2009, s.3.
[168] s.10.
[169] Constitutional Reform and Governance Act 2010, s.26.

means by which excess or abuse of power by the executive branch may be checked and it thus sits alongside other checks and balances described in chapter 5, as well as the mechanisms of administrative justice outlined above. Yet this form of check cannot be categorised as one exercised by the judiciary or the legislature. It is true that information obtained under the Act may be employed to assist in securing accountability either politically (through Parliament) or legally (in a courtroom). But the primary location in which government will be held to account as a consequence of information obtained under the Act, as the expenses scandal demonstrates, will be in the media and – by extension – at the ballot box in elections, as the public responds to what the media reports. Of course, the media has always played an important part in holding government to account: indeed, it can be regarded as a key component of the 'political constitution'.[170] Nonetheless, the enactment of the Freedom of Information Act has undoubtedly enhanced its capacity to play such a role and in this regard the legislation serves as a useful reminder that not all power which is of constitutional significance – nor the means to control that power – resides in the three branches of government.

E. 'Steering but not rowing': the regulatory state, 'contracting out' and the 'big society'

On a number of occasions in this book, and especially in chapters 1, 2 and 5, we have noted the existence of distinct perspectives upon the appropriate role for law in managing the relationship between the state and the individual. The traditional, Diceyan, perspective is that the function of law is to uphold individual autonomy against encroachment by the state, preserving a sphere of individual action which is free from governmental intrusion. Law therefore functions as a control mechanism. Alternatively, we have observed a more positive view of the role of the state, in which governmental action is not to be feared, but rather welcomed as a means of enhancing the capacity of individuals to function within society, for example by provision of education, health care or financial support to the disadvantaged. On such an analysis, law's role is not primarily to restrain governmental action, but rather to facilitate its use, particularly by prescribing standards for good administrative decision-making and ensuring that mistakes are avoided.

---

[170] Griffith, above p.13 (n.31), 16, 18 argues for the enlargement of the freedom of the press by 'the amendment of laws which restrict discussion' and for 'more open government'.

Both of these approaches are premised upon the existence of a significant role for government within society, although those subscribing to the first ('red light') approach would prefer it to play a smaller role, allowing individuals a greater degree of autonomy. But what if *government itself* decides to step back, handing more power to individuals, groups or the private sector and delivering fewer services itself? This is not merely a hypothetical question. The trend in many Western democracies over the past three decades has been for a gradual withdrawal of the state from activities which it had been performing in the mid-twentieth century. Such a withdrawal has related ideological and economic justifications. In enhancing the role of the free market, governments (particularly, although not exclusively, right-leaning governments such as those which were in power in the UK and US during the 1980s) sought to prioritise autonomy and freedom by breaking up state monopolies and providing individuals with greater choice, but also to enhance the efficiency of service delivery by opening services up to competition.[171] In some instances, it was possible to achieve these goals simply by privatising a particular activity, with government playing no future role in its delivery. However, in most cases, a complete withdrawal of government would not have been appropriate. This was, in part, because the service in question was, to some degree, socially valuable: some degree of governmental involvement was therefore necessary to ensure that free-market competition did not result in the 'public interest' elements of the activity in question being overlooked. It was also necessary to ensure that a genuinely competitive marketplace did, in fact, evolve and – conversely – that any tendency towards monopoly was controlled.

As an example, we may consider privatisation of the utility industries, such as gas, electricity, telecommunications and water, which took place in the UK during the 1980s. Privatisation in these cases was carried out through the sale of government-owned shares in enterprises which had previously been run as monopolies by the state, enabling the emergence of competition. This was viewed as beneficial both for consumers, because it would drive prices for such services down as companies were forced to compete with each other, and for government, as it would reduce bureaucracy and public expenditure. In order to stimulate competition, a price cap might be imposed upon the dominant (formerly state-owned) firm to ensure that its profits and prices were limited, and licences would be issued to new firms wishing to enter the market. But there was an obvious danger that it would not be financially viable for companies to provide services to

---

171 In the UK, the Conservative Governments of Margaret Thatcher drew upon the writings of Hayek as an ideology for many of their actions: see above, pp.49–50.

certain consumers, such as those living in remote parts of the country, those who required special equipment (for example, because they were disabled), or those who might have difficulty making payments. Since the service being provided was a utility which was necessary for human existence, government could not simply leave such consumers unprotected. It was also possible that greater efficiency in service delivery would have the negative consequence of driving down quality as companies sought to cut costs in order to remain competitive. For all these reasons, therefore, there existed a continuing need for *regulation* of the industries: that is, for 'sustained and focused control exercised by a public agency over activities that are valued by a community'.[172]

This is a somewhat different role for government than that to which we are normally accustomed. Rather than providing services itself, government creates a framework within which the private sector can deliver the services on a competitive basis. However, the market is not wholly free. The state continues to 'guide' the market in a particular direction so that certain objectives can be achieved. A useful metaphor for expressing this is to say that the state 'steers, but does not row'.[173] This may be done, as has been the case with regulation of the privatised utility industries in the UK, through a non-departmental public body which acts as a 'watchdog' over the market.[174] Alternatively, it may take the form of 'contracting out': central and local government may enter into contractual arrangements with private providers for the delivery of services, with performance standards being specified in the contract and ongoing monitoring of performance to ensure that such standards are being met.[175]

The difficulty which these developments present for public law has been touched upon in chapter 5. Is government by such means (or, perhaps more accurately *'governance'*, a word which has been coined to connote a 'broader notion than government, whose principal elements include the constitution, legislature, executive, and judiciary. Governance involves interaction between these formal institutions and civil society')[176] properly the subject matter of public law at all? Since power has, in effect, been transferred to the private sector, should not the source of rights and obligations lie in private law principles, primarily those of contract? And if this is correct, is this problematic?

---

[172] P. Selznick, 'Focusing organisational research on regulation' in R. Noll (ed.), *Regulatory Policy and the Social Sciences* (Berkeley: University of California Press, 1985), 363.

[173] The phrase originates in D. Osborne and T. Gaebler, *Reinventing Government: how the entrepreneurial spirit is transforming the public sector* (Reading, Mass.: Addison-Wesley, 1992), 32.

[174] For discussion, see T. Prosser, *Law and the Regulators* (Oxford: Clarendon Press, 1997).

[175] See I. Harden, *The Contracting State* (Buckingham: Open University Press, 1992); A. Davies, *Accountability: a Public Law Analysis of Government by Contract* (Oxford: OUP, 2001).

[176] G. Drewry, 'The Executive: Towards Accountable Government and Effective Governance?' in Jowell and Oliver (eds.), above p.39 (n.75), 285.

Of central concern is the nature and extent of accountability inherent in such arrangements. Where regulatory agencies are created, as in the privatised utilities, they are intended to operate at arm's length from central governmental control to enable the market to operate free of short-term political pressures. However, as noted in chapter 4, greater independence for such agencies tends to equate to diminished accountability to Parliament, and while judicial review remains available, 'there has been a reluctance to accept that the courts should play a central role in establishing principles for the operation of the regulatory bodies',[177] in part because of fears that the US experience of an overly legalistic approach will be repeated in the UK. Meanwhile, in the context of 'contracting out' of services, there has been 'judicial reluctance to apply to the contract function common law doctrines of judicial review that apply to other government activities'.[178] Thus, principles of the relevancy of considerations, rationality and fairness may not apply. Nor, indeed may Convention rights given effect by the Human Rights Act, as we noted in the context of the *YL* case in chapter 5.[179] It is true, as Lord Woolf argued in the *Leonard Cheshire* case, that judicial review does not provide the sole means of redress in such situations: his Lordship suggested there that an individual might oblige a contracting body (such as a local authority) to include contractual conditions which gave effect to public law principles or which protected human rights.[180] However, such a solution appears to understate the inequality of bargaining power between the individual and the public body, an imbalance which public law is, at least in part, able to redress. Furthermore, as discussed in chapter 5, public bodies stand in a distinct position to the private individuals or companies who are the usual subjects and beneficiaries of contract law because they are exercising powers, and spending money, *in the public interest*. Thus, even if they choose a 'private' means to discharge their functions, they should not be permitted to abuse their powers by (for example) acting unfairly or infringing individual rights. The focus upon the contractual nature of the public body's actions has, however, tended to obscure this principle, which might be regarded as a fundamental component of the rule of law.[181]

The partial withdrawal of British government to a 'steering' role appears likely to continue for the foreseeable future. The present Prime Minister, David Cameron, has spoken of his desire to create a 'big

---

[177] T. Prosser, 'Regulation, Markets and Legitimacy' in Jowell and Oliver (eds.), *ibid*, 353–54.
[178] C. Harlow and R. Rawlings, *Law and Administration* (London: Butteroworths, 2nd ed., 1997), 240.
[179] Above p.227 (n.209).
[180] Above p.227 (n.208).
[181] See S. Bailey, 'Judicial review of contracting decisions' [2007] *Public Law* 444, 463.

society'.[182] Arguing that 'big government' has served to decrease individual and social responsibility, 'because today the state is ever-present: either doing it for you, or telling you how to do it, or making sure you're doing it their way', he calls for 'a new focus on empowering and enabling individuals, families and communities to take control of their lives so we create the avenues through which responsibility and opportunity can develop'. In some instances, this can be achieved by full withdrawal of the state, but Cameron maintains that government will retain a role in

> 'galvanising, catalysing, prompting, encouraging and agitating for community engagement and social renewal. It must help families, individuals, charities and communities come together to solve problems. We must use the state to remake society. We must use the state to help stimulate social action.'

The details of how this will happen remain, as yet, somewhat unclear, although Cameron has spoken of encouraging 'social entrepreneurs' who are running community programmes by providing state funding, encouraging community activists (for example, by provision of training programmes and information), strengthening existing civic institutions, 'like local shops, the post office and the town hall', and establishing a 'Big Society Bank' to fund local projects, drawing upon dormant bank accounts and private sector investment.

However, what *is* plain is that the policy entails a further form of diffusion of power away from central government, albeit in this instance channelled towards individuals, groups and charitable organisations as distinct from private companies. This suggests that public law mechanisms will play a relatively minor role in any 'big society' if and when this does eventually emerge.[183] Here, therefore, at the very limits of our subject, we return to the question posed in chapter 1: what is public law for? Its most likely function would seem to be a facilitative rather than controlling one. First, it can establish the framework for the state's 'catalysing' role, for example, by way of legislation which makes it easier for individuals and groups to establish community projects and activities by reducing bureaucratic hurdles to doing so, transferring power from local government to community level on issues such as licensing, provision of information, and

---

[182] The following quotations are taken from the Hugo Young Memorial Lecture, 10 November 2009, available at http://www.conservatives.com/News/Speeches/2009/11/David_Cameron_The_Big_Society.aspx.

[183] Cameron has stated that 'This is not the work of one parliamentary term, or even two. Culture change is much harder than state control. It will take more than a generation': *id.*

encouragement of wider public participation.[184] Secondly, it can ensure that those decisions and actions which do remain at central governmental level are properly responsive to local interests (pointing to judicial enforcement of obligations to consult, rights to be heard and consideration of relevant factors). Elsewhere, it seems probable that legal rights and obligations may be largely matters of private, rather than public, law.

F. Conclusion

The developments outlined in this chapter serve to remind us that, as power shifts within the British constitution, both between the three branches of central government and away from them, so too must our understanding of legal principles and institutional mechanisms also continue to evolve. This is true whether we consider the primary objective of law in this field to be the control, or facilitation, of the exercise of such power. Thus, membership of the European Union and devolution (especially, to Scotland) have caused us to question the traditional reading of parliamentary sovereignty and the effectiveness of parliamentary forms of accountability of the executive, at least in the short to medium term. Reforms to the tribunal system enhance its role as a genuine institutional alternative to judicial review as a means of securing administrative justice, although we might have cause to be concerned at the prospect of too great an assimilation to the judicial branch. The Freedom of Information Act appears to offer a potent new means for holding government to account and invites us to consider the role of the media as a check upon the executive branch. Finally, the transition from 'government' to 'governance', from 'rowing' to 'steering', both introduces new institutional mechanisms and means by which services are delivered to the public (regulatory agencies and 'contracting out') and brings private law centre-stage as a means of regulating relationships between the individual and the 're-imagined state' (as the present Prime Minister has labelled it).[185]

In their emphasis upon shifting power relations, both this and preceding chapters present a view of the British constitution as being in a state of flux. It is important, therefore, to recognise that the 'map' which this book provides will frequently need to be redrawn as the constitution continues to evolve. This is no easy challenge. We need only contemplate the still present (though perhaps now fading), ghostly image of Dicey to understand quite how reluctant public lawyers have frequently been to call into

---

184 See Localism Bill, HC Bill 126 (2010–11).
185 Cameron, above n.182.

question approaches which have represented orthodoxy for many decades. Yet, as this book has shown, dramatic developments which have profoundly altered the character of the constitution and the balance of power within it have necessitated the significant rethinking of public law in recent years, extending even to its foundational principles. Since 'the only thing that is certain is that the British constitution is not going to stop changing',[186] it is inevitable that such a process of re-evaluation must remain ongoing.

---

[186] M. Glover and R. Hazell, 'Introduction: Forecasting Constitutional Futures' in R. Hazell (ed.), *Constitutional Futures Revisited: Britain's Constitution to 2020* (Basingstoke: Palgrave Macmillan, 2008), 2.

Index